T0330349

Funds

For other titles in the Wiley Finance Series
please see www.wiley.com/finance

Funds

Private Equity, Hedge and All Core Structures

Matthew Hudson

This edition first published in 2014 by John Wiley & Sons Ltd
© 2014 Matthew Hudson

Registered office
John Wiley & Sons Ltd, The Atrium, Southern Gate, Chichester, West Sussex, PO19 8SQ, United Kingdom

For details of our global editorial offices, for customer services and for information about how to apply for permission to reuse the copyright material in this book please see our website at www.wiley.com

Wiley publishes in a variety of print and electronic formats and by print-on-demand. Some material included with standard print versions of this book may not be included in e-books or in print-on-demand. If this book refers to media such as a CD or DVD that is not included in the version you purchased, you may download this material at http://booksupport.wiley.com. For more information about Wiley products, visit www.wiley.com.

Designations used by companies to distinguish their products are often claimed as trademarks. All brand names and product names used in this book are trade names, service marks, trademarks or registered trademarks of their respective owners. The publisher is not associated with any product or vendor mentioned in this book.

Limit of Liability/Disclaimer of Warranty: While the publisher and author have used their best efforts in preparing this book, they make no representations or warranties with respect to the accuracy or completeness of the contents of this book and specifically disclaim any implied warranties of merchantability or fitness for a particular purpose. It is sold on the understanding that the publisher is not engaged in rendering professional services and neither the publisher nor the author shall be liable for damages arising herefrom. If professional advice or other expert assistance is required, the services of a competent professional should be sought.

A catalogue record for this book is available from the British Library.

ISBN 9781118790403 (hardback) ISBN 9781118790380 (ebk)
ISBN 9781118790366 (ebk) ISBN 9781118790274 (obk)

Set in 10/12 Times by Sparks – www.sparkspublishing.com
Printed in Great Britain by CPI Group (UK) Ltd, Croydon, CR0 4YY

Contents

1

Introduction to Funds

1.1 WHY THIS BOOK?

I have sought to write the manual I always wanted to find on the shelves. In my career as both an asset manager and a legal adviser to asset managers and investors, I have often been asked to recommend a guide that covers the broad ambit of fund and manager structures.

In the world of asset management, knowledge is often assumed, jargon is sometimes opaque and there can be a tendency towards mystification. Frequently, for example, I am asked 'What is market?', and certainly one possible answer to that question is that 'market' means whatever is investment worthy at that particular moment in time and given the particular investment: following the money has, after all, always been a plausible strategy. However, in these fast changing times where the industry is being required to adapt to survive, it is more crucial than ever to understand the logic behind the structures that have come to dominate this sector.

Broadly, these pages are intended to function as a guide to all things funds and fund managers. Although approached principally from a United Kingdom (UK), United States (US) and European Union (EU) perspective, this book also references other core fund establishment locations, as well as core economic or asset jurisdictions such as China and Japan. The book approaches its subject from a structural, legal, tax and regulatory perspective. It is, however, a guide and not an in-depth review. The latter would require a number of separate volumes. I hope it succeeds in pointing the reader in the right direction.

1.2 ALTERNATIVE ASSETS

I am going to focus principally on funds comprising what are known as alternative assets. 'Alternative' as opposed to the mainstream world that is largely composed of listed equities and bonds. The phrase derives from the pension fund term 'alternative allocation', which refers to the proportion of a fund's portfolio that is invested in alternative assets.

This type of fund comprises principally private equity, hedge, venture capital, real estate, energy, infrastructure, credit and related funds. The managers of these funds tend to fall into the category of '2 and 20' managers, where the '2' refers to the annual percentage fee received by management of the cost or value of assets under management and the '20' refers to the percentage of profit to be made by the manager as a percentage of profit for investors as a whole.

A fund is a fluid concept. It can refer to any pooling of capital or assets. Historically, the concept of alternative assets and funds perhaps finds its origins in the age of exploration. At the heart of Christopher Columbus's expedition to the Americas was an agreement that is an example of financial pooling. Columbus was backed in part by a 'fund' from Italian financiers and was able to convince the King of Spain to provide the top-up funding required for the trip. Columbus and his 'management team' had their overheads covered and were promised a generous share of performance profits, as well as real management power within any newly discovered lands, the 'portfolio assets'. Success would also mean prestigious titles and backing for the next 'fund'. The agreement was in fact quite detailed. Together with any treasure looted, Columbus would receive 10% of revenues reaped from newly discovered lands as well as having a right of first refusal to invest at a discount in any commercial venture deriving from the newly discovered territories – the King of Spain apparently believed that success or indeed Columbus's return were unlikely investment outcomes. Management and co-investment opportunities rarely come better!

1.3   WHAT IS A FUND?

A fund is a broad term, but as we have seen is used to describe any pooling of assets. These assets may be cash, shares, loans or tangible or intangible assets. A fund can even be a vehicle that holds a single asset (such as Vallar (now Bumi plc) and Vallares (now Genel Energy plc) – both originally special purpose cash shells established by the financier Nathaniel Rothschild to acquire specific companies), although, typically, a fund is established to hold more than one asset.

The term fund can of course be applied to other industries and concepts, for example:

- a fund or 'stable' of pop artists, managed by an expert pop promoter, manager or agent. The more stars under management, the greater the diversification
- a fund or 'library' of knowledge or
- a fund or 'team' of football stars (where the assets are footballers) that are bought and sold.

Almost any economic gathering or pooling may be regarded in terms of a fund. A fund could almost better be defined by describing what does not constitute a fund, such as a single purpose operating company with a small balance sheet, unlike Rothschild's cash shells referred to above. Typically, a fund would not otherwise include a large single purpose operating company, unless of courses it uses off (or near-off) balance sheet side vehicles underpinned by external capital, a fairly common feature of large energy, real estate and infrastructure companies.

A fund may have one owner, or many owners who subscribe, acquire and sell positions, shares or units. One of the defining features of a fund is that it often has a professional fund manager (usually regulated) that manages and advises the fund.

Funds can be operated for a variety of different purposes:

- to make a profit
- or to be run on a not-for-profit basis (e.g. a charity)
- to spread risk
- to obtain leverage (by debt financing) on assets
- to take advantage of a specialist manager to operate the fund
- to attract investors (a bank may create a fund to house certain assets and then seek other investors to generate management fees for the bank)
- to build an asset management group (although mere 'asset gathering' is sometimes criticized by investors)

1.4   CATEGORIES OF FUNDS

1.4.1   Ways to categorize

It is clear the term 'fund' is a broad one. However, in this book we are considering funds that occur in the investment management or financial services industries. But even within these sectors the range of different types of fund is wide. Investors and managers refer to a 'hedge fund' or 'private equity fund' or 'mutual fund', descriptions which embrace many investment strategies, structures and management arrangements. I would categorize funds within the alternative asset sector using the categories below.

Categorization by industry (by example):

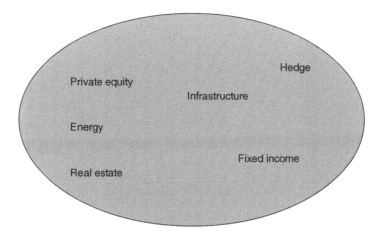

Table 1.1 Categorization by investor returns (or how they get their money back plus a profit)

Drawdown and distribution model	Tradable model	NAV or redemption model
Most private equity funds	*Many retail or tax-driven funds*	*Most hedge funds*
The fund 'draws down' money from investors when required for investment. Drawing down funds only when required as opposed to in their entirety in advance should have the effect of enhancing the fund's internal rate of return (**IRR**) when measured against the date of exit or realization of a particular investment.	A tradable fund is one where the shares or units in the fund are traded, usually on a public market. The capital is not distributed to investors although regular and larger one-off dividends can be made. The funds may or may not have a fixed life and gains and profits made within the fund should cause the fund's share price to increase. However, tradable funds are subject to the ups and downs of trading and:	This fund redeems or prepays units held by investors in the fund and on (or within a defined time of) redemption also pays investors any profit 'attaching' to those units. A share of the profits is paid as a performance fee to the fund's management team. Units are often redeemed at, or correlated to, the net asset value (NAV) of that unit. A unit's NAV is the total of the fund's gross assets, less leverage and liabilities, divided by the number of units in the fund. It is typically the manager or administrator and also third party valuers that calculate NAV.
On exits, the original cost and the capital gain or profits relating to each asset are then 'distributed' to investors and are seldom re-invested. The fund usually has a fixed life, and the intention is to invest and then 'return' the entire capital and profits, before winding up the fund. A share of the fund profits ('carried interest' or 'carry') is distributed to the management team. In a drawdown and distribution model fund, assets remaining after distribution at the end of the life of a fund can be sold on the 'secondary market', as can an investor's position.	• illiquidity • 'trading at a discount' to asset value • market, economy or investor sentiment. What this often leads to is a tradable fund trading at a premium to embedded value at moments of investor exhilaration, but at a discount the rest of the time. Sentiment or recognition can bear little correlation to actual asset value.	The fund is usually 'open' and not 'closed' (meaning the number of investors and amount invested fluctuate as investor commitments are made and redeemed) and can exist for an undetermined period of time, unless the fund is wound up.
Income generated from investments is usually distributed as it arises, for example, net yield from real estate, rental receipts or fixed-income gilts.		
The fund is usually 'closed' and not 'open' (meaning that the number of investors and amount invested are fixed and have a fixed life).		

Categorization by investment strategy (by example):

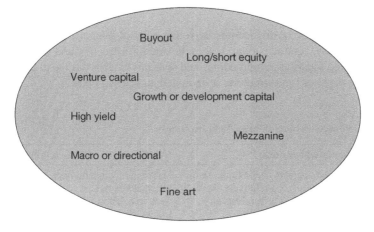

Categorization by vehicle:

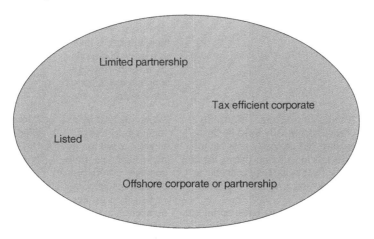

1.5   CHOOSING A VEHICLE

Choosing the correct vehicle for a particular fund will depend on a number of factors. Some to consider are:

- the vehicle that is most tax efficient for the target investor base and for the fund's management team (taking into account the fund's likely assets and their location)
- the regulatory regime that is least onerous while still providing an appropriate degree of credibility to the fund (taking into account the likely views of potential investors)
- any limitation on the target investors (either internal or external) or their ability to invest in certain vehicles
- the previous experience of the potential investors and the manager with different fund vehicles.

1.6   OPEN-ENDED AND CLOSED-ENDED FUND STRUCTURES

1.6.1   Introduction

Alternative assets can also be divided into two other types of categories, those that are illiquid such as private equity, venture capital, real estate and infrastructure and those that are more liquid such as listed securities, commodities and derivatives. This has led to the development of, broadly, two types of fund structure: open-ended and closed-ended.

Table 1.2   Open-ended and closed-ended fund structures

Type	Liquidity/investment	Assets	Further reading

Open-ended	The vast majority of the fund's assets are realized over a relatively short period of time. The fund has an indefinite life.
	
	    Investors may redeem their interest (wholly or in part) or increase their interest during the course of the fund's life.
		Typically a large number of small assets (for example, listed shares) or assets whose size can be readily adjusted (for example, derivative positions).
		
		    The fund can acquire new assets with additional proceeds invested. It funds withdrawals by investors through a partial realization of fund assets.
			Common with hedge funds – Chapter 3.

Closed-ended	An illiquid structure. The identity of investors usually fixed by final closing. Not generally possible for investors to withdraw during the life of the fund as the fund is unable to liquidate assets in order to finance withdrawals.
	
	    Only possible to invest during the first half or so of the fund's life to allow time to exit assets. The larger size of assets means that there are only, say, up to a dozen investments per fund.
	
	    The fund operates for a finite period, terminating once all of the assets are disposed of.
		Assets are held for a minimum period of time (for example, to restructure a portfolio company or refurbish a commercial property).
		
		    Usually a smaller number of larger assets are held, e.g. private equity portfolio companies or specific real estate.
			Closed-ended funds – Chapter 2.
			    Growth of secondary trading of illiquid fund interests – Chapter 5, section 5.11.

1.6.2   Impact of the credit crisis

This book was written during a period often described as the 'credit' or 'financial' crisis. For our purposes, this period started in February 2007 with HSBC reporting record losses for US bad mortgage debt and was quickly followed by the collapse of the sub-prime industry in the US. The crisis spread in the US with the implosion of leveraged Bear Stearns hedge funds, the capitulation of structured investment vehicles (SIVs), the contagion of many US, UK and European banks (Northern Rock being a notable example) and arguably reached what in retrospect was its early peak with the collapse of Lehman Brothers. The US, UK and European markets (which were considered more sophisticated than the rest of the world) were among the most seriously affected during the crisis.

Some hedge funds were wiped out during the peak of the crisis due to over-leverage and also by 'rehypothecation'. This was where the collateral pledged by funds with broker-dealers was called upon by those broker-dealers to satisfy their own liabilities. Lehman and Bear Stearns were market-dominant prime brokers at the time of their collapse. When the larger investment banks such as these two began defaulting, more hedge funds followed suit.

This 'credit crisis' usually refers to the period mid 2007 to late 2009 but was then eased by floods of central bank liquidity. Mid-to-late 2009 to the end of 2013 was a continuation of this period, known overall as the 'financial crisis'. The later period is marked by a certain stability returning in the US credit markets, but overall by poor growth and the Eurozone crisis. The later period of the financial crisis was characterized by:

- restructuring and huge mark-downs (sometimes overdone in my view)
- continued bank weakness
- increased regulation – again in my view, often driven by headline-seeking politics and naïveté and leading to the disinclination of banks to lend on a scale that might otherwise have restimulated economies.

All manner of funds were impacted by the financial crisis. Despite negative publicity about the sector, funds themselves (whether private equity, hedge, or otherwise) were not a root cause of the crisis. Instead, funds were caught in the pre-crisis enthusiasm, over-leveraging and over-pricing funds and assets. The adverse effects on funds have since been keenly felt. During the crisis, funds found that fund-raising became more difficult as investment in general slowed, which was aggravated by the difficulty of borrowing.

Private equity funds are, by their nature, long-term investments. To an extent they have been able to ride out the financial storms. Some managers have been criticized for not continuing to invest during what might come to be viewed as vintage years for investment. Hedge funds adapted relatively quickly owing to their shorter-term investment horizons with rights to redeem (despite manager rights to 'gate', that is to say restrict withdrawals, or lock up investments), scaling down, reducing in size, investing differently, usually with much less leverage, as well as adapting their structure to managed accounts (see Chapter 4, section 4.7 for a full definition) and other more transparent investment programmes.

Alternative asset allocation is now starting to increase. The denominator effect has largely run its course (for the moment) as listed markets start to rebound. Funds are being sought out by investors:

- hedge funds as adjuncts to broader investment strategy
- private equity funds for growth
- credit funds for better than dismal bank interest and
- real estate, infrastructure and energy for the anticipated asset valuation rebound.

It is too easy to be a doom-monger, although some highly intelligent people believe we have entered a new low growth paradigm. However, I believe cycles will always exist, and that trends overshoot.

1.7   CONTENTS OF THIS BOOK

To help you find your way through this book, the main contents are set out below.

Table 1.3   Main contents of the book

Chapters	Contents
2 and 3	Dedicated to two types of funds that are significant in this book: private equity funds and hedge funds, although the structures for each are also used for other alternative asset strategies such as real estate, infrastructure, credit and energy. These chapters also cover the two principal structures of alternative investment funds, being closed-ended funds (Chapter 2) and open-ended funds (Chapter 3). The chapters dedicated to these types of funds go into detail about the most common structures, jurisdictions and the market terms
4	Analysis of other private fund structures
5	Investment strategies employed by different funds with an analysis of each
6	Key jurisdictions for funds to list on stock exchanges and the key types of listed funds and the regimes that apply to them
7	Principal 'offshore' fund locations and a summary of their regulatory and tax regimes and stock markets
8	Key global economies, the type of fund entities that exist there and the prospects for investors
9	Large investor players: sovereign wealth funds, state funds, pension funds and charities
10	Fund managers – the common investment manager structures and their commercial operations
11	Taxation of funds, investors and managers
12	Regulation of funds and managers
13	Conclusion – reviews the ground covered and remarks on future trends

2

Limited Partnerships – Use in Alternative Asset Funds

2.1 INTRODUCTION TO LIMITED PARTNERSHIPS

2.1.1 Suitability of limited partnerships for alternative asset funds

A limited partnership is the vehicle most commonly used for closed-ended funds investing in the less liquid alternative assets, including private equity, venture capital, real estate, infrastructure and energy.

2.1.2 Benefits of limited partnerships

A limited partnership offers a range of benefits in this context including:

- tax transparency (a limited partnership is effectively ignored for tax purposes and amounts received by the partnership (e.g. capital gains) retain their character when allocated to individual partners)
- the liability of investors can be limited to the amount which they agree to contribute to the partnership and
- a limited partnership is very flexible and subject to relatively few restrictions in terms of governance and profit sharing arrangements, which allows fund managers greater freedom than may be the case for other types of vehicle.

2.1.3 Types of limited partnerships

Limited partnerships are available across a range of different jurisdictions. The two most commonly used onshore jurisdictions are the UK and the US (typically Delaware). Commonly used offshore jurisdictions include the Cayman Islands and the Channel Islands (Guernsey and Jersey). Other jurisdictions such as Luxembourg are also available.

There are many similarities between limited partnership structures across jurisdictions. The fact that many offshore jurisdictions (including the Channel Islands and the Cayman Islands) have legal systems closely related to English law assists in this regard.

2.2 STRUCTURE OF LIMITED PARTNERSHIP FUNDS

2.2.1 Role of general and limited partners

Participants in a limited partnership are called partners and fall into two categories.

(a) Limited partners (LPs)

The limited partners are the partners whose liability is, broadly, limited to the amount of their investment, provided that they do not take part in the management of the partnership. Therefore, the investors in a fund participate as limited partners. Limited partners are typically required to make a capital contribution to the partnership. The carry vehicle (as described below) is also often a limited partner.

(b) General partners (GPs)

The general partner has unlimited liability for the debts and liabilities of the partnership (i.e. the fund) but is able to undertake the management of the partnership. There must be at least one general partner although in practice, in the context of alternative assets funds, there will only be a single general partner which will normally be an entity with minimal assets (as those assets will be at risk in the event that the fund becomes insolvent).

Typically, each partnership will have its own general partner which will not carry out any activities unrelated to the fund of which it is the general partner. The use of a separate general partner for each fund reduces the risk of cross-contamination, which is the risk that the insolvency of one partnership leads to the insolvency of its general partner which could, in turn, adversely affect other partnerships of which it is also the general partner.

2.2.2   Management and operation of the partnership

In a limited partnership structure, it is the general partner that is responsible for and is permitted to undertake the management and operation of the partnership. However, it is common either for a separate manager to be appointed or, where the general partner does manage the partnership, for it to be advised by a separate investment adviser or even a combination of both a separate manager and an investment adviser.

There are a number of reasons for adopting these more complex structures:

- separate management or investment advisory entities in turn allow the management/advisory functions for multiple funds to be contained in a single holding entity which facilitates building up value in the fund management/advisory business
- the general partner may need to be located offshore and may be reliant on an onshore investment adviser to provide it with advice on the acquisitions, management and disposal of investments
- there may be regulatory or tax reasons for having a separate manager/investment adviser and
- it can protect the management vehicle from the unlimited liability nature of the general partner.

In the rest of this chapter (and book) references to 'manager' are, depending on the structure of an individual fund, to the general partner/manager in conjunction with any investment adviser. The management structure adopted in US and UK limited partnership structures is discussed in more detail in sections 2.2.4 and 2.2.5 below.

2.2.3   Remuneration

There are broadly three forms of remuneration that are generated by a fund structured as a limited partnership for the benefit of the fund manager (or its principals):

- management fees
- carried interest and
- transaction or monitoring fees.

These are discussed in more detail under section 2.6 of this chapter (Economics) below.

In terms of a UK fund's structure, it is worth noting that management fees are typically structured as a share of the fund's profits (if there are no profits, the amounts can be drawn down from the investors, so while technically a profit share it still operates much like a fee), which is paid to the general partner and by the general partner to the manager in the form of a fee. For limited partnerships established in the UK, this means that no value added tax (VAT) should be payable on the 'management fee' as no VAT is payable for a share of profits paid to a partner and VAT is also not payable in respect of the subsequent payment of that amount from the general partner to the manager provided that they are grouped for VAT purposes.

For offshore funds in jurisdictions where there may be no VAT payable, the management fee may be paid by the fund directly to the manager as a fee for its services and not via a profit share to the general partner.

The carried interest is the performance-based remuneration received by the management team. It is a share of the profits paid to a partner in the partnership, which is called the founder partner, carry partner or carry vehicle. This entity is often a Scottish limited partnership – as either a limited partner in an English limited partnership or an offshore limited partnership. For the distinction between English and Scottish limited partnerships, see below in section 2.2.4(a) of this chapter. Each member of the fund manager's management team who is entitled to receive a share of the carried interest is then a limited partner in the carry vehicle. As it is another limited partnership, the carry vehicle also requires its own general partner, called the carry general partner, which is usually a limited company in the same jurisdiction.

Transaction or monitoring fees are received by the manager or its affiliates from entities in which the fund has made an investment or third parties and may be shared between the fund and the manager.

2.2.4   UK limited partnerships

(a) Legal background

In the UK, partnerships originated under common law (that is, legal practice developed by the courts) rather than being established by legislation (as is the case for companies). For example, unlike a company, a partnership in the UK can be established by an agreement between the relevant partners without the need to apply to a government authority or register the existence of the partnership. Such a partnership is a general partnership, that is, one in which all the partners are general partners and have unlimited liability for the debts and obligations of the partnership.

However, all UK partnerships are now subject to the Partnership Act 1890. While fundamental to the law on partnerships in the UK generally, this Act has little day to day impact on the use of partnerships as a vehicle for alternative asset funds.

More relevant to alternative asset funds is the Limited Partnerships Act 1907. This Act allows a general partnership to be registered with Companies House in the UK as a limited partnership. This allows some (in practice all the partners who are investors) to be registered as limited partners with the consequence that their liability is limited as described in section 2.2.1 of this chapter. The Limited Partnerships Act 1907 imposes relatively few requirements on limited partnerships. Those that are most relevant relate to registering the fund with Companies House and notifying certain changes in the partnership such as the addition of new limited partners.

Technically, limited partnerships established in the UK can be divided between those that are English (or Welsh) and those that are Scottish. The principal difference is that English limited partnerships do not have separate legal personality (that is, no legal entity distinct from its partners) while a Scottish limited partnership is such a distinct legal entity. While largely a legal technicality, the effect of this is to make Scottish limited partnerships more appropriate for partnerships that will invest into other partnerships (for example, carry vehicles (described below) and fund of funds) or partnerships that invest in registerable assets (as property funds for example).

Therefore, while it is necessary to distinguish between English and Scottish limited partnerships, this chapter uses the term 'UK limited partnership' to refer to them generically.

In Figure 2.1, the fund uses special purpose vehicles (SPVs) to act as liability blockers, or vehicles into which different levels of investment are made.

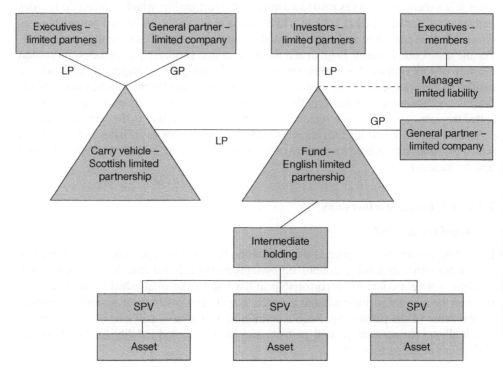

Figure 2.1   Typical English limited partnership structure with a separate manager and Scottish carry vehicle.

(b) Management

An alternative asset fund structured as a UK limited partnership will normally have a separate manager that is appointed by the partnership (see Chapter 10, section 10.2 for more information). The reason for this is that acting as a manager and operator of an alternative asset fund is an activity which if carried on in the UK requires authorization by the Financial Conduct Authority (FCA) (see Chapter 12 for more detail).

(c) Loan/capital split

An investment in a limited partnership fund is normally structured as a commitment that is drawn down over time (see section 2.5.1 below). The amounts actually contributed to the fund are usually referred to as capital contributions. However, one unusual feature of UK limited partnerships is that the commitment made by an investor is split between a capital contribution and a loan.

The reason for this is that under the Limited Partnerships Act 1907, while a limited partner is required to make a capital contribution to the partnership, that capital contribution can only be repaid to the investor on the liquidation of the partnership or, if it is repaid early, the investor remains liable to re-contribute it if required in order to meet the partnership's liabilities. So, if part or all of an investor's capital contribution is repaid prior to the liquidation of the fund, that investor has no certainty that they will not be required to pay it back to the fund if a liability arises (for example, litigation against the fund from a purchaser of one of its investments). This is clearly an undesirable consequence of using a UK limited partnership as a fund vehicle.

In order to avoid this problem, in a UK limited partnership, an investor's commitment is divided into a capital contribution and a loan. The capital contribution is nominal (either say 0.01% or 0.001% of their commitment) and is subject to the restrictions set out above. However, as the amount of the capital contribution is so small this restriction is of no practical importance. The rest of an investor's commitment is then a loan to the fund. The loan can then be repaid together with any profits during the life of the fund as it disposes of assets or receives income from them without being recalled (unless the fund's terms specifically allow such recall). However, as the loan is repayable only to the extent that there are such proceeds available to do so, the loan/capital split has very little economic significance on the operation of the fund.

2.2.5 US limited partnerships

As discussed above, the most common vehicle for an onshore closed-ended fund in the United States is a limited partnership organized under the laws of the State of Delaware. Delaware is commonly used in large part because the Delaware Revised Uniform Limited Partnership Act (DRULPA) includes some management-friendly provisions, and Delaware has a well-established body of partnership law and a focused and specialized court (the Delaware Court of Chancery) that is widely thought of as the forum of choice for litigation of corporate and partnership issues, including the scope of duties and liability of executives. A Delaware limited partnership is a separate legal entity, unlike an English limited partnership.

Management-friendly provisions include the following.

(a) Exculpation

DRULPA provides that the duties, including fiduciary duties, of the general partner or any other person may be limited or even eliminated if so provided in the limited partnership agreement, provided that the limited partnership agreement may not eliminate the implied contractual covenant of good faith and fair dealing.

(b) Indemnification

A limited partnership has broad power to indemnify the general partner or any other person and advance costs and expenses to any indemnified person.

(c) Access to information

DRULPA permits a limited partnership to restrict the access of a limited partner to information, to a reasonable extent. Additionally, a limited partner's request or demand for information must be reasonable and for a purpose reasonably related to the limited partner's interest as a limited partner.

(d) Certain flexibilities

The limited partnership agreement may provide specified penalties or specified consequences that arise from or are related to a breach of the limited partnership agreement and for different classes of interests that have different rights, benefits, obligations, restrictions or limitations. This gives the sponsor the ability to 'pre-game' the results of certain events, such as a failure to contribute capital and the statutory authority to assert a penalty, although courts in some states will not enforce penalty or forfeiture provisions.

Typically, the sponsors will control the limited partnership through a general partner that is organized as a Delaware entity – typically an entity with limited liability. The general partner or an affiliate will also act as the carry vehicle.

The typical structure for a US private equity fund is illustrated by Figure 2.2. The fund is a limited partnership. The general partner of the fund is a limited liability company (LLC). An affiliate of the general partner will hold the carried interest and makes the investment in the fund on behalf of the sponsor. This figure illustrates a structure in which there is not a separate investment adviser and the assets or operating companies are held through separate special purpose companies.

Structures often include holding companies so that the sponsor or certain parts of the management team form an entity, typically a limited liability company, which holds all of the interests in the general partner, the special limited partner and the investment manager. The primary reasons to include a holding company structure are to provide greater flexibility in management, compensation and other specified relationships among the management team. A holding company structure may also be used to implement tax efficient structures that consider state and local (e.g. New York City) tax regimes.

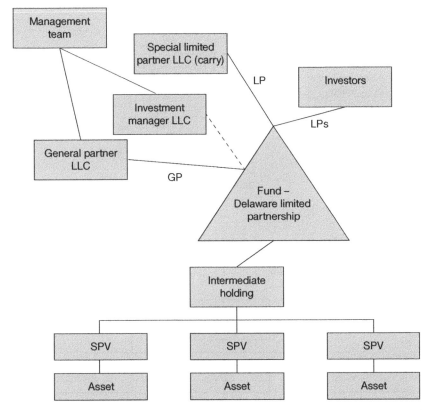

Figure 2.2   Typical US Delaware limited partnership structure with a separate manager, a special partner that receives carried interest and a general partner.

2.2.6   Parallel funds

While an investment fund structure often employs a single limited partnership (the discussion below refers to limited partnerships but the same principle is equally applicable to other types of entities such as limited liability companies or indeed a combination of different types of entities), investment funds that accommodate tax and certain regulatory or investment policy concerns of the investors often employ more than one limited partnership (or other entities) which invest alongside each other in parallel (see Figure 2.3).

There are a number of different situations that give rise to the need for a parallel structure. One of the common situations is where taxpaying and tax exempt US investors require the partnership in which they participate to make different elections for US tax purposes (US tax exempt investors that do not want to have unrelated business taxable income (or UBTI) will generally want their partnership to elect to be treated as a corporation or hold investments through a corporation, while US taxpaying investors will generally want their partnership to be treated as a partnership). An organization that is recognized as a tax exempt entity under the US Internal Revenue Code (IRC) may be liable for tax on its unrelated business taxable income and be required to file certain returns or forms with the US Internal Revenue Service (IRS). This area of US taxation is subject to complex rules and regulations that are beyond the scope of this book. The concern for sponsors of investment funds is to determine whether

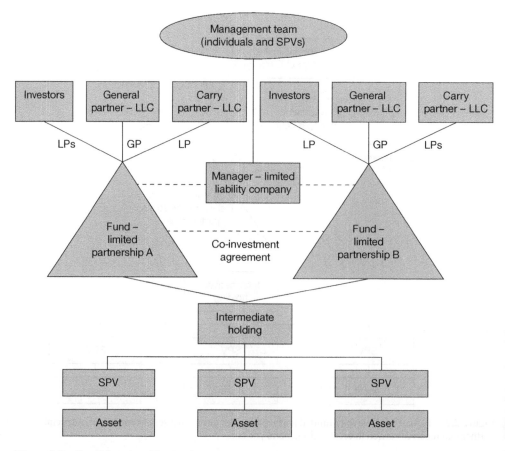

Figure 2.3 Parallel partnership structure.

investment will be solicited from such investors, including charities, pension funds and state funds, and then to use corporations in the investment fund structure to block or shield such investors from unrelated business taxable income to the extent so desired by the investors. Similarly, non-US investors often have US tax and tax withholding issues and will employ parallel funds or other tax-sensitive structures to reduce their overall income tax and/or avoid the requirement to file a tax return with the IRS.

In a parallel fund structure, each limited partnership or fund provides similar terms to their respective investors (other than any differences necessary to overcome the relevant regulatory or tax issues that have led to the parallel structure in the first place). One of the significant differences between the terms is that the calculation of the carry interest payable to the special limited partner or general partner is grossed up (increased) by the corporate income tax payable within the structure, so that the carry is not reduced by the investment fund structure accommodating the investor tax issues.

The separate affiliated limited partnerships enter into a co-investment agreement, which requires each limited partnership to acquire and dispose of investments at the same time and on the same terms pro rata to their investment commitments that may be drawn and deployed to the investment. The investment allocation between the separate limited partnerships is typically based on the amount of investment capital that may be deployed in the specified investment, after consideration of any regulatory, tax or other applicable limitations or restrictions. Therefore, the use of several parallel partnerships as opposed to a single large partnership should make little practical difference to investors and has the advantage that the documentation for each partnership (other than in respect of the relevant tax or regulatory issues) is identical.

The parallel vehicles will provide for the allocation of costs and expenses among the vehicles so that the resulting economics among the investors are substantially the same as an investment structure that has only one vehicle. Typically, the allocation is based on the investment funds available for deployment or aggregate investment commitments. In addition, the voting of the investors is often structured so that the investors of all of the parallel investment vehicles vote as a single class.

2.2.7   Master/feeders

An alternative to a parallel structure is a master/feeder structure (shown in Figure 2.4). Under this structure, there is a single 'master' limited partnership in which some of the investors participate. One investor is another limited partnership (or other vehicle) in which

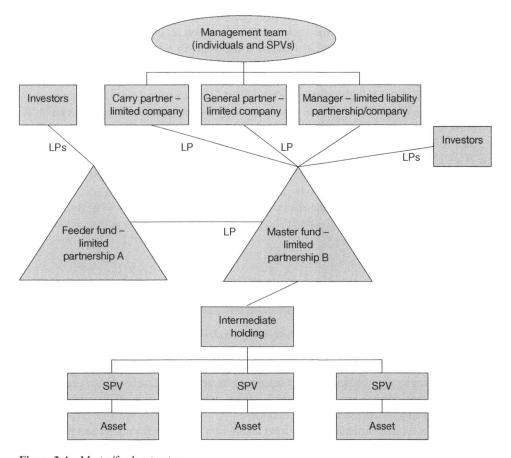

Figure 2.4   Master/feeder structure.

the remaining investors participate. The feeder partnership will invest solely in the master partnership. Both partnerships will be managed by the same entity or an affiliate.

Whether a master/feeder structure is effective will depend on the particular issues for the fund. For example, a master/feeder can be used to resolve the different tax elections required by taxable and non-taxable US investors by treating the master fund as a partnership for US tax purposes and the feeder as a corporation (taxable investors participate in the master and tax exempt in the feeder), although the reverse arrangement is not effective as once the master fund elects to be treated as a corporate, the feeder cannot benefit from tax transparency through to the master fund's assets even if it elects to be treated as a partnership. The feeder fund often will have a subsidiary that is a US entity that is treated as a corporation for US federal income tax purposes, referred to as a 'blocker corporation'.

There can be advantages to a master/feeder structure compared with a parallel structure. For example, it means that all the investors participate (directly or indirectly) in the master fund. That can be useful if an investor in the master fund cannot make up more than a certain percentage of the vehicle that they are participating in (for example, due to internal investment restrictions or regulatory reasons). Additionally, US investors that are pension funds subject to ERISA (Employee Retirement Income Security Act) present certain issues to the investment fund managers. If the business of the feeder fund is limited to investments in the master fund, then a position may be taken under ERISA that there is no investment discretion exercised by the investment manager or general partner with respect to the feeder fund. This is helpful if the sponsors are relying on an exemption from the master fund constituting 'plan assets' under ERISA, which requires that the aggregate amount of investment in the master fund subject to ERISA is less than 25%. Under a master/feeder structure all the investors in the feeder count as investors in the master fund, which would not be the case with a parallel structure. In addition, with a master/feeder structure there is only one partnership instead of two, which can simplify the acquisition and disposition of investments and other administrative matters.

The documentation for the two partnerships will generally differ as fees and carried interest are often charged only to the master fund (in order to avoid duplication so that all investors' investments are subject to the same economics) and, therefore, are not present in the feeder fund. Voting issues will also need to be addressed, for example, by allowing investors in the feeder to direct the exercise of the relevant proportion of the feeder's voting rights in the master so as to place them in effectively the same position as if they participated directly in the master.

2.3   ESTABLISHMENT OF THE FUND

2.3.1   Process

The process for establishing a limited partnership fund will involve the following steps:

(a) develop concept for fund including investment objective/strategy/target returns
(b) pre-marketing with key investors to determine interest in fund, refine fund concept
(c) identify and appoint key advisers and service providers (e.g. legal and tax advisers, placement agent, administrator and auditors)
(d) develop a suitable structure for the fund taking into account relevant tax and regulatory issues

(e) prepare more detailed terms for the fund. The key factors in determining the terms will be the fund's investment strategy (for example, is the fund investing in buyouts, venture capital, real estate, infrastructure or debt?) as well as the relative negotiating positions of the manager and the investors

(f) draft marketing material for the fund (e.g. one or two page 'teaser' document, presentation for roadshow, formal offering document)

(g) distribute marketing material and conduct initial discussions with potential investors

(h) investors consider the terms of the fund and conduct due diligence

(i) draft legal documentation for the fund (see section 2.3.2 below)

(j) investors (and/or their lawyers) review legal documentation and provide comments on it

(k) negotiations between the manager and investors (fund documentation amended where necessary and side letters prepared)

(l) investors complete subscription documents and

(m) first closing.

2.3.2   Documentation

A fund established as a limited partnership will generally require the following key documents.

(a) Offering document (or the Private Placement Memorandum – PPM)

This contains information on the fund such as its investment objective and strategy, a summary of its terms, background on the management team and its track record together with more technical information such as risk factors, a summary of the tax consequences of investing and details of restrictions on the marketing of the fund.

(b) Limited Partnership Agreement (or the LPA – in fact, normally a deed)

It is entered into between the general partner and each limited partner. It is the principal document governing the partnership and sets out all of the fund's terms in detail.

(c) Investment Management Agreement (if required)

It is entered into between the fund and its manager. It provides, among other matters, for the appointment of the manager and the circumstances in which the manager's appointment can be terminated. As set out above, the manager is either paid a fee by the fund or remunerated by the general partner out of its general partner's priority profit share. In the latter case, the actual amount to be paid is generally not specified in the management agreement.

(d) Investment Advisory Agreement (if required)

It is entered into between the manager and the investment adviser. Its content is similar to the Investment Management Agreement. It deals with the adviser's appointment, its termination and its remuneration.

(e) Subscription agreement

Each investor will sign a subscription agreement under which they agree to be bound by the partnership agreement (which is more convenient than each investor actually signing the limited partnership agreement). Each investor will also provide information about themselves (contact information, bank account details) and give representations and warranties about themselves, including eligibility to invest in the fund.

(f) Carried interest documentation

Where another limited partnership has been established to act as a carry vehicle, it will require its own limited partnership agreement and management agreement.

(g) Side letters

In the course of negotiations, the manager may agree certain matters with individual investors that are consistent with the partnership agreement (for example, specific reporting information that is required by an investor). Such agreements with individual members are set out in side letters with the relevant investors.

2.4 INVESTING

2.4.1 Investment objective and returns

The investment objective (set out in the PPM) is the result that the manager aims to achieve for investors (for example, long-term capital gain, generation of income) together with either a target return or a range of target returns. Returns are generally expressed as an internal rate of return (IRR; care should be used as to whether a target IRR is expressed as being gross or net of amounts such as management fees, carried interest or tax). Investors will generally be interested in the net amount that they receive from the fund.

2.4.2 Investment strategy

The investment strategy (set out in the PPM) establishes the investment criteria and types of investment to be made. Examples of investment strategies are set out in Chapter 5.

2.4.3 Investment period

This is the period of time during which the fund is able to make new investments. It will start from the date when the first investor is admitted to the partnership (each occasion on which an investor is admitted is called a closing and the first of these is called the first closing) and for a private equity fund typically lasts for a period of five years, sometimes with the ability of the manager to extend that either unilaterally or with the consent of investors.

The investment period will terminate earlier if the fund is fully invested. This is normally deemed to be the case when 75% (or a higher percentage) of commitments have been invested or reserved for investments (for example, this could include additional investments (called 'follow-on investments') in the fund's existing investments which the manager intends the fund to make).

The investment period will need to be consistent with the investment strategy, that is, to allow a reasonable period of time for the manager to fully invest the fund. In addition, the investment period has to close soon enough, to allow the 'harvesting' period to exit each investment within the target life of the fund. What constitutes a reasonable period of time will depend on the size of the fund, the frequency with which the manager anticipates sourcing suitable investment opportunities and the likely time required to consider those opportunities, carry out due diligence and actually make an investment. Where a fund intends to take advantage of particular circumstances (for example, an economic downturn that is (hopefully) short lived), the investment period may differ.

2.4.4   Term

This is the period of time from the first closing until the termination of the fund. This period of time will need to cover the acquisition of the investments (that is, the investment period) and then be sufficient to allow for their subsequent disposal in accordance with the fund's investment strategy.

For a private equity fund, this is typically 10 years, often subject to the manager's right to extend the term for up to two additional one-year periods with the approval of either the investors or the advisory committee. Other investment strategies may differ, for example, infrastructure funds investing in mature assets may have terms of 15 to 25 years.

Many 10-year funds are simply not long enough, and are too optimistically targeted, as it is deemed easier to sell to LPs with a 10-year target life. This has proven to be the case, especially with venture capital funds.

2.4.5   Fund borrowing

The fund may be entitled to borrow money, generally only on a short-term basis pending drawing down commitments from investors, although in some cases borrowings may be on a longer-term basis. Such borrowings together with any guarantees given by the fund are usually capped at a percentage of total commitments (e.g. 20%) and often require the manager to reserve a portion of the undrawn commitments equal to the amount borrowed plus any guarantees, so that the fund will always have sufficient undrawn commitments to repay the amount borrowed.

Amounts borrowed by the fund are generally secured against the fund's investments and the undrawn commitments of the investors. In the event of a default, the lender will generally want the right to draw down commitments from LPs.

2.4.6   Investment restrictions

In addition to the investment strategy, investors will normally require a fund to have specific restrictions on the investments that it can make. These are usually set out in the PPM and/or the LPA. While they will vary depending on the investment strategy and the requirements of investors, they could include the following:

- the maximum proportion of commitments that the fund can invest in a single investment (e.g. 20%), often referred to as a diversification or a concentration limit
- limits on the investments that can be made in particular countries or geographic areas
- limits on certain types of investments (for example, for a buyout fund, no more than 40% of commitments to be invested in retail companies or, in a real estate fund, no more than 25% of commitments to be invested in non-commercial property and
- prohibitions on particular sectors, for example, no investments in manufacture of weapons or in tobacco.

2.5 COMMITMENTS BY INVESTORS

2.5.1 Commitments/drawdowns

Limited partnership funds will generally operate on a drawdown/distribution basis. This means that when they are admitted as investors, limited partners make a commitment to contribute up to a certain amount when they are required to do so. They do not pay the total amount of their investment to the fund at that time. Instead the manager is entitled to send investors notices (called drawdown notices) from time to time requiring them to pay a portion of their commitment in order to fund the acquisition of investments or other costs or liabilities associated with the operation of the fund.

Drawdown notices typically set out the purpose for which the amount is being drawn down (subject to confidentiality restrictions) and investors have a period of time (generally 10 business days) in which to pay the relevant amount to the fund.

Any proceeds from investments' exits are then distributed back to investors once the fund receives them. Therefore, amounts committed by investors are used or invested only once and cannot be re-used (subject to certain agreed recycling items – see below). This is in contrast to other types of funds (for example, listed funds or open-ended funds like hedge funds) where once an investment is sold or has generated income, those proceeds can then often be re-invested by the fund.

2.5.2 Recycling

As discussed above, once commitments are drawn down from the investors and invested (or used to meet costs and liabilities of the fund), they generally cannot subsequently be re-used. However, there are often a small number of situations where this rule does not apply and amounts that have been drawn down can be re-used:

- underwriting or bridging investments (that is, investments made by the partnership in excess of that which the fund would ordinarily make) which are sold down or syndicated within say 12 months of the investment or underwriting commitment being made
- investments which are realized within 12 months and before the end of the investment period, sometimes subject to a limit
- amounts which are drawn down to pay the general partner's share
- amounts drawn down to fund an investment that does not proceed or that are in excess of the amount actually required and
- amounts that are returned to investors as part of the equalization process – see section 2.5.5 below.

2.5.3   Default

In the event that an investor fails to contribute an amount due under a drawdown notice by the required date, there are a number of actions that the manager can take to deal with that default. These are typically as listed below.

(a) Payment of interest

The defaulting investor is liable to pay interest on the amount outstanding from the date of default, until the default is remedied (this is an interim measure which assumes that the investor will eventually pay the amount which is due).

(b) Payment of costs

The defaulting investor is liable to pay any costs incurred by the fund as a result of its default (for example, costs related to any borrowing by the fund to cover the shortfall caused by the default).

(c) Sale of interest

If the default is not remedied within a stated period of time, the manager may sell the interest in the fund of the defaulting investor (this would include the amount already funded by the defaulting investor together with the obligation to fund further drawdowns including the drawdown that resulted in the default).

(d) Forfeiture of interest

The manager may forfeit the interest of the defaulting investor. The effect of this is that the size of the fund is reduced and the defaulting investor no longer has any interest in the fund or entitlement to distributions provided that it will be paid the amount of its commitment that has been drawn down but not already repaid after the commitments of the other investors have been repaid.

(e) Breach

A failure to meet a drawdown will constitute a breach of contract (i.e. of the LPA), which would also entitle the fund to take action against the defaulting investor to recover any loss suffered.

Historically, it has been uncommon for investors to default on their commitments to the limited partnership fund (given the consequences outlined above as well as the reputational issues for investors who would like to participate in other funds). Anecdotal evidence suggests that the number of defaults did increase during the recent financial crisis. In practice, investors who are going to have difficulties in meeting drawdowns would typically negotiate a sale of their interest in the fund (a secondary trade) prior to actually defaulting.

2.5.4   Management team's commitment

Investors will generally expect the fund's management team (that is, the institution or individuals that are responsible for sourcing, managing and exiting the fund's investments who are typically employees, directors or members of the manager) to make a commitment to the fund in order to align their interests with those of the investors and to demonstrate their faith in the fund and its investment strategy.

This is often referred to as the 'general partner's commitment' or 'general partner's co-investment' and is typically a percentage of the size of the fund, often subject to a cap. The size of the management team's commitment that investors expect varies depending on the nature and financial situation of that management team. For example, a first time fund where the management consists of a small number of individuals will be expected to contribute much less than a fund sponsored by a major financial institution. In the former case, a minimum of 1% of commitments is typically required (1% was an historic US tax requirement) whereas in the latter case amounts of 10% or more are not uncommon. That said, in the recent financial crisis, the amount a general partner commits has risen quite considerably.

2.5.5   Closings/equalization

As discussed in section 2.4.3 of this chapter, each occasion on which an investor is admitted as a limited partner is called a closing and the first occasion on which this happens is the fund's first closing. Typically, the last of the closings or final closing must happen within 12 months of the first closing.

Despite the fact that investors are admitted on different closings, all investors are treated for the purposes of the fund's economics as if they had been admitted on the first closing. This reflects the approach that all investors should participate in all of the fund's investments pro rata to their commitments (subject to some limited exemptions) and also simplifies the administration of the fund.

In order to achieve this, there is a process called equalization where the positions of all investors are adjusted to put them in the same position as if they had all been admitted at the first closing. This process is generally relevant only where investors are admitted after the fund has already drawn down commitments, although most funds will generally do this at or very soon after a closing to at least pay the fund's organizational costs.

When investors are admitted after the first closing, they are then drawn down for an amount equal to the amount that they would have contributed had they been admitted at the first closing. That amount is then distributed to the other investors pro rata to their commitments such that each investor has then had the same percentage of their commitment drawn down. These amounts that are 'refunded' to the earlier investors are then available to be drawn down subsequently from them and used for other investments (that is, it is as if those amounts had never been drawn down at all).

In addition, investors admitted after the first closing pay interest on the amounts that are initially drawn down from them which is paid to the earlier investors and is in addition to their commitment. As the net effect of investors being admitted at subsequent closings is that they acquire a proportion of the fund's assets from the existing investors, this interest payment compensates the earlier investors for the use of their funds in the intervening time. The amount of interest is normally calculated on the basis of a percentage above the relevant base rate (e.g. LIBOR or EURIBOR).

The general partner's share or management fee (see section 2.6.1 of this chapter) is also calculated on the basis that all investors are admitted at the first closing. Therefore, investors admitted at a subsequent closing are required (as part of their initial drawdown) to pay the general partner's share from the date of the first closing to the date of their admission together with interest (to compensate the general partner for the delay in receiving it).

2.5.6   Investor clawback

This is a controversial issue. It involves redrawing distributions already made, sometimes a long time after the distribution. The principal example is where a liability arises later in the fund – for example, a litigation claim from the sale of a portfolio company, and a recent example is of a pension claim relating to a previously sold portfolio company. Other examples have included environmental or regulatory issues.

2.5.7   Withdrawals

As a closed-ended fund, it is not generally possible for investors to withdraw from it. There may be some circumstances where withdrawal is permitted but they are generally only in exceptional circumstances such as regulatory or tax issues that might make continued participation by an investor in the fund unlawful or materially adverse either for that investor or for the fund. Even in these situations an investor may have to wait until investments are realized before they are paid the value of their investment in the fund. The lack of liquidity for investors is primarily driven by the illiquid nature of the fund's investments.

2.5.8   Transfers

Although investors are, as discussed above, typically unable to withdraw from a fund, there is no particular obstacle to transferring an interest (or part of an interest) either to another existing investor or to a new investor. The main proviso is that any new investor must be able to meet any regulatory or other requirements that applied to original investors in the fund.

The LPA may set out various requirements that transferees must meet. In addition, the manager of the fund may have discretion to approve transfers. This may be done to ensure that any remaining regulatory or other impediments to a transferee participating as an investor can be properly dealt with. In addition, it may be done so that the manager can control the identity of investors, for example, a manager may not want an interest in the fund to be held by a potential competitor.

A transfer is typically effected by an agreement between the transferor and transferee which would, for example, set out the purchase price and a separate document under which the transferee adheres to the LPA and makes the same representations (for example, with respect to their eligibility to be an investor) as other investors made when they originally invested in the fund.

2.6   ECONOMICS

2.6.1   Management fee/priority profit share

As discussed above, instead of being a fee payable directly by the fund to the manager, in a UK partnership, the management fee is typically structured as a priority profit share that is paid by the fund to the general partner and then by the general partner to the manager or investment adviser.

(a) During the investment period

The management fee is generally calculated during the investment period as a percentage of the fund's total commitments. It is typically between 1% and 2% depending on a number of factors including the fund's size and investment strategy. The management fee will typically be lower for a fund of funds, reflecting the fact that making investments into other funds is less costly than making investments into underlying assets such as portfolio companies and also in recognition of the fact that the underlying funds will also charge management fees.

(b) After the investment period

The management fee is typically calculated as a percentage of the acquisition costs of the investments that the fund continues to hold (for this purpose an investment that has been written off is treated as having been disposed of, so no management fee is payable in respect of it). An alternative formulation is to charge a management fee based on a reduced percentage of all commitments drawn down.

2.6.2   Distributions/carried interest

As a limited partnership fund typically operates on a drawdown/distribution model, the fund will typically distribute any income or capital gains that it receives to investors periodically in the case of income (often quarterly) and as soon as possible in the case of capital gains. The fund is generally permitted to retain amounts to meet its ongoing expenses and liabilities and potentially to keep a reserve for future expenses and liabilities but is not otherwise permitted to retain amounts in the fund or to re-invest them. There are typically certain exceptions to this rule – see section 2.5.2 of this chapter.

The amounts that are available for distribution are split between the investors and the carry vehicle. The amount paid to the carry vehicle is called carried interest and is the performance-based remuneration that the management team is eligible to receive. The provisions in the LPA which deals with the calculation of these distributions are commonly referred to as the waterfall (Figure 2.5).

There are a number of different ways in which the waterfall can work. The most common arrangement and the one that is used in the vast majority of private equity funds involves distributions being made in the following order:

(a) first, to pay the general partner's share (if applicable, see section 2.6.1 of this chapter)
(b) second, to the investors (pro rata to their commitments) until the amounts drawn down from them have been repaid

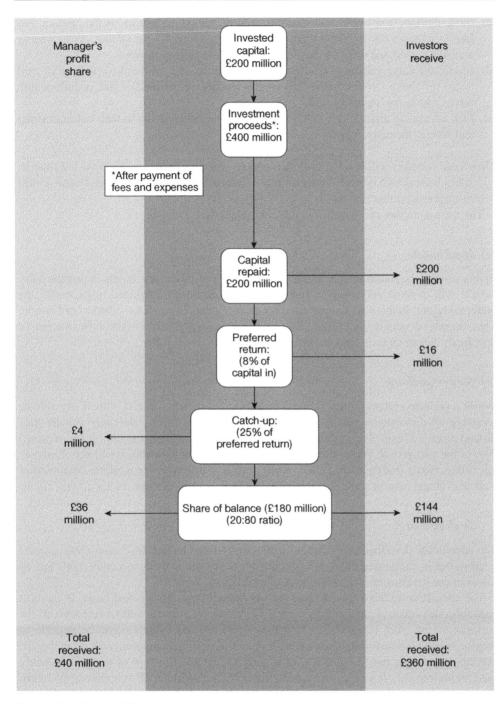

Figure 2.5   The waterfall structure.

(c) third, the investors are paid a return (called the preferred return) on the amount that has been drawn down from but not repaid to them (often 8% per annum, compounding annually, calculated daily on the amount of outstanding drawdowns)

(d) fourth, the carry vehicle is paid an amount equal to 25% of the preferred return paid under (c) above (so that it has 20% of the 'profits' of the fund) – this is colloquially referred to as the 'catch-up' and

(e) fifth, remaining amounts are paid 80% to the investors (pro rata to their commitments) and 20% to the carry vehicle.

Therefore, investors will receive back the amount that they have actually invested (that is, which has been drawn down from them) plus a return on that amount (the preferred return) before any carried interest is paid.

There are a number of variations to this basic approach.

(a) Hard hurdle

In this variant, the fourth step of the catch-up is removed. The effect of this is that the carry vehicle will at most only ever receive 20% of the amounts distributed in excess of the preferred return. In this case the preferred return is often more correctly called a hard hurdle. This variant is generally used for limited partnership investing in real estate, infrastructure or debt funds, where an investor 'coupon' is expected.

(b) Slower catch-up

Where a preferred return (and not a hard hurdle) is being used, instead of the carry vehicle receiving all distributions until it has received 20% of the profits, the carry vehicle may instead receive a lesser proportion (for example, 60% of distributions) until it has received 20% of the total profits. Where the distributions are sufficient to do this, it will not ultimately affect the amount that the carry vehicle receives. It is likely, however, to affect the timing of their receipt and may, in some circumstances, affect the actual amount.

(c) Deal-by-deal

The approaches described above are all variants of what is called 'fund as a whole' carried interest, that is, the carried interest is calculated by reference to the fund's entire portfolio, so losses in one investment offset gains in another and vice versa.

The alternative to this is to calculate carried interest on a deal-by-deal basis. In its most pure form this involves applying the waterfall to each investment without reference to the performance of other investments. This means that carried interest could be payable in relation to one high performing asset, even if other low performing investments mean that the portfolio as a whole has failed to reach the preferred return. This type of waterfall is rarely used and historically has been applicable to only certain types of US venture capital funds. Deal-by-deal was more common at the origins of the private equity 'industry' when discrete investment clubs were formed. During the recent financial crisis, as more flexible variants of the traditional fund model have been raised (see common examples in Chapter 4), deal-by-deal has somewhat re-emerged.

More commonly deal-by-deal carry refers to a waterfall where, on the realization of an investment, proceeds are paid to investors until they have received all of their commitments that have been drawn down and used to fund the cost of only that investment which is being realized, and any losses on other investments which have already been realized together with any write-downs on unrealized investments (managers will prefer that the calculation of write-downs also takes into account any write-ups). Any surplus is then split 80:20 between investors and the carry vehicle, subject to the investors first receiving their preferred return. Therefore, the key difference between this and fund as a whole carried interest is that on the realization of an investment that has performed well, the fund does not have to return to investors amounts drawn down to fund the acquisition costs of investments that have not yet been realized (except to the extent of any write-down) prior to paying carried interest.

(d) Distributions in specie

As discussed above, distributions are made to investors in cash following the disposal of an investment or the receipt of an income from an investment. However, in some limited circumstances funds may also make distributions in specie (that is, instead of distributing cash, securities such as shares following an initial public offering (IPO) are distributed). Many investors do not wish to receive distributions in specie because of the administrative costs involved, the potential difficulty in disposing of the assets and the uncertainty as to what those assets might actually be (for example, if the fund can invest in a large number of countries, an investor could potentially receive a distribution in specie of securities in any of those countries).

Therefore, during the life of the fund, distributions in specie are typically allowed only (if they are allowed at all) where the relevant securities are freely transferable. During the liquidation of the fund, there may be more flexibility in making distributions in specie. There will also need to be an agreed approach to valuing any assets distributed in specie so that they can be properly taken into account in the fund's waterfall.

(e) Other variants

There are a number of other commercial variants, such as more 'steps' being introduced into the waterfall, as is common in secondary direct portfolio transactions (see Chapter 5, section 5.11), or higher or lower percentages of the carry, the hurdle or the earlier returns to investors.

2.6.3   Carried interest, escrow and clawback

It is possible that too much carried interest could be distributed or, more precisely, that the amount of carried interest distributed exceeds the amount that would have been distributed if all the distributions have been at the same time on a consolidated basis. This is often due to the timing of investments and subsequent exits.

Upon termination of the fund, the carry limited partner will be required to repay any distributions it received in respect of its 'carried interest' (the 'clawback') to the extent that such distributions exceed (as is most common) 20% of the fund's cumulative net portfolio gains. A further protection for LPs on carried interest overpayment is holding part of the carried interest in escrow until the fund's end returns are known.

2.6.4   Carried interest structure

In the UK, the carry vehicle is, like the fund, often a collective investment scheme (CIS) and hence needs to be managed by an FCA-regulated manager (the manager, again, in this structure). Carry holders are the principals of the fund manager. See Chapter 11, section 11.5.3, which explains that the carry should be treated as capital rather than income. The carry deed governs the terms of the principal's returns with the manager, such as share of income, joiners and leavers, consents, etc. Further information is provided in Chapter 10.

2.6.5   Expenses

(a) Establishment expenses

Normal market practice is that the costs related to the establishment of the fund will be borne by the fund itself once it has been established. In practice this means that the first time that commitments are drawn down from investors (normally shortly after the establishment of the fund) that drawdown will include the establishment expenses. The fund will then either pay the establishment expenses or, to the extent that the manager has already borne those expenses, refund them to the manager.

The establishment (or organizational) expenses generally include costs incurred by the manager such as advisory fees (legal, tax, etc.) as well as costs of travel, meetings, printing and other administrative expenses related to the establishment of the fund. They do not include day to day costs of the running of the manager or its affiliates, for example rent, salaries and utilities.

(b) Ongoing expenses

The fund is responsible for all of the expenses incurred during the life of the fund. These include administrative expenses such as ongoing legal fees, fees of auditors, accountants and fund administrators as well as all costs associated with investments including potential investments that are not completed (that is, abort costs). As with establishment expenses, these do not include the day to day expenses of the manager or its affiliates, such as the costs of office premises and salaries. It is anticipated that these will be met out of the management fee paid to the manager.

(c) Variants

Especially during the recent financial crisis, there has been greater investor scrutiny of expenses, and variants or tougher caps have developed, also in conjunction with budgeted manager fees.

2.6.6   Transactional or monitoring fees

These occur during a fund's life and relate to investments and portfolio companies. They encompass entry and exit fees, monitoring of investment fees, directorship fees and other types of deal or consulting type components. In better economic times where access to certain fund managers was harder, a manager might expect to keep some of their fees (sometimes

20% for leveraged buyouts or LBOs, 50% for venture capital or even 100%). A combination of some high profile abuses (or just massive GP 'takes') and the recent financial crisis has largely stopped the manager taking any or most of these fees, and instead in an LPA, they now are largely set off against the general partner's share, and thus not kept by the manager.

2.7   GOVERNANCE

2.7.1   Removal of the general partner/manager

The investors will have the right to remove the general partner for cause and, typically, in more limited circumstances, without cause. The removal of the general partner will result in the removal of any affiliated manager or investment adviser who provides services in respect of the fund.

(a) Removal for cause

The circumstances which constitute 'cause' will vary from fund to fund and are often the subject of detailed negotiation with investors, but the following are typical of the events that will constitute cause in respect of the general partner or, if applicable, the manager or investment adviser:

- insolvency or an equivalent event
- engaging in fraud, wilful misconduct, (gross) negligence or an illegal act
- ceasing to hold any regulatory authorizations necessary to carry out their role (e.g. the manager ceasing to be FCA authorized) or
- a material breach of either the LPA or, in the case of the manager, the management agreement.

The right to remove for cause can generally be exercised by investors holding a percentage of commitments to the fund. As a limited partnership must have a general partner, removal will necessarily involve the investors identifying a replacement general partner (and manager/investment adviser where relevant). Instead of a right of removal, investors may instead have a right to terminate the fund, a concept more prevalent in recent LPAs.

(b) Removal without cause

The removal of the general partner (and manager) without cause (often referred to as 'no-fault divorce') does not (as the name suggests) require the investors to demonstrate any failing on the part of the general partner. However, the investors' ability to exercise this right is generally limited in two ways:

- timing – often removal without cause can only take place after a certain period of time, for example, two or three years after the final closing
- investor approval – a much higher proportion of investors is typically required for removal without cause, typically investors holding 75% or even 85% of commitments.

(c) General partner's share and carried interest following removal

Where the general partner is removed for cause, the general partner will only typically be entitled to receive its general partner's share (and, therefore, the manager any management fee) up until the date of its removal. Similarly, on the general partner's removal, the carry vehicle might also cease to be entitled to receive any carried interest.

On removal without cause, the situation is more complex. In addition to the general partner's share up until the date of its removal, it is common for it to be entitled to receive compensation of one to two years' worth of general partner's share. Such compensation is often justified by the longer-term costs incurred by the manager (e.g. lease of premises, employment of staff), which means that it would incur costs in winding down its operations in the event of its removal. The amount of general partner's share is often the subject of negotiation with investors.

The position on carried interest is less clear and common approaches include:

- the carry vehicle remains entitled to receive distributions of carried interest as if the removal had not occurred
- the carry vehicle remains entitled to receive distributions of carried interest as in (a) but only in respect of investments made prior to its removal
- the carry vehicle may be entitled to receive only a proportion of future distributions of carried interest or
- the entitlement to carried interest is calculated at the date of removal on the basis that all of the fund's investments were liquidated on that date (the methodology used to value the fund's investments is obviously very important in this case).

2.7.2 Key person

In many cases investors will want to ensure that certain individuals (typically, members or employees of the manager) whom they regard as 'key' are involved in the day to day management of the fund. A 'key person' provision will typically provide that if a particular number of specified individuals (the key persons) cease to be involved in the affairs of the fund, the fund will no longer be able to make new investments (that is, the investment period will be suspended). The key persons will be listed in the LPA.

The identity of the key persons will be the subject of negotiation between the manager and the investors and will depend on the size of the management team and the extent to which only one or two members of the management team have particular skills or experience that are considered critical to the success of the fund. The number of key persons who have to cease being involved before the investment period is suspended will, similarly, depend on the exact composition of the management team. In some circumstances, the departure of even one individual could be sufficient. The amount of time which key persons are required to dedicate to the affairs of the fund can also vary.

Once the investment period has been suspended, there is a procedure that allows it to be restarted if the investors so approve, for example, on the basis that a replacement individual(s) has been recruited by the manager or, on reflection, that the manager is able to continue to satisfactorily invest and manage the fund in the absence of the relevant individual. There is often a time limit on this, so that the manager has only a set period of time (for example, six months) in order to find a replacement individual and seek approval from the investors, otherwise the investment period terminates.

In addition to the suspension of the investment period, a key person provision could have other consequences, for example, giving investors a right to terminate the fund or remove the general partner. This is becoming more common in the current financial crisis.

2.7.3   Advisory committee

Many funds have a committee or board made up of representatives of certain investors, often called an advisory committee or investors committee. The composition of this committee may be at the discretion of the manager (in which case major investors are likely to negotiate a seat on the committee when they invest in the fund). Alternatively, investors may be automatically entitled to nominate a representative if they make a commitment above a certain amount.

The role of the advisory committee is limited to being consulted on matters such as conflicts of interest, approving exceptions to the investment restrictions and potentially certain other matters set out in the LPA and discussing the performance and operation of the fund. The advisory committee is generally not involved in making any decisions relating to the making or realization of investments (involvement in such decisions could compromise the limited liability of those investors represented in the advisory committee).

2.7.4   Reports and meetings

Investors will generally receive an annual report with audited accounts prepared in accordance with an agreed accounting standard including valuations of the investments, together with details of investments and their progress. Semi-annual or quarterly statements are usually also provided which contain unaudited financial information and commentary on investments.

Managers may also organize annual meetings of investors in order to update investors on the progress of the fund and provide them with a forum to ask questions or request further information. Such meetings may be held in conjunction with a meeting of the advisory committee.

2.8   SOME CONCLUSIONS

A limited partnership structured private equity fund provides a number of important advantages for both investors and managers. They are tax transparent, but at the cost of investor control, and management liability can easily be isolated through the use of a subsidiary company acting as the general partner of the fund partnership.

The management, structure and internal economics of a fund are likely to change as regulation such as the Alternative Investment Fund Managers Directive (AIFMD) (see Chapter 12, section 12.6) comes into force after transitional periods, and in particular, when private placement regimes are abolished (if indeed they are). Regulatory change will be the single most influential driver of change in this sphere rather than market pressures, although existing trends also suggest that investors will drive down the economic rewards for managers as much as remuneration regulation.

3

Hedge Funds

3.1 INTRODUCTION

A hedge fund can be used as a vehicle in relation to a wide scope of investment strategies. Broadly, this type of fund could be categorized as an actively managed portfolio of investments that uses a range of instruments and investment strategies with the goal of generating returns.

The returns of hedge funds generally fall into two broad categories of return type. Hedge funds may seek to operate an 'Alpha' return, namely an exceptional return that an investor or portfolio manager is looking to achieve due to the application of what is a unique market view, for example by exploiting a specified market inefficiency. A 'Beta' type return, meanwhile, is a measure of a hedge fund's returns relative to a given index or benchmark. This approach exposes a fund's portfolio value to asset price movements recorded on a given index or by a particular benchmark.

In terms of legal structure, hedge funds often use offshore structures to allow investors to create tax efficiencies and to provide managers with investment flexibility, which advantages would otherwise not be available if using the type of regulated onshore structure that is frequently designed to protect retail investors.

3.2 TYPES OF HEDGE FUND STRATEGIES

3.2.1 Market neutral or directional

Hedge fund strategies are described as absolute return strategies, in that they seek to deliver positive returns regardless of market performance, and can be described as directional or market neutral.

A market neutral fund will seek a lower correlation to the current markets and will be less exposed to volatility in the markets. Directional funds are often exposed to market movements, as they seek to follow the direction that a particular market is moving and exploit any inconsistencies in the market movements.

3.2.2 Discretionary or systematic

The way a hedge fund implements its chosen strategy and makes investments into its chosen instruments can also be divided into how the hedge fund operates when analysing the markets and selecting investments. They are known as either discretionary/qualitative strategies, under which investments are selected by managers who tend to rely on a fundamental or qualitative approach to their decision making, or systematic/quantitative strategies, under which investments are selected using a systematic model.

3.2.3   Strategy implementation and instruments

The strategies set out above can be further broken down into how they implement this strategy to achieve the required level of returns and will depend on:

- the chosen market
- the approach to the market
- the types of instrument used to generate returns
- the method and analytics used to select investments and
- the desired level of asset diversification.

In addition, the level of diversification within a fund can vary dramatically.

3.2.4   Typical strategies

Hedge funds cover a range of strategies and are often evolving. This makes it difficult to categorize a typical hedge fund strategy; however, as a rough guide typical strategies fall into the following categories.

(a) Global macro

Hedge funds utilizing a global macro investing strategy take a view on an industry sector as opposed to individual companies in order to generate a risk-adjusted return. Global macro fund managers use macroeconomic ('big picture') analysis based on global market events and trends to identify opportunities for investment that would profit from anticipated price movements. Global macro is often categorized as a directional investment strategy.

(b) Directional

Directional investment strategies utilize market movements, trends, or inconsistencies when picking stocks across a variety of markets. Systematic models can be used, or fund managers will identify and select investments. These types of strategies have a greater exposure to the fluctuations of the overall market than do market neutral strategies. Directional hedge fund strategies include US and international long/short equity hedge funds, where long equity positions are hedged with short sales of equities or equity index options.

(c) Event-driven

Event-driven strategies concern situations in which the underlying investment opportunity and risk are associated with an event. An event-driven investment strategy finds investment opportunities in corporate transactional events such as consolidations, acquisitions, recapitalizations, bankruptcies and liquidations. Managers employing such a strategy capitalize on valuation inconsistencies in the market before or after such events, and take a position based on the predicted movement of the security or securities in question. Large institutional investors such as hedge funds are more likely to pursue event-driven investing strategies than traditional equity investors because they have the expertise and resources to analyse corporate transactional events for investment opportunities.

Corporate transactional events generally fit into three categories – distressed securities, risk arbitrage and special situations.

(i) Distressed securities

Distressed securities include such events as restructurings, recapitalizations and bankruptcies. A distressed securities investment strategy involves investing in companies facing bankruptcy or severe financial distress, when these bonds or loans are being traded at a discount to their value. Hedge fund managers pursuing the distressed debt investment strategy aim to capitalize on depressed bond prices. Hedge funds purchasing distressed debt may prevent those companies from going bankrupt, as such an acquisition deters foreclosure by banks.

(ii) Risk or merger arbitrage

Risk arbitrage or merger arbitrage includes such events as mergers, acquisitions, liquidations and hostile takeovers. Risk arbitrage typically involves buying and selling the stocks of two or more merging companies to take advantage of market discrepancies between acquisition price and stock price. The risk element arises from the possibility that the merger or acquisition will not go ahead as planned; hedge fund managers will use research and analysis to determine whether the event will take place.

(iii) Special situations

Special situations are events that impact the value of a company's stock, including the restructuring of a company or corporate transactions including spin-offs, share buy-backs, security issuance/repurchase, asset sales, or other catalyst-oriented situations. To take advantage of special situations the hedge fund manager must identify an upcoming event that will increase or decrease the value of the company's equity and equity-related instruments.

(iv) Other event-driven strategies

Other event-driven strategies include:

- a 'credit arbitrage strategy', which focuses on corporate fixed-income securities
- an 'activist strategy', where the fund takes large positions in companies and uses the ownership to participate in or influence the management and
- a 'legal catalyst strategy', which specializes in companies involved in major lawsuits.

(d) Relative value arbitrage

Relative value arbitrage strategies take advantage of relative discrepancies in price between securities. The price discrepancy can occur due to mispricing of securities compared with related securities, the underlying security or the market overall. Hedge fund managers can use various types of analysis to identify price discrepancies in securities, including mathematical, technical or fundamental techniques. Relative value is often used as a synonym for market neutral, as strategies in this category typically have very little or no directional exposure to the market as a whole.

(e) Convertible arbitrage

Convertible arbitrage is an equity long-short investment strategy which involves taking a long position in convertible securities of a company, while at the same time taking a short position in the shares of the same company. Convertible securities often take the form of bonds which may be converted to shares at a set time and price, usually at a discount to the market value of the company's shares.

The idea behind the convertible arbitrage strategy is that if a company's share price falls, the hedge fund will benefit from taking a short position in the company, and in addition the value of the convertible bonds should decrease less than the company's share price. However, if the company's share price rises, a loss will be made in relation to the fund's short position of selling the company shares, but the hedge fund will benefit from taking a long position, as it may convert the convertible bonds to shares and sell at market price, hopefully making a gain overall.

(f) Fixed-income arbitrage

Fixed-income arbitrage is an investment strategy that seeks to profit from arbitrage opportunities between fixed-income securities. Fixed-income securities, such as government bonds, are debt instruments which provide a fixed stream of periodic payments to investors. A common fixed-income arbitrage strategy entails 'swap-spread arbitrage'. Swap-spread arbitrage involves betting on the likely direction of credit default swap rates and other similar rates. A credit default swap is a type of credit derivative, and is a contractual agreement whereby the risk of a reference entity defaulting is transferred from a seller to a buyer. Payments are made by the buyer to the seller, but in the event the reference entity defaults on the loan, the seller agrees to compensate the buyer for the loss.

(g) Multi-strategy funds (and fund of funds)

Fund of hedge funds (multi-manager) are hedge funds with a diversified portfolio of numerous underlying single-manager hedge funds. Essentially the investment is spread across separate sub-managers that invest in their own strategy.

Alternatively a multi-strategy hedge fund is a hedge fund that uses a combination of different strategies to reduce market risk.

(h) Commodities trading advisers (CTA) strategy

CTA funds use futures and options (more information in relation to futures contracts can be found in Chapter 5, section 5.9.5(c)). In the early stages of the execution of the strategy, managers of CTA funds tended to focus upon commodity-based investments. CTA funds tend to do well when the prices of securities are falling, and tend to underperform when the prices of securities rise. The investment strategies of a CTA fund fall into two categories:

(i) Systematic trading
Systematic CTAs rely on computer programs to provide analysis of market data and to identify and make trades. Systematic trading is the most common CTA strategy, although it has

drawbacks in that it can take a long time to implement changes to the computer programs, where changes in market or economic conditions occur.

(ii) Discretionary trading

A discretionary CTA which employs discretionary trading relies on its investment decisions being made by management based upon 'real-time' market data. While a discretionary CTA is able to react to changes in market or economic conditions, they are less likely to be able to make an unbiased decision in the manner in which a systematic CTA can.

3.3   WHERE ARE HEDGE FUNDS LOCATED AND WHAT ARE THE TAX DRIVERS?

Hedge funds are commonly located in an offshore jurisdiction such as the British Virgin Islands, the Cayman Islands or Jersey. An alternative is to domicile the fund in Europe in either Ireland or Luxembourg. Luxembourg is a particularly popular hedge fund jurisdiction for US investors. US hedge funds are often domiciled in Delaware. One of the key drivers is that these jurisdictions typically offer zero-tax regimes and lighter regulation of investment strategy. For the managers it is better to be subject to fewer regulatory constraints in respect of investment strategy than are imposed in other jurisdictions (especially considering the incoming Dodd–Frank Act (see Chapter 12, section 12.5.3) and the AIFMD (see Chapter 12, section 12.6), which will alter the regulatory landscape further). It is important to note that the corporate governance regulation in these jurisdictions can be stricter than in onshore counterparts. This section will outline and compare the regulatory and tax regime of the British Virgin Islands, Cayman Islands and Jersey. Additional detail is available on these jurisdictions in Chapter 7. In addition, for regulated UCITS funds that are generally based in Luxembourg or Ireland see section 3.6.3 of this chapter.

3.3.1   Cayman Islands

In the Cayman Islands (Cayman), open-ended funds are governed by the Mutual Funds Law (MFL) unless they are exempted. The MFL defines a 'mutual fund' as a company, unit trust or partnership that issues equity interests, the purpose or effect of which is pooling of investor funds with the aim of spreading investment risks and enabling investors in the mutual fund to receive profits or gains from the acquisition, holding, management or disposal of investments.[1]

There are three types of regulation for open-ended mutual funds, together with exempted funds. The categories are:

- Licensed Mutual Fund[2] – funds which hold a Mutual Funds Licence granted by the Cayman Islands Monetary Authority (CIMA)
- Administered Mutual Fund – funds for which the principal office is provided by a CIMA-licensed mutual fund administrator in Cayman and therefore do not need to apply separately for a mutual fund licence and

---

[1] Part 1 (2) MFL

[2] Section 4(1) MFL

- Registered Mutual Fund – funds which are registered and require a minimum initial subscription of USD 100,000 per investor.

Other than exempt mutual funds, all Cayman mutual funds require regulatory approval by CIMA. Broadly speaking, funds that qualify as exempt mutual funds under section 4(4) of the MFL are those where (a) the equity interests are held by fewer than 15 investors, a majority of whom are capable of appointing or removing the operator of the fund; or (b) the fund is not incorporated in Cayman and makes a public offering to the public in Cayman to subscribe for its equity interests.[3] The 'operator' of the fund is either the directors of a company, the general partner of an exempted limited partnership, or the trustee of a unit trust, where appropriate.

Cayman has a tax system attractive to companies and funds operating in Cayman. No income tax, corporation tax, capital gains tax (CGT) or inheritance tax is payable and Cayman is not party to any double taxation treaty. Exempted companies are entitled to apply for undertakings from the Governor-in-Cabinet of Cayman should local taxes be introduced for a maximum of 20 years, undertakings which maintain their exemption for that period of time. For partnerships and trusts, the length of the undertaking is 50 years.

3.3.2   British Virgin Islands

In the British Virgin Islands (BVI) all funds that fall within the definition of a 'mutual fund' or 'fund' under the Securities and Investment Business Act, 2010 (SIBA) require regulatory approval by the BVI Financial Services Commission (the BVI-FSC). The definition, set out in Chapter 7, section 7.13.3, captures open-ended funds (the key element being investors' entitlement to redeem their interests). For funds falling within the definition, there are no exemptions from the approval requirement which, depending on the type of open-ended fund established, is termed 'recognition' or 'registration'.

In turn, SIBA distinguishes three different types of indigenous mutual fund, all of which are subject to approval and oversight by the BVI-FSC, as follows:

- Public funds – being funds which may offer their shares to the public, and any offers they make must be contained in a prospectus registered with the BVI-FSC
- Professional funds – being funds available only to 'professional investors', which are defined as persons whose ordinary business involves the investment in the same kind of property as the fund's, either on their own account or on behalf of others, or who have declared a net worth over the specified regulatory minimum (currently USD 1 million), and where the minimum initial investment by investors unrelated to the fund is USD 100,000 (or its equivalent in another currency) and
- Private funds – being funds whose constitutional documents specify that the fund cannot have more than 50 investors or that any invitation to potential investors is made on a private basis only – being an offer made either to specified persons that is not calculated to result in fund interests becoming available to other persons or by reason of a close business connection between the offerer and the investor.

---

[3] s4(4) Mutual Funds Law 2012 (Cayman Islands)

Mutual funds must have a registered office and registered agent within the BVI, as well as an authorized representative in the BVI. They must also have at least two directors (who must be individuals in the case of a public fund); however, there are no requirements for mutual funds to have locally based directors, service providers or auditors. While SIBA includes a licensing regime that covers certain fund service providers (including investment managers and advisers), provided the service provider is not based in the BVI, it normally will not need to be licensed. However, the BVI-FSC must be satisfied that a fund manager has the requisite experience to carry out its management role.

The BVI tax regime is neutral with respect to mutual funds, which are exempt from all provisions of the Income Tax Act of the BVI (the BVI-ITA), including with respect to all dividends, interests, rents, royalties, compensation and other amounts payable by them to persons who are not persons resident in the BVI. Likewise, capital gains realized with respect to fund interests by persons who are not persons resident in the BVI are also normally exempt from the provisions of the BVI-ITA, and no estate, inheritance, succession or gift tax, rate, duty, levy or other charge is normally payable by persons who are not persons resident in the BVI with respect to such interests.

3.3.3   Jersey

Jersey offers a broad range of open- and closed-ended funds including public and private funds. The legislation governing Jersey based funds is predominantly the Collective Investment Funds (Jersey) Law 1988, as amended (CIF Law), which governs public funds, and the Control of Borrowing (Jersey) Order 1958 (COBO), which governs private funds. The Jersey Financial Services Commission (JFSC) is the financial authority responsible for the regulation of all funds with the exception of Unregulated Eligible Investor Funds established under the Collective Investment Funds (Unregulated Funds) (Jersey) Order 2008 which, as the name suggests, are free of regulation. Some examples of typical fund types are as follows:

- Expert funds – a type of semi or non-retail public fund which is available to 10 categories of expert investor, for example those investing at least USD 100,000. Although expert funds have no investment restrictions, they do have strict requirements as to the experience and domicile of managers and some service providers
- Unregulated eligible investor funds – as above, these public funds are free of regulation and have no investment or borrowing restrictions. Such funds are often used for hedge funds and
- Unclassified funds (unrecognized funds) – funds similar to expert funds which are regulated under CIF Law.[4] However, unclassified funds must fall within prescribed investment criteria and are subject to certain investment restrictions. These funds must have a manager or administrator domiciled in Jersey.

As for the jurisdictions examined above, the Jersey taxation regime does not, broadly speaking, require limited companies to make income tax, corporation tax, CGT or inheritance tax payments unless the company is a financial services or utilities company whose place of

---

[4] s8 CIF Law

business is Jersey. Similarly, only income derived from a trade carried on in Jersey is subject to taxation. Income from international business activities is excluded from tax.

3.4   HEDGE FUND INVESTORS

Hedge funds are designed for professional investors and not the general public, and typically these include pension plans, institutional investors, sovereign wealth funds and wealthy individuals.

3.4.1   Seed and cornerstone investors

Raising early stage capital is one of the most challenging aspects of starting a hedge fund. Investors will often prefer to invest with an established fund manager as this will be viewed as less risky than investing with a new fund or manager. Typically, early stage investors have a strong negotiating position and can therefore obtain significant fee discounts in terms of both management fees and performance fees. Such a discount is often regarded by managers as fair compensation for the crucial role seed investors play in the establishment of a fund. Many cornerstone investors will be able to negotiate an equity stake or preferential terms with the fund manager, such is the importance of their investment. Established seed investors also take not only an equity stake in the manager but a share of all fees generated. A future put or call is also often negotiated to buy out the seed investor later.

3.4.2   Incubator funds

Given investors' reluctance to invest with untested funds or managers, incubator funds are an increasingly popular investment vehicle for new managers to adopt when starting out with a new fund. Typically, the general manager will contribute a significant proportion of their own capital to the incubator fund and manage the investments for around a year or so. This provides a test to prove the manager's investment strategy. Once a successful track record has been established, incubator funds are then opened up to further investment and so can become fully fledged hedge funds. Certain institutions provide an incubator environment and capital to early stage managers.

3.4.3   Fund of funds

A fund of funds is an investment vehicle that allows investors to invest capital over a number of different funds or hedge funds. The benefit to investors is that they can diversify their investment, manage their risk and utilize different managers. Further, by effectively pooling their resources in a fund of funds, independent investors may be able to access a particular fund that would ordinarily be denied to them due to that fund's minimum investment. Typically, overall management fees charged to investors in funds of funds are higher than other hedge funds, as management fees are charged by the manager of the fund of funds that is also charged a management fee by the individual funds in which they invest.

3.4.4   Individual investors and family offices

Despite the high levels of volatility seen in the financial markets since 2008, high net worth individuals and family offices continue to be attracted to investing in hedge funds. Such an investment strategy allows their own choice of strategy managed by experienced professional managers. The diversification of investments offered by hedge funds allows individual investors a degree of risk management, particularly in order to avoid index-linked investments, or Beta.

3.4.5   Platforms

A platform is a partnership between an existing manager or financial institution and a newly formed manager (whether a spin-out of the existing manager or independent of it). For a newly formed manager it allows it access to capital, operational oversight and experience in risk management and fund-raising. The existing manager can benefit by gaining exposure to new and/or alternative sources of Alpha generation.

3.5   PRINCIPAL VEHICLES

3.5.1   The fund vehicle

The typical vehicles used to structure hedge funds are limited partnerships or corporate vehicles, based in the favoured offshore jurisdiction. Limited partnerships are tax transparent, whereas offshore companies generally pay little or no tax at fund level. For UK-based investors it may be more favourable for the fund not to be structured as a tax transparent vehicle as Her Majesty's Revenue and Customs (HMRC) treats hedge fund activity as 'trading' rather than 'investing', meaning taxation of the investors as partners is on the basis of income rather than capital gains. In the alternative, if a hedge fund achieves 'reporting fund' status from HMRC, the distributions to investors are treated as capital rather than income. Hedge funds may be structured so as to incorporate various vehicles in accordance with the requirements of key investors or a large number with shared needs.

Funds that employ an open-ended structure (issuing and redeeming units or shares in the fund in accordance with demand) are the most common structure used, enabling the fund to raise further funds and enabling investors to request that their money to be returned. The value of a share in an open-ended fund is calculated in accordance with the fund's net asset value, divided by the number of shares in issue at that given time.

If in the alternative, a fund is structured as a closed-ended vehicle, there is reduced liquidity for an investor's commitment and there may be limited options to sell the interest to a secondary investor. Side pockets to open-ended hedge funds (see section 3.10, below) can be structured as closed-ended vehicles owing to the reduced liquidity of their underlying investments.

3.5.2   Offshore management vehicle

When a fund is established in an offshore jurisdiction it is common for the manager of the fund to be established in the same jurisdiction, and often this is a requirement of the local jurisdiction's regulations. It may still be possible (and desirable) for the investment advice to be provided by an associated advisory entity onshore, where the prime markets for recruiting investment professionals are located. Being an offshore manager may also entail the appointment of at least one director who is resident within that jurisdiction. For more detail on the regulatory requirements of the primary offshore jurisdictions, see section 3.3 of this chapter (above) together with Chapter 7.

The manager entity is typically structured as either a limited liability partnership (LLP) (or its offshore equivalent) or a limited liability company. Within the fund structure, if the fund is a limited partnership, the manager will be engaged by the partnership by agreement to provide services but can also act as the general partner. If it is a corporate structure fund there will be a bilateral agreement between the fund and the manager.

The fund manager may be made up of various entities if the commercial, regulatory or taxation considerations require it. Often, the investment advisers will be individuals who are based onshore in financial centres such as London or New York. In the UK, for example, if an adviser were to conduct more of the functions typically associated with a manager that may be enough for the fund to be considered established within the UK and attract greater taxation for its activities (see Chapter 11, section 11.2.4 for more information).

3.5.3   Onshore advisory entity

The advisory entity, if based in the UK, would typically be structured as a limited liability partnership. This is the most common structure used to create an onshore UK advisory group to advise offshore funds, and would house the investment team (however, see Chapter 10, section 10.2 on the UK HMRC's review of LLPs). The structure of the limited liability partnership would also typically include corporate members to act as an onshore 'profits trap' and secondly to take on liabilities not wanted in the regulated entity.

It would also need to be authorized and regulated by the FCA to arrange transactions of finance, and may also seek further permissions to manage and operate a CIS.

3.6   TYPES OF HEDGE FUND STRUCTURES

There are several different fund structures which are available for hedge funds to use.

3.6.1   Simple hedge fund

A simple hedge fund structure uses only a single vehicle to act as the fund. Some examples of commercial requirements that would enable such a simple structure would be a fund entirely marketed to US taxable investors (or alternatively US tax exempt investors) where no variation is required to accommodate other investors. This arrangement does not preclude the requirement that the manager-adviser structure is complex as it will remain the case that the advisory functions are best performed by onshore experts and the regulatory demands of the local offshore jurisdiction of the fund require an offshore manager. A simple hedge fund may even be based onshore if it suits the regulatory and taxation requirements of the manager-adviser and the investors.

Like a UK limited partnership, a Delaware limited partnership that is a hedge fund will also typically have a separate investment manager appointed under a management agreement between the fund and the investment manager. The investment manager will normally be a

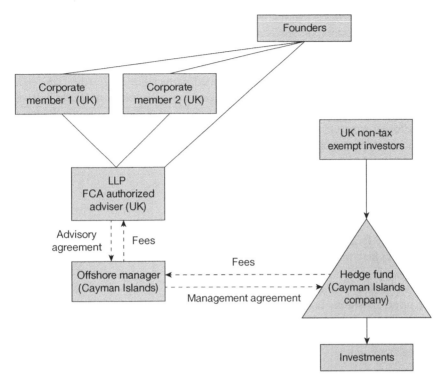

Figure 3.1   Simple hedge fund structure.

Delaware limited liability company or corporation and an affiliate of the general partner. The major considerations in choosing a suitable vehicle to act as an investment manager are tax efficiency for the owners of that vehicle and providing them with limited liability and the flexibility for defining the relationships among the management team. The use of a separate investment manager provides a structure that will more easily comply with the requirements under the Dodd–Frank Act, which requires that the investment manager be registered under state authorities or the Securities and Exchange Commission (SEC). Additionally, the investment manager may be used to provide investment advice to several portfolios or investment funds while it is more typical that the general partner entity is the general partner for only one investment fund.

With UK-based investors as an example (namely those who are not tax exempt), the fund will need to be based offshore to avoid the investors being taxed for the fund's income at the higher income tax rates, and to avoid double taxation if a corporate structure was to be used. As an example, the offshore fund vehicle could be a Cayman-registered limited company. As an example, the fund is managed by a Cayman limited company too but the investment advisory functions could be conducted onshore, say in the UK, by an associated entity. Figure 3.1 sets out this structure.

3.6.2   The master/feeder structure

The master/feeder structure is a common hedge fund structure used in recent years, in which two feeder funds co-invest through a jointly owned master or hub fund (the 'master fund').

The benefit of this model is that it allows the fund to effectively source investment from both US and non-US investors, or between other groups of investors who have different requirements for the structuring of the fund or its vehicles.

Using a Cayman fund and the needs of US investors as an example, one feeder vehicle will commonly be a Delaware-registered limited partnership entity (the 'US feeder') and the other will be a Cayman-registered limited company (the 'offshore feeder'). Both the US feeder and the offshore feeder will invest substantially all of their assets into the master fund. A master/feeder structure enables the investment manager to manage the assets of the fund, the offshore feeder and other current or potential future investment vehicles on a combined basis.

(a) Common advantages

(i) One account
The manager effectively manages all assets in a single account, which avoids the need to allocate individual transactions between two or more parallel funds.

(ii) Automatic rebalancing of accounts
The securities positions held by each feeder fund indirectly through the master fund are automatically rebalanced relative to each other every time either feeder fund experiences subscriptions or redemptions, thereby avoiding the need to adjust individual security positions in each account.

(iii) Customized feeder funds
Customized feeder funds can also be created under different names, with different economic terms (such as different fees or lock-up provisions), or structured to meet specific tax, regulatory or business concerns of investors in specific jurisdictions.

(iv) Non-US person status
The master fund will likely qualify as a non-US person for SEC regulatory purposes, which would permit it to participate in certain securities offerings limited to non-US persons.

(b) Common disadvantages of master/feeder structure

(i) Cost
The principal disadvantage of the master/feeder fund structure is the added expense and administrative burden of organizing and administering the master fund, since an additional legal entity must be created and administered.

(ii) Tax strategies
The master/feeder structure permits less flexibility to make decisions providing tax savings to certain investors, because the master fund cannot specifically allocate either the cost or the benefit of the tax savings to a particular feeder fund. Non-US investors and US tax exempt investors in an offshore feeder fund will have to bear part of the costs of US tax savings strategies without necessarily sharing the benefit.

Figure 3.2 sets out a common master/feeder structure.

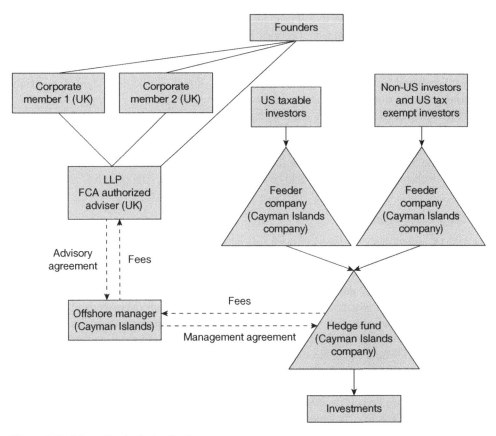

Figure 3.2   Master/feeder hedge fund structure.

3.6.3   EU UCITS-compliant funds

(a) Introduction

Undertakings for Collective Investment in Transferable Securities (UCITS) funds are hedge funds established under the EU UCITS Directive.[5] Having met the requirements of the directive, and becoming registered in an EU country, a UCITS fund can be freely marketed across the EU, through the 'European passport'.[6] UCITS are designed to enhance the single European market while maintaining high levels of investor protection.

The UCITS regime is flexible enough to allow multiple sub-funds, giving scope for the master/feeder structure described above in section 3.6.2. A UCITS-compliant fund will be domiciled in an EU country and so the domicile will usually be one of the European jurisdictions described in Chapter 7: typically Luxembourg or Ireland as these are low tax jurisdictions within the EU. The structure chosen will again depend on the choice of domicile and the taxation requirements of the investors. A Luxembourg-domiciled UCITS may take either a contractual or a corporate form.[7] If domiciled in Ireland, a UCITS will typically use

---

[5] Undertakings for Collective Investment in Transferable Securities Directive 85/611/EEC (UCITS I)

[6] http://ec.europa.eu/internal_market/investment/index_en.htm

[7] http://www.alfi.lu/setting-fund-luxembourg/investment-funds/ucits-funds

a public limited company structure. For more information on these domiciles and corporate structures, please refer to Chapter 7, sections 7.6 and 7.5, respectively. The increased regulatory standards are also appealing to investors outside of Europe, in particular following high profile scandals such as Madoff. UCITS funds are also popular in Asia and South America[8] and are distributed for sale in many non-EU countries – largely due to their regulation, which is considered to be transparent, tried and tested.

Investors in UCITS may redeem units or shares on demand, in other words, UCITS must be open-ended. A UCITS fund must have sufficient liquidity to support redemptions in the fund on at least a fortnightly basis. In practice, the vast majority of UCITS funds are daily dealing, which can be an attractive proposition for certain investors. Assets must be entrusted to an independent custodian or depositary and held in a ring-fenced account on behalf of investors.

(b) The UCITS regime

The UCITS regime has developed through several iterations. The first UCITS Directive was adopted in 1985 in order to harmonize the regulation of open-ended funds across the EU. In the 1990s there was a proposed UCITS II Directive that did not progress as no common position was found. It was not until 2003 that UCITS I was amended by a new regulatory regime, UCITS III, made up of two directives: the Product Directive and the Management Directive.[9]

The Product Directive expanded the type and range of investments that a UCITS could hold. The Management Directive sought to give a European passport to management companies of a UCITS fund to enable them to operate throughout the EU as well as tightening up risk management frameworks and increasing managers' capitalization requirements. The combined directive was intended to widen consumer choice and consumer protection.

Newcits is a term coined in reference to UCITS funds that are compliant with the combined UCITS III Directive. In general Newcits benefit from wider investment powers.

UCITS III expanded the range of available investments to include derivatives for investment purposes, other UCITS and cash. This dramatically increased investor choice, allowing for cash funds, funds of funds and mixed asset funds.

(c) Types of assets

The Product Directive expanded the type of available investments to allow a UCITS to invest in derivatives not only for efficient portfolio management (EPM) or hedging purposes but for investment purposes as well.

The eligible assets that a UCITS can invest in now include:

- transferable securities (i.e. publicly traded equities or bonds, listed on the recognized stock exchanges)
- deposits and money market instruments (i.e. cash deposits with credit institutions, treasury bills or commercial paper)
- mutual funds – UCITS have always been able to invest in other funds; however, this was somewhat restricted. UCITS III relaxed this restriction, with further ability to invest in other open-ended mutual funds whether other UCITS or non-UCITS funds with UCITS-like traits. This has allowed the development of UCITS funds of funds and

---

[8] http://lexicon.ft.com/Ter?term=UCITS
[9] The Undertakings for Collective Investment in Transferable Securities Directive 2001/107/EC and 2001/108/EC

- financial derivative instruments – under UCITS I, derivatives could only be used for hedging and EPM (i.e. to reduce risk or cost, or to replicate a position that could otherwise be achieved through investing in the underlying asset). With the advent of UCITS III, UCITS are able to use derivatives for investment purposes, using either exchange traded or over-the-counter instruments (see Chapter 5, section 5.12), with some limitations.

(d) Restrictions

The original directive required 90% of a UCITS' assets to be invested in transferable securities, while the remaining 10% could be placed in certain other investments.[10] Earlier UCITS regulations also greatly limited borrowing powers of funds[11] and prohibited certain speculative investments such as shares of other funds, derivative products or money market instruments.

Assets ineligible for UCITS funds include (i) real estate, (ii) bank loans and (iii) commodities. This may result in a number of hedge fund strategies being unable to be replicated in a UCITS form.

For many hedge fund managers, short selling often forms part of their trading strategy, and while physical short selling is not permitted, it can be achieved and is allowed through the use of derivatives such as contracts for difference.

(e) Risk spreading

A significant requirement of UCITS is that investments are properly diversified. There are a number of different limits, all of them in place since UCITS I, but the best known is the 5/10/40 Rule. This states that a UCITS cannot invest more than 5% of its assets in securities issued by a single issuer. However, this limit can be increased up to 10% provided that where the 5% limit is exceeded, the exposure to these issuers, when added together, does not exceed 40% of the fund's assets.

The regulatory regime requires an appropriate level of cover for the derivative risk, which can mean that on the opposite side of the exposure there must be cash, a similar asset or balancing derivative giving an opposite exposure to a similar underlying asset to cover the original derivative exposure. It can also mean that some UCITS III funds may have high levels of gross exposure.

(f) Liquidity

UCITS must also be open-ended, so that investors redeem their shares or units on demand, and crucially they must be liquid. A key point in this regard is that they must be able to support redemptions on at least a fortnightly basis. This can be attractive for investors in the current climate, as investors will not be subject to any gating provisions that they may encounter in a typical hedge fund. Not all hedge fund managers will market UCITS funds due to the added cost and administration to operate such funds and because certain strategies may not fit within the UCITS guidelines.

---

[10] Art. 19(2)(b), UCITS I
[11] Art. 36, UCITS I

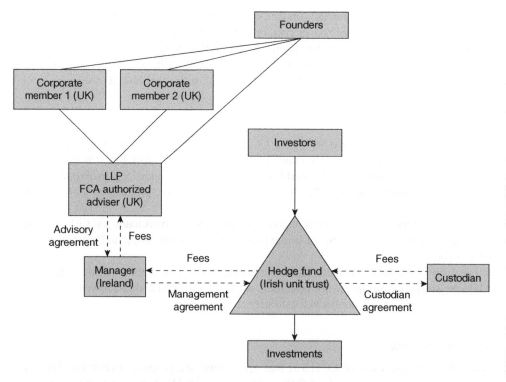

Figure 3.3   UCITS hedge fund structure.

(g) UCITS IV

The UCITS IV Directive was implemented in EU member states on 1 July 2011. It has received a mixed response from asset managers since its implementation.[12] It allows master/feeder structures and for the passporting of management companies. There are also provisions for the merger of funds, but the uptake of these opportunities has been low and the increased regulatory burden has led some asset managers to question the necessity of the new regime.[13]

As an example, Figure 3.3 shows a UCITS-compliant hedge fund domiciled in Ireland with a unit trust structure. For more information on Ireland and the vehicles available see Chapter 7, section 7.5.

3.7   ESTABLISHMENT OF THE FUND

3.7.1   Process

The process for establishing a hedge fund will often involve the following steps:

---

[12] http://www.ft.com/cms/s/0/1f067d7e-b14f-11e1-bb9b-00144feabdc0.html#axzz2UaULI9uo
[13] Ibid.

(a) develop concept for fund including investment objective/strategy/target returns

(b) pre-marketing with key investors to determine interest in fund, refine fund concept

(c) identify and appoint key advisers and service providers (e.g. legal and tax advisers, placement agent, prime broker, custodian and auditors)

(d) develop a suitable structure for the fund taking into account relevant tax and regulatory issues

(e) prepare more detailed terms for the fund. The key factors in determining the terms will be the fund's investment strategy, as well as the relative negotiating positions of the manager and the investors

(f) draft marketing material for the fund (e.g. one or two page 'teaser' document, presentation for roadshow, formal offering document)

(g) distribute marketing material and conduct initial discussions with potential investors

(h) investors consider the terms of the fund and conduct due diligence

(i) draft legal documentation for the fund (see section 3.7.2 below)

(j) negotiations between the manager and investors

(k) investors complete subscription documents and

(l) closing.

3.7.2   Documentation

A fund established as a limited company will generally require the following key documents.

(a) Information Memorandum (IM or PPM)

This contains information on the fund such as its investment objective and strategy, a summary of its terms, background on the management team and its track record together with more technical information such as risk factors, a summary of the tax consequences of investing and details of restrictions on the marketing of the fund.

(b) Fund constitutional agreements

These set out the running and governance of the fund, and will include articles of association and a shareholders' agreement if the fund is a company, or a limited partnership agreement if the fund is a limited partnership.

(c) Investment management agreement

It is entered into between the fund and its manager. It provides, among other matters, for the appointment of the manager and the circumstances in which the manager's appointment can be terminated.

(d) Investment advisory agreement (if required)

It is entered into between the manager and the investment adviser. Its content is similar to the investment management agreement. It deals with the adviser's appointment, termination and remuneration.

(e) Subscription agreement

Each investor will sign a subscription agreement under which they acquire shares in the fund. Each investor will also provide information about themselves (contact information, bank account details) and give representations and warranties about themselves, including eligibility to invest in the fund.

(f) Prime brokerage and custodian agreements

Key supplier and leverage provider agreements to be finalized.

(g) Custodian and administrative agent

For custody and administrative terms, and NAV calculations.

(h) Side letters

In the course of negotiations, the manager may agree certain matters with individual investors that are consistent with the partnership agreement (for example, specific reporting information that is required by an investor). Such agreements with individual members are set out in side letters with the relevant investors.

3.8   MANAGEMENT AND PERFORMANCE FEES

Hedge fund managers charge fund management and performance fees to the fund for their services, and a summary is detailed below. For more information in relation to fund management and performance fees, please see Chapter 10, sections 10.5 and 10.6, respectively.

3.8.1   Management fee

The management fee is designed to cover the costs of operating the manager and is typically set at 2% per annum (but can vary between 1% and 4% depending on the fund manager and strategy) and is charged on the NAV of the fund's assets. While represented as an annual charge, the management fees are often paid monthly or quarterly.

3.8.2   Performance fee

The second level of fees is the 'performance fee' which is designed to be an incentive for the manager and reward out-performance. A typical performance fee will be set at 20%; however, this can range from as little as 10% up to 50%.

3.8.3   Hurdle rate

Often built into the performance fee mechanism is what is known as the 'hurdle rate', which is a rate of return that must be paid to investors before the manager can claim its entitlement to the performance fee. The hurdle rate can also either be soft or hard; 'soft hurdle' being that after the hurdle is cleared a catch-up mechanism applies so that the performance return is calculated on all returns once cleared, or alternatively the 'hard hurdle' only allows the performance fee to be calculated on the returns above the hurdle.

3.8.4   High water mark

Most performance fees also include a 'high water mark', which essentially works to carry forward any losses from the manager to ensure that the manager only receives a performance fee over its highest performance level, essentially meaning that any previous losses must first be recovered.

3.8.5   Redemption fees

An additional layer of fees also deals with where an investor seeks to withdraw its funds. In such circumstances the investor may be charged a fee to withdraw, which generally operates to charge investors a redemption fee if they withdraw money within a 12- or 18-month period. Redemption fees may also be applicable where an investor seeks to withdraw a large amount from the fund, as they may be limited to withdrawing a fixed amount or percentage at any given time.

3.9   OTHER KEY TERMS

In addition to the fees detailed above there are a number of key terms, which would be incorporated into a formal PPM or offering documents, forming the basis upon which investors would invest into the fund.

3.9.1   Liquidity

The liquidity of a hedge fund is generally linked to the investment strategy, type of assets invested in and market liquidity. Hedge funds often offer investors the option to redeem their investment on a monthly, quarterly or annual basis, subject to a minimum amount of notice being provided.

3.9.2   Lock-ups

Some hedge funds will impose lock-ups whereby an investor will not be able to redeem their investment for a fixed period of time. This can be broken down into 'hard' and 'soft' lock-ups. Under a 'hard lock-up' investors will not be able to take out their funds for a fixed period of time, whereas under a 'soft lock-up' investors will be able to redeem but will be able to do so only upon the payment of a redemption fee and liquidity being available. It may also be that hard and soft lock-ups are combined, providing that an investor cannot redeem for a period of time (e.g. one year), and then be subject to redemption fees on a sliding scale following the expiry of the hard lock-up.

3.9.3   Gating provisions

Gating provisions provide redemption on certain dates for investors, such as annually or quarterly, and can in addition limit the amount of the funds that can be returned to investors at any given time.

This effectively means that investors will be able to take their money out of funds on fixed dates only, and if the fund has a large number of investors seeking to redeem their investments simultaneously, then investors may be able to obtain access to only a portion of their investment at any given time, with the remainder only being repayable in the subsequent gate.

3.9.4   Capacity

The offering documents of a hedge fund will set out its capacity limits, and this will be based on numerous factors including the fund's target market and investment strategy. As a hedge fund approaches its capacity limit, the manager may choose to have a 'hard close', by closing investment in the fund to all investors, or alternatively may decide to have a 'soft close' whereby investments in the fund will be closed to new investors only.

3.9.5   Early stage or seed investors

To create an incentive for investors to commit to investing in a hedge fund at an early stage, more favourable terms may be offered (including reduced payment of management and performance fees) and this can be done, for example, by way of issuing a separate class of shares to early stage investors. Such investors are often known as 'seed' investors, and in addition to receiving more favourable terms, they may expect to share in the top-line revenue of the hedge fund together with management. Such investors will, however, be expected to agree to certain terms, such as contributing a substantial investment in the fund, and to lock up their investment for a set period of time.

3.9.6   Key man

Hedge funds often have certain individuals who are essential to the investment management of the fund and the implementation of its investment strategy. If this is the case key man clauses can be added to protect investors and to help to keep key individuals managing the fund. In the event of a key man departing then investors may have the option to exit the fund.

3.9.7   Equalization

In the context of hedge funds, and indeed any open-ended fund that pays incentive or performance fees, the term 'equalization' refers to an accounting methodology, designed to ensure not only that the investment manager is paid the correct incentive, performance or profit sharing fee, but also that the incentive fees are fairly allocated between each investor in the fund. This is done by adjusting the price at which shares are issued and/or adjusting the holdings of investors in the hedge fund, by calculating a per share fee at the fund level and then compensating each investor for the portion of fees that they should or should not have been charged.

3.10 THE USE OF SIDE POCKETS

As part of a hedge fund's portfolio of assets, it may hold private assets that are difficult to value or are considered to be illiquid. Managers will typically invest in such assets under a belief that there may be a future opportunity for them to exit the investment once a particular trigger event has caused the investment value to increase significantly. Private investments of this nature are generally held on the fund's balance sheet at cost until the trigger event.

In such a situation the fund may carry out an accounting provision to segregate these illiquid assets from the remainder of the assets in the portfolio. This practice is known as 'side pocket' accounting. Following the investment into the segregated asset, the fund will often issue investors with a new class of shares relating to the side pocket. The objective of this practice is to fix the ownership of these assets to only the investors in the fund at the particular point in time when the investment was made.

The new shares issued for the side pocket investment do not usually have redemption rights attached to them. This is on the basis that the assets will need to be held for a longer period of time to obtain a realization. As a result the investor will get the related return only when the fund is able to sell those assets, and the assets are therefore locked up indefinitely.

To achieve a fair result for investors in terms of the NAV valuation and related management and performance fees, the side pocket will be separate from the remainder of the portfolio. As a result any performance fees payable in relation to the side pocket would not be on a NAV basis.

When additional investors invest into the fund they will not participate in the side pocket and the existing investors will not have their interest diluted. The creation of side pockets with a separate class of shares will also mean that if any investors redeem their investments, the remaining investors will not be left holding a disproportionately high percentage of the side pocket.

The effect of the development and increased use of side pockets is that funds are creating private equity vehicles that sit within their fund structures. This evolutionary step is an interesting reflection of how investment managers have to continuously develop their products and increase their range of investments in order to maintain profits. However, since the credit crisis, the use of side pockets and private equity style structures by hedge funds has anecdotally decreased.

3.11 REGULATION

In general hedge funds are considered to be lightly regulated investment fund structures. The extent to which this is true depends on the type of investors being sought for the hedge fund and the number of investors.

A hedge fund management company established offshore may require authorization from its local regulator or may be able to apply for an exemption. The onshore adviser in the UK will be required to be authorized and regulated by the FCA (or other local regulators) to provide advice in relation to advising and arranging financial transactions. More detail in respect of authorization and regulation can be found in Chapter 12.

At the opposite end of the spectrum, a hedge fund structured as a UCITS fund will be subject to stricter regulatory requirements, from a portfolio construction, administrative and marketing perspective. This is mainly due to the fact that the UCITS regulatory regime is principally targeted at retail investors.

3.12 SOME CONCLUSIONS

As we have seen, hedge funds require flexible structures and the domiciles of choice are offshore. Taxation and regulatory constraints on investment policy rather than corporate governance are the main drivers of funds going offshore.

In the following chapter, we take a look at alternative fund structures – for both private equity and hedge investment strategies.

4

Structural Variants and Alternative Structures to Chapters 2 and 3

4.1 INTRODUCTION

In this chapter we build on those structures discussed in Chapters 2 and 3, and discuss some structural, regulatory and tax-driven variants and other structures that are used in the market as financing vehicles. This chapter only explores certain more common variants or structures used in the UK, the US and the EU: it is not exhaustive.

4.2 PLEDGE FUNDS

Pledge funds are funds where investors have not contractually committed to invest, but have pledged or ring-fenced certain money to invest in specific deals sourced and to be managed by a manager as the investor chooses from time to time.

Each investor can either enter into a separate but identical agreement with the manager, often called a 'participation agreement', or alternatively might invest a small initial sum into a fund or vehicle managed or advised by the manager, with a further pledge. Under the structure, each investor can pay some form of participation fee to the manager for a set period of time. In return, the manager undertakes to source and offer all the investment opportunities of a particular type to those investors.

When the manager has identified a potential investment, there is typically a two-stage process. First, the manager will provide each investor with a 'teaser' containing a summary of the proposed investment. The manager will ask investors to indicate whether they are interested in participating in the opportunity and, if so, for what amount.

Each investor then has a period of time to decide whether it wants to participate in that investment; to opt in or out. Investors will be able to invest up to a pre-agreed proportion of each investment (based on the proportion of the total fee for the fund which each investor pays) and may often have the right to participate in a greater proportion if other investors decline the opportunity.

For each investment, a separate limited partnership or other vehicle is often set up (unless the pledge fund is a vehicle already established) and those investors who wish to participate in that investment become limited partners or investors in it. The documentation for that vehicle will normally have been agreed when investors sign up to the arrangement, and it may be annexed to each investor's participation agreement.

While investors may be under no obligation to participate in any investment, there may be incentives for them to do so. Various 'sticks' and 'carrots' can be included in the terms of the pledge fund such as:

- 'three strikes and out' or
- fees and carry can increase (stick) or decline (carrot) or
- future investments may become committed or
- the investor can be 'thrown out' of the fund.

The management fees are often on actual drawn capital and/or monitoring or similar fees from the portfolio companies. The carried interest is often paid on a 'deal-by-deal' basis, which is a major advantage of the pledge fund structure to managers.

4.3   'COMBO' FUND STRUCTURE

4.3.1   Introduction

A 'combo' fund (a term coined at MJ Hudson) is an investment club or programme which combines the benefits of 'blind' committed capital with significant 'sighted' co-investment for investors. Two limited partnerships or other vehicles can be established simultaneously, with one operating as the committed capital fund and the other as the pledge fund, both together constituting the 'combo' fund itself.

4.3.2   The blind-pool or committed capital fund

The committed capital fund would be more or less in standard form in most areas and it would have, subject to possible adjustments depending on the context outlined below, the usual features:

- a management fee on committed capital
- the carry interest paid on a 'fund as a whole' basis to the executives of the manager
- commitments from investors up to a stated amount and
- investors are committed to provide their funds without an option to hold them back.

The extent to which these standard features would be varied depends on the purpose of the particular committed capital fund. If it is to be a source of guaranteed funds, there would be a strong preference for a larger funding pool. If it is to be 'flash cash' (an enticement to potential portfolio companies, sellers or other investors) the size of the pool matters less. The committed capital might be needed in full if investors invest less in a transaction from the 'pledge' pot.

4.3.3   The pledge fund

The principal features of the pledge fund are set out at the beginning of this chapter. When used as part of the combo fund structure there are a number of additional considerations.

Investors who opt in should be able to pick up the 'slack', on a proportionate basis, of the commitments of investors who have declined to invest. To the extent any slack is not covered, the shortfall could come from the committed capital fund as a source of funds of last resort. There may be a limit to the investment from the pledge fund as against the committed capital fund. The more an investor invests into the committed capital fund, the more pre-emption rights the investor will obtain to further invest through the pledge fund.

All investors, whether they opt in or opt out in relation to any investment, will be limited partners of that limited partnership, but to ensure that returns on any investment flow only to those investors who opted in, returns will usually be applied on a 'deal-by-deal' basis.

4.3.4   The combined (or 'combo') fund

A combined structure would represent the fund as one overall entity, but made up of the pledge fund and the committed capital fund as set out in Figure 4.1.

The combining of the pledge fund and the committed capital fund needs to be carefully considered and the key issues include (Table 4.1):

(a) the termination of the two funds should, preferably, be kept separate. This is to avoid the situation where if all investors decline to invest under the pledge fund, the investment period of the blind-pool is truncated

(b) the removal of the manager, whether for cause or otherwise, could be contemporaneous across both funds and

(c) the disparity in investments in each deal made through the pledge fund as a result of some investors potentially opting out will result in returns being assessed on a 'deal-by-deal' basis. This works in favour of the 'carry' for the executives and it may be possible to apply the same 'deal-by-deal' basis in the committed capital fund.

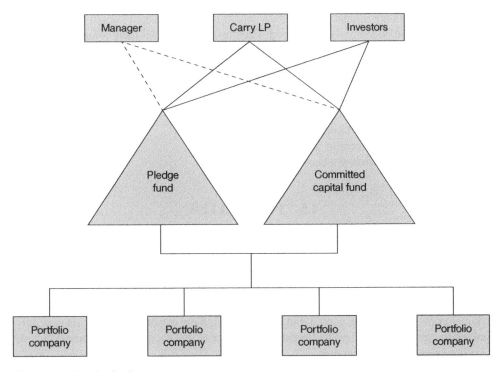

Figure 4.1   Combo fund structure.

Table 4.1   Key points for pledge fund and committed capital fund

Key points for pledge fund	Key points for committed capital fund
• No management fee until drawn	• Management fee of say 2% p.a. on committed capital
• Transaction fee and monitoring fee	• If lower management fees, transaction fees and monitoring fees
• Commitments of say ×3 of committed capital fund	• Commitments of say ¼ pledge fund – this reduces management fee on overall capital to 0.5% p.a.
• Commitments by way of pledge: that is, capacity to opt in or opt out	• Fixed commitment in usual form: can be used as 'flash cash'
• Carry – often deal-by-deal	• Carry – often fund as whole

4.4   INVESTMENT CLUBS

Investment clubs are more informal than funds. Here a manager pools money into deals. A club 'investor' can pay some form of fee and is invited into deals. On closing a deal more fees are paid. They are common in angel investing and are also moving up the size curve in the current tricky markets.

Deal-by-deal funds are another variant. Here a 'sponsorless GP' will raise money for each transaction. One of the practical difficulties in 'deal-by-deal' funds is the attitude of the investors, who might seek greater control over the fund due to their commitment to provide all of the capital.

Other constructs are annual programmes, where investors commit capital annually, and carried interest can be similarly annualized. Each investor can 'pull their commitment' each year, or elect for it to be rolled over for a further year.

The credit crisis has caused managers to become more imaginative in structuring vehicles to assist investors with:

- transparency
- ability to slow investment rate
- investors' overcommitment to funds and
- reduction in fees on undrawn capital.

4.5   FUND-LITES

4.5.1   Introduction

Fund-lites (again, a term invented at MJ Hudson) are typically single-investment funds which accommodate both investor demand for visibility of the underlying target company before investing and a reluctance to commit to a blind-pool of capital. Fund-lite structures are not only used by first-time managers to provide a base from which to build a track record and a bridge to larger pools of committed capital, but also by larger, more established managers generally looking to create a bridge until their next fund-raise or to make a one-off investment outside their fund's investment parameters.

A fund-lite, which is in many ways similar in structure to a standard private equity limited partnership, features a GP/manager managing the fund entity through a management agreement and a separate carry limited partnership to reward the manager (through which the carried interest would be paid, on a de facto deal-by-deal basis as there is only one investment in a typical fund-lite structure).

The key differences between a fund-lite and a more traditional blind-pool fund are to be found in the detail of the LPA. There are some surprisingly beneficial terms for GPs in these structures, but at the same time they can also contain enticing terms for the fund investors. The terms can also address some of the current concerns of investors investing into private equity funds. The key differences are discussed below.

4.5.2   Shorter life of the fund

Fund-lites typically have durations of 5–7 years compared with 10 years for a typical blind-pool fund, as the investment period is effectively immediate – with the exception of buy-and-build or venture capital strategies. Investors benefit from having their funds tied up for a shorter period of time, creating greater visibility for future allocations.

4.5.3   Reduced scope of the investment objective

A fund-lite is formed to invest in a single company (or buy-and-build), and the scope of the fund's investment objective will be limited to the specified target company. This is a key difference as the fund investor will know from the outset the identity of the target that the fund will be investing in. Having a clear view of the target company, therefore, serves to reduce part of the risk of investors being unhappy with the fund's investment, as may happen in a blind-pool fund. As a result, detailed investment objectives of larger blind-pool funds, which would include the sector, exposure limits and geographic locations of investments, will not be required.

4.5.4   Fees

In a fund-lite arrangement management fees are charged on drawn capital only. Investors can complain about excessive fees payable on committed capital that remains undrawn for some time in a traditional pooled fund.

4.5.5   No key man clause

As investors know the identity of the target company from the outset, by agreeing to invest in a fund-lite they expressly approve the underlying investment in the target company. As a result, key man clauses are either reduced in scope or removed entirely.

4.5.6   No escrow or clawback for carry

As the carried interest is effectively paid on a deal-by-deal basis under the fund-lite model and is only in relation to the target company, neither an escrow account nor any carry retention is required. As deal-by-deal carry on blind-pool funds has become increasingly difficult to obtain from investors, the fund-lite structure is beneficial for managers as it rewards them for each successful deal.

4.5.7   No re-investment of realized funds

Given the deal-by-deal nature of the fund-lite, any realizations are distributed to the investors and further re-investment is generally not permitted, save for buy-and-build strategies or certain venture capital investments.

4.5.8   No restrictions on future funds

A manager will also generally be free to raise successive funds following the investment. This has the benefit for the manager of being able to seek further investment opportunities following an investment in a target company and allows the manager to raise a series of fund-lite structures to build out its investment programme or to provide a bridge until the next fund.

4.5.9   Fund-lites: some conclusions

As discussed above, the fund-lite structure offers managers and fund investors a number of advantages, and more specifically can align many of the interests of both parties. While the fund-raising process for managers on a deal-by-deal basis can be time-consuming when simultaneously balancing the related negotiations for a target company, there are significant advantages. These advantages include the opportunity:

- to create a track record
- to invest in the best vintages

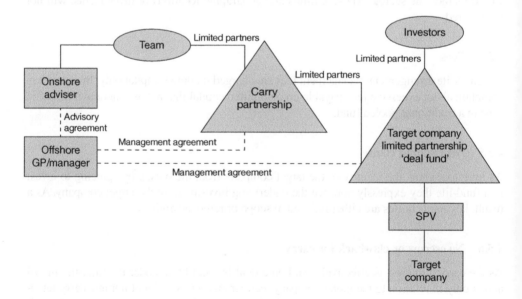

Figure 4.2   Fund-lite structure.

- to cement investor relationships
- to enjoy benefits of the deal-by-deal carry.

A limited partnership structure, rather than a corporate SPV, is preferable for a GP, as investors in a corporate SPV can seek to manage or restrict the GP, whereas they are largely prevented from doing so in a limited partnership structure due to the risk of losing their limited liability status.

For new and emerging managers that are seeking to launch first-time funds, fund-lite structures allow managers to launch an investment programme in a challenging economic climate. In addition, the management entities formed as part of the structure will form the basis of their management group for future funds. A typical fund-lite structure, together with related management entities, would be in a similar form to that set out in Figure 4.2.

4.6   TOP-UP, BRIDGE AND SIDE POCKETS

Top-up funds delay the requirement to raise a further fund. Existing investors 'top-up' and invest further, and some new investors can invest.

Bridge funds (or opportunistic funds) can act as a bridge between funds, and are specifically helpful when there is a real opportunity to raise money and invest quickly.

Side pockets are discussed more in Chapter 3, but act more like a closed-ended parallel fund to the main hedge fund.

4.7   MANAGED ACCOUNTS

4.7.1   Introduction

The increasing popularity of managed accounts is partly in response to investors' decreased risk appetite post-2008, although managed accounts are also a useful structure for certain larger investors. They are compatible with private equity, hedge fund and other alternative asset investment strategies. With broad parallels to a hedge fund, a fund manager is responsible for a segregated portfolio and makes investments in accordance with the given policy. The investment strategy of the fund manager is deployed in the usual fashion, as is management of the portfolio; however, an independent third party has overall control of the account but the investor invariably still 'owns' the account with the assets in it. In other words the fund manager buys and sells, including determining quantity and frequency on behalf of the account while the third party deals with the other business of the account, for example reporting.

Managed accounts can be directly with an investment manager or alternatively through a managed account platform (see Figure 4.3). Under a managed account platform, investors would invest into the platform which would have a separate investment agreement with the investment manager, who would be responsible for managing the funds in a managed account. These structures reduce the administrative burden of managed accounts for investors, as many aspects of the operational infrastructure (for example custody, administration and valuation) are delegated to the platform or aggregated independent third party providers. In addition they can allow investors to gain access to certain strategies with lower levels of capital, and often with enhanced redemption rights.

Managed accounts can be a useful alternative to mutual funds or other pooled vehicles and more closely align with an investor's own specific return objectives, risk tolerance and special circumstances.

4.7.2   Comparison with funds

(a) Investor lock-in

Investors in a typical fund would be locked into that particular fund and managers may seek to lock in investors to managed accounts on a similar basis. Without this requirement an investor could redeem or terminate its managed account shortly afterwards.

(b) Termination

In a closed-ended fund, 'no-fault divorce' or termination without cause would generally be permitted only after 2–5 years from the creation of the fund and even then with a decent notice period (i.e. 12 months). Managers may seek to protect themselves with similar provisions in a managed account.

(c) Investment discretion

In a fund the manager will have discretion to invest in accordance with the parameters of the related investment policy. However, the scope of a managed account can be tailored to meet individual investor requirements.

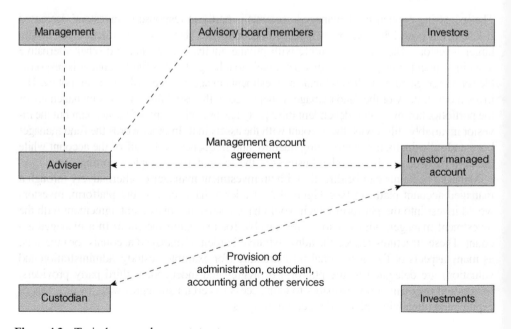

Figure 4.3   Typical managed account structure.

(d) Access to further capital

In a closed-ended fund money is typically drawn down over a five-year period, whereas managed accounts can be drafted so that investors have the ability to continually 'top-up' their accounts.

(e) Management fees

The management fees and performance fees in a managed account can be structured on a similar basis to those in a fund.

4.7.3   Advantages

One key advantage of this structure is that investors often have a greater degree of control and it allows investors to retain direct ownership of the assets. Investors can also control the liquidity of their investment as the structure and the terms will more easily accommodate a withdrawal of funds. In a traditional fund structure capital access is restricted by the terms and the only source of liquidity for closed-ended funds is on the secondary market. Also in certain managed account platforms investors will be able to obtain significantly enhanced redemption (biweekly or even daily) on the basis of modified investment strategies through the managed account.

As the investor's portfolio is segregated, the investor has greater sight of the composition of the account and is able to better judge risk while having a more transparent understanding of their holdings.

The investor has a much greater level of control over their account in terms of directing the fund manager as to what products the investor would or would not like to invest in. These can be dealt with as caveats at the beginning of the account or put directly to the manager during the arrangement.

There are advantages to fund managers also. As this arrangement becomes ever more popular, managers with a reputation for providing a viable alternative to the traditional fund structure will in turn be able to attract more investors. This is not limited to individuals either; larger institutional investors are also making use of this platform. This approach can provide a more constant source of capital for investment as new investors and investor 'top-ups' can be easily accommodated. The need to go through a fund-raising process on a frequent basis can also be avoided. The accounting complexities of operating closed-ended limited partnerships with a range of separate interests is removed; additionally, with the agreement of the investor, profits can be easily 'recycled' back into new investments, thereby growing the account over time.

4.7.4   Disadvantages

Despite the advantages detailed above, investors must accept an increased administrative burden in exchange for having their account managed separately. Managed accounts may be subject to increased fees given that they cannot take advantage of the economies of scale offered by a pooled fund. Investors must also make sure that their manager is devoting sufficient resources to their account equitable to the other funds/accounts the manager handles.

Investors must also guard against their account being used for cross-trades, i.e. their account being used to acquire an asset being disposed of by the pooled fund at an unfair value. It is important for investors and managers to clearly define any strategy and restrictions early in the arrangement to avoid unnecessary disputes later. This point is as important to managers as it is to investors.

There is the additional administrative burden on the manager of having to perform trades on behalf of multiple accounts. Managers also risk exposing closely guarded investment strategies given the higher levels of transparency. Termination provisions for the manager are generally more onerous in a managed account as opposed to those commonly associated with managing a fund. Multiple accounts can lead to a more expensive structure to operate.

Not all hedge funds are willing to operate on a managed account basis – as a result investors may not be able to gain access to some of the best fund managers. In addition this may depend on the investment strategy pursued, as strategies that invest into private companies and other less liquid assets would be less suited to managed accounts. This is on the basis of the difficulties in valuating these positions, and the difficulties in splitting the allocations across different pools.

4.7.5 Some conclusions

Large institutions, endowment funds and pension plans with substantial assets under management benefit from managed accounts as they offer heightened transparency, risk mitigation and understanding and control. I would also suggest that historic fund of fund managers should evolve to manage significant managed accounts. However, given the additional costs associated with the managed account platform, for both the investor and the manager, it is unlikely that this avenue will be available or prudent for all investors in alternative investments.

4.8 CORPORATE VEHICLES

Funds may also be structured as a corporate SPV for private equity or other investments. In this situation the fund would not be a typical limited partnership where investors receive interests, but a company where investors receive shares. There would also be a separate class of share to provide the carried interest/performance return to the manager.

The shares would not be redeemable by the investors, but only on the sale of the target company or at the discretion of the manager. To avoid double taxation, the SPV would commonly be offshore. This structure is often used for longer-term investments, e.g. a private equity investment. The structure could be set out as shown in Figure 4.4:

- **A shares** – for new investors and could be subject to a 2% management fee and 20% carried interest/performance fee
- **B shares** – for funds managed by the same manager and would not be subject to management or carried interest/performance fees
- **C shares** – for a cornerstone or strategic investor and would have a lower level of fees attached
- **D shares** – shares held by the manager entitling it to the 20% carried interest/performance fee.

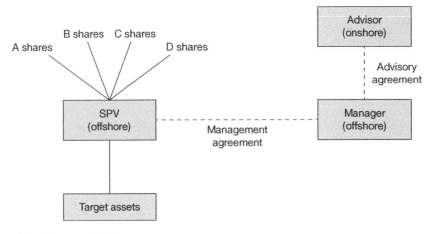

Figure 4.4   Corporate SPV structure.

4.9   SPECIAL PURPOSE ACQUISITION COMPANIES (SPACS) OR CASH SHELLS

SPACs are a form of 'cash shell'. Cash shells are listed entities that do not have any business or assets of their own. They are companies incorporated and listed for the sole purpose of making investments. The cash shells are usually set up to buy other companies, businesses or assets. Part of the consideration for the acquisition is often by issuing new shares in the cash shell. Cash shells can take advantage of available funds as well as their listing on a stock exchange by raising further equity capital to acquire assets.

Cash shells can be dedicated to a particular acquisition but are also used for a series of deals, often focused on geographical regions or a certain industry or sector. The offering document will set out the acquisition strategy.

As a cash shell has no business or assets, they are typically supported by one or more sponsors/founders, which increases the attraction for investors. The sponsors' track record is detailed in the prospectus or admission document which is then verified during the listing process. To add further weight to their credibility, sponsors often take a capital stake in the company as well as providing undertakings. Founders/sponsors are usually restricted in relation to disposals. This is often expected by both investors and stock exchanges alike. The listing rules of the UK stock exchange expect either the target company to not be known or full disclosure of the target.

In the US, SPACs grew to become quite significant since 2003 and the Millstream Acquisition Corp of Earlybird Capital, and grew a body of rules, such as:

- money being raised would be held on trust
- a defined period of time to close the acquisition
- prescribed stepped value performance shares and options.

When structuring a new cash shell, founders consider tax implications and potential regulatory issues, as well as the expectations and preferences of investors. Figure 4.5 shows a common structure.

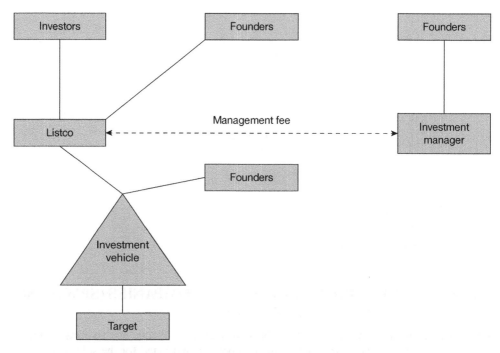

Figure 4.5   Cash shell structure.

4.10   UK ENTERPRISE INVESTMENT SCHEME

4.10.1 Introduction

The UK Enterprise Investment Scheme (EIS) was devised in 1994 to encourage investment in small, higher risk British companies by way of tax relief. For a company to be eligible it must meet certain conditions with regard to its trading activities, structure and the amount of money that can be invested in a company. The company must satisfy HMRC that it is a qualifying company.

Investors may also invest in EIS funds which invest in qualifying companies on behalf of the investors. The investors are the beneficial owners of the shares in the qualifying companies and claim relief in the same way as individuals investing directly in those companies would. EIS funds are similar in many respects to venture capital trusts, which are discussed in Chapter 6, section 6.3.3(f).

4.10.2 Legislation

Part 5 of the Income Tax Act (ITA) 2007 provides the framework for the EIS and sections 150A to 150C of, and Schedule 5B to, the Taxation of Chargeable Gains Act (TCGA) 1992 provide for the capital gains reliefs.[1]

---

[1] As amended by the Finance Act 2009 and 2012

4.10.3 Conditions

(a) The investor

The investor must own the shares in a qualifying company, or if invested through an EIS fund, beneficially own those shares.[2] The investor must be investing in the qualifying company for genuine commercial reasons and not for the purpose of avoiding tax.[3] The shares must be held by the investor for at least three years in order to obtain income tax relief and the capital gains exemption.[4] The investor cannot hold, either alone or with 'associates', shares equivalent to 30% of the ordinary share capital or 30% of the issued share capital, or be entitled to exercise 30% of the voting rights.[5]

For shares issued before 6 April 2012 an investor cannot claim EIS relief if he holds a combined 30% of both the loan capital and the issued share capital.[6] For shares issued on or after 6 April 2012, this does not apply.[7]

Finally, EIS is not available where the investor was previously connected with the qualifying company (as either an employee or a paid director) or was involved in carrying on the whole or any part of that trade to be carried on by the qualifying company or its subsidiaries.[8]

(b) The qualifying company

There is a series of complex rules which determines whether or not a company is a qualifying company.

(i) The gross assets test

This means that for shares issued on or after 6 April 2012, the gross assets of the investee company must not exceed pound sterling (GBP) 15 million immediately before the shares were issued and GBP 16 million immediately afterwards.[9]

(ii) Unquoted

The company must also be unquoted at the time of the issue of the shares, and there must be no arrangements in place for it to become quoted at that time. Admission to AIM is not regarded as quoted for these purposes.[10]

(iii) Qualifying trade

The company must exist wholly for the purpose of carrying on a qualifying trade during the period commencing with the issue of the shares and terminating immediately before the third anniversary of that issue.[11] Most trades are qualifying trades if they are conducted on a commercial basis with a view to earning profit, and during the three-year period from issue

---

[2] Sections 131 and 157 ITA 2007 and section 150A and Schedule 5B TCGA 1992
[3] Section 166 ITA 2007
[4] Sections 159, 209 and 256 ITA 2007, section 150A TCGA 1992
[5] Section 170 ITA 2007
[6] HMRC v Taylor and Haimendorf (Appeal FTC/43/2010)
[7] Schedule 7, paragraph 4 to the Finance Act 2012
[8] Sections 166–169 ITA 2007
[9] Section 186 ITA 2007, amended by Schedule 7, paragraph 11 to the Finance Act 2012
[10] Section 184 ITA 2007
[11] Sections 159, 181 and 256 ITA 2007

the trade does not consist either wholly or substantially of carrying on excluded activities.[12] Excluded activities include dealing in land, financial activities and receiving royalties.

(iv) Independence
A qualifying company must satisfy the requirement of independence.

(v) Exception to qualifying trade
The shares must have been issued in order to raise money for the purpose of a qualifying business activity (or trade) (see paragraph 4.10.3(b) (iii)) but an insignificant amount may be used for any other business purpose.[13] A company may hold the funds on instant access deposit if for the relevant period the company has earmarked them for a specific purpose and is holding them on deposit in anticipation of that purpose.[14] All money must be used in the qualifying trade within two years of the issue.[15]

(vi) Permanent establishment in the UK
The investee company must have a permanent establishment in the UK throughout the three-year period from the issue of shares.[16]

(vii) Number of employees
The investee company (or group) must have fewer than 250 full-time employees (or part-time equivalent) where shares were issued on or after 6 April 2012.[17] This test is applied only once for the investor in question, when the shares are first issued.[18]

(viii) Amount investee company can raise
The investee company or group cannot raise more than GBP 5 million in total within a 12-month period under the EIS, a venture capital trust (VCT) scheme or any other similar scheme.[19]

(ix) Investee company must not be in financial difficulty
The investee company must not be in financial difficulty at the time of the issue of shares in order to be a qualifying company.[20] Financial difficulty is defined in reference to a Community Guideline.[21]

(x) Disqualifying arrangement
An investee company must not be established in order to access tax relief.[22]

---

[12] Section 189 ITA 2007

[13] Section 175 ITA 2007

[14] Richards & Skye Inns Ltd v HMRC FTC/37/2010

[15] Section 175 ITA 2007, as amended by paragraph 7, Schedule 8 to the Finance Act 2009

[16] Sections 180–180B and 191A ITA 2007, as amended by s5 and Schedule 2 to the Finance (No 3) Act 2010

[17] Section 186A ITA 2007, as inserted by paragraph 2, Schedule 16 of the Finance Act 2007 and amended by paragraph 12, Schedule 7 of the Finance Act 2012

[18] Enterprise Investment Scheme Summary of responses document, Appendix B

[19] Section 173A ITA 2007, as amended by paragraph 7, Schedule 7 of the Finance Act 2012

[20] Section 180B ITA 2007, as inserted by paragraph 1, Schedule 2 to the Finance (No 3) Act 2010

[21] 2004/C 244/02

[22] Section 178A ITA 2007, as inserted by paragraph 9, Schedule 7 of the Finance Act 2012

4.10.4 EIS funds

In an EIS fund, a nominee company holds the issued qualifying shares on trust on behalf of the individual investees. The fund is structured to ensure that the investees have a beneficial interest in the qualifying shares as EIS relief is available only for those that do.

EIS funds have no legal personality and are contractual creations. Each investor will enter into an individual agreement with the fund manager that in turn engages a custodian. The custodian organizes the holding of the shares which comprise the fund, and deals with the administration of matters such as settling transactions and collecting dividends and other income. The custodian will use a nominee company (or may comprise it itself) to buy the shares on behalf of the investors.

The manager will often charge investors several fees. There is an initial charge to cover the costs of establishing the fund, normally between 2% and 5% of an investor's investment. The manager will charge an administration fee annually in the range of 1.5% p.a. and 2.5% p.a. of an investor's investment. The final charge is a performance fee, often a 20% share of the investor's return, with or without a notional rate of return. Hence the fees are pretty high in these funds.

EIS funds can apply for approval from HMRC which allows investors to claim income tax relief in the tax year in which the approved fund closes.[23] To be approved, the fund must invest in at least four companies, and the investment in any one company must not exceed 50% of the capital in the fund. The investments must be allocated pro rata in proportion to their contribution to the fund. There can be no investment until the fund closes and at least 90% of the funds should be invested in qualifying companies within 12 months of the closing date. The fund must also show intent to invest entirely in qualifying investments. EIS funds can also be unapproved – that might have some reduced tax advantages over an approved fund, but an unapproved fund is less restricted in its investment strategy.

4.10.5 Tax

Income tax relief is available to individuals who subscribe for shares in an EIS, at a rate of 30% of the cost of the shares with an investment cap of GBP 1 million.[24] This is set against the individual's tax liability for the tax year in which the investment is made.

An exemption from CGT is available on the disposal of shares after they have been held continuously for three years from issue. This is conditional on the income tax relief being claimed for that period.[25]

If there is a loss on disposal of the shares, the loss, less any income tax relief claimed, can be set against income in the year of disposal, or against income in the previous year, as well as being set against any capital gains in the year of disposal.

---

[23] Section 251(2) ITA 2007
[24] Section 158 ITA 2007
[25] Section 150A TCGA 1992

4.11   UK UNIT TRUSTS

4.11.1 Introduction

A unit trust is a portfolio of holdings divided into units which are sold to investors that can be bought and sold directly from fund managers. A unit trust differs from an investment trust (these are described more fully in Chapter 6, section 6.3.3(d)) in that the size of the fund can both increase and decrease (in terms of asset volume, rather than value). An investor can buy additional units from the managers, which increases the size of the fund accordingly, and if the investor wishes, the unit can be sold back to the manager at the NAV – which is how the investor makes a profit (or loss). A unit trust can either be authorized or unauthorized. If authorized, there is greater regulation but the units can be sold to a wider range of investors, and a CGT exemption can apply, although the trust's income is often taxable. An unauthorized unit trust is unattractive to investors often due to the absence of the CGT exemption except for those who are already tax exempt, for example charities and UK pension funds. The investors (unit holders) are the beneficiaries of the trust deed made between the managers and a trustee. They have a beneficial interest in an undivided proportion of the total assets and liabilities of the trust fund and the interest is in proportion to the number of units held by the investor against the total number of units.

4.11.2 Legislation

A unit trust is a CIS[26] under which the property is held on trust for the participants. A CIS is any arrangement by which property (including money) is pooled and run by an 'operator' (manager) with the purpose of enabling the participant investors to receive profits or income from the holding and disposal of property.[27] The investors must have no day to day control over the management of the property, regardless of their right (or absence of a right) to be consulted or give directions. There are exclusions to the definition of a CIS, notably where investors retain ownership in their portfolios but use the manager's services as if an ordinary investor, on the condition that the investor has the right to withdraw that part at any time.[28]

4.11.3 Authorized unit trusts

An authorized unit trust (AUT) is one that has been approved by the FCA in accordance with section 243 of the Financial Services and Markets Act (FSMA) 2000. The application is made jointly by the manager and trustee, who must be separate persons.[29] The FCA directs the form of application and may request information as it reasonably requires for determining the application. If satisfied that the proposed trust complies with the FSMA 2000 rules, complies with the trust scheme rules and if presented with a copy of the trust deed certified by a solicitor that it complies with both sets of rules, the FCA may make an order declaring the scheme an AUT scheme.[30] The 'trust scheme rules' are set out in the FCA's Collective Investment Schemes handbook (COLL).[31]

---

[26] Section 237(1) of the FSMA 2000
[27] Section 235 FSMA 2000
[28] Section 235(5) FSMA 2000 and paragraph 1 to the CIS Order, SI 2001/1062
[29] Section 242(2) FSMA 2000
[30] Section 243(1) FSMA 2000
[31] Established by section 247–248 FSMA 2000

On approval the scheme is subject to the COLL rules, the rules of FSMA 2000 and the FCA's Conduct of Business Sourcebook (COBS) rules on an ongoing basis. A prospectus must also be produced. A benefit of being an AUT is that it can be promoted and sold to retail investors in the UK[32] whereas an unauthorized unit trust cannot. An additional benefit of being an AUT is that any gains accrued are not subject to chargeable gains tax,[33] although tax is paid on any income. An unauthorized unit trust is not subject to the COLL rules, and so the trust deed is more detailed because the rules set out in COLL refer to matters such as pricing and investment restrictions. Unauthorized unit trusts cannot be promoted or sold to retail investors, and there is no exemption for CGT, making them attractive to only a limited range of investors.

4.11.4 Undertakings for collective investment in transferable securities

AUTs may also be structured to comply with the EU UCITS Directive in order to be promoted in other member states of the EU without the need to seek the approval of any authority other than the fund's home authority. Once an AUT complies with the rules of the UCITS Directive set out in FSMA 2000 and COLL it may be authorized by the FCA. The fund must be open-ended,[34] with the sole objective of investing pooled capital in transferable securities based on the principle of risk spreading,[35] and the head office of the fund must be located in the same member state as the registered office.[36]

There are several exclusions, which preclude certain unit trusts. The unit trust must be directly available to the public, which is why only AUTs can be a UCITS scheme. Unit trusts that invest in physical assets such as commodities or real property cannot be a UCITS scheme.[37] Investments made by a UCITS scheme are not just limited by the type of investments made, but also by the spread of the investments. Among a long list of rules, no investment can be made that amounts to more than 20% of the trust assets deposited with a single body.[38] Nor can more than 20% of the trust assets consist of transferable securities and approved money market instruments that are issued by the same group,[39] and no more than 10% of the investment can be in one security.

Some AUTs are not brought within the UCITS framework. These are known as non-UCITS retail schemes (NURS). NURS have greater investment flexibility than UCITS schemes, but they cannot be sold to investors across the common market without seeking approval from each member state concerned. NURS can invest in the same assets as a UCITS scheme, as well as investing in unapproved securities, unregulated schemes, gold and immovable property. NURS can also borrow on a non-temporary basis where there is no specific time limit for repayment.[40] Some of the investment limits for NURS are also increased over those within UCITS schemes. Overall, managers have greater flexibility over the scope of their portfolios by being NURS, but will have a narrower pool of investors and a more expensive and time-consuming process to broaden that pool.

---

[32] Section 238(1) and (4), FSMA 2000
[33] Section 100(1) Taxation of Chargeable Gains Act 1992
[34] COLL 6.2.16R(3)
[35] COLL 5.2.6A R
[36] Article 7(1)(d) UCITS IV Directive 2009/65/EC
[37] COLL 5.2.6A R
[38] COLL 5.2.11R(3)
[39] COLL 5.2.11R(8)
[40] COLL 5.6.2G(b), (d), (e) and (f)

4.11.5 Pricing

The price of a unit of a trust is linked to the value of the underlying assets, the NAV. The price of a unit is usually calculated daily, and presented as two prices. The price at which the investor can buy a unit is the offer price, and the price at which an investor can sell is the bid price. Unlike an investment trust, a unit trust is open-ended and so the price is not affected by the number of units available. When an investor chooses to invest, his investment increases the overall value of the fund, and when he sells, the value of the fund decreases. So the price is only linked to the underlying assets and the costs of the manager, trustee and custodian.

4.11.6 Risk

The risk for the investor depends in part on the management of the fund. Some funds are actively managed, that is to say that a manager will pick which investments to invest in from time to time, and so there will be risk inherent in the wisdom of the decision. Other funds are passively managed, that is they are linked to an index (for example the FTSE 100) and the success or failure of the investment is linked to the performance of that index. The choice of index will also affect the risk. The pricing of unit trusts is less susceptible to swings in pricing (which do not match the NAV) compared with investment trusts as the price is affected only by the underlying assets rather than the scarcity of the units (or shares).

By contrast to investment trusts, a trustee can only borrow money for the use of the authorized fund on a temporary basis and the borrowings must not be persistent.[41] It is the responsibility of the manager to ensure that the borrowing is not in breach of COLL or the trust deed. The borrowing must also not exceed 10% of the value of the fund on any day.[42] The restrictions on borrowing mean that the investors in unit trusts are less exposed to the risk of the exaggerated reduction of the value of the fund when money is borrowed due to gearing.

4.11.7 Fees

The manager of a retail unit trust will charge an investor an initial charge to cover the establishment of the unit to be purchased. The initial charge is usually calculated as the spread between the offer price and the bid price which means the charge can vary. The ongoing costs of managing the fund are covered by an annual fee. The fee varies depending on whether the fund is actively or passively managed, but is typically 1.5%, which is split between the manager and the other advisers who work to maintain the trust. Trustee and auditor fees are taken directly out of the fund.

4.11.8 Taxation of unit trusts

AUTs do not pay CGT on any gains, but do pay income tax.[43] The tax is deferred until the investor disposes of his interest in the AUT instead of on the disposal of underlying assets. If the AUT is made up of several sub-funds as part of an umbrella scheme, each sub-fund is treated as a separate AUT for tax purposes,[44] so if there is a transfer between sub-funds, a chargeable gain or allowable loss may arise.

---

[41] COLL 5.5.4R (1) and (4)
[42] COLL 5.5.5R (1)
[43] Section 100(1) TCGA 1992
[44] Section 99A TCGA 1992

The income of an AUT is treated as if it was a company and the unit holders are shareholders. It is liable to pay tax on income at the basic rate of income tax rather than the corporation tax rates.[45] The management expenses are deductible during the calculation of tax because an AUT is treated as a company with an investment business.[46] Generally speaking, an AUT must either accumulate or distribute the whole of its distributable income as a dividend or yearly interest, although there can be a minimum below which income does not have to be distributed.[47]

For an individual UK-resident investor in an AUT, income distributed as interest by a tax elected fund will be treated as yearly interest and will be deducted at source at the basic rate. For any higher rate taxpaying investor, the shortfall is taxed on the grossed up figure for the distribution. If the fund is not a tax elected fund the dividend payment is treated as a UK company dividend[48] and so carries a tax credit equal to 10% of the grossed up distribution.

A UK-resident unauthorized unit trust is treated as a company for corporation tax on chargeable gains, and the rights of the unit holders are treated as shares in the company. That being said the trustees are subject to chargeable gains tax on chargeable gains rather than corporation tax[49] and so the unauthorized unit trust is liable to CGT on the disposal of underlying investments. If the only investors in an unauthorized unit trust are UK resident and tax exempt then the trust will be exempt from the tax arising from the disposal of its investments.[50] If the units in the trust are temporarily held by the trust managers in anticipation of resale then this exemption still applies.[51]

If the unit trust is unauthorized and is UK resident, the income is taxed as income of the trustee rather than of the unit holders at the basic rate of income tax. Tax credits on UK dividends do not apply to dividends in these circumstances.[52] In contrast to an AUT, an unauthorized unit trust is not treated as a company, and so management expenses are not deductible for the purpose of its own income. If the management expenses are deducted before the computation of distributions, it is treated as reducing the income available for payment to unit holders. But if the expenses are recovered by the unit holders (and only certain investors, such as authorized registered pension funds can do so) out of the amounts available for distribution it maximizes the recovery of tax by increasing the taxable income accordingly.

The unit holder will be treated as receiving income that has been deducted at the basic rate,[53] so income is taxed as it arises and cannot be turned into capital. The tax already paid by the trustees allows a UK-based unit holder to obtain a tax credit at the basic rate. If the unit holder is exempt, it should be able to claim back the tax to the extent that it exceeds their UK tax liability. A unit holder who disposes of units will be liable to tax on chargeable gains accruing on the disposal.

The income of the unit trust's manager derives from the margin on dealing in a unit and from the periodic management charge (such as an annual fee). The dealings in units by both

---

[45] Sections 617 and 618 Corporation Tax Act (CoTA) 2010
[46] Section 1219 CoTA 2009
[47] Regulation 23, Authorised Investment Funds (Tax) Regulations (AIF) 2006
[48] Regulation 22 AIF 2006
[49] Section 99 (1) TCGA 1992
[50] Section 100(2) TCGA 1992
[51] Section 100(2A) TCGA 1992, as inserted by the Finance (No 2) Act 2005
[52] Section 504 ITA 2007
[53] Sections 941–943 ITA 2007

an AUT and an unauthorized unit trust are exempt from VAT.[54] The management activity of an AUT is also exempt from VAT. The management activity of an unauthorized unit trust is treated by HMRC as taxable. Generally, any VAT incurred by the trustees will be an absolute cost due to the trustees not being registered, and being therefore unable to recover any input tax.

4.12   OFFSHORE ALTERNATIVES

4.12.1 Unit trusts

Unit trusts in offshore jurisdictions such as Jersey or Guernsey are no longer a common choice for retail investors. A key practical benefit which led to their popularity was the redeemability of units such that the fund did not have to issue new units or realize assets in order to do so. This was an advantage over corporate structures, which did have to effectively issue new shares in order to redeem others. Since the introduction of offshore corporate structures with zero par value shares, this advantage has gone. Additionally, the lack of flexibility when choosing a unit trust structure compared with corporate structures has meant that their popularity has dwindled. They are still common in certain sectors, such as property (see section 4.13 below), and are used in private capital contexts.

4.12.2 Cell companies

Cell companies are corporate entities which are composed of a 'core' and an unlimited number of 'cells'. These cells are isolated from each other (allowing losses to be insulated from other investments) but remain part of the same company. The cells can be used to invest in different assets, or to be invested in by various investors on different terms. Cell companies are described in more detail in Chapter 7, section 7.2.2(a)(i) (Jersey), section 7.2.2(b)(ii) (Guernsey) and section 7.3.2(b) (the Isle of Man).

4.13   JERSEY PROPERTY UNIT TRUSTS

4.13.1 Introduction

A Jersey property unit trust (JPUT) is a unit trust governed by Jersey law and used to hold real estate. This is a very popular structure for European real estate managers.

A unit trust is not a legal entity: under a unit trust, legal ownership of the trust assets is vested in a trustee, who holds them on trust for the benefit of holders of units in the trust (unit holders) in accordance with the terms of the trust instrument.

In setting up a JPUT, the initial step is to choose the trustee. Where the JPUT is an investment fund, there will also typically be a separate manager who is also a party to the trust deed. The manager directs the investments of the JPUT and is usually owned by the promoter of the fund.

There are a number of benefits to using JPUTs for investment in property, including:

---

[54] Items 6 and 9, Group 5 of Schedule 9 to the Value Added Tax Act 1994

- tax transparency – income can be treated as directly attributable to unit holders, allowing them to set off JPUT expenses against that income
- deferral of CGT – if managed and maintained offshore, CGT can be deferred or avoided
- no UK Stamp Duty Land Tax on a transfer of property from the unit trust (this typically results in an uplift of the sale price for the seller)
- Jersey tax exempt provided there are no Jersey-resident unit holders or Jersey-source income (other than bank deposit interest)
- units in JPUTs are easily transferable in the same way as shares
- there is no statutory framework as for companies so, for example, there are no restrictions on financial assistance or distributions
- different classes of units can be issued.

4.13.2 Jersey FS law

Trust companies domiciled in Jersey are subject to and regulated by the FS Law. Those executing the business of the trust company are obliged to register (there are some exceptions) and to comply with the Codes of Practice issued under the Financial Services (Jersey) Law – FS Law. Dedicated trustee companies usually maintain such a registration but where the JPUT is to be a stand-alone property holding structure, the unit holder may incorporate a private company for the purpose of holding the property and make the private company the trustee.

In this stand-alone scenario, the unit holder can exercise control over the board by populating it with specific members. There is an added advantage on sale of the JPUT: because the trustee company can be sold along with the JPUT, as opposed to using a dedicated trustee company, any underlying contracts need not be assigned to a new 'trustee' as for these purposes the trustee is the company that is sold along with the JPUT.

Provided that:

- the sole purpose of the private trust company is to provide trust company business services to a specific trust(s)
- the private trust company does not solicit from or provide trust company business services to the public and
- the private trust company's administration is carried out by a person registered under the FS Law.[55]

The private (stand-alone) trustee companies are exempt from the requirement to register under the FS Law.[56] This exemption further extends to the applicable Codes of Practice.

4.13.3 Types of JPUT

Depending on the type and number of investors, there are varying levels of regulatory control to which the JPUT will be subject as well as the relevant authorization required of the JFSC. If the JPUT has 15 or fewer investors and does not issue an offering document to potential investors, it will be a very private unit trust (VPUT). Before a VPUT can raise funds and

---

[55] Article 4, Financial Services (Trust Company Business (Exemptions) (Jersey) Order 2000) (FSO)
[56] Article 2, FSO

then issue units it must seek the consent of the JFSC.[57] This is usually only a formality following confidential disclosure of ultimate beneficial ownership to the JFSC. Once consent is obtained, there is no ongoing monitoring of the VPUT by the JFSC.

If the JPUT involves the pooling of funds, and issues an offer document to potential investors, or if there are more than 15 investors (subject to the units being offered to no more than 50 investors or being listed on a stock exchange) then the JPUT will be designated a 'COBO-only' fund (a fund regulated by COBO).[58] As with VPUTs, consent of the JFSC is required to raise money and issue units; in giving its consent, the JFSC will review the offer document. An additional requirement of the JFSC is that the trustee must have two Jersey-resident directors on its board and potentially have a Jersey manager. The JFSC also maintains a policy regarding promoters which it will judge the promoter against.

If the units in the JPUT are to be offered to more than 50 investors or are to be listed on a stock exchange then the JPUT will be a collective investment fund (CIF).[59] Under COBO, a CIF requires consent to raise funds and issue units. The trustee, the manager and any administrator or custodian (collectively known as the Jersey functionaries) must obtain permits from the JFSC.[60] The JFSC will scrutinize the promoter as well as the JPUT documentation before issuing such permits. Such permits will include conditions placed by the JFSC to enable ongoing monitoring. The JFSC also requires for CIF JPUTs that the trustee have two Jersey-resident directors and a Jersey manager. Certain additional documentary and structural requirements also apply if the CIF is open-ended.

If each of the investors is an 'expert' then the JPUT will be an expert fund. An expert is defined as:

- someone whose initial minimum investment is more than USD 100,000 (or equivalent) or
- someone whose ordinary business is that of buying/selling investments or providing advice to the same or
- a person with a net worth of more than USD 1 million (individually or jointly with a spouse and excluding their place of residence) or
- an entity with assets available for investment of USD 1 million (or equivalent) or more or of which every member/partner is an expert investor or
- a person connected with the trustee, manager, administrator or custodian of the fund.

4.13.4 Some JPUT conclusions

Given the high standards applied to expert investors, expert funds enjoy a lighter regulatory regime. Despite this, an expert fund still needs consent under COBO to raise funds and issue units and still requires two Jersey-resident directors on the trustee's board. The requirement to have a Jersey manager will be waived if the fund is open-ended and has a separate Jersey-based administrator, or if it is closed-ended and the trustee undertakes the function of manager as well.

[57] Article 9, Control of Borrowing (Jersey) Order 1958 (COBO)
[58] Article 3, Collective Investment Funds (Jersey) Law 1988 (CIF Law)
[59] Article 3, CIF Law
[60] Article 5, CIF Law

Following regulatory approval, the trust instrument can be executed; however, the JPUT is not technically in existence until the trustee holds assets on trust for the unit holders. For this reason, property acquisition is a prerequisite to the establishment of the JPUT.

A property manager is usually appointed to deal with routine management of the property and while major decisions relating to the trust assets remain the preserve of the trustee or manager, the property manager can, through the trust instrument, be required to provide advice. Similarly, the trust instrument can require the consent of the unit holders before the taking of certain major decisions.

4.14   SOME CONCLUSIONS

The variety of alternative investment structures in the market is growing. This is partly down to the fact that managers are adapting to the demands of investors and are seeking new ways to overcome the limitations of orthodox structures such as the limited partnership model.

As it has generally become a more difficult market in which to raise funds, this has had the effect of pushing managers into offering tailored vehicles to meet specific situations or to provide investment strategies in which the investors are not fully committed in respect of capital.

In my view, structures such as the managed account, which provides a single investor with direct ownership of an asset, are likely to grow in popularity with both investors and managers. This is also partly because new laws such as the AIFMD are tightening the regulatory straightjacket around collective pooled investments. Under the AIFMD, so long as an investment vehicle only represents the interests of a single investor, it cannot be said to be a collective fund.

Whether the administrative burden of managing multiple small vehicles, which is often the case for a structure like a managed account, turns out to be less than the burden of compliance with the regulations applicable to pooled investments remains to be seen.

5

Investment-specific Strategies

5.1 INTRODUCTION

This chapter focuses on the principal investment strategies for alternative assets in order to place the structuring, legal and tax reviews described earlier in this book into context.

5.2 PRIVATE EQUITY/VENTURE CAPITAL

5.2.1 Introduction

Private equity is a general term for investments made into companies which are either un-listed private entities, listed entities with the intention of delisting the target company or those that behave more like a private equity-backed business (for example a buy-and-build strategy). The aim of private equity investment is to in some way restructure or redirect the target business which results in an increase in the value of the business, which can then be sold on to the profit of the investors, typically within three to five years of its acquisition or investment.

5.2.2 Strategies

There are various strategies deployed by private equity investors or funds in order to maximize their gains.

(a) Buy-out

The most common is the leveraged buy-out (LBO) by which investment is made combining private capital with debt financing. The rationale is the classic justification for leveraging or gearing, that once the fixed cost of debt borrowing is paid for by the returns, the remaining capital gains from an investment are pure profit for the investors. The greater the ratio of debt to equity, the greater the return for the equity investors (in theory). LBO deals are more common when acquiring larger and more mature companies, as the proven track record of income and perceived lower risk will reduce the borrowing costs, and in today's economic climate will increase the likelihood that debt financiers will commit to lending. The most common criticism of the LBO strategy is that it can encourage more financial engineering, with little operational or strategic value.

(b) Growth capital

Here an established business is seeking to expand and requires investment. The aim is not necessarily to relinquish control of the company to the incoming investors, who may instead acquire only a minority stake (with appropriate safeguards). The existing business may or may not be listed. Where it is listed the transaction commonly takes the form of private investment in public equity (referred to as a PIPE) whereby the incoming private equity investors acquire convertible or preferred security that is unregistered with the markets for a period of time.

(c) Venture capital

Venture capital concerns the financing of start-up or early growth stage businesses by equity rather than debt. Venture funding is typically associated with capital-intensive industries such as technology, biotechnology and health care, where the high start-up costs are unable to be met by debt financing (which is usually cheaper than venture capital) and the revenue streams and even the success of the concept are likely unproven.

(d) Development capital

Development capital is like growth capital, but is not so limited to high growth of the portfolio company, but more to a new 'development' of the business or a new business line.

5.3 PUBLIC EQUITIES

5.3.1 Introduction

Equity investment is the classic form of investment, and not really very 'alternative' at all, until it becomes 'hedged'. Shares which are traded on the various stock exchanges across the world are the headline figures for day to day economic news reporting and this is where many first thoughts about investing stray. The common view on equity investment is to 'pick a winner': investing in the shares of a company in the expectation that they will increase in value over time. This is a fairly simplistic approach to investing and inevitably leads to as much success as failure as share prices rise and dip due to myriad economic factors (many of which do not concern the direct performance of the portfolio shares).

5.3.2 Strategies

Other approaches to equity investment include tracking a particular index: this may be accomplished by investing in all of the equities within a particular index (such as the FTSE 100) or a representative sample of them; the aim with either approach is to obtain portfolio growth in line with the growth in the market overall, rather than relying on a handful of equities beating the market trend.

Some more advanced strategies towards equity investment have been adopted more commonly in the world of hedge funds. A primary example is that of long/short equities. The core approach is to buy long equities which are expected by the investment manager to increase in value and to sell short equities which are expected to decrease in value. When buying long, the investor (or manager) will agree a derivative contract (see section 5.12 of this chapter for more detail on derivatives) with a counterparty to buy a specified number of shares of a company at a specified price on a future date. If the prediction holds and the market value of the shares increases, the investor exercises the contract and buys the shares at the now lower than market price. Selling those shares immediately following acquisition generates profit. Where the investor is to sell the equities short in anticipation of a falling market, he enters into a contract to sell a specific number of shares on a specified date at a specified price higher than that which is predicted for the future. When the market falls, he acquires the shares at the new lower price and then exercises the option (compelling the counterparty to buy) and makes a profit on the higher price paid for the shares. Sometimes the hedge fund will buy the stock both long and short, to 'hedge' its position (the origin of the term hedge fund).

5.4   BONDS

Bonds are again not usually 'alternative' but 'mainstream', unless hedged or leveraged, or used as derivatives or derivative benching. Bonds are debt securities issued by either a company or a public body, such as central government or municipal authorities. Bonds are typically medium- to long-term investments, with a maturity of anything from a year up to 30 years. They are often negotiable instruments, which are easily sold between investors on a secondary market. Traditionally, interest and capital repayments were made to the bearer of the bond (hence the now outdated term 'bearer bond'), although nearly all bonds are held and traded electronically through clearing houses and depositaries such as Euroclear.

The interest rate or the 'coupon' on bonds is dependent on several factors: the creditworthiness of the issue, the maturity date of the bond and the prevailing market conditions at the time of issue. Some bonds carry an interest rate which is not fixed – these are technically floating-rate notes rather than bonds and the interest rate is typically expressed as, for example, LIBOR + 125 basis points. The note will stipulate how often the interest rate is to be recalculated.

Bonds can be rated by rating agencies such as Standard & Poor's or Moody's. The lower the perceived risk, the lower the yield. Bonds that are rated below 'investment grade' ('BBB' by Standard & Poor's or 'Baa3' by Moody's is the lowest investment grade) were historically referred to as junk bonds, or high-yield bonds. These carry a higher risk of default, but offer higher returns. Investment grade bonds range from AAA to BBB (Standard & Poor's) or from Aaa to Baa3 (Moody's).

5.5   CREDIT FUNDS

5.5.1   Introduction

A credit fund invests in fixed-income loan instruments ranging from senior and mezzanine debt to bonds and other short-term borrowings as well as securitized products such as collateralized debt obligations. Generally speaking the cost of running a debt fund is lower than other funds, and so the management fees are correspondingly lower. Debt funds focus on preserving capital returns and will return a lower income than other investments. Funds will generally aim for absolute returns rather than returns relative to a benchmark. Credit funds can be structured as open-ended, closed-ended or listed.

5.5.2   Senior debt

Senior debt is debt that has the highest priority relative to other commitments of the investee or target. This priority is often secured by way of a lien over the investee's assets, which gives the lender the right to possess and sell those assets in the event of default. The senior creditor is also paid first compared with other creditors when interest payments or capital repayments are made. Although senior debt was typically provided by commercial banks, in the past decade an increasing amount has been provided by non-bank sources, such as institutional investors and hedge funds. This has only increased following the financial crisis as banks are subject to tighter regulation on their investments and exposure and are generally more reluctant to lend.

The yield from senior debt is typically lower than other forms of debt where it is secured by collateral. Senior debt can often return from 5% to 7% of capital.[1] The risk profile is low for senior debt because along with potential security, the legal systems in well-developed economies for dealing with the priority of creditors are sophisticated and can provide a fair degree of certainty. The presence of security alone is not determinative of the interest rate, as factors such as credit history, projected income and ability to pay are also considered.

5.5.3 Mezzanine debt

Mezzanine debt is debt that is subordinated to other commitments, such as senior debt. Generally speaking it is only senior to contributions to shareholders in the distribution of the assets of a company when it is wound up; therefore it is between the two levels of senior debt and equity, or 'mezzanine'.

The mezzanine debt market can be divided into two broad sectors:

- the traditional mezzanine debt which is accompanied by equity or warrants to increase blended returns and
- larger scale 'institutional' mezzanine finance which is not secured by warrants and is often syndicated.

The institutional finance transactions are typically 10 or greater times larger than traditional mezzanine deals. Institutional investors prefer warrantless debt because it comes with a greater interest rate and such investors typically have yield targets that their investments must meet. Equity sponsors also prefer warrantless mezzanine debt because the uptake of warrants will often dilute the equity holdings of other investors.

Mezzanine debt is a riskier investment than senior debt as it is not always fully secured and distributions are made only after the higher priority debts have been satisfied. To compensate the yield on mezzanine debt is often higher, frequently in the range of 12% to 15%.[2] Some issues of mezzanine debt carry warrants which allow the debt holder to elect to convert part of the debt into equity after a period of time, although this is restricted to smaller transactions.

Payment in kind (PIK) investments do not pay a current yield, but rather roll yield up, and therefore the coupon is higher than current yielding debt.

[1] Source: Partners Group and *Wall Street Journal* – http://blogs.wsj.com/privateequity/2012/08/23/partners-group-chart-should-single-handedly-make-every-debt-fund-oversubscribed/

[2] Source: Partners Group and *Wall Street Journal* – http://blogs.wsj.com/privateequity/2012/08/23/partners-group-chart-should-single-handedly-make-every-debt-fund-oversubscribed/

5.5.4   Bonds

Credit funds will typically invest in bonds as they are the most common forms of debt financing freely traded on the market. Many bonds are seen as 'safe' investments due to the creditworthiness of the borrower and can be utilized to shore up the diversity of a portfolio. For more information on the nature of bonds and bond investment, see above in section 5.4 of this chapter.

5.5.5   Asset-backed securities (ABSs), collateralized loan obligations (CLOs) and collateralized debt obligations (CDOs)

ABSs are bond issues by SPVs into which a financial institution has transferred secured assets such as mortgages. The aim is in part to take low value debts off a bank's balance sheet and the bond's interest payments and capital repayments are financed by the income stream from the underlying assets. The underlying assets do not have to be mortgages; ABS issues have been funded by a range of income streams such as recording royalties, credit card receivables and life insurance premiums. The financial institution maintains its client relationships and simply diverts the income into the SPV.

The issue of ABSs can also be structured into more complex instruments. CDOs are issues of bonds derived from pooling various debt obligations into an SPV financed by the stream of income from this pool. The assets that are pooled are segregated according to their creditworthiness. The division of assets is described as the difference between senior CDOs and junior CDOs; senior CDOs are the highest quality whereas junior CDOs are the poorest. This segregation allows for the pools to be tranched, and for CDO securities to be issued that have varying yields and risk profiles.

CLOs are similar to CDOs in structure; they are structured as SPVs which acquire debt obligations and issue securities (debt or otherwise) to investors to fund the acquisition of said debts. As a form of CDO, CLOs are a distinct subclass as they are syndicated bank loans rather than any other form of debt obligation. The loans are often highly leveraged: that is, the borrowers are borrowing much more than their equity.

An underlying flaw in ABSs, CDOs and CLOs was exposed and partly precipitated the financial crisis of 2008, where a large number were backed by sub-prime mortgages, and when it became clear that a large number of the mortgage borrowers would default, the holders of these securities (primarily banks and institutions that the bank sold these on to) found themselves with near worthless assets and large losses. Over-leveraging of such investments was also rife pre-credit crisis, which meant that only a small movement in the 'equity' of such investments took the investment under water. The market for CLOs and CDOs also ground to a halt during the credit crisis and there is still much stigma attached to these asset classes. Very few CDO or CLO funds were likewise raised. Despite this, in the past year a greater number of CDOs and CLOs have been established and successfully marketed to investors and the market is currently at its highest since the crisis.

5.5.6   Fund diversity

A debt fund's investment strategy will inevitably involve a degree of diversification in order to spread risk and still find investments that will deliver absolute returns. Government bonds and senior debt are examples of the more prudent debt investments to be found, but for many such as institutional investors the returns offered are simply not high enough. In order to attract a broader base of investors, investments in the higher yield securities such as mezzanine debt and high-yield corporate bonds (or indeed some sovereign debt) would need to be made. Given the current low interest climate, these riskier investments may make up 50% or more of the investment portfolio.

5.6   SHADOW BANKING

5.6.1   Introduction

Shadow banking is an aspect of the financial markets which replicates traditional credit facilities and intermediation outside of regulated banks. Avoiding the regulatory regime applicable to banks is largely done by not accepting insured deposits. Subsidiaries and divisions of otherwise regulated banks also engage in the shadow banking sector. Participants in the shadow banking sector include hedge funds, money market funds, investment banks and other entities that hold financial assets.

The commercial attraction of shadow banking is that with the right expertise, credit intermediation can be achieved with much greater efficiency than highly regulated banks can offer. It is also an attractive option for investors, as cash can be put to use cheaply and (with the right intermediaries) for a good low risk return. There are risks attached with the market that should be considered by potential investors. The shadow banking system is often highly leveraged by comparison with regular banking, which is helped in part by the absence of the regulation that traditional banks must comply with on borrowing and other ratios. The leveraged funds are often from short-term sources and the fund's investments are frequently in long-term and illiquid assets.

5.6.2   SIVs/conduits

An SIV is an SPV established (often in the Cayman Islands or Jersey) by financial institutions to function in a similar way to a bank but without being subject to such heavy regulation. Typically, SIVs were funded by a combination of investment from the original investors and by issuing short- or medium-term debt instruments called 'commercial paper' at low interest rates. The issue of commercial paper is effectively a cheap way of borrowing cash from the financial markets. The SIV then uses the capital derived from the issue of commercial paper to purchase longer-term securities which earn rates of interest higher than the cost of servicing the original debt. Essentially, the SIV then derives profit from the difference between the rates of interest it has borrowed at and the interest the assets earn.

SIVs were a controversial instrument in the early months of the credit crisis because if the value of the SIVs investments falls and they encounter a lack of liquidity (i.e. through little take-up by investors) then the SIV will be insolvent. SIVs are structured so that if they become insolvent the original investors will not be liable for the SIV's debts. This is usually achieved by granting security over the SIV's assets including its securities portfolio to a trustee to hold for the benefit of the investors. SIVs were also structured so as to benefit from a capital markets exemption under section 72B of the UK Insolvency Act 1986. This exemption provides that if an SIV is facing financial difficulty or insolvency, the security trustee can block the appointment of an administrator by appointing an administrative receiver. Following the 2007 financial crisis, many SIVs did in fact fail and the model has subsequently been discredited.

Conduits are very similar to SIVs in that they are structured as SPVs established and administered by banks and financial institutions. Conduits issue asset-backed commercial paper in which the underlying assets include receivables generated from trade, credit cards, leasing and other collateralized debt obligations.

5.6.3 Perceived risks

When combined with the lack of central bank support and deposit protection, if creditor confidence in the value of the invested assets drops, there is little to stop a 'run' on these shadow banks. This in part contributed to the financial crisis of 2008. The market survived the crisis, and (somewhat ironically) has since grown in terms of asset value larger than it was prior to the crash as traditional banking has shrunk. From a systemic perspective, shadow banking and other non-bank sources of finance can be considered beneficial for the economy overall – the FCA has stated in the past that fewer risks are introduced into the financial markets by non-bank entities and that it can introduce stability. Paul Volcker, former Chairman of the US Federal Reserve, famously said that banks should not act as if they were hedge funds.

However, what has since happened is that shadow banking has now grown in scope (partly as the banks are being heavily restricted by regulations) to the point where it has introduced the same systemic risks that banks introduced, by going from credit intermediation into finance. The market in shadow banking only looks set to grow faster as the regulation of traditional commercial banks limits the capacity to lend to riskier borrowers, to leverage their activities and liquidity and capital restraints which require investment in more liquid assets, although increased regulatory scrutiny could easily curtail it or drive it deeper underground. By financing unsecured lending such as credit cards or car loans, those investors involved in shadow banking can often obtain high rates of return efficiently. Another attractive investment is in repurchase agreements (repos) which are secured on the assets they represent. These can provide an efficient source of income, as the repurchase price effectively amounts to interest, but as the 2008 crisis showed, if the underlying assets are overvalued or worthless, the security itself is of little worth as an asset or collateral.

Shadow banking activities can certainly increase systemic risk. The lack of central funding support or deposit guarantees hinders liquidity in a crisis moment, reflecting the risks that banks undertook before the current financial crisis and the advent of greater regulation. When an operator in the market finds that its short-term liabilities are due, its credit can be at risk as its own assets are most often illiquid. Another concern about the shadow banking sector is that it can operate alongside regulated banks without being subject to the same controls, which can bring systemic risks into the regulated system. There are also concerns about the effect of arbitrage when the two systems operate side by side. That being said there are suggestions that non-bank credit sources can be a source of systemic stability in certain limited circumstances.

A risk of investing in shadow banking is also the leverage of the fund's dealings. As the sector is unregulated, there is no limit to the amount of borrowing that funds the acquisition of assets. This leveraging can increase returns in a financial boom, but if the markets crash the exposure is much greater. The risk of the market crashing is actually increased by excessive leveraging reducing liquidity. Further, the regulated banks use the shadow banking operators as investment opportunities, widening the potential contagion when the market crashes.

The concerns for regulators are the aspects of shadow banking that create the same risks as regulated banks would, which (for regulated banks) are either monitored by regulatory disclosure or restricted by regulation. A specific example is maturity transformation. If investors have placed readily accessible cash in a fund, which acquires short-term (e.g. 15 day) commercial paper from an issuer, that in turn uses the proceeds to invest in mortgage-backed securities which mature in 25 years' time, that effectively recreates bank maturity transformation. Borrowing short and lending long killed Northern Rock. The investors who originally have instant access to cash have – in the worst case scenario – lost that access because the fund's own investments have defaulted. Prudential regulation of the banking sector aims to reduce the exposure to these risks, but at present the shadow banking sector is not so regulated.

There is, and will be going forward, some headline news around shadow banking charging excessive returns to consumers, and 'baseball bat' collecting of liabilities. These headlines (note the Church of England versus Wonga in mid 2013) will only encourage regulators to attempt to stifle shadow banking, as if they don't need any more encouragement for systemic risk issues. Thus as mainstream banks recover, shadow banking will either largely become institutionalized and regulated or be driven underground to payday lenders and mobsters.

5.6.4   Proposed added US regulation

Elements of the US Dodd–Frank Act, signed into law by Barack Obama in 2010, may provide for some regulation of the shadow banking sector. One of the provisions is for the Federal Reserve to act as a lender of last resort in exceptional circumstances to participants in the market. Although this could reduce the damage from spreading in the event of another crisis in the shadow banking sector, there is no provision for preventative regulation so there is no incentive to drop the investment policies that create the risks. There is also a potential moral question of a central bank lending to market participants who are unregulated and often the architects of their own downfall. Some bankers consider that the regulations imposed on regulated banks by the Dodd–Frank Act will actually drive business into the shadow banking sector.

The Financial Stability Board (FSB) is in the process of drafting proposals for the regulation of shadow banking for members of the G20 (and it is hoped other states) to implement. It is important for the regulations to be widely adopted across key markets to reduce the risk of arbitrage. The regulations do not seek to overly hamper the shadow banking sector, acknowledging that it can have a key economic role to play. The areas of concern it seeks to address are:

- to reduce the risks inherent in shadow banking spilling over into the 'regular' banking sector
- to reduce the risk of a run on money market funds
- to assess and mitigate systemic risks posed by other shadow banking operators
- to assess and align the incentives associated with securitization
- to dampen risks and pro-cyclical incentives associated with instruments such as repos that exacerbate credit strains during a run.

The aim of the FSB is to have a 'surgical' approach to regulating and overseeing shadow banking. It seeks only to target the areas which are vulnerable or liable to induce wider systemic risk into the market. On 29 August 2013, the FSB published a policy framework which aims to put into place a global set of rules regulating the sector by 2015.

5.7   REAL ESTATE AND INFRASTRUCTURE

5.7.1   Introduction

Real estate and infrastructure funds operate with certain similar objectives and risk management profiles. Both fields can offer the reward of a long-term return on an investment, and
depending on the willingness to undertake risk, they can deliver substantial rewards. The
risks which underline both are also similar: they are sensitive to the property market, they
are largely illiquid and it can be difficult to assess how the fund's investments are performing
until they have been realized. The time it takes for each investment to mature is significant
too; it could be up to a period of 10 years. Most investors in real estate funds are pension
funds, insurance companies, hedge funds, sovereign wealth funds and other shadow banking
operators that can play a long game. Some investors have recently taken on the acquisition
and development in-house rather than by an intermediary, which adds to the risk and the cost
of getting a management and development team in place, but can return a greater proportion
of the income and capital profit. A lot of infrastructure projects are public–private partnerships with the government and local authorities, which can lead to conflicts of interest in
seeking a return and the publication of results.

5.7.2   Real estate strategies

Real estate funds invest in a wide range of property types: housing, retail, commercial and
industrial. The return depends in part on the investment strategy and on whether the market
grows during the period of investment. The main strategies are known as 'core plus', 'value
added' and 'opportunistic'. Real estate funds are typically structured as a specialized vehicle.
Popular publicly available structures are the JPUT described above in Chapter 4, section
4.13 and the real estate investment trust (REIT) which is common in the US (see Chapter 6,
section 6.4.3(b)) and a recent development in the UK (see Chapter 6, section 6.3.3(e)). The
use of these specialized structures is not necessary; many private funds are still structured as
limited partnerships or as any other suitable structure, depending on the usual range of factors
such as taxation of the investors or regulations.

Real estate funds can be more of a 'business' than other fund structures. What this means
is that the assets are managed on a more concentrated level with issues such as planning, construction, maintenance, insurance and wider regulatory concerns and specialized tax regimes
for property.

The real estate market took a hit during the financial crisis (it does in most financial crises),
especially as one of the triggers was the collapse in house prices in 2008 and the subsequent
widespread default on mortgage payments. It has since recovered to an extent in both the UK
and the US.

A 'core plus' strategy is conservative, investing in high value property that does not need a
large investment, with modest but safer and more immediate returns. The properties acquired
will require little in the way of development and often have tenancies soon up for negotiation. This may be an opportunity to increase rents, although it may appear to be a less stable
investment on acquisition.

The 'value added' strategy will look to properties which require more development and can
offer greater returns. It may not be limited to the physical state of repair; some value added
properties may be so because of low occupancy rates. Such properties may be available at

a discount and offer an opportunity to increase rent profit income along with capital growth where development is necessary.

The 'opportunistic' approach will often invest in greenfield sites, niche sectors or emerging market properties that require the greatest amount of development, planning and investment. Undeveloped and underdeveloped sites will often be unoccupied or have very low occupancy rates, and so this will present an opportunity to greatly increase the rental income and the overall value of the property (occupancy often increases market value). They target the greatest return but the investment period is longer and there are greater risks involved.

5.7.3   Infrastructure strategies

The term 'infrastructure' encompasses a broad and diverse range of physical structures and services required for the functioning of a modern economy. This may include projects such as transport education and health care facilities, but also telecommunications, water supply and waste disposal. Certain types of infrastructure are not obviously recognizable as such. For example, scientific research facilities, banking, finance and regulatory systems may all fall into the infrastructure bracket. Infrastructure is closely connected with energy, as discussed in section 5.8 of this chapter. Infrastructure investment can take place at different phases of the development cycle. Riskier investments can be made such as greenfield sites and projects that have yet to receive authorization, which will suffer from a longer period of time before they generate returns. The profit margin for such projects can be greater. Alternatively, investment can be made in the later stages of development, or when the project itself is complete. These can be safer investments but are often expensive, and the investor will have had no control over the previous development process.

Infrastructure funds seek to invest in developments as diverse as the projects themselves. Infrastructure projects are frequently developed as public–private partnerships (PPPs) with the government or local authorities investing alongside institutional investors and banks. PPPs are often created following private finance initiatives (PFIs) driven by the state. PFIs are somewhat controversial in that private sector debt and equity are used to finance public projects but are underwritten by the public purse. This concept of underwriting of projects with public finances, together with the generation of profits for private interests and high profile failures, has led to PFIs and PPPs being perceived as politically unpopular. Equally they can be unpopular with investors that do not believe public policy should interfere with investment strategy.

PFI contracts are usually awarded by public authorities to privately held SPVs in order to utilize private sector project and financial management expertise. Contracts usually have a lifespan of between 20 and 30 years. Prior to the 2007 financial crisis, PFI infrastructure projects were overwhelmingly bank funded. However, more recently the infrastructure funding market has seen a retreat by banks, which are faced with regulatory capital concerns and the regulation of the liquidity of their assets. The advent of shadow banking operators (as described above in section 5.6 of this chapter) coupled with the withdrawal of banks has seen an increase in pension and hedge fund investment into PFIs.

Infrastructure initiatives such as PPPs and PFIs can deliver a high rate of return for investors in terms of the capital investment and, where appropriate, the receipt of ongoing contractual fees for the management of the facilities. Because initiatives are often underwritten by public authorities, they are regarded by investors as a relatively low risk asset class which delivers long-term yields through contractual cash flow (which is often inflation-linked).

Effectively, this means that infrastructure investments are more recession resistant than more short-term focused investments and above inflation returns are virtually guaranteed. Further, because returns are based on facilities rather than usage, changes to the economic landscape are less likely to adversely impact returns. Certain infrastructure investments, such as utilities and public transport projects, are seen as particularly stable because they often have a natural monopoly status and operate within highly regulated sectors. An additional factor which makes infrastructure projects attractive to investors is that returns have a low market correlation and are not connected to investments in other asset classes such as bonds or equities. All that sounds great, but there have been high profile mistakes and government-led or regulatory interference, leading to the building blocks of certain investment strategies being knocked, in turn leading to losses, which are exasperated by the 'thinness' of allowable risk or equity. A good example is a government changing agreed rebates or tax allowances after the event.

5.8   ENERGY FUNDS

5.8.1   Old energy

The old energy sector is made up of crude oil (in its various forms, such as Brent Crude and West Texas Intermediate), heating oil, natural gas, ethanol and coal. It is a vital sector for the global economy as it is made up of the fuels that have historically fired industrial growth as well as transportation, heating and electricity. The market in old energy has seen a large growth in both prices and supply, as the appetite of developing industrial economies such as China consumes vast resources. That being said, China's latest five-year plan has set targets to reduce fossil fuel dependency and increase the relative consumption of natural gas, two moves which are likely to have an effect on the old energy markets if they are implemented.

The growth of new technologies such as fracking and more economic means of locating reserves both onshore and in deep water for the extraction of oil and natural gas has provided new impetus to the old energy market. The US in particular has seen an expansion in its position as a globally prominent supplier of these forms of energy, although there is no consensus on the strength of this boom and whether it is a bubble or genuine growth. Private equity investment in these sectors often takes the form of investing in the pioneers of exploration and extraction technologies rather than the energy output instead, as exploration and technology can deliver the higher returns.

5.8.2   New energy

New energy concerns the development of alternative sources of energy from the old energy stalwarts. It is not only the development of renewable electricity or thermal energy generation such as hydro-electric, wind and solar, but also alternative sources of fuels and other hydrocarbons such as the sourcing of ethanol from crops, wood and agricultural waste. The industry saw large growth at the beginning of the 21st century as both investors and existing energy giants responded to public demand for reduced dependency on hydrocarbons and predictions that the reserves of old energy resources were limited, with scarcity driving up future prices. However, recent developments in the old energy sector have resulted in more economic access to known deposits and have revealed greater deposits of these resources. This has had an impact on investing in new energy.

Various government policies may help the economic growth in this sector by the provision of tax incentives and subsidies but the benefit of new energy sources (reduced air pollution) is not factored into the market value of the energy produced, and they are still arguably expensive sources of energy compared with the old energy sources. Also, as with infrastructure projects, they can be dented by government or other interference after the event.

5.9   COMMODITIES FUNDS

5.9.1   Introduction

The commodities market is divided into three broad classes of asset – agriculture, metals and energy. Agriculture encompasses basic foodstuffs such as corn, wheat, soybeans and sugar. The metals market ranges from aluminium to zinc and includes precious metals such as gold and silver. Energy is dominated by crude oil, natural gas and coal; refined products such as heating oil and petrol; and alternative energies. Investing in commodities is traditionally seen as a hedge against inflation, and it is not often considered sound to invest too heavily in commodities due to the fluctuations in price that can occur. An investment in the commodities market can be made by directly purchasing the physical goods themselves, investing in the equities of companies which are involved directly in the trade (such as mining or oil companies), investing in exchange traded funds (ETFs) or exchange traded commodities, or speculating in the futures market. Each strategy varies the risks and rewards of investing but all are fundamentally linked to the prices themselves, which have over the last decade continually increased in what has become known as a 'supercycle'.[3] This supercycle may be coming to an end or at least a lull.

5.9.2   Agriculture

Like all commodities, the agriculture sector can often see volatile swings in prices. Long-term trends which are affecting prices include the desire for biofuels, pushing up the price as more staple foodstuffs such as corn and sugar are fermented for use as energy. It can also spike when there is a crisis in the oil markets, as consumers look for cheaper alternatives. The agriculture sector can also be affected by more traditional factors such as poor harvests, population growth and political and social upheaval.

5.9.3   Metals

The market in metals commodities can be divided into precious metals and base metals. Precious metals include gold, silver, platinum and palladium. Base metals include iron, copper, zinc, tin and aluminium. Although all have industrial purposes which can fuel demand and supply constraints, precious metals are also used as investments – gold is the best example, which is often used as a hedge against inflation or the decline of other investment markets. The market in base metals has seen price rises as part of the supercycle, with growth in demand fuelled by industrial growth, which has recently shown signs of slowing down. The situation is underlined by the volume of metals registered on the London Metal Exchange – it rose from 1.5 million tonnes in 2008 to 7 million tonnes in 2012.[4] This shows a greater number held by investors rather than being put to use by the industrial sector, and this reduction

---

[3] *FT* – Special Report: Commodities 2012
[4] *FT* – Special Report: Commodities 2012

in demand may lead to greater price drops. Base metals will see a growth in demand as more developing economies grow their industrial sectors, despite short-term cycles in pricing. Precious metals have some industrial applications and will see their prices affected by industrial growth as well, although they still will be valuable investments as hedges.

5.9.4   Energy

See section 5.8 above.

5.9.5   Direct or indirect investment

Investing in commodities can take various forms. An investor or manager can invest directly into commodities by trading them through the various markets. Alternatively a manager can seek exposure to the commodities markets in the following ways.

(a) Exchange traded funds

Investment can be made through an ETF (see Chapter 6, section 6.5.2) which is linked to the sector. Such an ETF may invest in one commodity or be spread across many. If it tracks just one, it may maximize its returns where there are good returns, but equally, where there is a poor return, the whole fund suffers due to the limited portfolio. A more diverse portfolio of commodities would spread the risk of losses more widely but reduce the maximum return where one has a standout performance.

(b) Indirect investment in operating companies

Investments can be made in the commodities sector indirectly by investing in the equity of companies that operate in it. There is exposure to the movement of prices and where prices increase, in general the revenues and profits of the producers rise too. There are some factors with regard to equity investments in commodity producers that should be considered. The movement of the spot price of a commodity can affect a company's profit and loss profile in proportion to the company's size. Much like an ETF portfolio, the range of commodities that a company extracts or produces can also affect its susceptibility to market movements. An energy company dealing in crude oil and natural gas would suffer less in a crash in the price of crude oil than a company operating purely in crude.

(c) Futures

Rather than dealing in the commodities themselves or an ETF linked to them, some investors operate by investing in the futures markets. A futures contract is an agreement for the supply of a fixed amount of a commodity at a fixed price on a fixed date. Not all futures contracts are settled by physical delivery but by cash instead. They are useful for suppliers, for example farmers, as they allow them to guarantee a price for their crops when they expect prices to be low (provided that the crop is good and sufficiently bountiful), but could result in having to sell at less than the market rate if their judgement is wrong. The other side of a futures contract is often entered into by speculators who believe the price will rise, and that therefore they will make a profit selling at the market price (or spot price) once they have acquired the commodities or equivalent. A speculator of course has no intention of taking physical delivery of the crop. When the expiry date of the contract arrives, the investor will close the position by entering into a contract to sell the same amount of the crop. The movement of the price from the original position to the second closing position is the measure of the speculator's gain or loss. Most futures contracts are made exclusively between speculators, and are settled by cash rather than delivery.

5.9.6   Regulation

(a) Current regulatory environment

Other than the usual fund and fund manager regulations, specific regulation of the commodities markets has historically been in reaction to market manipulation, such as the establishment of the Commodity Futures Trading Commission (CFTC) in the US in 1974 in reaction to the increase in agricultural futures prices in the early 1970s, which was attributed in part to excessive speculation. In the years preceding the crisis of 2008, prices in the market rose consistently and then sharply leading up to the crisis. After the crisis most prices shrank back to the level of a few years prior.

(b) Market concerns

The concerns about food prices are humanitarian and economic. Given the extent of global poverty, the continual increase in the price of basic agricultural commodities is considered to have a disproportionate negative effect on the world's poorest. The increase in energy and industrial prices is a concern as it may hinder economic recovery by increasing base manufacturing costs and requiring higher levels of investment. Another concern is that speculation will lead to a widening gap between the natural price of the commodity and its market price, which would then result in a loss of confidence in the market price.

(c) Proposed regulation

The CFTC proposed position limits in January 2012 which would cap the holdings of commodities and their derivatives and prevent single traders from controlling too much of the market. The proposal was overturned in September 2012 by a federal court and in November 2012 the CFTC announced it would appeal the decision. This appeal failed and on 5 November 2013 the CFTC approved a new position limits rule in a 3–1 decision. In our view it is likely to be challenged by the industry again, given the opinion of Commissioner Scott O'Malia, who voted against the rule on the grounds that it did not sufficiently address the objections raised by the federal court.[5] The uncertainty surrounding the rule has in itself led to complaints from the investment industry about the costs of putting into place contingencies for compliance and has faced opposition from Wall Street groups as a flawed and unnecessary rule. The legislative bodies of the EU are currently debating Markets in Financial Instruments Directive (MiFID) II. MiFID II would also introduce position limits for traders of commodities and their derivatives. As part of the legislative process, the rapporteur of the

---

[5] http://www.ft.com/cms/s/0/ad1a6360-4617-11e3-b495-00144feabdc0.html?siteedition=uk#axzz2kXPgYNWu

European Parliament's committee on development has conceded that the only consensus is that there is a 'lack of comprehensive and granular information' on the subject.[6]

5.10   SOCIAL IMPACT FUNDS

5.10.1 Introduction

Social impact investing aims to generate a positive social and/or environmental return along-side a financial return. It should be distinguished from socially responsible investing, which typically aims to avoid harmful consequences, rather than fostering a positive outcome. A fund may invest in a wide range of activities, or may specialize, but the typical investments are in housing, rural water supplies, maternal health, primary education and financial services. The expected financial return will depend at first glance on the investor base. Some may want investments which outperform traditional investment classes, others may allow for a reduced return as the price to pay for the social impact. Most funds instead aim to compete with the returns typically offered by other classes by looking at whether the venture will have a positive social impact first, and then looking at the commercial viability second.

The range of participants in social impact investment is wide; it can include development finance institutions, private foundations, large-scale financial institutions, private wealth managers, commercial bankers, pension fund managers and companies. There is a nascent field of regulatory and oversight committees, such as the Global Impact Investing Network (GIIN) established by JP Morgan, the Rockefeller Foundation and the United States Agency for International Development. Another landmark body of principles is the United Nations' Principles for Responsible Investment, which since its launch in 2006 has seen over 1000 asset owners and investment managers become signatories to it.[7]

5.10.2 The rewards of social impact funds

The rewards of social impact investing are often divided into those which are financial and those which are social. There need not be a trade-off between the two if the investment is right, but sometimes the reduction of the financial reward can be offset by the social reward. What this takes is the kind of reporting that quantifies the social returns and allows for the best comparison with financial returns by expressing those returns with reference to cash. Such a subjective valuation could of course lead to distortions in the values given, especially so where individual groups use their own standards. If there is an industry-wide standard or standards (such as that provided by GIIN), there is both a greater pool of contributors to those standards (reducing the tendency towards bias) and a clearer system for comparing returns.

Most investors still seek reasonable rates of return versus traditional investments such as bonds or equities, within the range of 5–10% per annum as opposed to the higher returns offered by hedge funds and private equity. Some investors will have restrictions on the minimum amount of returns to be sought, which may price them out of the social impact market. This would be true of pension funds, where a duty of the trustees is to seek the best return for the beneficiaries.

---

[6] *FT* – 1 December 2012
[7] www.unpri.org

The use of auditing methods such as the GIIN's metric will help drive up investor confidence in the social impact investment market. It is important to develop a stable and consistent way of comparing the social return with the financial one. This in part may justify a lower rate of return if it can be said that the social benefit created was equivalent to (for example) a return of 30% in cash. For some charitable foundations which are investing in the social impact market, this is the key return. Some may look for a minimal financial return if it increases the social return, depending in part on the wealth and background of its backers (such as the Rockefeller Foundation or the Bill & Melinda Gates Foundation that want to 'give it away').

5.10.3 The risks of social impact funds

The risks involved in social impact investing are not too dissimilar from existing classes of investment. They are still influenced by factors such as sector, location and the stage in which the investment is made, but there are elements that increase the risk. A lot of the activities backed by social investing take place in less economically developed countries, and as such should be treated as similar to high-yield emerging market investments (in terms of risk profile, but not necessarily return). The risks involved can be legal, as the regulatory infrastructure may not be in place to seek redress and ensure the appropriate channelling of investment. It may also impede any necessary construction or other works. Other typical risks are company risk, currency risk and other financial risks. Not all social impact investing takes place in such places though; there are projects that deal with urban infrastructure and a wide range of voluntary sector organizations in more developed nations, although the risks will be reduced in scope and will still merit consideration. It should also be noted that given the current economic climate, many more developed countries are at risk of becoming poor targets for investment. This is especially clear for sovereign debt, which is a factor to consider as many impact investments are made in conjunction with state funding or agencies.

There are also reputational risks involved in social impact investing. There are critics who suggest that private equity investment in otherwise charitable ventures leads to the risk of exploitation and 'mission drift', especially as the target groups are often the impoverished and potentially less well educated.

The terminology and the goals set are important too. There is a difference between 'output' and 'outcomes'. The output of the investment is more easily quantified – the number of development loans provided to farmers, for example. The outcome is less easy to quantify, and requires precise definition.

5.11   SECONDARIES FUNDS

5.11.1 Introduction

Secondary investments in private equity (or real estate or hedge, for that matter) are effectively buyouts by a second private equity fund of private equity assets from a first private equity fund. This can also include the buyout of a position in a fund as a limited partner or a direct acquisition of equity stakes in portfolio companies. These methods of acquisition can be broken down further.

(a) The sale of limited partnership interests

- Straight sale – for cash of a limited partnership interest at or around the GP NAV
- Structured joint ventures – an agreement that does not completely relinquish the seller's interest
- Securitization – the process by which an interest in the fund is transferred to a special purpose vehicle which issues loan notes to generate liquidity. Equity in the new vehicle may also be offered to investors
- Stapled secondaries – where a new fund is being raised by the general partner of the existing fund, a secondary interest in the existing fund may be offered to investors in the new fund as an additional incentive.

(b) The sale of direct investments

- Secondary direct – the sale of direct portfolio assets
- Synthetic secondary/spin-out – the sale of portfolio assets to a fund partnership into which the secondary investors invest, which is managed by the previous manager
- Tail-end – the sale of assets during the winding up of a fund
- Structured secondary – where the incoming investor agrees to provide the seller's capital contributions in the future in exchange for a preferred return on the portfolio income.

Secondaries are becoming more important as an exit route for private equity investors (and other long-term investment) for several reasons. They shorten deal lifetimes and help achieve early exits for what are otherwise very illiquid investments, and many managers seek a more active portfolio policy in order to achieve the greatest returns possible. The regulatory landscape for investors such as banks and insurance firms is changing too – the Basel III and Solvency II regulations, respectively, will limit the investments these firms can invest in due to capital adequacy restrictions and rules on the risk weighting of assets, which in turn leads to secondary sales of alternative assets.

5.11.2 Key legal points

When making a secondary investment in a transaction there are several key points to note. One is the warranties and other protections which a buyer will seek from the seller to protect its investment. Typically, a seller will be reluctant to give extensive protection to the buyer in any transaction but with a secondary sale the seller will not have been involved in the management of the firm in a direct manner and so is even more reluctant to guarantee the buyer's purchase. An alternative route would be to seek warranties from the management of the fund or portfolio company (as appropriate) but this is often inadvisable where the management is retained, as it could potentially strain relations irrecoverably if enforced. The management also frequently cannot afford to cover the cost of the secondary deal out of its own resources, making it an unreliable source of redress. A solution is often to put a price adjustment mechanism in the contract, which holds some of the purchase price in escrow or is otherwise deferred for a period of time, after which it cannot be recovered. During that time, if there is a defect in the investment made (or earning targets are not met), then the purchase price can be recovered in accordance with agreed mechanisms.

A further key legal point is whether the buyer steps into the shoes of the seller and assumes all liabilities both historic and going forwards. In addition, the date of the key pricing points, as well as who takes the benefit and burden of further distributions and drawdowns, are hotly debated.

5.11.3 Aspects of secondaries investment

The key feature of portfolio or fund secondaries is the offsetting of risks involved in investing in private equity at the primary stage. Secondary investment can reduce the effect of the 'j-curve'. The j-curve is the cash flow of a fund over time represented graphically. The initial outlays of the construction of the fund mean that the cash flow is negative for the first years, before returning to a positive line of growth later in the life cycle. Secondary investments often take place during the latter part of the construction phase or after, so the secondary investor should experience a positive cash flow either immediately or within a short period of time.

A secondary investment also mitigates the risks associated with blind-pools, where an investment fund has no specific investments lined up on creation. The secondary investor has an advantage in that it can analyse the historical performance of the current investments and decide whether or not to invest on that basis, and also potentially negotiate a better price. Secondary investments are less 'blind' than primary investment.

Another benefit is that it is easier to diversify a portfolio with acquisitions of secondary interests than with a primary investment. When investing at the initial stage, the high commitments required prevent a quick diversification of the portfolio and the similar vintage years will often mean that it is harder to spread the volatility of returns and the lack of initial positive cash flow. Mature primary investment funds do not have such problems, but for newcomers it is easier to establish this diversity with secondaries.

5.11.4 Some criticism of secondaries investment

Secondary funds in themselves can be blind-pools, especially when large funds are raised that take, say, five years to invest. In addition, as the demand for secondary investment increases, if the market of sellers (or primary direct funds) does not grow at the same rate, a greater proportion of secondary capital will be available and it will become more of a seller's market and the cost of acquisition will increase.

There is also the possibility of paying higher fees for secondary investments than for primaries. The investment in the primary fund requires the payment of fees to the managers of that fund. As most secondary investments are made through funds, the management of those funds in turn also charges fees. Also the larger secondary funds are effectively becoming an index for the wider private equity asset class where the secondary manager hardly influences returns (other than through sharper or structured entry pricing).

Finally, 'pass the parcel' secondary investing (especially of single assets) is seen by some LPs as lazy, non-proprietary investing, and a means of extending management fees for an asset.

5.12 DERIVATIVES FUNDS

5.12.1 Introduction

Derivatives are investment products which are based on an underlying asset, index or other product. To buy oil is to acquire the asset. Agreeing to buy oil at a future date is the derived product. Derivatives originally developed to allow suppliers or purchasers of products to purchase the products they need and to simultaneously hedge against price volatility, in the belief that the price will increase or decrease. The derivatives market has now grown to encompass nearly any financial product, for example: equities, bonds, interest rates and currencies. The counterparty to the derivative believes that the price will move in the opposite direction. The counterparty is often a speculator, and they often trade not to acquire or sell goods but only to make a profit by second-guessing the price movements. That is not to say they are unpopular, as their presence often provides liquidity in the market and a greater range of derivative options for those who are dealing directly in the products traded. Some of the recent regulatory interest, however, is investigating and seeking to regulate the perceived volatility that an excess of speculation can bring into a market. Derivatives are either traded through exchanges following a standard form, or are traded over-the-counter (OTC derivatives) where the form is often designed to the requirements of the parties.

Funds have in the past decade begun to take an interest in the use of derivatives as sources of income. There are funds that invest solely in derivatives as their investment strategy, whereas others hold them as part of the portfolio or use them to hedge against portfolio risk. The attractiveness of derivatives funds is on the increase as interest rates remain stagnant and other opportunities for investment income remain low.

5.12.2 Issues around derivatives

Derivatives carry general risks. There is counterparty risk where the contracting party that has unlimited exposure defaults on its obligations, leaving the other without the expected return, which can often be a vital hedge. Exchange traded derivatives are guaranteed by the clearing house, which mitigates the risk of default. OTC derivatives, however, are not normally traded through a clearing house and therefore carry no implicit protection. Large-scale default by counterparties can cause wider market problems such as the bailout of US insurance company AIG in 2008. As OTC derivatives are not frequently traded through a clearing house they are potentially more difficult to value, transfer or liquidate.

Investing in derivatives by a fund can potentially create risk. Their use frequently involves leverage – enabling a fund to participate in gains or losses far beyond the initial investment. Instruments such as purchased call options do not expressly involve leverage, but can create an economic equivalent of leverage. Although leverage can allow gains far in excess of capital commitment, a fund stands to lose a large amount of its portfolio when at a loss.

One of the risks of funds for a stock market fund is where the equity markets grow at a rate which causes the losses on the call options sold to outweigh the gains the portfolio naturally makes. Derivative enhanced funds may however be better investments in a stagnant or bearish equity market.

5.12.3 Specific regulation

The derivatives market came under close scrutiny following the recent financial crisis. Derivatives are seen as risky investments which were misused to excess, leading to some of the highest losses during the crisis. Not only that, but derivatives are often misused by traders to conceal losses, such as the case of Jérôme Kerviel of Société Générale, which resulted in losses of euro (EUR) 4.9 billion for the bank. OTC derivatives are regulated more extensively now in the US and the EU. The Dodd–Frank Act has brought in sweeping reform, meaning derivatives known as 'swaps' are regulated by either the CFTC or the SEC, or in some cases both. Private funds will be regulated as 'financial entities' such that funds will not be able to take advantage of an exception, known as the 'end-user' exception. The regulations under the Dodd–Frank Act require: reporting of each swap entered into, that the board or other appropriate committee approves uncleared swaps and that other documentary requirements are fulfilled. The EU has also issued rules regulating the use of any derivative contract, the European Market Infrastructure Regulation (EMIR). These rules require the reporting of any derivative contract entered into to a trade repository and require that users implement management risk standards. They also introduce a category of OTC derivatives which must be cleared via a central counterparty (CCP). Both the provisions of the Dodd–Frank Act and EMIR will have indirect extraterritorial effect, affecting counterparties which are based outside of the applicable jurisdictions.

The SEC also considered direct regulation of the use of derivatives by funds. This was initiated by an announcement in March 2010 of a moratorium on the registration of new exchange traded funds which were actively managed or leveraged and utilized derivatives. A consultation was launched in August 2011 exploring the benefits and risks of using derivatives in funds and whether or not there was a need for further regulation than that already required under US law. In December 2012 the SEC announced that it would lift the moratorium but would attach conditions to future registrations: an issuer would have to represent that it would assess and disclose its use of derivatives in accordance with relevant Commission guidance. The moratorium was only partially lifted, and ETFs which are leveraged by derivatives will continue to be prohibited.

5.13   CURRENCY FUNDS

5.13.1 Introduction

Some funds will use currency investments as a core strategy whereas others look to currencies to hedge portfolio risk – for example an investor in foreign currency denominated bonds would hedge against an adverse currency shift by investing in a currency derivative. Investment strategies rely on a variety of methods to calculate or predict changes in the exchange rates – some analyse market trends and the base statistics such as power purchasing parity to predict changes in the rates, whereas others look to investor psychology and behaviour to determine how the rates will shift on the premise that the majority of trades are conducted between investors rather than those using the markets in the course of their business. Many of the more sophisticated investors will use a blend of both techniques.

Investors in currencies who are seeking a return rather than to hedge against currency risk often seek to exploit changes in the exchange rates or differences in interest rates in different currencies. Most investments make use of derivative instruments linked to the currency trade.

Another technique is the 'carry trade' – borrowing money in a currency with a low interest rate, and then purchasing another currency with a higher interest rate and then investing in bonds denominated in that currency. The transaction is at risk of exchange rate fluctuations, which could wipe out the gain on interest. To protect against this, the arrangement to buy back the initial currency borrowed is made in advance by a forward contract. As long as the premium paid for the contract is less than the gain expected from the interest rates, the investor has a guaranteed return.

5.13.2   Issues around currency funds

Currency trading is notoriously difficult to succeed in or predict. The wealth of macroeconomic factors which affects the exchange rates in the first instance is difficult to predict but understanding and anticipating the psychology of the markets is an even more exotic art form. The volatility inherent in the markets is a key driver for commercial success but is also where big losses can be made. One of the recent problems arising from the economic downturn is that the euro, dollar and yen have all been subject to low interest rates and low swings of volatility, pushing investors into emerging market currencies, which often carry greater currency risk. As currency trades are frequently executed by derivatives there are also the risks attached to those instruments, such as counterparty risk, as mentioned above.

5.13.3   Specific regulation

Foreign exchange markets are regulated, along with the traders that operate them. Regulatory bodies include the National Futures Association and the CFTC in the US and clearly the FCA in the UK. There is no direct regulation of the use of currencies as investment objects by funds, although most types of funds must show that they spread their investment risk.

5.14   HEDGE FUND STRATEGIES

Hedge funds employ various strategies such as global macro, event-driven, directional and arbitrage. These strategies are described more fully in Chapter 3 alongside hedge funds as a whole.

5.15   SOME CONCLUSIONS

The diversity of investment strategies is such that it stretches categorization to breaking point in certain circumstances. Many generalized funds will diversify their investment strategies in order to provide a balanced portfolio. This is not the case with niche strategies.

The following chapter looks at listed fund structures as opposed to the private models within Chapters 2, 3 and 4.

6
Stock Markets and Listed Funds

6.1 INTRODUCTION

Obtaining a listing for a fund is advantageous for a fund manager as it allows marketing of the fund to a wider range of investors. Listed funds are much more liquid than their unlisted counterparts and as such can be seen by investors as a less risky investment with a lower tied in commitment being required.

Listed funds are typically the only way for smaller scale and individual investors to obtain exposure to certain markets and product types, although, as with most listed companies, the bulk of share ownership in listed funds is held by larger scale investors such as pension funds and insurance companies.

The five largest stock exchanges in the world by market capitalization are the NYSE Euronext, NASDAQ, the Tokyo Stock Exchange, the London Stock Exchange (LSE) and the Hong Kong Stock Exchange. The size of market alone does not necessarily mean that it is attractive in the world of listed funds – for example the LSE was regarded as a poor choice for listing funds until necessary reforms were made in 2007.

While it is true that the majority of companies still choose to list on their domestic stock exchanges, the globalization of capital has broadened listing options around the globe. Funds can therefore now shop for a suitable market, with each exchange offering its own particular profile in terms of visibility to investors, strategic focus, disclosure standards, costs, listing timeline, regulatory control and also valuation. There is intensified competition between exchanges in these product areas as can be seen in the way exchanges now seek cross-border mergers, demutualize and go public to win market share.

Several of the European markets are regulated by EU-wide rules, although many of the markets (including the LSE, NYSE Euronext and the Deutsche Börse) operate a primary market with rules that supersede the European rules and a junior market that is outside the scope of those rules.

This chapter focuses primarily on those exchanges in the UK, US and Europe where investment funds are listed, along with an outline of those vehicles used when listing a fund. Hong Kong and Tokyo are dealt with in Chapter 7, section 7.15.4 and Chapter 8, section 8.3.4, respectively.

6.2 LISTINGS OF PRIVATE FUNDS

In addition to providing fund managers with another source of capital, there are longer-term benefits including increasing fee income and greater exposure to investors worldwide, as well as investor side benefits. By being able to re-invest realized investments on an indefinite basis, managers can continue to benefit from fees earned from the realized value of the investors' initial investment, without the need for further fund-raising.

6.2.1   Introduction

In a typical private (i.e. non-listed) hedge fund structure, subject to certain periodic and redemption limits, investors may redeem their investment on periodic redemption dates. A listing, however, allows investors to realize their investment on a sale of (all or most of) their shares in the fund and at the same time does not reduce the capital base of a fund, unlike redemption in a private open-ended fund or distributions in a private closed-ended fund.

Listed funds may provide alternative investments to investors that may have otherwise been inaccessible because, for example, they were closed to new investors or had a high minimum investment. Liquidity provided through a listing also gives what some investors require as a prerequisite to making an investment.

6.2.2   Direct funds

Private equity, infrastructure, hedge and other funds seek listings to diversify their investor base away from just private fund investors. Commonly, infrastructure funds with a yield are popular in the UK for this reason. Hedge fund managers will list funds where certain types of investors require listed investments. Most of these listed entities are offshore companies with sometimes intervening limited partnerships.

6.2.3   Feeder funds

Similarly, a desire to diversify the investor base and access new investors (as well as seek more permanent capital) leads managers to list feeder vehicles. These feeders behave like fund of funds, and they invest in the underlying units of other funds that the manager manages, and indeed in funds managed by other managers. They tend to go in and out of favour and the discount to NAV of the share price and lack of trading and liquidity can haunt these vehicles. When the market opens for these vehicles, a lot of money can get raised quickly.

6.2.4   Taxation

In the same way as for a non-listed private equity structure, one of the listed investment fund structure's key objectives is tax efficiency. Consideration needs to be given to whether the listed fund may not be more tax transparent than a non-listed limited partnership private equity structure, or not as efficient as private companies that can avoid the second tax charge at fund level. However, as with typical private funds, this can still be mostly achieved through using tax transparent or tax exempt vehicles established in offshore jurisdictions, sometimes with a combination of a listed offshore company with a limited partnership underneath it. That structure is used by certain listed private equity and infrastructure managers and gives investors a choice to invest in the Topco shares or in the underlying partnership interests.

There are numerous available listed structures. One of the possible structures is for a manager to establish a company or partnership, or a series of partnerships, from which the manager then channels investors' funds into other vehicles, usually managed by that same manager. Tax efficiency is therefore achieved by investing through mostly tax transparent entities.

Alternatively, closed-ended companies can act as feeder funds to provide investors with access to pre-existing single or master funds. The closed-ended companies are tax exempt and the funds are invested into tax exempt or tax transparent funds already under management.

6.3   UK MARKETS AND LISTED FUND STRUCTURES

6.3.1   Background

London is one of the world's leading financial centres (I am a Londoner, so I would say post the (New York-triggered) credit crisis that London is now the leading financial centre) and the LSE has the principal bond and equity exchange. It is consequently one of the main markets where investment funds seek a listing. The LSE comprises several markets. All are subject to regulation by the FCA, the UK Listing Authority (UKLA) and the LSE itself. The relevant LSE markets for investment funds are the Main Market, AIM and the Specialist Fund Market (SFM).

6.3.2   The London markets

(a) Main Market

The Main Market of the LSE, established in 1698, is the primary market. In 2012 the capital raised on this market was GBP 31.5 billion.[1] The securities which may be admitted to the Official List include closed-ended investment funds (CEIFs), open-ended investment companies (OEICs) and other types of investment vehicles under a 'super-equivalency basis', broadly meaning high regulatory standards that are internationally recognized, and which are more stringent than the minimum standards required by pan-EU regulatory harmonization.

For a company to obtain a quotation on the Main Market, it must apply to UKLA for admission to the Official List and to the LSE for admission to trading on the Main Market. A sponsor is required to facilitate the admission process, as well as the publication of a prospectus.

(b) AIM

AIM (formerly known as the Alternative Investment Market) was founded in 1995 to provide an opportunity for smaller entities to raise capital and trade on the markets. The capital raised on AIM in 2012 totalled GBP 3.1 billion.[2] Securities listed on AIM are subject to less regulation and are regulated separately under the UKLA and the LSE. Application procedures are similar to those for the Main Market, but some of the more stringent requirements have been relaxed in order to encourage smaller and less established entities to seek a listing. For example, a reduced historical accounts record may be acceptable and there is no need to have an established management team. Low listing costs and regulatory compliance expenses have also been themes of AIM.

(c) Specialist Fund Market

The SFM was opened in 2007 and the debutant admission was in May 2008 (not the best timing!). The SFM was created for highly specialized investment entities targeting professional, knowledgeable and institutional investors. The market is not open to the general public. A

---

[1] Main Market Factsheet December 2012 – www.londonstockexchange.com/companies-and-advisors/mainmarket/main-market/home.htm (10 January 2013)

[2] Main Market Factsheet December 2012 – www.londonstockexchange.com/companies-and-advisors/mainmarket/main-market/home.htm (10 January 2013)

wide range of securities may be listed on the SFM, including hedge funds and property investment funds.[3] The application procedures are much less rigorous than for either the Main Market or AIM. The main requirements are proof of transferability, compliance with the Admission and Disclosure Standards of the LSE and approval of a prospectus by the UKLA. The SFM was established with the intention of competing with the Euronext markets.

6.3.3   Vehicles in London appropriate for listing investment funds

(a) Introduction

The Listing Rules are a set of regulations applicable to any company listed on a UK stock exchange. They set out mandatory standards for any company wishing to list its shares or securities for sale to the public. The rules are published by the FCA.

(b) Closed-ended investment funds

(i) Defined
Listing Rule 15 applies special listing rules to a CEIF, which it defines as an undertaking with limited liability such as a company, limited partnership or limited liability partnership. The primary objective of the CEIF must be to invest and manage assets with a view to spreading investment risk. This would include pooled funds contributed by the holders of its listed shares or securities invested in any form of property.[4]

These securities must have a premium listing (see paragraph (iii) below) on the Official List, where the rules are stricter than the requirements of the relevant EU directives.

(ii) General requirements for standard listing
All issuers must comply with certain rules, including being a duly incorporated or validly constituted issuer with securities in issue which conform to the law under which the issuer is constituted.[5] If a prospectus is required for the issue and listing of securities, it must be approved by the FCA (or the relevant competent authority in another EEA state) and published in accordance with relevant local applicable law.[6]

(iii) Premium listing
Where the CEIF is a new applicant, in order to list its securities it must also comply with the rules for a premium listing.[7] The CEIF must also meet certain working capital requirements. This requirement may be dispensed with where there has been a previous listing of equity shares and the prospectus outlines suitable proposals to address any working capital shortfall.[8] Any shares in the CEIF must also be sufficiently distributed to the public in at least one EEA state. The threshold amount is 25% of the class of shares admitted to trading which is required to be in public hands.[9]

---

[3] From the list provided on www.londonstockexchange.com/companies-and-advisors/sfm/about/sfm-guidance-for-admission.pdf
[4] LR App 1
[5] LR 2.2.1R and LR 2.2.2R
[6] LR 2.2.4R, LR 2.2.7R, LR 2.2.8R and LR 2.2.10R
[7] LR 15.2.1R
[8] LR 6.1.3R (d) and (e), LR 6.1.16R and LR 6.1.17G
[9] LR 6.1.19R

The CEIF must comply with the above examples at all times and must notify the FCA as soon as possible where it does not.[10] The FCA has the discretion to cancel the CEIF's listing for non-compliance.[11]

(iv) CEIF investment policies

A CEIF must invest and manage its assets in line with the objective of spreading investment risk and in accordance with its published investment policy.[12] The published investment policy should enable an investor to assess the investment opportunity, identify how the risk spreading objective is to be achieved and evaluate the significance of any proposed change in investment policy.[13]

(v) Cross-holdings

A CEIF should not invest more than 10% of the aggregate of its total assets on admission in other listed CEIFs unless, as an exception to this rule, the CEIF has published an investment policy stating it will not invest more than 15% of its total assets in other listed CEIFs. This rule needs to be considered by the CEIF management whenever they make an acquisition.

(vi) Master funds

If the CEIF principally invests its funds in another company or fund that invests in a portfolio of investments (a master fund), the CEIF must at all times ensure that the stated investment objectives and policies of the master fund are compatible with its own published investment objectives and policies, and that the master fund acts in accordance with those objectives and policy in practice.[14]

(vii) Independence

The board of directors of a CEIF (or equivalent body if the CEIF is not a corporate vehicle) must be able to act independently of any investment manager appointed by the CEIF and also independently of the master fund (if there is one), unless the master fund is a subsidiary of the CEIF.[15] The chairman of the board must be independent, along with a majority of the board.

(viii) Application for listing

The application process for listing a CEIF is much the same as for other companies. The CEIF is required to comply with the rules on listing applications and where it is listing equity shares it is required to retain a sponsor. If the CEIF is constituted as what is known as a 'multi-class' fund or as an 'umbrella' fund, the CEIF must provide details to the FCA of the various classes of securities that will be issued in connection with that CEIF.[16]

(ix) Transactions

There are rules which restrict the freedom of premium listed companies to enter into sufficiently significant transactions by calculating the ratio of the price paid (in cash or in kind)

---

[10] LR 9.2.15R and LR 9.2.16R

[11] LR 9.2.17G

[12] LR 15.2.2R and LR 15.4.2R

[13] LR 15.2.8G

[14] LR 15.2.6R

[15] LR 15.2.11R

[16] LR 15.3.1G, LR 15.3.2G and LR 15.3.4R

to certain financial indicators of the CEIF. The CEIF will have to (depending on the ratio output) publish a notification through a regulated information service (RIS) and/or seek shareholder approval if it meets the threshold ratio output. A CEIF does not have to comply with the rules (regardless of ratio output) for transactions carried out within the scope of the published investment policy.[17]

(x) Financial reporting

The annual financial report of a CEIF must include a statement on how it has invested in line with the objective of spreading investment risk and its stated investment policy. It must also contain a prominently placed and reasoned opinion about whether or not in the view of the board (or its equivalent body) the employment of the investment manager on the agreed terms should be continued in the interests of the shareholders as a whole.

(c) UK open-ended investment companies

(i) Introduction

An open-ended investment company (OEIC) is a pooled collective investment vehicle introduced to the UK in 1997. It is also referred to as an investment company with variable capital, and the terms are used interchangeably. It is a type of open-ended collective investment and is formed as a corporation under the Open-Ended Investment Companies Regulations 2001 in the UK. In the UK, OEICs are the preferred legal form of new open-ended investment over the older unit trust. OEICs were developed to be similar to the European SICAV or the US mutual fund.

Unlike a unit trust, an OEIC can have an umbrella structure where there are several sub-funds which can operate towards their own investment objectives. An investor is free to move their investments between the different sub-funds. Investors have shares in the OEIC which owns the investment assets outright. For example, one OEIC may hold a sub-fund called 'UK smaller companies' and another sub-fund called 'UK equity income'. Each sub-fund has its own investment aims and is held separately from other sub-funds within the same OEIC. This has some cost savings for the investment manager.

It is open-ended (like a unit trust) so it expands and contracts in response to demand and (unlike an investment trust) does not generally trade at a discount. The price is calculated by reference to the underlying NAV divided by the number of shares on offer. There is no separate offer and bid price; only one price is quoted. Each time money is invested new shares are created to match the prevailing share price. Each time shares are redeemed the assets sold match the prevailing share price. In this way there is no supply or demand created for shares and they remain a direct reflection of the underlying assets. An OEIC may be single-priced (there is one price at which shares may be bought or sold) or dual-priced (there will be a buying price and a selling price, with the difference between the two being the bid-offer spread).

(ii) Legislation

OEICs are formed under the OEIC Regulations[18] (OEICR), which define their creation and structure. The conduct of running an OEIC as an investment product is regulated by the FCA's COLL.

---

[17] LR 15.5.2R
[18] SI 2001/1228

(iii) Creation

To establish an OEIC, an application must be made to the FCA under regulation 12 of OEICR. The application must be accompanied by a copy of the proposed instrument of incorporation together with a certificate signed by a solicitor affirming that it complies with OEICR and COLL. When the FCA is satisfied with the application it will issue a certificate of incorporation.[19]

(iv) Structure

An OEIC is a body corporate with a separate legal personality, in comparison with a unit trust created by deed between the manager and the proposed trustee. The OEIC must hold the beneficial interest in the underlying assets which are managed with the purpose of spreading investment risk and passing on the benefit of the resulting income or capital to its members.[20] The investors only have shares in the OEIC, with no beneficial interest in the investments. The OEIC must also satisfy the investment condition that a reasonable participating investor would expect to realize their investment in a reasonable period of time and be satisfied that the return would be calculated with reference to the performance of the underlying assets.[21] The head office of an OEIC must be located within England, Wales or Scotland.[22]

The OEIC can be made up of a single fund or several sub-funds under an umbrella scheme. The different sub-funds may have different investment objectives and target investors, but since 21 December 2011 (when new rules were introduced) sub-funds are protected from the failure of other sub-funds under the same umbrella. The assets and liabilities of each sub-fund are legally separated,[23] so the OEIC does not have to reduce other sub-funds to cover losses in the one that is struggling.

There must be at least one director to run the day to day business of the OEIC and there must be at least one corporate director who is an authorized person (an authorized corporate director) with permission to act as a sole director of an OEIC. As mentioned above, there must also be a depositary, to which the assets are entrusted.[24] The depositary must be a person authorized by the FCA and must be independent of the OEIC and the persons appointed as directors(s) of the OEIC.[25]

Once authorized the OEIC is subject to OEICR and COLL on an ongoing basis. They can promote and sell to the general public in the UK[26] so long as they are compliant with both COLL and the FCA's COBS rules. OEICs can be 'passported' across the EEA by compliance with the UCITS regulations.

(v) Pricing

The price of a share in an OEIC is determined initially by reference to the NAV of the fund or sub-fund to which the share relates. The price actually paid by an investor for the share when purchased from the management will be higher than the price based on the NAV because it will also include an initial charge and a possible dilution levy (which covers the dealing cost of acquiring new securities). When an investor sells his shares back, he is paid the NAV

---

[19] Regulation 14 OEICR 2001
[20] Section 236(2) FSMA 2000
[21] Section 236(3) FSMA 2000
[22] Regulation 15(3) OEICR 2001
[23] Regulation 3 of the Open-Ended Investment Companies (Amendment) Regulations 2011 – SI 2011/3069
[24] Regulation 5 OEICR 2001
[25] Regulation 15(8) OEICR 2001
[26] Section 238 FSMA 2000

price less an exit charge and a possible dilution levy. The dilution levy can be considered an artificial 'spread' between the entry and exit prices, which diminishes the difference between OEIC pricing and unit trust pricing.

(vi) Fees and charges

Most fees are clearly itemized on the contract note and will be calculable in advance by an investor as the charges and fees are required information in the prospectus.[27] The main charges are an initial charge to cover the costs of the acquisition of the underlying investments and an exit charge for similar expenses when leaving the scheme. The exit charge may be scaled in relation to the time invested in the fund, to prevent short-term investors taking advantage of attractive returns. There will also be an annual management fee which is for the running costs and commission fees for the depositary and other advisers.

(vii) Investment strategies

OEICs and sub-funds can be managed actively or passively. Passive funds can track a particular index like the FTSE 100, which can lead to artificial price movements, for example, when it has to buy or sell investments which are departing from or joining an index, as the price may be artificially deflated or inflated by all other passive investors selling or buying and other market participants such as speculators. There are statistical indications that passively managed funds outperform most actively managed funds, but the most successful actively managed funds perform much better than passive ones. As a result of these considerations, there are some passive tracker funds offered which have an element of active management to offset the shortcomings of a purely passive fund.

(viii) Taxation

Taxation of the fund

One tax advantage is that when an OEIC makes a chargeable disposal of assets, the disposal is exempt from corporation tax.[28] This tax is deferred until the individual investor disposes of shares in the OEIC.

Taxation of the investor

The investor's non-dividend income from a tax-elected fund (TEF) is treated as yearly interest, subject to a 20% rate of withholding on account of income tax.[29] A dividend payment to an investor from a fund (whether or not it is a TEF) with a predominately equity-based portfolio is treated as a UK company dividend[30] and so the distribution comes with a tax credit equal to 10% of the grossed up dividend.

Taxation of the management

For the management, the main sources of income are the dilution levy and the annual and initial management fees. The dealings in shares in an OEIC by the management are considered exempt from VAT.

---

[27] COLL 4.2.5R, entries 18 (dilution), 21 (preliminary charge) and 22 (redemption charge)
[28] Section 100 TCGA 1992 and regulation 92 of the Authorised Investment Funds (Tax) Regulations 2006
[29] Section 874 Income Tax Act 2007
[30] Regulation 22 AIF Regulations

(ix) Listing
Requirements for listing
An OEIC must comply with the requirements of obtaining a listing which apply to all applicant companies (see paragraph (b) (ii) above). An OEIC must satisfy only two of the rules for a premium listed company:[31]

- the total of all issued warrants or options to subscribe for equity shares must not exceed 20% of its total issued equity share capital and
- the shares in issue and the constitution of the company must be compatible with electronic settlement.[32]

Application for listing
The application for listing shares in an OEIC must comply with Chapter 3 of the Listing Rules (see paragraph (b) (viii) above). The FCA will admit to listing more shares than the OEIC plans to issue immediately on approval of the application, which allows for future growth of the fund without the need to go back to the FCA for approval in the short term. Where the OEIC consists of multiple funds within an umbrella structure, or is seeking to become such a fund, and the OEIC is planning to issue new classes of shares without increasing the share capital for which the listing has previously been granted, then on notification to the FCA of the intended structure, no further application is necessary.[33]

OEICs and the Listing Rules
The continuing obligations set out in Chapter 9 of the Listing Rules apply to OEICs with the following exceptions:

- an OEIC does not have to comply with the requirement that 25% of its shares are in public hands
- an OEIC does not have to ensure that the discretion of its board on making strategic decisions is not limited or transferred out of the group structure and
- when issuing shares of a class already in existence, an OEIC does not have to offer the existing shareholders the shares on a pre-emptive basis.[34]

Financial reporting
The OEIC must comply with the rules regarding financial reporting in Chapter 9.8 of the Listing Rules along with the requirement that it reports any change in its tax status to an RIS as soon as possible.[35]

---

[31] LR 16.2.1R
[32] LR 6.1.22R and LR 6.1.23R
[33] LR 16.3.6R
[34] LR 16.4.1R(1)
[35] LR 16.4.1R(3)

(d) UK investment trusts

(i) What are investment trusts?

Investment trusts are not, as the name suggests, trusts at all but are in fact UK-resident companies, constituted as a public limited company.[36] Their shares must be admitted to trading on a regulated market and their purpose is to invest in a variety of shares, securities and other assets, enabling investors to spread their risk and gain exposure to a diversified and managed portfolio of investments.

An investment trust is a closed-ended fund. This means that the amount of equity investment available to the fund manager is fixed, until it raises further capital.

The board will typically delegate responsibility to a professional fund manager to invest in the stocks and shares of a wide range of companies.

The share price does not always reflect the underlying value of the share portfolio held by the investment trust. In such cases, the investment trust is referred to as trading at a discount or premium to net asset value.

One of the key differences between an investment trust and a unit trust is that an investment trust manager is legally allowed to borrow capital to purchase shares. Investment trusts can borrow money to invest. This leverage may increase investment gains but also increases investor risk.

Provided that it is approved by HMRC, an investment trust is taxed in the normal way on its investment income (other than approved dividends) but its capital gains are not taxed. This avoids double taxation on investment gains in the portfolio.

(ii) Legislation

The treasury implemented the Investment Trust Regulations[37] in 2011, which govern the establishment and operation of investment trusts in such a way as to maintain their tax status. The regulations are made under the Corporation Tax Act (COTA) 2010.[38] Previously, investment trusts were regulated under the Income and Corporations Tax Act 1988 as amended.

The regulations apply to investment trusts with a first accounting period which begins on or after 1 January 2012. There were a number of reasons why these regulations came about. One of the intentions of these relaxations and improved flexibility was to encourage the listing of investment trusts on mainland UK stock markets as opposed to seeking an offshore investment vehicle. Essentially, the new rules sought to make investment trusts more attractive as a fund structure for investment managers.

(iii) Approved investment trust conditions

There are three principal conditions that must be met by an investment trust before it is in a position to apply for approval as an investment trust.[39] The Investment Trust Regulations provide further detailed conditions.

Condition A

Condition A states that the business of the investment trust must consist of investing its funds in shares, land or other assets with the aim of spreading investment risk and giving members of the company the benefit of the results of the management of its funds.[40]

---

[36] Section 1158 COTA 2010 as amended by section 49 Finance Act 2011
[37] Investment Trust (Approved Company) (Tax) Regulations 2011
[38] Section 1158 COTA 2010 as amended by section 49 Finance Act 2011
[39] Section 1158 COTA 2010
[40] Section 1158(2) COTA 2010

When making an application for investment trust status, a copy of the published investment policy must be provided. This will include details on asset allocation, risk diversification, gearing and details of maximum exposure. Any changes to the published investment policy must be notified to HMRC.

Condition B
Condition B states that shares making up the company's ordinary share capital (or, if there are shares of more than one class, those of each class) must be admitted to trading on a regulated market.[41]

Condition C
Condition C states that the investment trust must not be a VCT (see section 6.3.3(f) of this chapter) or a UK REIT (see section 6.3.3(e) below).[42]

(iv) Investment Trust Regulations – further conditions
The investment trust must not be a 'close company' (as defined in Appendix I of this book) at any time during the relevant accounting period (there are certain companies that are exempt from this definition). An investment trust must not retain more than 15% of its income in any accounting period, although this test will not apply if it would require a distribution of less than GBP 30,000.

Previously, an investment trust's articles of association had to prohibit the distribution of profits made on the disposal of investments. This is no longer required and returning profits to shareholders can be done through the payment of dividends. However, in circumstances where the shareholders of the investment trust are predominantly UK resident, it may remain preferable for them to receive these as capital rather than as income. This provides even greater flexibility for investment trust structures.

(v) Advantages of the new regime under the Investment Trust Regulations
The new regime has made clear what transactions comprise 'trading transactions' rather than 'investment transactions'. This distinction is particularly important due to the fact that gains made on disposal of assets that are 'investments transactions' are capital gains, and therefore exempt from tax, whereas profits made on disposal of assets that are 'trading transactions' are income and taxable. The Investment Trust Regulations provide a 'White List' of transactions which will provide certainty to directors and investment managers. The list also includes 'relevant contracts', which is defined broadly as an option, a future or a contract for differences.

Previously HMRC approval was granted retrospectively for each accounting period. Now the company will make a single application to HMRC which must be received within 90 days after the end of the first accounting period of the company for which investment trust status is sought. Shares are deemed to be admitted to trading on a regulated market (for 60 days), if, on the date of application, the applicant has started the procedure for admission to a regulated market. This means a period of time is given to meet Condition B above.

The rules on breach of an investment trust condition have become much less severe and distinguish between a minor and a serious breach. Previously a breach of a condition would usually result in the company ceasing to be an approved investment trust for the whole of the accounting period. A minor breach will not result in loss of investment trust status unless the breach is repeated over a 10-year period.

---

[41] Section 1158(3) COTA 2010
[42] Section 1158(5) COTA 2010

(vi) Split capital investment trusts

Traditional investment trusts issue just one type of share whereas split capital investment trusts are a type of investment trust that issues more than one type of share, depending on what type of return the investor is looking for, namely capital or income. The most simple split capital investment trusts will have two types of shares – one allowing investors to receive income during the trust's life, and the other receiving capital growth. Holders of these two share classes are known as 'income shareholders' and 'capital shareholders', respectively.

Most split capital investment trusts will issue more than two types of shares. The most common are known as zero dividend preference shares (or zeroes). Zeroes are aimed at individuals who wish to receive a specific sum on a date in the future as they pay no income but offer a fixed return when the trust is wound up. Therefore, on winding up, holders of zeroes are usually paid out first, after repayment of loans.

In 2001/2002, many investors lost a lot of money in split capital investment trusts because they were not correctly structured to handle the downside or a declining market. Split capital investment trusts do not guarantee to return capital in the future, so it is possible for an investor to lose their entire investment. The split capital investment trust sector still exists today, but is aimed more towards expert investors.

(vii) Pricing of investment trusts

An investment trust uses NAV. Investment trust share prices can fluctuate (and tend to more often than units in unit trusts) because they are affected in part by supply and demand. Because there are a fixed number of shares in issue, the more popular the investment trust, the higher the price of the share. This means that the trust could have a share price higher than the NAV of the trust (trading at a premium).

(viii) Gearing and risk

Investment trusts can borrow money to invest in shares and other securities. This is useful and improves an investment trust's performance when they are doing well. However, when the market falls, and investments are not doing well, gearing will increase loss, meaning that generally the higher the gearing rating, the riskier the investment trust.

A gearing rating of 100 means the trust does not borrow and a rating of, for example, 120 means that the trust has a gearing of 20% of total assets.

(ix) Regulation of investment trusts

As investment trusts are closed-ended companies, they are not CISs and therefore not subject to FCA regulation as a CIS. However, they are subject to the listing rules of UKLA.

Ultimate responsibility for management rests with the board of directors, which is accountable to the shareholders, although the investment trust will usually appoint an investment manager which will be regulated by the FCA. However, the UK Listing Rules require that the board will act independently of any investment manager, and therefore a majority of the board should not be linked to the investment manager.

The marketing and promotion of investment trust shares must be performed by an entity which is authorized by the FCA.

(x) Investment manager fees

The investment manager usually charges an annual management fee which is between 0.5% and 1.5% of assets under management.

A small number of investment trusts charge a performance fee which is usually paid only if the investment trust out-performs a given benchmark. Performance fees are payable on alternative asset trusts, such as private equity, hedge or real estate.

(xi) Taxation of investment trusts
For the purposes of UK taxation, investment trusts are treated like any other company within the charge to corporation tax other than that they are exempt from tax on chargeable gains.[43] Investment trusts are subject to corporation tax on their income at normal corporation tax rates. However, dividend income will usually be exempt as a result of the dividend exemption from corporation tax.

Approved investment trusts also enjoy exemption from tax on certain capital profits arising from loan relationships and derivative contracts which would otherwise be taxable as income.[44]

On 28 June 2007 the European Court of Justice ruled that the exemption from VAT for the investment management of 'special investment funds' should extend to closed-ended investment trusts,[45] and the UK Treasury extended the VAT exemption for fund management to cover UK listed entities (including investment trusts).[46]

As investment trusts are generally subject to tax on income, they would be subject to tax on a disposal of an interest in a non-reporting offshore fund. This is because any gains on such a disposal would be recharacterized as an offshore income gain. However, if certain conditions are met throughout the period of ownership, an investment trust can avoid giving rise to a taxable income gain on the disposal of an interest in an offshore non-reporting fund.

(e) UK real estate investment trust

(i) Introduction
REITs were introduced in the UK in 2007 to allow investors to obtain broadly similar returns from investing in the trust as though the investor had acquired the underlying property itself. A UK REIT is a company that owns and often operates income-generating real estate. REITs can own many types of commercial real estate, ranging from office space to hotels. Some REITs also participate in financing real estate. The UK REIT structure was designed to provide a real estate investment vehicle similar to the structure of a US mutual fund for investing in shares. Much of the US regime has inspired the UK's own REIT regime, for example the minimum distributions and the balance of business conditions.

UK REITs can be publicly or privately held. A public REIT would be listed. Following the passage of the legislation laying out the rules for REITs in the UK, nine UK property companies converted to REIT status, including five FTSE 100 members at that time: Slough Estates, Land Securities, British Land, Hammerson and Liberty International.

REIT tax incentives aim to make the vehicle as tax neutral as possible. They also allow individuals to invest who would not otherwise be able to afford the high initial cost of investing in property. In addition, the requirement for the vehicle to be listed provides liquidity to investors. UK REITs must be approved by HMRC and are subject to rigorous regulation on

---

[43] Section 100(1) TCGA 1992
[44] Parts 5 and 7 COTA 2009
[45] JP Morgan Fleming Claverhouse Investment Trust Plc and another v HMRC
[46] Value Added Tax (Finance) (No 2) Order 2008

application and during their lifespan, along with regulation applicable to a publicly listed company.

(ii) Legislation

The legislative framework for REITs is set out in Part 12 of COTA 2010. Legislative amendments in the Finance Act 2012 brought important changes to the REIT regime, including: (i) the abolition of the 2% entry charge to join the regime – this made REITs more attractive due to reduced costs; (ii) relaxation of the listing requirements so that REITs could be AIM quoted, which meant a listing was more attractive due to reduced costs and greater flexibility; (iii) a REIT now has a three-year grace period before having to comply with close company rules; and (iv) a REIT is not considered to be a close company if it can be made close by the inclusion of institutional investors. These relaxations had the effect of allowing smaller REITs to join the regime.

(iii) Conditions for approval for single company vehicles

Application is made to HMRC for approval as a REIT. Before making the application the company must satisfy two conditions: (i) that it is resident in the UK; and (ii) that it is not an OEIC.[47] These conditions must be met in relation to each successive accounting period during which the company wishes to remain a REIT. The applicant company must be ready to meet the following conditions on the date on which it becomes a REIT, subject to dispensation or a grace period:

- Shares must be admitted to listing on the Official List of the London Stock Exchange (or overseas equivalent) or are traded on a recognized stock exchange, which has been extended to include AIM.[48]
- The company must not be a close company (excluding institutional investors).[49] A REIT also has a three-year grace period in which to cease to be a close company. If it fails to achieve this within the grace period it will lose its status as a REIT going forward.[50]
- The company must have only two classes of shares in issue – ordinary voting shares and non-voting restricted preference shares.[51] A non-voting restricted preference share is one that does not carry a right to acquire shares or securities and carries a restricted right to dividends, but can be converted into other shares or securities in the company.[52]
- The company may not enter into a loan on terms where:
  - the creditor is paid interest which is calculated with reference to the company's financial performance or the value of its assets or
  - the creditor is paid interest or a return on repayment which exceeds a reasonable commercial return.[53]
- The REIT must operate a property rental business in the UK or overseas. A property rental business consists of every business carried on by the company which generates income

---

[47] Section 524 COTA 2010
[48] Sections 528(3) and 528A COTA 2010 as inserted by paragraph 16 of Schedule 4 to the Finance Act 2012
[49] Section 528(4) COTA 2010 as amended by paragraph 4 of Schedule 4 to the Finance Act 2012
[50] Section 527 COTA 2010 as amended by Schedule 4 to the Finance Act 2012
[51] Section 528 (6) COTA 2010
[52] Sections 160 and 528(6) and (7) COTA 2010
[53] Section 528(8) COTA 2010

from property and every transaction which that company enters into for that purpose.[54] Certain business activities and sources of income are excluded.

- One condition to be met for an accounting period is the balance of business conditions. The profits of the property rental business must be at least 75% of the aggregate profits of the company, calculated in accordance with GAAP (generally accepted accounting principles; the 'profits test'). The assets of the company relating to the property rental business at the beginning of each accounting period must be at least 75% of the total assets of the company (the 'assets test').[55] For the calculation of the assets test, any cash holdings are considered part of the property rental business.[56] The Finance Act 2013 amended the regulatory framework so that an investment in a REIT will be treated as an asset of the investor REIT's property rental business for these purposes, but will be tied into a requirement that the investing REIT distributes 100% of the income it receives to its own investors.[57]

(iv) Flexibility of the conditions
A breach of any of the company conditions during an accounting period ordinarily results in the automatic termination of the company's or the group's participation in the regime as of the end of the previous accounting period,[58] but there are exceptions when automatic termination does not apply.

(v) Breaches of conditions which give rise to a tax charge
For accounting periods (beginning on or after 17 July 2012) there are three conditions, set out below, which give rise to a charge to corporation tax if they are breached.

- The REIT company or principal company is required to distribute 90% of the net income profits of the tax exempt UK property rental business within three months of the filing date for the tax return of the accounting period in which the profits occurred (or six months in exceptional circumstances).[59]
- REITs are subject to a restriction on borrowing. In relation to the property rental business, the REIT's property profits to property financing costs ratio cannot be lower than 1.25.[60]
- The maximum shareholding condition is that a corporate shareholder cannot own or be entitled to 10% or more of the shares or of the receipt of dividends, nor control 10% or more of the voting rights. A charge arises where the company or principal company has not taken reasonable steps to prevent the distribution to such a shareholder.[61]

(vi) Ring-fence
One of the key principles of the UK REIT regime is the ring-fencing of the property rental business. The ring-fence serves to separate the corporation tax treatment of the property rental business from the rest of the company's activities, primarily to prevent advantage being taken of the corporation tax reliefs.

---

[54] Sections 205 and 206 of the COTA 2009 and section 520 COTA 2010
[55] Section 531(1) and (2) COTA 2010
[56] Sections 531 (5) COTA 2010 as amended by paragraph 27 of Schedule 4 to Finance Act 2012
[57] Section 39 and Schedule 19 to the Finance Act 2013
[58] Section 578 COTA 2010
[59] Section 530 (1), (4), (6C) and (6D) COTA 2010 as inserted by paragraph 4 of Schedule 4 to the Finance (No 3) Act 2010 and amended by paragraph 22 of Schedule 4 to the Finance Act 2012
[60] Section 543 COTA 2010
[61] Section 551 COTA 2010

- The property rental business is treated as a separate business for corporation tax from:
  - the business of the company or group prior to the date on which it became a REIT
  - the residual business (all non-property rental business) of the company or group and
  - the business of the company or group after it has left the regime.

The company or group, so far as it carries on a property rental business, is treated as a separate company or group from its pre-REIT, residual and post-REIT company or group.[62] This means that the losses made outside of the property rental business cannot be set off against the profits of the property rental business, and more significantly the losses of the property rental business cannot be set off against the profits of the other businesses.

(vii) Taxation of the investor
When the REIT company or principal company makes a property income distribution (PID) – a distribution in respect of the profits and gains of the tax exempt property rental business – it is generally treated as UK property income rather than dividend income. If the investor is a corporate body, the PID is treated as the profits of a UK property business.[63] Where the REIT makes a distribution in respect of profits and gains from the residual business, it is taxed as dividend income.

Where an investor sells his shares in the REIT he will be subject to tax for capital gains in the normal way along with stamp duty or stamp duty reserve tax (as applicable).

(f) UK venture capital trusts

(i) Introduction
A venture capital trust (VCT) is viewed as a tax efficient UK closed-ended CIS. It is structured to provide private equity capital for small expanding companies and tax efficient capital gains for investors. VCTs are publicly traded. Introduced in 1995, they can invest in other companies which are not themselves listed.

Like investment trusts, they are in fact listed companies and not trusts. This encourages investment as it increases the liquidity of an individual's investment. There are tax advantages available to an investor in a VCT. There are several conditions to be met in order for a company to be an approved VCT, which are drawn up by HMRC.

The managers of the VCT have three years in which to choose companies to invest in and during this time often place the money into cash, gilts or bonds. As they become more sophisticated, VCTs are investing in funds such as smaller company funds or funds of hedge funds, to maximize returns. Typically VCTs aim to invest the majority of assets in qualifying companies, 80% of which are established companies or management buyouts. VCTs are usually separated into three different types: limited life, specialist and generalist. Generalist VCTs invest in a range of companies in different sectors and stages of investment. Specialist VCTs tend to invest in just one sector such as technology, health care or environmental infrastructure. Limited life VCTs also tend to invest in just one area or theme and will look to wind up in the fifth or sixth year. Normally a large percentage of any potential profit from a limited life VCT is from the initial tax rebate, so they might appeal to investors looking for a comparatively lower risk VCT.

---

[62] Section 541 COTA 2010
[63] Section 548 COTA 2010

(ii) Legislation
Part 6 of the ITA 2007 sets out the conditions for becoming an approved VCT and the tax advantages. The capital gains benefit is set out in section 151A and 151B of the TCGA 1992.

(iii) Approved VCT conditions
The conditions which a VCT must comply with must be satisfied in each successive accounting period in order to retain approval. A company seeking to be a VCT must obtain approval from HMRC and not be a close company[64] (there are companies that are exempt from this definition). In addition, VCTs must also comply with the Listing Rules, which require 25% of shares in public hands.[65]

The approval conditions include the listing condition; that the ordinary shares or each class of share will be listed during the relevant period of time on the Official List of the London Stock Exchange or any other EU Regulated Market.[66] The company's income must be derived mainly from investments in shares or securities and the company must distribute at least 85% of its income from shares or securities to its investors. No more than 15% of the total value of investments may be invested in any one company.

At least 70% by value of the VCT's investments must be represented by shares or securities in specified qualifying companies (see below) and at least 30% by value of the VCT's qualifying holdings has been or will be represented by holdings of eligible shares.

The VCT's investment in a company (together with any other investments made in that company in the 12 months prior to that investment) must not exceed the annual investment limit, which is currently GBP 5 million.[67]

(iv) Qualifying investee companies
Within three years of the share issue at least 70% of the VCT's assets must be invested in 'qualifying' holdings. The rules for being a qualifying investee company (QIC) are much more complex than for a VCT and careful consideration must be given when formulating an investment strategy. One of the purposes of the VCT scheme is to encourage investment in small and start-up businesses. Therefore, a QIC (or its group) must have no more than GBP 15 million in gross assets before the investment is made, and no more than GBP 16 million immediately afterwards, for shares issued on or after 6 April 2012.[68]

For shares issued on or after 6 April 2012, the QIC cannot raise more than GBP 5 million in total from any number of VCTs, through the EIS or from qualifying state aid in the preceding 12-month period[69] and any investment which causes this limit to be breached will be wholly ineligible for the VCT scheme.

The QIC must not be in financial difficulty at the time of the issue of shares.[70] Financial difficulty is defined with reference to the Community Guideline.[71] Circumstances in which HMRC will not consider a company to be in financial difficulty include a company which is able to raise funds from its existing shareholders or from the market sufficient to meet its

---

[64] Section 259(1) Income Tax Act (ITA) 2007
[65] LR 6.1.19R
[66] s274 ITA 2007
[67] Section 292A ITA 2007, as amended by paragraph 6 of Schedule 8 to the Finance Act 2012
[68] Section 297 ITA 2007, as amended by paragraph 8, Schedule 8 to the Finance Act 2012
[69] Section 292A ITA 2007 as amended by paragraph 6 of Schedule 8 to the Finance Act 2012
[70] Section 286B ITA 2007, as inserted by paragraph 2, Schedule 2 to the Finance (No 3) Act 2010
[71] 2004/C 244/02

anticipated funding requirements at that time, or a company within the first three years of its operations.

The QIC must not have its shares quoted in the Official List of the LSE or on any other EU Regulated Market, but they can be listed on other markets such as AIM.[72] The QIC must also be independent, and the QIC or the QIC's group (if a holding company of a group) must not employ more than 250 employees or part-time equivalents.[73]

The QIC must carry on a qualifying trade, or be the parent or holding company of a group which wholly carries on a qualifying trade.[74] A qualifying trade is one which is carried on with a view to making a profit and is conducted on a commercial basis. If the trade involves 20% or more of excluded activities it will not be a qualifying trade.[75] The list of excluded activities includes farming, dealing in land, shares or commodities, financial activities, property development, operating or managing hotels or nursing homes, ship building, coal and steel production and feed in tariffs.[76]

(v) Pricing and management fees

On average the initial charge for investing in a VCT is around 5%. Annual running costs can amount to 3.5%. Most funds have a performance fee for the management if certain investment targets are met. Funds typically have a minimum investment for an individual investor, often between GBP 2000 and GBP 5000. On the secondary market, prices are quoted much as listed companies are, with reference to the NAV, the dividend yield, availability of shares and the expectation of future performance. As such the prices can be somewhat volatile and often trade at a discount.

(vi) Risk

VCTs are inherently risky due to the small size of the enterprises which are invested in. Due to the requirement of keeping the money invested for at least five years in order to keep reliefs, a VCT is an illiquid investment despite the fact that it is listed. Some VCTs are structured to seek maximal rates of return (at a greater risk) while others are more conservative and seek to exploit the tax rebate together with low growth and a lower risk portfolio; for example a GBP 10,000 investment, with a return of GBP 3000 of income tax relief and 10% growth over five years, would return GBP 11,000 for an effective GBP 7000 investment.

(vii) Taxation

If the VCT is a UK resident for taxpaying purposes it will not pay tax on any dividends received from its UK-resident QICs or from any of its non-UK-resident investee companies, subject to certain conditions.[77] The VCT does not have to pay any tax on chargeable gains that arise on disposal of investments.[78] However, on any interest payments received, the VCT will be taxed.

When an investor in a VCT makes a chargeable disposal of their shares in the VCT that disposal is exempt from CGT.[79] The investor is also entitled to an exemption from income

---

[72] Section 295 ITA 2007

[73] Section 297A ITA 2007 as amended by paragraph 9 of Schedule 8 to the Finance Act 2012

[74] Sections 290, 291 and 294 ITA 2007

[75] HMRC – VCM17040

[76] Section 303 ITA 2007

[77] Chapter 3 of Part 9A of the Corporation Tax 2009

[78] Section 100 (1) TCGA 1992

[79] Section 151A TCGA 1992

tax on dividends received from the VCT on shares acquired within the annual maximum for income tax relief.[80] For any shares issued after 5 April 2004 deferral relief is not available.[81]

An investor in a VCT is entitled to income tax relief at a maximum rate of 30[82] up to an investment of GBP 200,000 per tax year on the condition that the shares are held for at least five years.[83] The relief is only available on the issue of new shares.[84] Therefore an investor who buys the shares on the secondary market is not entitled to claim income tax relief for the cost of the acquisition, but is entitled to the exemption from capital gains on disposals and income tax on dividends.

6.3.4   Obtaining a London listing – Main Market and AIM[85]

Obtaining a listing on the main market of the LSE can be a lengthy process, often beginning 12 months before the day of first trading. Dealings with the Stock Exchange and the required parties begin three to six months before the date of listing.

The listing process on AIM is far more flexible. Generally, only an AIM admission document is required rather than a prospectus that must be vetted by the UKLA. An admission document is exempt from submission to the UKLA if the offer is not made to more than 150 persons other than 'qualified investors'. A company's sponsor, on AIM referred to as the nominated adviser or 'Nomad', will generally seek to ensure that the deal is structured to qualify for this exemption to avoid the time and expense of UKLA vetting. In addition, AIM rules on historical accounting records are more flexible.

6.4   NEW YORK

6.4.1   Background

New York is another global leading financial centre. There are several markets on which funds may list, and indeed fund managers too. The principal markets are the New York Stock Exchange (now merged with Euronext to operate as NYSE Euronext) and NASDAQ, the first electronic exchange. The New York markets are regulated by the SEC and the markets themselves under the auspices of the SEC.

6.4.2   The New York markets

(a) NYSE Euronext

NYSE Euronext was launched in 2007 from the merger of the New York Stock Exchange (NYSE) and Euronext N.V. (Euronext). It operates exchanges in New York and across Europe. The exchange positions itself as the world's largest and most liquid market.

NYSE Euronext formed a strategic alliance with the Tokyo Stock Exchange in 2007, prioritizing the mutual listing of REITs and ETFs.

---

[80] Chapter 5, Part 6 of the Income Tax (Trading and Other Income) Act 2005
[81] Schedule 5C TCGA 1992
[82] Section 263 ITA 2007
[83] Section 262 and 266 ITA 2007
[84] Section 261 ITA 2007
[85] London Stock Exchange, www.londonstockexchange.com

Exchange traded securities, including ETFs, are traded on the NYSE Arca exchange. The NYSE is regulated by NYSE Regulation, the SEC and the Financial Industry Regulatory Authority (FINRA) both during the application process and once listed. An application for listing must be approved by NYSE Regulation and with an effective registration statement from the SEC.

(b) NASDAQ

NASDAQ was established in 1971 as the world's first electronic stock market. It is regulated by the SEC and FINRA. NASDAQ operates several different markets on a tier system, with the more stringent requirements for the higher tiers (such as for market value). Funds listed on NASDAQ must be approved by the SEC and FINRA in a similar process to funds listed on the NYSE, subject to the unique rules of NASDAQ.

The exchange has made client services a point of differentiation. It has developed various offerings to assist listed vehicles with investor relations and post-listing needs.

6.4.3   Vehicles in New York appropriate for listing investment funds

(a) US mutual funds

(i) Introduction
'Mutual fund' refers to an open-ended pooled investment structure that is subject to significant regulatory oversight and invests in non-controlled positions in securities that satisfy the specified investment objectives. An open-ended company provides investors with the right to purchase equity from the fund or sell to (i.e. redeem their equity interest) the fund at a price equal to the net asset value (or NAV) of the fund as of the close of business of the purchase or redemption date. A mutual fund investment portfolio is 'managed' by an investment adviser that is registered with the SEC. That is, a registered investment adviser provides the investment advice to the mutual fund with respect to the securities included in the portfolio. A mutual fund is governed by its board of directors, or if the mutual fund is organized as a trust, the board of trustees. The professional management and collective or pooled investment structure is similar in some respects to a hedge fund. There are however significant differences. First, there are different regulatory characteristics. The mutual fund is subject to extensive regulatory oversight and available to purchase or distribute to the general public in a continuous public offering. By contrast, a hedge fund was, prior to the Dodd–Frank Act, largely unregulated and is now regulated through certain provisions of the Jumpstart Our Business Startups Act 2012 (JOBS Act) and the Dodd–Frank Act, through specified registration requirements and supervision of the investment adviser, and with respect to the distribution of the investment interests. Second, the investment interests are not subject to variation through 'side letters' and participation in parallel investment vehicles, side funds and other vehicles.

A mutual fund is a company that is defined as an investment company and is subject to the provisions of the Investment Company Act of 1940, as amended (the ICA). The investment adviser to the mutual fund, as noted above, must be registered under and subject to the provisions of the Investment Advisers Act of 1940, as amended (the Advisers Act). The ICA promotes the protection of investors through numerous provisions discussed in greater detail below.

Shares in a mutual fund can be listed on an exchange (referred to as ETFs – exchange traded funds) or unlisted. Section 6.5.2 (below) discusses ETFs. This section will deal with mutual funds as an unlisted entity.

In the US alone there are over 7000 mutual funds with combined assets worth more than USD 12.8 trillion. There are four general types of mutual funds based on the investment strategy and securities held by the fund. There are numerous variations of investment strategies, risk criteria and other factors within each category. For example, a bond fund could focus its investment portfolio on high-yield or 'junk' bonds, non-US bonds, short-term or long-term maturities, etc. Investment strategies are discussed in more detail in Chapter 5.

(ii) Legislation

Mutual funds are subject to significant regulatory oversight. The primary federal law impacting mutual funds is the ICA, which imposes a broad range of substantive requirements on organization and operation of mutual funds along with granting the SEC authority to regulate them. Other laws to which they are subject are the Securities Act 1933 (governing the documentation and sale of shares to the public), the Securities Exchange Act 1934 and the IRC (which imposes requirements for tax relief to be made available). The regulatory framework is overseen by the SEC, FINRA and the CFTC (where applicable).

(iii) Structure

A mutual fund may be structured as a business or statutory trust, a corporation, a limited partnership, a limited liability company or any other suitable US business entity. Many funds are structured as a Massachusetts business trust, a Delaware statutory trust or a Maryland corporation. These structures provide flexible governance structures and arrangements and do not require annual shareholder meetings.

Under the ICA, a mutual fund must comply with certain restrictions on investments:

- investors must receive a prospectus that includes:
  - specified disclosures and subjects specified persons to liability for failure to properly discuss the material facts relating to an investment in the fund
  - the past performance of the fund and
  - other material facts about the investment adviser and executives
- out of the whole of a diversified fund's assets, of 75% of those assets no more than 5% can be invested in a single issuer (other than the government or another investment company), nor can an investment in a single issuer amount to more than 10% of its voting rights
- the remaining 25% is not subject to this restriction and can be invested freely
- there are restrictions on transactions with affiliates
- there are extensive record-keeping requirements
- there are limitations on investments in other investment companies, securities-related businesses and illiquid securities
- funds which invest in the money markets are restricted in their portfolio holdings in terms of diversity, quality, maturity and liquidity
- the full disclosure of its investment policy in relation to investments such as real estate and commodities, which can only be modified with shareholder approval
- it cannot borrow money by the issue of securities and can only borrow a certain amount in relation to its assets.

(iv) Pricing

The price of a share in a mutual fund is determined by its NAV. This is the total of all the assets under management minus liabilities divided by the number of issued and outstanding shares at the date the NAV is computed. The price does not vary according to investor perception due to the open-ended nature of the fund.

(v) Risk

As the price of the mutual fund's shares is set at the NAV, the risk of investing is reduced partly because the price will not fall below this figure in response to supply and demand. The risk of the underlying assets failing remains and so investors must be aware that even though the price does not deviate from the NAV, the NAV itself can still change. It is partly for this reason that the fund must disclose its investment strategy and that the strategy is difficult to amend: investors will want to know what the risks associated with the fund's policy are and to know with certainty the future policy of the fund.

The risk of investing in a mutual fund also depends in part on the asset class on which its policy is focused. Exposure to one single asset class is sometimes considered too much of a risk, although each class has varying degrees of risk and reward. For example, a bond fund faces both interest rate risk and income risk – the price of a bond is inversely related to the prevailing rates of interest and the income yield is directly related to a change in the interest rates at the time. Some mutual funds are focused on specific sectors – such as agriculture – rather than a particular asset class. Hybrid funds are often marketed to take advantage of many different asset classes and sectors and to hedge against the risks involved in each.

(vi) Fees

The management fees and operating expenses of a mutual fund are typically deducted from the fund's return and are typically calculated as a percentage of the fund's assets spent on operating expenses, often with a wide range of between 0.2% and 2%. There are frequently on-off fees for certain events. A front-end load is a fee charged to the investor on the purchase of shares in the fund or when re-investing proceeds into the fund. A back-end load is charged when the investor redeems shares in the fund and is often based on the length of time that the shares have been held, with longer-term holdings receiving a discounted rate. A level load is a fee charged annually and deducted from the fund's assets to cover marketing and distribution costs and to pay commissions to the advisers – the broker and the financial adviser. A redemption fee may also be possible when the shares have been held for a short time, in order to discourage short selling.

(vii) Taxation

Most mutual funds seek to qualify as regulated investment companies under the IRC. Generally, this effectively exempts the fund itself from federal income tax on its income and capital gains.

US-resident investors

The distribution of investment income and net short-term capital gains are taxed as ordinary income at the applicable federal income marginal tax rate. The distribution of net capital gains which have been properly reported is taxed as long-term capital gains at the applicable federal income tax rate. Any distribution of investment income received from qualifying dividend income is, subject to qualifications, taxed at rates applicable to long-term capital gains. Any income received by an individual is also subject to a Medicare contribution tax and any state or local taxes.

Non-US-resident investors
The dividends (other than capital gains) paid to non-resident investors are subject to a withholding tax of 30%, subject to a lower rate if there is an applicable tax treaty. A properly reported distribution of US sourced interest income or net short-term capital gains is subject to a special exemption from the withholding tax. This exemption is due to expire on 31 December 2013 if it is not renewed by Congress (which it has done before). When the Foreign Account Tax Compliance Act (better known as FATCA) withholding provisions come into force in phases from 1 January 2014, an additional 30% withholding charge will be levied on investors who do not comply with FATCA's reporting provisions.

(b) US REITs

(i) Background and overview
The US is the birthplace of the REIT. The US enacted a law authorizing REITs in 1960 and in 1965 the REIT was first traded on the NYSE. Much of the US regime has inspired the UK's own REIT regime, for example the minimum distributions and the balance of business conditions (as referred to in the UK legislation).

There are two primary concerns when determining whether to form a real estate investment entity as a REIT: (i) US federal income tax and (ii) securities laws.

The primary benefit of a REIT is its tax efficiency. A large number of investors are able to participate in real estate focused investments with only one level of federal income taxation. An oversimplification of the federal taxation of entities is that: (i) corporations pay federal income tax; (ii) partnerships effectively pass-through federal income tax obligations including the character and amount of income, gains, losses, deductions and credits; and (iii) a REIT is in between. A REIT is a structure embodied in the US IRC that has specified characteristics and consequences for its investors. A REIT may result in a favourable tax structure because:

- a REIT's taxable income will be reduced by the amount of the dividends that it pays to its investors. REITs are obligated to distribute 90% of their earnings and profits on an annual basis; accordingly, the maximum effective current federal income tax rate that could be applicable at current rates to a REITs earnings and profits is 3.5%
- the REIT investors are taxed on distributions at ordinary federal income tax rates, other than for the applicable rate for qualified dividends to the extent the income was taxed at the REIT level, and
- because a REIT is not a 'pass-through' entity like a partnership, investors are not required to make state and local tax filings, pensions and tax exempts may invest in REITs without adverse obligations and (a significant benefit for a US REIT attracting capital from non-US sources) non-US investors are not effectively connected with a trade or business in the United States which requires the filing of tax returns and subjects the investors to the US tax regime.

The US federal securities laws are also a significant consideration when evaluating whether a real estate focused investment should be pursued through a REIT. Shares in a REIT may be offered in a public offering that is registered under the Securities Act of 1933, that is, a public offering. This provides the REIT with the opportunity to increase its capital sources, as investment is not limited to institutional investors or a limited number of investors; these restrictions are applicable to private equity investment funds.

A REIT acquires capital from its investors and, directly or indirectly, owns and controls the real estate assets. This structure is similar to an operating corporation. There are two general alternative structures of a REIT: an 'UpReit' and a 'DownReit'.

In an 'UpReit', the REIT investors own the entity that is a REIT and the REIT owns an investment in a limited partnership that owns the investments in the real estate assets. In a 'DownReit', the investors own the entity that is a REIT and the REIT owns and controls several single purpose limited partnerships ('properties'). The other limited partners in the limited partnerships are the contributors of the applicable property.

There are three general types of REITs:

- publicly traded REITs
- public non-traded REITs and
- private REITs.

Each type of REIT must comply with the requirements set forth in the IRC. The public REIT (traded and non-traded) is subject to the reporting and other requirements of a public company under the Securities Exchange Act of 1934 and the publicly traded REIT is subject to additional regulatory requirements of the applicable exchange, such as the NYSE.

(ii) Conditions

To qualify as a REIT there are certain conditions that must be met which are set out in the IRC.[86] The REIT must distribute, on an annual basis, at least 90% of the sum of all earnings and profits, and pay corporate income tax on the amount that is not distributed if it retains any. A REIT will often distribute 100% of its earnings and profits. It must use a structure that is taxable as a corporation (which also includes a trust or association and should include other entities) that is managed by directors or trustees. The investors must hold fully transferable shares or certificates of beneficial interest. After the first year of being a REIT there must be at least 100 shareholders and five or fewer shareholders cannot hold more than 50% of the value of stock. The UpReit structure noted above can be used to comply with this requirement. The initial contributors of the property can participate in the REIT portfolio through the limited partnership owned by the REIT and the other investors can participate in the REIT. This permits investors with a larger share value to contribute to the property and receive an investment interest pro rata. The REIT must receive at least 75% of its gross income from real estate income (commonly referred to 'good REIT' income) such as rent, the interest from mortgage secured property and gains from certain sales of real property. The REIT must also receive at least 95% of its gross income from sources including the real estate income described above and other sources including dividends from certain stocks. At least 75% of the assets must be real estate assets and the REIT cannot own more than 10% of another corporate body. Finally, no more than 5% of the REIT's gross assets can be invested in another corporate body (other than other REITs and qualifying subsidiaries) and a REIT may not engage in certain specified prohibited transactions.

---

[86] § 856

(iii) Publicly traded REITs

Publicly traded REITs are subject to the greatest amount of regulation. They are subject to the Securities and Exchange Act of 1934 and, accordingly, must adhere to the regulatory oversight of public companies. The majority of publicly traded REITs are listed on the NYSE. The investor benefits from the greater requirements for transparency and corporate governance, as well as the increased liquidity of their investment. The management of the investments is typically overseen by the directors of the company and operated in-house, rather than by outside agencies. The NYSE's rules require a majority of the directors to be independent by having no material relationship with the REIT as an investor or former employee, or by having an interest in a body which has a relationship with the REIT.[87] The investors have a degree of control over the directors because they have the power to re-elect the board. The SEC rules and stock exchange rules also regulate corporate governance and require that the company has its own policy on corporate governance.[88] The costs associated with investing in a publicly traded REIT are mainly in brokerage fees when buying or selling the shares. The Securities Exchange Act of 1934 also requires companies to make periodic public disclosures of financial performance[89] and yearly audited financial results must be filed with the SEC. Additionally, prompt public disclosure of significant events affecting the REIT must be made.

(iv) Public non-traded REITs

REITs may also be public entities but not listed on a stock exchange, known as non-traded REITs or non-exchange traded REITs. They are still required to file with the SEC. A non-traded REIT is a riskier investment because it is less liquid than its traded counterpart, and the value of the stocks is not calculated as frequently as it would be on the market. The management of a non-traded REIT is often by an external investment manager, in contrast with a public REIT, which can reduce the amount of profit available for distribution by dividend and could potentially lead to a conflict of interests. Non-traded REITs often have redemption procedures in place to allow an investor to dispose of their stocks, but the process is not as quick as on the markets and could cost an investor more in fees than brokerage costs would. The composition of the board is still regulated for its independence, but it is by the regulations of the North American Securities Administrators Association. Although there is the requirement to file accounts with the SEC there is no requirement to disclose to the investment community.

(v) Private REITs

There are some REITs which are private; they are not traded on a stock exchange nor are they registered with the SEC. They are primarily aimed at institutional investors and high net worth individuals and provide the least amount of liquidity. It is generally difficult to have the stocks redeemed and they are often redeemed at a high cost. They are typically run by outside investment managers and there are no requirements for independent directors or regulation of corporate governance and disclosure.

---

[87] NYSE Listed Company Manual (LCM), section 303A.02
[88] NYSE LCM section 303A.09
[89] NYSE LCM section 203.01

6.5   EUROPE

6.5.1   The European markets

(a) Euronext

The European market places under the NYSE Euronext umbrella are in Amsterdam, Brussels, Paris, London and Lisbon. They are all regulated markets under MiFID, and are subject to regulation similar to (but less onerous than) that of the LSE's Main Market. An advantage of NYSE Euronext markets over the LSE is that they permit the listing of non-corporate entities whereas only incorporated investment vehicles can be listed on the Main Market, although the establishment of the SFM (with reduced regulation and more flexibility in terms of the kind of investment vehicle that can be listed) means there is now greater competition.

(b) German stock exchanges

There are several stock exchanges operating within Germany. Many of them are named simply after the city in which they are located (e.g. Börse Berlin, Börse Stuttgart and Börse München). This similarity of naming does not mean that they are under common ownership. The largest stock exchange in Germany is the Frankfurt Stock Exchange, which is also one of the world's largest stock exchanges, competing for global issuance. Its share turnover accounts for more than 90% of turnover in the German equity market. It is now owned and operated by Deutsche Börse which also operates the Frankfurt-based Eurex market, one of the global market leaders in the trading and clearing of futures and options, and Clearstream, the European clearing house based in Luxembourg that provides integrated banking, custody and settlement services.

For further information on the various German business vehicles and German stock exchanges, see Chapter 8, section 8.8.4.

6.5.2   European exchange traded funds (ETFs)

(a) Introduction

ETFs were devised and refined in the US in the late 1980s and early 1990s. The purpose of an ETF is to have investments that can be bought and sold freely which are linked to underlying interests in markets or indices. They are similar to an OEIC as the shares can be redeemed (giving the fund its open-ended character). Some ETFs are actively managed rather than simply passive, although an original attraction of the ETF was that it was a cheaper investment than other funds, and active management pushes the fees up.

An ETF holds assets such as stocks, currencies, commodities or bonds, and trades close to its NAV over the course of the trading day. Most ETFs track an index such as a stock index or bond index. ETFs can be attractive to investors because of their low costs, tax efficiency and stock-like features.

A share in an ETF represents an interest in a unit of securities. The unit of securities can be all the shares of the tracked market or index in proportion to their weighting, a sample of the shares that aims to imitate the index, or made up of swaps or other derivatives. An ETF is priced continuously throughout the day, which makes it more attractive to short-term investors, along with the low management fees. It is however more expensive with regard to dealing costs, as there is a cost when selling the share or the bundle of securities it represents (on redemption).

Only authorized participants, which are large broker-dealers that have entered into agreements with the ETF's distributor, actually buy or sell shares of an ETF directly from or to the ETF. Authorized participants may wish to invest in the ETF shares for the long term, but they usually act as market makers on the open market, using their ability to exchange creation units with their underlying securities to provide liquidity of the ETF shares and help ensure that their intraday market price approximates to the net asset value of the underlying assets. Other investors, such as individuals using a retail broker, trade ETF shares on this secondary market.

(i) Legislation

Most European ETFs are structured to fall within the UCITS IV Directive to take advantage of the EEA-wide freedom to sell and market them without reference to each national authority. In the UK they are regulated by the FCA. The ETF will also be regulated by the exchange on which it is listed, and by the relevant law for the corporate vehicle and domicile chosen. Most European ETFs are domiciled in Ireland or Luxembourg with a public company structure.

(ii) Structure

The basic structure of an ETF entails several relationships between different parties. Firstly, the market maker uses cash to create a 'basket' of securities that represents the index or market tracked by the ETF by purchasing them on the market. That basket is then exchanged with the ETF sponsor (fund manager) for shares in the fund, and the shares are kept or sold to an investor on a secondary market. The investor may sell his shares to a third party or redeem his shares, whereby they will be sold back to a market maker.

Not all ETFs involve the acquisition of shares representing either a full or partial representation of the market. There are synthetic ETFs available which use derivatives to imitate a basket of assets without having to acquire them. The money passes directly from the market maker to the sponsor/fund manager who enters into a total return swap with a counterparty: a derivative contract for the underlying assets. The fund manager issues shares in the ETF in return to the investor, but retains the cash. This is an unfunded swap. In a funded swap, the swap counterparty deposits collateral in a separate account with a custodian. The cash passes to the swap counterparty and the fund manager receives an equity-linked note.

(iii) Pricing

The price can vary in accordance with investor demand. If the price is pushed up a market maker can purchase new baskets of securities and exchange them with the fund manager for shares in the fund. This increase of supply will reduce the price accordingly. When demand falls and prices drop, market makers can redeem the shares which will increase the share price. With this open-ended approach, the shares in the fund are often quoted at close to NAV although there can be brief fluctuations.

The shares are not purchased or sold at the NAV. When sold on the secondary market there will be dealing costs as with any quoted share, and when the shares are redeemed with the fund manager there may be additional redemption costs.

(iv) Risk

Investors have the ability to trade shares in the fund more frequently than with units of an investment trust, resulting in more flexible investments. This implies that these short-term trades will lead to greater returns; however, with the brokerage fees and potential fluctuations in price there is a risk that short-term gains are reduced significantly by the cost of frequent trading in comparison with a longer-term investment.

There is also a risk with regards to the synthetic models of an ETF that, as with any derivative product, the counterparty's collateral is dubious and the underlying investment fails.

(v) Regulation

In the US, ETFs are typically structured as open-ended retail funds. The primary source of law in respect of such funds is the ICA. Under the ICA, the SEC is empowered to regulate ETFs and the ICA also imposes substantive requirements on ETFs. In addition, as ETFs are by their nature exchange traded, the funds must be compliant with the applicable securities laws (the Securities Act 1933 and the Securities Exchange Act 1934) and the relevant exchange's rules.

European ETFs are normally structured to comply with the UCITS IV Directive as mentioned above. They will also need to gain approval from the ETF's home authority. ETFs are considered UCITS where the sole object is the collective investment in transferable securities or other liquid financial assets, by capital which is raised from the public, that is operating on the principle of risk spreading and the units can be redeemed or cancelled out of the fund's assets.[90] Steps taken by the fund manager to issue or redeem units in order to keep the price of the shares as close to NAV are acceptable. A fund which is closed-ended and either does not offer shares to the public or does so outside of the EU only, or which is prescribed by the home member state for the impropriety of its investment objectives or borrowing policy, cannot be a UCITS.[91]

The fund will be authorized and regulated by its home member state for its compliance with UCITS (article 5, UCITS IV). Most European ETFs are domiciled in Ireland or Luxembourg for taxation purposes and so will be regulated by those countries, both as a UCITS and for their compliance with local laws with regards to their corporate structure. They will also be regulated by the markets on which their shares are traded.

The regulatory landscape for ETFs may change in the near future. Several bodies at UK, EU and international level have expressed concern about ETFs and the consequences of their activities on the markets for the underlying assets. For example, ETFs which invest in the commodities markets are considered to be affecting prices and reducing liquidity by holding onto assets. The FCA has identified that ETFs are putting investors at risk as well as market stability.[92]

Retail investors are considered at risk, as the market for ETFs has grown rapidly in the past 10 years and there are concerns that regulations have not kept up with this rapidly evolving market. Investors are at risk due to the increasing complexity and the increasing reliance on derivatives in synthetic ETFs. There is concern that despite the low fees and the ability to place the shares in tax exempt accounts, knowledge of the underlying risks (especially with derivative products) remains low.

---

[90] Article 1, UCITS IV Directive – 2009/65/EC
[91] Article 3, UCITS IV Directive
[92] The FCA's Retail Conduct Risk Outlook 2011

Regulators are also concerned about the effect of ETFs on other markets. The Financial Stability Board in 2011 published concerns that illiquidity, counterparty risk and transparency issues connected with ETFs were connected to increased financial instability. It recommended a further study into whether further regulation was necessary.

(vi) Management fees

ETFs are often promoted for their low management fees over some of the competitor funds. Expenses for passive funds are typically in the range of 0.5–1%. If there is an element of active management in the fund the fees can increase. Most fees are simply to deal with the cost of trading in the underlying securities, and investors can expect to pay brokerage fees when purchasing shares on the secondary market from the market makers. Some funds employ an 'all in one' fee system, where the expenses of the fund are deducted as a single flat fee calculated as a percentage of the NAV and paid monthly out of the fund. Many funds do not charge entry and exit fees.

(vii) UK taxation

There are three potential taxable levels.

Investment level

First, the fund is taxed at the investment level. For example, if the fund tracks the shares quoted on the FTSE 100 and those shares pay out a dividend, there will be a tax on the payment, depending on the domicile of the fund and the investment.

Fund level

There will also be a tax at the fund level. That is to say the fund will be taxed for corporation tax for its income and gains on the sale of its assets.

Investor level

Investors will be taxed on the sale of their shares in the fund and for any income by the way of dividends which represent each share's interest in the total profit of the fund (less expenses).

6.6   ALTERNATIVE OFFSHORE STOCK EXCHANGES

Many investment funds are listed on so-called 'offshore' exchanges. Fund managers choose to go offshore for a variety of reasons.

There may have been a specific reason for the decision to go offshore. For example, historically, a fund may have opted to list in the Channel Islands as opposed to on the UK mainland on the LSE. This decision may have been taken in the period before the LSE offered the option to list CEIFs and OEICs. At that time the LSE did not permit the listing of non-corporate fund structures unless they were first listed on another exchange. In addition, another hurdle sometimes seen as unfavourable on the LSE was that corporate entities were required to have a three-year accounting track record, which could prove prohibitive.

Often the reasons for seeking an offshore exchange are associated with greater tax or regulatory efficiencies. One example of this might be a US fund seeking to avoid adverse tax consequences for non-US investors. In addition, a fund might need a listing to evidence listing status for certain types of investors. An offshore listing enables the fund to satisfy this requirement by an easier process.

However, I would argue that all offshore exchanges do not offer enough liquidity to be a true exchange (within the usual meaning of the term, dating back to the 17th century London coffee houses, that implies regular trading or exchanging of securities). Offshore exchanges can offer a valuable service providing easier, faster listings, especially where other non-exchange inspired legislation or regulations or investors require those securities to be listed.

For more details of some of the primary offshore listing locations, see Chapter 7.

6.7   SOME CONCLUSIONS

In this chapter we have reviewed some of the more commonly used 'onshore' fund vehicles and stock exchanges, how those fund vehicles are typically used and their regulatory and tax regimes.

In the next chapter we take a look at the so-called 'offshore' alternatives to these structures.

7

Principal 'Offshore' Fund Locations

7.1 WHAT ARE THE CHARACTERISTICS OF AN ATTRACTIVE INVESTMENT FUND LOCATION?

In recent times we have seen an increase in global competition from countries that seek to attract investment funds and companies. For example, in Europe, Ireland offers a corporate tax rate of 12.5%;[1] however, recent reports have suggested that subsidiaries of Apple Inc. were offered a corporate tax rate of less than 2%.[2] In the UK the present corporate tax rate is 23% (down from 24% in 2012), and is due to decrease to 20% in 2015. Evidently there is competition from jurisdictions to provide an attractive tax environment for companies and investment funds, hence the focus for fund managers and investors in analysing the taxation regime, as well as the regulatory environment and ease of incorporation and administration of funds within a jurisdiction. In addition, rules around permanent establishment and the investment managers' exemption (see Chapter 11, section 11.2.4) seek to encourage fund managers to locate onshore and advise funds that are offshore. In this chapter I will review a number of attractive investment fund locations, and the review will include an analysis of the regulatory and tax environments of the various locations.

Many of the jurisdictions in this chapter are often identified as offshore. The term 'offshore' has been used by some to refer to a jurisdiction perhaps perceived to be a 'tax haven' and certain political parties across the world attack these tax havens from time to time, on various grounds, including lack of taxation and transparency. However, a combination of factors, including global competition for lower headline corporation tax and rules to encourage fund management to their country, is leading in my view to the onshore/offshore distinction becoming redundant. I would suggest that another definition of an 'offshore' location could refer to any location outside of a fund manager's home jurisdiction. I analyse the onshore/offshore distinction more in Chapter 13. As opposed to just seeking tax advantages, many fund managers also see a strategic advantage in basing an entity in an offshore location in an attempt to target new markets. For example, an entity may be formed in Mauritius with an intent to target the African market, or an entity may be formed in Hong Kong to target the Chinese market, although the origin might have been tax driven (for example Mauritius' use of double taxation treaties).

I have divided this chapter into five parts. I commence the analysis in part (A) with an overview of the offshore crown dependencies of Jersey, Guernsey, Isle of Man, and a number of the other Channel Islands. I have provided an overview in part (B) of the specifically regulated EU fund jurisdictions of Ireland, Luxembourg, Malta, Cyprus and Gibraltar, and in addition I have listed a number of other countries forming the rest of Europe within part

---

[1] HMRC website: http://www.hmrc.gov.uk/rates/corp.htm: last accessed 7 June 2013
[2] The *Telegraph* website: http://www.telegraph.co.uk/finance/personalfinance/consumertips/tax/10083323/Ireland-goes-on-offensive-to-counter-US-tax-haven-claims.html: last accessed 7 June 2013

(C), being Switzerland and the Netherlands. I have also provided an overview in part (D) of those countries located within the Caribbean and the Atlantic, detailing the Cayman Islands, BVI and Bermuda. I have concluded the chapter with part (E) which provides an overview of Asia, detailing Hong Kong, Singapore and Mauritius. I apologize for categorizing Mauritius within Asia; however, I have done so by reason that Mauritius is a popular fund location to invest into Asia (and Africa).

(A)   OFFSHORE CROWN DEPENDENCIES

7.2   THE CHANNEL ISLANDS

7.2.1   Background

Jersey, Guernsey and some smaller islands form part of a group of islands that makes up the collective body known as the Channel Islands, which are situated in the English Channel. While they remain loyal to the British Crown, they are self-governing, and set their own taxes. The relationship between the Islands and the EU is set out under Protocol 3 to the United Kingdom's Act of Accession 1972. The effect of Protocol 3 is that although the Islands are neither a member state nor an associate member of the EU, they are part of the customs territory of the EU. It follows that there is free movement of industrial and agricultural goods between the Islands and the EU member states. The Islands retain their fiscal independence meaning that they contribute nothing to, nor receive anything from, the EU. The legal systems of both Jersey and Guernsey draw on influences from Norman customary law and also English common law. Both Jersey and Guernsey are parliamentary representative democracies, and they are also British Crown dependants, meaning that the UK is responsible in respect of defence and international relations.

7.2.2   Common structures

(a) Jersey

The most common Jersey investment fund structures include the following.

(i)   Companies

The legislation which governs the formation and operation of companies in Jersey is the Companies (Jersey) Law 1991. Under the legislation it is possible to create the following types of company: a public or a private company, a limited company with par value or no par value,[3] an unlimited company,[4] or a limited life company whereby a company will be wound up or dissolved upon the death or bankruptcy of a member or the occurrence of some other event specified in the company's articles or memorandum. With effect from 1 February 2006, the Companies (Amendment No 8) (Jersey) Law 2005 introduced incorporated and protected cell companies. Cell companies have the ability to create cells separate from themselves, each of which can hold separate assets. A protected cell company (PCC) is a separate legal entity, but the individual cells do not have a separate legal identity independent of the PCC. By contrast the various cells of an incorporated cell company (ICC) form an independent

---

[3] Companies (Jersey) Law 1991; Article 3C
[4] Companies (Jersey) Law 1991; Article 3D

legal personality. A benefit of a PCC or an ICC is that the assets of each individual cell are made available only to the shareholders/creditors of that particular cell.

(ii) Unit trust

As discussed in Chapter 4, section 4.11, unit trusts are limited in their application to specific investment classes or private capital arrangements. One asset class which remains popular is real estate; for more information on Jersey property unit trusts, see Chapter 4, section 4.13.

(iii) Limited partnership

A limited partnership may be formed under the Limited Partnerships (Jersey) Law 1994. The partnership must contain at least one limited partner and there is no maximum number of limited partners.[5] Providing administrative ease, accounts need not be audited,[6] and subject to the event of insolvency, the legislation provides for the unrestricted return of partnership contributions[7] and distribution of profits. The only document that needs to be publicly filed to form a partnership is a short declaration, and this does not need to disclose the identity of the limited partners, the business of the limited partners, or the partnership contributions.[8]

(iv) Limited liability partnership

A limited liability partnership enables a fund to be established with a separate legal person which is not a corporate. It enables the partners to have limited liability while engaging in the management of the fund.

(v) Separate limited partnership

A fund structured as a separate limited partnership is a legal person but is not a body corporate. With tax transparency, it is analogous to a Scottish limited partnership (see Chapter 2, section 2.2.4(a)) or a Delaware limited partnership (see Chapter 2, section 2.5).

(vi) Incorporated limited partnership

A fund structured as an incorporated limited partnership has legal personality and is a body corporate. This is beneficial to US investors whose tax arrangements require their investment income to derive from a corporate entity rather than be treated as income of the partnership direct in their hands.

(b) Guernsey

Similar to Jersey, there are five main types of entity which may be used to form an investment fund.

(i) Limited company

A limited company is formed pursuant to the Companies (Guernsey) Law 2008, and may be incorporated either as a company limited by shares or by guarantee.[9] A company limited by

---

[5] Limited Partnerships (Jersey) Law 1994; Article 3(2)
[6] Limited Partnerships (Jersey) Law 1994; Article 9(2)
[7] Limited Partnerships (Jersey) Law 1994; Article 17
[8] Limited Partnerships (Jersey) Law 1994; Article 4
[9] The Companies (Guernsey) Law, 2008, section 2)2)(a)

shares must have a share capital[10] and must only have members whose liability for the company's debts is limited to the amount, if any, unpaid on their respective shares.[11] A company limited by guarantee may have a share capital if it so decides[12] and the liability of the members will be limited to the amount the member has undertaken to contribute to the company in the event of winding up.[13]

(ii) Incorporated cell companies and protected cell companies

ICCs and PCCs are governed under the Companies (Guernsey) Law 2008. An ICC consists of a number of incorporated cells, each of which is separate from the incorporated cell company.[14] By contrast while a PCC is a separate legal person, its individual cells are not legal persons in their own regard.[15]

(iii) Unit trust

A unit trust is formed under the Trusts (Guernsey) Law 1989 by an instrument in writing[16] and the concept is that the trustee (who quite often is a trust company) holds the assets of the fund on behalf of the beneficiaries, who will be the investors.

(iv) Limited partnerships

A limited partnership is formed under the Limited Partnerships (Guernsey) Law, 1995. A limited partnership may be formed in Guernsey for the purposes of carrying on a lawful business there, or outside of Guernsey.[17] It must consist of one or more general partners, who will be jointly and severally liable for all the debts of the partnership, and one or more limited partners. Under the 1995 law, it is also a requirement that every limited partnership has a partnership agreement.[18]

7.2.3   Regulation of the fund

(a) Jersey

Jersey-based funds are subject to regulation by JFSC. There are a large number of regulatory options available to funds in Jersey, some of which are briefly listed below.

(i)   Unregulated funds

Unregulated funds, which are either structured as an eligible investor fund or an ETF, are not subject to any requirement to apply for authorization from the Financial Services Commission. An eligible investor fund is open to investors each investing a minimum of/or the equivalent of USD 1 million, or investors who are defined as a professional investor. ETFs must be closed-ended and listed on an approved exchange.

---

[10] The Companies (Guernsey) Law, 2008, section 6(1)
[11] The Companies (Guernsey) Law, 2008, section 6(2)
[12] The Companies (Guernsey) Law, 2008, section 7(1)
[13] The Companies (Guernsey) Law, 2008, section 7(5)
[14] The Companies (Guernsey) Law, 2008, section 474
[15] The Companies (Guernsey) Law, 2008, section 441
[16] The Trusts (Guernsey) Law 1989, Section 6(2)
[17] The Limited Partnerships (Guernsey) Law 1995, section1(1)
[18] The Limited Partnerships (Guernsey) Law 1995, section 3(1)

(ii) Very private funds

Very private funds are collective investment arrangements which do not require ongoing regulation and only require consent under COBO. However, it is imperative that there are fewer than 15 investors and investors must be restricted to professional investors, and the minimum investment of each investor to the fund must be GBP 100,000, but preferably GBP 250,000.

(iii) COBO-only funds

COBO-only funds are funds that are offered to not more than 50 investors and which are not listed upon any stock exchange. A private placement memorandum must be provided to the JFSC and their consent to the fund is required under the COBO. If it is targeted at more experienced investors, the JFSC may be more flexible with the regulatory requirements which apply.

(iv) Unclassified collective investment fund

Unclassified collective investment funds are under the same general regime as COBO-only funds, but as these funds are able to offer to a wider range of investors, the regime is enhanced in its regulatory requirements.

(v) Expert funds

Expert funds are subject to less stringent regulation provided that the investors of the fund qualify as expert investors, being those investors able to prove an investment of/or equivalent to USD 100,000.

(b) Guernsey

The Protection of Investors (Bailiwick of Guernsey) Law 1987 applies to both open-ended and closed-ended funds. For regulatory purposes the legislation puts funds into two categories:

- authorized funds and
- registered funds.

Both categories of fund are subject to ongoing supervision by the Guernsey Financial Services Commission (GFSC). Registered funds benefit from a fast-track application process with GFSC (registration usually takes three days from the filing of the application). There is also a fast-track regime for authorized funds, available if the investors fall within certain categories of qualifying investor.

Closed-ended authorized funds are subject either to the Authorised Closed-Ended Investment Scheme Rules 2008 or the Registered Collective Investment Scheme Rules 2008, and are subject to supervision by the GFSC on a continuing basis.

Open-ended authorized funds may be established in Guernsey as Class A, Class B or Class Q schemes.

(i) Class A schemes

These schemes are those recognized under the Commission's Collective Investment Schemes Rules 2002 and they may be sold to the UK public as they are recognized by the FCA.

(ii) Class B schemes

These schemes are normally targeted towards institutional investors as the rules governing them do not include specific investment, borrowing or hedging restrictions. The flexible nature of the governing rules is reflective of the fact that Class B funds are targeted towards innovative products.

(iii) Class Q schemes

These seek to provide clear guidance in relation to professional investment funds. Each scheme must be authorized and continually supervised by the Commission and an offering document must be produced which contains sufficient information to allow an investor to make an informed decision.

Authorized open-ended funds can benefit from a fast-track application regime if their committed investors fall into certain prescribed categories.

Open-ended funds may alternatively be established as registered open-ended schemes, which allows a fast-track application, although such funds cannot be marketed inside Guernsey.

7.2.4   Stock exchange

Jersey and Guernsey are both members of the Channel Islands Stock Exchange (CISX), which is based in St Peter Port, Guernsey. The CISX has concentrated on several core products including specialist securities and investment funds since it commenced operating in October 1998. The CISX was recognized by the SEC as a designated offshore securities market in September 2002, and as a designated investment exchange by the FCA with effect from 1 February 2004. CISX is regulated by the GFSC and is also a member of the Association for Financial Markets in Europe.

Trading members of the CISX do not need to be established in the Channel Islands; however, they must be a corporation, partnership or legal entity which is licensed, regulated or supervised by a regulated body which operates in a recognized jurisdiction, or must be a member of a professional body approved by the CISX. In addition, an applicant for membership must be of sound financial standing, be fit and proper, and be in compliance with the rules of the CISX.[19]

7.2.5   Taxation

(a) Jersey

In relation to both open-ended and closed-ended funds, regardless of the structure which the fund takes, it will generally not attract any form of taxation, unless the fund invests in Jersey-based property. There is no corporation, capital gains or inheritance tax payable when issuing or realizing investments.

(b) Guernsey

At fund level, in relation to both open-ended and closed-ended funds, regardless of the structure the fund takes, it will generally not attract any form of taxation, as it may elect to apply

---

[19] CISX Listing Rules

for tax exempt status in Guernsey. If an application for tax exemption is granted then an annual fee will be payable in respect of the fund.

7.3   THE ISLE OF MAN

7.3.1   Background

The Isle of Man (IOM) is a self-governing dependent territory of the British Crown. It is located in the Irish Sea and is geographically part of the British Isles; however, it is not part of the United Kingdom (UK) and as such it has full autonomy in relation to its domestic affairs, including tax. It is not a member of the EU and consequently it is not obliged to give effect to EU directives on tax harmonization, company law and financial services. The IOM's parliament (Tynwald) makes its laws and oversees its internal affairs. Its legal system is effectively based on the English common law.

The IOM was the first overseas territory to obtain 'designated territory status' under what is now Section 270 of the UK Financial Services and Markets Act 2000 (FSMA), having satisfied the UK Government that the law under which certain CISs (authorized schemes – see below) are authorized and supervised in the IOM affords investors protection at least equivalent to that provided for them under the law of the UK.

The regulatory authority in the IOM is the Financial Supervision Commission (FSC).

7.3.2   Common structures

In the Isle of Man the most popular fund structures include the following.

(a) Isle of Man Company

The IOM has two separate companies acts: the Companies Acts 1931–2004 (under which 1931 Act Companies are formed) and the Companies Act 2006 (2006 Act Companies). The 2006 Act is completely different to the UK Act of the same name. Most funds are 2006 Act Companies. The 1931 Act is similar in principle to the UK Companies Act 2006, although much less detailed. The 2006 Act was designed for ease of administration: for example, there need only be one director and the sole director may be a body corporate; and there are less stringent filing requirements with the Companies Registry.

(b) Protected cell companies

A PCC can be either a 1931 Act Company or a 2006 Act Company. A PCC is a company limited by shares; however, a PCC is able to divide the assets of the company into separate cells. Each cell is ring-fenced against the liabilities of the other cells within the company. The assets of a particular cell will only be made available to the shareholders and creditors of that cell.

(c) Limited partnerships

Limited partnerships are governed by the Partnership Act 1909. A fund constituted as a limited partnership must have at least one partner (the general partner) who is liable for all its debts and obligations. Limited partners have limited liability. Pursuant to a special regulation, funds constituted as limited partnerships may have more than 20 partners.

7.3.3 Regulation

(a) Authorized schemes

Authorized schemes are formally authorized and subject to prescriptive regulation. Authorized schemes are retail-focused and may be marketed directly to the general public in the Isle of Man as well as the UK, Hong Kong, Australia, Jersey and Guernsey.

No minimum investment is specified and retail, high net worth and institutional investors may invest. There are detailed investment and borrowing restrictions. The manager must hold an IOM licence and must ensure that an appropriate investment adviser/asset manager is appointed. The custodian must be an IOM bank with an appropriate licence. An auditor must be appointed.

The manager and the custodian both have a duty to ensure that the fund is managed and compliant with its constitutional documents. The manager must provide quarterly statistical information to the FSC. The fund's offering document must provide sufficient information to investors to allow them to make an informed judgement in relation to participating in the fund.

Authorized schemes benefit from an Isle of Man investor compensation scheme.

(b) Regulated schemes

Regulated funds are subject to a relatively high level of oversight by the FSC.

To establish a regulated fund, the FSC must be sent pre-notification together with draft documentation, agreements and information.

The members of the fund's governing body (directors, trustee, or general partner) must be vetted by the FSC and the governing body must sign a statement of responsibility. There must also be at least one member of the governing body who resides in the IOM.

Minimum subscription is set by the governing body and there are no investor criteria or qualifications except as set by the fund itself.

The manager must hold an IOM licence and must ensure that an appropriate investment adviser/asset manager is appointed. The custodian must be regulated in the Isle of Man, the UK, Ireland, Luxembourg, Jersey or Guernsey or otherwise acceptable to the FSC. An auditor must be appointed.

The directors, manager and custodian are responsible for the proper operation of the fund and must submit an annual compliance declaration to the FSC.

(c) Qualifying funds

A qualifying fund offers flexibility in relation to investment advisory and asset management requirements. For example, the governing body of the fund does not need to be vetted by the FSC and the minimum investment level of the fund will be agreed between the fund manager and the governing body of the fund. However, the fund is restricted to qualifying investors, i.e. those who self-certify that they have the expertise, experience and knowledge adequately to appraise the investment risks of a qualifying fund.

The governing body must include at least one non-executive director who is independent of the promoter and at least one Isle of Man-resident natural person (this can be the same person). The fund must appoint a manager licensed in the Isle of Man who must approve any asset manager or investment adviser who is appointed. A suitably experienced custodian regulated in the Isle of Man or in a jurisdiction acceptable to the FSC must also be appointed. The fund must be audited.

(d) Specialist fund

The specialist fund is commonly regarded as the fund structure of choice for alternative investments as there are no restrictive regulations in relation to trading strategies, leverage or asset classes of the fund.

Specialist funds are not suitable for retail investors: the minimum investment level is at least USD 100,000 and investors must be 'specialist investors', defined as institutions with assets available for investment of not less than USD 1 million and individuals with a self-certified net worth (excluding principal residence) of not less than USD 1 million. Investors are required to certify that they are specialist investors, that they are sufficiently experienced to understand the risks associated with an investment in the fund, that they have read and understand the offering document and accept the risks and that they have taken independent advice where appropriate.

The fund's governing body must include at least one non-executive director who is independent of the promoter; where the administrator is not in the Isle of Man, that director must be a suitably regulated Isle of Man-resident individual. The governing body must ensure that a suitable asset manager and/or investment adviser is appointed. An administrator regulated in the Isle of Man or a jurisdiction accepted by the FSC as imposing an appropriate standard of regulation must be appointed. There is no express requirement to appoint a custodian but the fund's offering document must contain a description of the arrangements for the custody of its assets. The fund must be audited.

(e) Exempt schemes

The exempt scheme is not subject to regulation by the FSC; rather, it is regarded as a private arrangement.

Provided that an exempt scheme has an express prohibition in its constitutional documents excluding offerings to the public anywhere in the world, and provided that it has fewer than 50 participants at any time, it can operate outside of the scope of Isle of Man fund regulation.

There are no restrictive regulations in relation to trading strategies, leverage or asset classes of the fund and there is no minimum subscription requirement.

An exempt scheme may not be constituted as a PCC.

7.3.4   Taxation

A fund based on a company vehicle is subject to a zero rate of income tax in the IOM. The same applies to a fund management or administration company based in the IOM.

No value added tax is payable in the IOM on fees charged by investment managers and fund administrators based in the IOM in relation to services to CISs, other than exempt schemes.

7.4   OTHER CHANNEL ISLANDS

7.4.1   Alderney

Alderney is the third largest of the Channel Islands. It is a self-governing democratic territory with its own government,[20] and its legal system draws influences from Normandy customary law and English common law. Most companies are subject to 0% corporation tax, subject to a number of exceptions, and there is no CGT or VAT. Individuals pay a flat rate tax on income of 20%.

7.4.2   Isle of Sark

The Isle of Sark is the second smallest of the Channel Islands. It has its own government and its legal system is based on Normandy customary law. The island has no form of taxes.

7.4.3   Herm

Herm is the smallest of the Channel Islands, measuring only a mile and a half long and half a mile wide. It is a dependency of Guernsey.

(B)   SPECIFICALLY REGULATED EU FUND JURISDICTIONS

7.5   IRELAND

7.5.1   Background

The Republic of Ireland (ROI) constitutes the substantial proportion of the island of Ireland, with the remainder of the country being Northern Ireland (which is part of the UK). The ROI was part of the United Kingdom of Great Britain and Ireland until 1922 when it attained independence. It is a parliamentary republic with a president serving as the head of state and a 'Taoiseach' serving as head of government. The legal system of the ROI is derived from English common law, though unlike the UK, the ROI has a written constitution which enshrines the rights of Irish citizens.

The growth of the ROI as a centre for the establishment of investment funds commenced with the introduction of the International Financial Services Centre in 1987, which among other things introduced tax incentives for the establishment of companies providing international financial services.

7.5.2   Common structures for funds

The following legal structures may be used to constitute investment funds in the ROI.

(a)   Investment company

Investment companies are incorporated as public limited companies and are governed by Irish Company Law, with appropriate exemptions to facilitate funds.

---

[20] States of Alderney website: http://alderney.gov.gg/article/4063/Government-and-Administration: last accessed 12 December 2012

(b) Unit trust

Unlike a company or an LLP, a unit trust is not a separate legal entity in law, as the trustee holds the assets of the fund on behalf of the investors who are the trustees.

(c) Common contractual fund

A common contractual fund (CCF) is established through contractual deed made between the management company and the investors who participate as co-owners of the fund assets. Like a unit trust, it does not have separate legal personality.

(d) Investment limited partnership

An investment limited partnership is formed by two or more persons, consisting of one or more general partners and one or more limited partners. An investment limited partnership may be formed as a non-UCITS under the Investment Limited Partnership Act 1994; however, such a structure is not permitted for UCITS funds.

In addition to the legal structure it is necessary to select the form of regulatory authorization under which a fund, regardless of structure, will be authorized. The following are available.

(i) UCITS

UCITS are established pursuant to the European Communities (Undertakings for Collective Investment in Transferable Securities) Regulations 2011, which implement the European UCITS Directives in Ireland. The key advantage to such funds is the pan-European passport which they afford funds.

(ii) Non-UCITS

Non-UCITS are established under domestic Irish legislation and may be authorized as retail, professional investor funds or qualifying investor funds (QIFs). The QIF, targeted towards sophisticated and institutional investors, has been the most popular choice of non-UCITS as the investment restrictions of the Central Bank do not apply. Following implementation of the AIFMD in Ireland, the QIF's successor will be the qualifying investor alternative investment fund or 'QUAIF' and this is expected to be the leading category of European alternative fund.

7.5.3 Regulation

Investment funds in Ireland are regulated by the Central Bank of Ireland (CBI), and its regulatory duties include granting approval of the fund manager, fund promoter and the management company, as well as having the ongoing obligation to regulate Irish funds.

In relation to the fund manager, European Economic Area (EEA)-based fund managers which are on the CBI's MiFID register do not require approval, although EEA fund managers not listed on the same will not be approved until their State regulator provides the CBI with confirmation that the fund manager meets the applicable home-State requirements. For non-EEA fund managers, a detailed review of the applicant must be made by the CBI.[21] In relation to fund promoters, the CBI does not require that the same be located in Ireland (and almost

---

[21] Central Bank of Ireland website: http://www.centralbank.ie/regulation/industry-sectors/fund-service-provider/investment-manager/Pages/approval.aspx: last accessed 28 November 2012

99% of currently authorized promoters are not), although the CBI requires that the promoter has relevant experience, is of good repute and has sufficient financial resources. In relation to a management company (if any), the CBI requires that the company be incorporated within Ireland (unless it is availing of a UCITS passport), and the level of regulation will depend on whether the relevant fund is structured as a UCITS or non-UCITS.

7.5.4   Stock exchange

The Irish Stock Exchange, which has been in existence since 1793, is an EU-recognized stock exchange and is also recognized by the securities markets of countries including the United States. It has three markets: (1) the Main Securities Market (MSM); (2) the Enterprise Securities Market (ESM); and (3) the Global Exchange Market (GEM). The MSM admits securities including investment funds, and is the principal exchange in the world for the listing of Irish and non-Irish funds. The ESM is the primary market for the listing of growth companies. Its rules allow for the dual admission of investment funds on the ESM and the AIM. The GEM is a specialist market aimed towards professional investors.

7.5.5   Taxation

Irish regulated funds are exempt from tax on their income and gains irrespective of an investor's residency. No withholding tax is applied on income distributions or the redemption of units by a fund to a non-Irish-resident investor, provided that a relevant declaration is in place. No Irish stamp duty is applied on the establishment, transfer or sale of units or shares in an Irish regulated fund and no ongoing or yearly tax is charged on the NAV of the fund. The standard corporate tax rate of 12.5% is levied on fund management companies, fund managers and service providers to the Irish fund industry. Ireland has signed comprehensive double tax treaties with 69 countries.

7.6   LUXEMBOURG

7.6.1   Background

Luxembourg is a constitutional monarchy at the heart of Europe. It is landlocked by Belgium, France and Germany and is one of the smallest EU member states. As an EU member state it is therefore required to comply with all EU directives and regulations. It is a parliamentary representative democracy and is the only remaining Grand Duchy, being a territory whose head of state is a monarch. Its legal system is a hybrid system based substantively on the French Napoleonic Code, though the commercial and penal divisions are based on Belgian law.

7.6.2   Common structures

In Luxembourg, funds may be created under either a contractual form or a corporate form.

(a) Common fund – fonds commun de placement

Fonds commun de placement (FCP) is similar in structure to a UK unit trust. It is established by contract (the management regulations) drawn up by a management company, and has no legal personality. Therefore, it is a requirement that it has a regulated management company. It is a co-proprietorship and the liability of the parties to the contract is limited to their respective contribution to the same.

(b) Investment funds with a corporate form

The most common corporate forms in Luxembourg used to set up investment funds are as follows.

(i) Société anonyme (SA) (public limited liability company)

SAs are the most common corporate legal form in Luxembourg. To incorporate an SA, there must be at least one shareholder who is a natural or legal person, and the liability of shareholders is limited to their contribution to the share capital of the SA. The minimum share capital of an SA is EUR 31,000. The management of an SA can be either a one-tier or two-tier structure. A one-tier management structure will consist of a single director or a board of at least three directors. A two-tier structure will have a management board of at least two members who are supervised by a board consisting of at least three members. It is possible to list an SA.

(ii) Société à responsabilité limitée (Sàrl) (private limited liability company)

A Sàrl resembles a company in that the liability of shareholders is limited to the amount they contribute to the share capital, but also bears traits of a partnership, as prior approval of the existing shareholders is required to transfer shares to non-shareholders. To incorporate a Sàrl, there must be at least one shareholder, though no more than 40. The minimum share capital of a Sàrl is EUR 12,500. In relation to internal governance, a Sàrl is managed by one or more managers. It is not possible to list a Sàrl.

(iii) Société en commandite par actions (SCA) (partnership limited by shares)

An SCA is the form of choice for funds where tight control of management is required. To incorporate an SCA there must be at least one unlimited shareholder, and two or more limited shareholders. Unlimited shareholders are jointly and severally liable for the company's debts, and they have unlimited liability as the name suggests. The liability of limited partners is capped to their contribution to the company share capital. An SCA is managed by one or several managers, being unlimited members or not. In practice, if the SCA is managed by its unlimited member, in order to limit its liability, it is structured as a company under the form of an SA or a Sàrl. The minimum share capital of an SCA is EUR 31,000. It is possible to list an SCA.

(iv) Société en commandite simple (SCS)

An SCS is a limited partnership and is taxed at partner level rather than at partnership level. To incorporate an SCS there must be at least one general partner who has unlimited liability for the debts of the partnership, and it will have at least one limited partner, who is liable only up to the amount it has contributed to the SCS. An SCS is managed by one or several managers, being unlimited members or not. In practice, if the SCS is managed by its unlimited member, in order to limit its liability, it is structured as a company under the form of an SA or a Sàrl.

(v) Société en commandite spéciale (SCSp)

The SCSp is a newly created legal form in Luxembourg. The SCSp has no legal personality. To create an SCSp there must be at least one general partner who has unlimited liability for the debts of the partnership, and it will have at least one limited partner who is liable only up to the amount it has contributed to the SCSp. The SCSp is managed by its general partner or by one or several managers who do not need to be a general partner. In practice, if the SCSp is managed by its general partner, in order to limit its liability, the general partner is structured as an SA or a Sàrl.

Investment companies may be structured either with a variable capital (SICAV) or with a fixed capital (SICAF), depending on the legal form adopted.

The share capital of an investment company created as a SICAV is always equal to its net assets. There are no formalities required for any alterations in share capital. By contrast, any change of the share capital of an investment company organized as a SICAF requires a resolution of the extraordinary general meeting of shareholders deciding upon: (i) the issue of new shares or redemption and cancellation of shares and (ii) the amendment of its articles of association to reflect the change of capital.

7.6.3 Regulation

Luxembourg regulated funds will be established under:

- the law of 15 June 2004 on the investment company in risk capital, as amended (2004 Law)
- the law of 13 February 2007 on specialized investment funds, as amended (2007 Law) or
- the law of 17 December 2010 on undertakings for collective investment, as amended (2010 Law).

(a) Investment company in risk capital (SICAR)

Investment companies established under the 2004 Law are known as SICARs, the object of which is to invest in risk capital. The SICAR is an attractive vehicle for private equity investments.

A SICAR may be created under the form of an SA, a Sàrl, an SCA, an SCS or an SCSp. The SICAR shall be created under the corporate form, either as a SICAV or a SICAF (it may not be constituted as an FCP). The minimum subscribed share capital of a SICAR is EUR 1 million and must be reached within 12 months from the authorization of the Commission de Surveillance du Secteur Financier (CSSF), the Luxembourg supervisory authority.

(b) Specialized investment fund (SIF)

Funds established under the 2007 Law are known as SIFs, for which there are no investment restrictions but risk spreading requirements. SIFs may only be sold to well-informed investors.

An SIF may be created under the contractual form of an FCP or under the corporate form (either as a SICAV or a SICAF) as an SA, a Sàrl, an SCA, an SCS or an SCSp. The minimum net assets of an SIF under the form of an FCP or the subscribed share capital of an SIF under the form of a SICAV is EUR 1.25 million and must be reached within 12 months from the authorization of the CSSF.

(c) Undertakings for collective investment

Funds established under the 2010 Law will be either UCITS (see further Chapter 3, section 3.6.3), submitted to Part I of the 2010 Law, or undertakings for collective investments (UCI), submitted to Part II of the 2010 Law.

Funds established under the 2010 Law may be sold to both retail and institutional investors and have specific investment restrictions.

The minimum net assets of a UCITS/UCI under the form of an FCP or the minimum subscribed share capital of the UCITS/UCI under the form of a SICAV is EUR 1.25 million and must be reached within six months from the authorization of the CSSF.

7.6.4 Stock exchange

The Luxembourg Stock Exchange was founded in 1928 and it is the largest European stock exchange in relation to the listing of international bonds. The Luxembourg Stock Exchange operates two markets, the Bourse de Luxembourg which offers a European passport, and the Euro MTF which is a multilateral trading facility. The listing of securities in relation to both of the above requires prior approval of the respective prospectus. Further to this, there are certain legislative requirements to be met before admission to the Luxembourg Stock Exchange may take place.[22]

7.6.5 Taxation

There is no corporate income tax in respect of funds established under the 2007 Law or the 2010 Law. However, there is an annual fund subscription tax which is levied at a rate of 0.01% per annum in relation to funds established under the 2007 Law, and 0.05% per annum in relation to funds established under the 2010 Law (for the funds under the 2010 Law, the subscription tax could be reduced under certain circumstances to 0.01% or 0%).

7.7 MALTA

7.7.1 Background

Malta is a small island situated in the Mediterranean Sea. It is a member state of the EU and is also a member of the Eurozone. By population and area, it is the smallest member of the EU. Malta is a former British colony, gaining independence in 1964, and it is therefore unsurprising that while its legal system is predominantly a codified civil law system based on the Code Napoleon and with ample influences of Roman civil law, its public law and corporate law are predominantly based on English law. Its political system resembles the Westminster model, having a separation of powers of the legislative, executive and judicial branches. It is a democratic republic, with a President as the head of state and a Prime Minister as the head of the government.

---

[22] Luxembourg Stock Exchange website: https://www.bourse.lu/about: last accessed 28 November 2012

7.7.2 Common structures

The following are the most common structures for setting up Maltese alternative investment funds.

(a) Investment companies

(i) SICAV

The most popular structure for Maltese-based hedge funds and other alternative investment funds is the SICAV. It is structured as an investment company with variable share capital which can be either a private or a public limited liability company. A SICAV can be set up as a multi-class company and can be also set up as a multi-fund company with one or more sub-funds each comprising one or a group of classes of shares. Each sub-fund can hold discrete assets. A SICAV is ideal for an open-ended scheme as its shares are not assigned a nominal value.

As set out by the Maltese Companies Act 1995, the memorandum of a SICAV should limit the objects of the company to 'the collective investment of its funds in securities and in other movable and immovable property, or in any of them, with the aim of spreading investment risk'.[23] This means that the SICAV structure permits a great degree of flexibility regarding investment strategies.

(ii) INVCO

An investment company with fixed share capital (INVCO) is defined under the Maltese Companies Act 1995 as a public company, the business of which entails 'investing in funds mainly in securities with the aim of spreading investment risk and giving members of the company the benefit of the results of the management of its funds'.[24] Further to this an INVCO must:

- not hold more than 15% by value of its investments in other companies which are not themselves an INVCO[25]
- prohibit in its memorandum the distribution of the company's capital profits[26]
- not retain more than 15% of the income it derives from securities.[27]

(b) Limited partnership

Under the Maltese Companies Act 1995, a commercial partnership may be formed as a partnership en commandite or limited partnership, which can have its capital divided into shares or a capital not so divided. It may be formed by two or more partners having its obligations guaranteed by unlimited joint and several liability of one or more general partners and by the liability of the unpaid contribution of one or more limited partners.[28] A deed of partnership must be entered into by the partners and a signed certificate of registration must be issued by the Registrar of Companies to form a partnership en commandite or limited partnership.

---

[23] Companies Act 1996; Article 84(2)(b)(i)
[24] Companies Act 1996; Article 194(6)(a)(i)
[25] Companies Act 1996; Article 194(6)(b)
[26] Companies Act 1996; Article 194(6)(c)
[27] Companies Act 1996; Article 194(6)(d)
[28] Companies Act 1996; Tenth Schedule, Part I(2)(1)

At the time of writing a review of the current legal framework is being undertaken to adapt and align the limited partnership structure in Malta with the structural and operational flexibility and needs of promoters of funds who are familiar with this structure, especially those involved in the private equity business, so as to make the Maltese limited partnership more appealing to these.

(c) Unit trust

Unit trusts are created by trust deed and are made between the fund manager, the investors and the trustees (who usually act as custodians of the trust property). Under Maltese Law, a unit trust can be a tax transparent structure, provided that the investors of the trust are non-Maltese residents and the fund's income is not derived from Maltese-based income.

(d) Contractual funds

Contractual funds are governed under the Investment Services Act (Contractual Funds) Regulations (Legal Notice 3 of 2011). It is a collective investment scheme which is formed by a deed of constitution. This agreement is entered into by the manager and the custodian of such a collective investment scheme. The investors participate and share in the property of the scheme by units issued by the manager, and such unit holders are statutorily bound by the deed of constitution as if they were parties to such deed.

7.7.3 Regulation

The principal legislation governing the Maltese fund industry is the Investment Services Act 1994, and the single financial services regulator is the Malta Financial Services Authority (MFSA).

A CIS is defined under the Investment Services Act as 'any scheme or arrangement which has as its object or as one of its objects the collective investment of capital acquired by means of an offer of units for subscription, sale or exchange'[29] and which is operated according to the principle of risk spreading and satisfies at least one of the following three alternative characteristics: (a) pooling of contributions of investors and of profits or income out of which payments are made to them; (b) units are redeemed by the scheme at the request of investors continuously or in blocks at short intervals; and (c) units are issued continuously or in blocks at short intervals. A fund which comes under this definition and which intends to issue or create any units or carries any marketing activity in or from Malta is obliged to acquire a collective investment scheme licence from the MFSA. In considering an application, the MFSA will have regard to the experience and suitability of the applicant and the other parties to the scheme and also have regard to the protection of investors and the protection of Malta's reputation.

Having received a licence from the MFSA, the scheme is subject to reporting obligations including *inter alia* the submission of reports on a biannual basis and must in respect of every financial year submit audited financial statements to the MFSA and to its investors.

For regulatory purposes, a distinction is made between: (i) retail collective investment schemes that are available to the general public comprising UCITS and retail non-UCITS

---

[29] Investment Services Act; Article 2

schemes; (ii) professional investor funds being non-retail collective investment schemes that are available only to investors satisfying specified eligibility criteria; and (iii) private collective investment schemes which are limited to 15 investors (related to or friends of the promoters) and which do not require a licence but need to be recognized by the MFSA.

7.7.4   Stock exchange

The Malta Stock Exchange (MSE) has been established for over 20 years (having commenced operation in 1992) and is regulated by the MFSA. There is also an Alternative Companies List (ACL) which commenced operations in 1999 and which provides a means of listing to companies that do not qualify for listing upon the MSE. The main participants in listed securities are issuers, stockbrokers and investors, and the financial instruments which may be admitted to the MSE include equities, bonds, corporate bonds, government stocks and treasury bills. An application must be signed by the sponsor and the directors of the applicant, accompanied by an Offering Memorandum and Board Resolutions authorizing the issue of financial instruments which are freely transferable.

The transfer of shares and securities listed on the Malta Stock Exchange is exempt from CGT, and from the payment of stamp duty.

7.7.5   Taxation

The level of taxation of a fund will depend upon whether the fund is prescribed or non-prescribed. A prescribed fund will have been incorporated in or formed in accordance with the laws of Malta, and will have declared that 85% of its fund assets are Maltese-based. A prescribed fund will be exempt from income and CGT. However, there is a 10% withholding tax on certain defined investment income including interest, discounts or premiums derived by the fund from government stocks or bonds, and also from bonds issued by listed companies. There is a 15% withholding tax on bank interest, and income or capital gains derived from immovable Maltese property are taxed at 35%. A non-prescribed fund will include all funds not qualifying as a prescribed fund. They are exempt from income and CGT, though taxes derived from immovable Maltese property remain applicable.

Additionally collective investment schemes licensed under the Investment Services Act benefit from a blanket stamp duty exemption in respect of any acquisitions or disposals of marketable securities.

7.8   CYPRUS

7.8.1   Background

Cyprus is an island located in the Eastern Mediterranean Sea, and is a member of both the EU and the Eurozone, having adopted the euro as its currency in 2008. It is geographically situated at a cross-road between Europe, Africa and the Middle East, and given its strategic location is a popular destination for fund management. Cyprus is a presidential republic akin to the US, whereby the president is both the head of state and head of the government. Cyprus was ruled by Britain from 1878 until 1960, and it is therefore unsurprising that the English legal system has been predominantly preserved, with the legal system being based upon the principles of common law and equity.

Due to Cyprus' request for an EU bailout from the International Monetary Fund (IMF) in March 2013, its appeal as an investment location was initially shaken, although confidence seems to be slowly returning.

7.8.2   Common structures

Common structures for Cypriot-based investment funds include the following.

(a) Companies

Under the Companies Law (Cap 113 as amended) any seven or more persons (excepting private companies where it will be one or more persons) can form a company with limited liability – either as a company limited by shares, whereby the liability of the members will be capped at the amount unpaid on the respective shares, or as a company limited by guarantee, where the liability of the members is set at the amount undertaken by the members to contribute to the company assets in the event of the company being wound up.[30]

(b) Limited partnerships

A Cypriot limited partnership may be formed under the Partnership and Business Names Law (Cap 116 as amended). It must consist of one or more general partners, who will be liable for all the debts and obligations of the partnership, and one or more limited partners who will be liable only up to the amount contributed by that partner.[31]

7.8.3   Regulation

Cypriot funds may be set up as an open-ended UCITS or alternative funds may be structured as an International Collective Investment Scheme (ICIS). Unlike a UCITS, an ICIS is established under the local rules set out in the International Collective Investment Schemes Law (No 47(1)/1999 as amended). An ICIS can be set up with unlimited or fixed duration and can take the form of either: (i) an International Fixed Capital Company, which issues shares of a specific nominal value; (ii) an International Variable Capital Company whose capital is equal to the net value of the shares issued from time to time; (iii) an International Unit Trust Scheme in which the Trust Scheme holds the assets on behalf of the trust beneficiaries; or (iv) an International Investment Limited Partnership in which a general partner must be appointed to manage the fund and whose liability is unlimited. ICISs are regulated by the Central Bank of Cyprus (CBC), which requires that only non-residents, offshore enterprises and other ICISs can be unit holders of an ICIS. Prior approval of the CBC is required to set up an ICIS and to make any proposed changes to its structure. Information must be provided to satisfy the CBC as to the competency of the promoters, managers and trustees of the ICIS, or any replacements from time to time. According to the ICIS Law, an ICIS can be set up as either (a) an experienced investor ICIS, for which a minimum subscription of USD 50,000 per investor applies; (b) a private ICIS with a maximum of 100 unit holders; or (c) an ICIS marketed to the public. In practice, the CBC has been approving only private ICIS funds.

---

[30] The Companies Law, Cap 113 as amended; section 3
[31] The Partnership and Business Names Law, Cap 116 as amended; section 47

It is expected that, in the not too distant future, the ICIS regime will be subject to change, as new legislation is proposed to meet the compliance requirements of the AIFMD. ICISs would then become subject to regulation by the Cyprus Securities and Exchange Commission, and they would have the option of either maintaining their existing structure subject to compliance with the new regulatory regime or adapting their structure so that they can expand their investor base.

7.8.4   Stock exchange

The Cyprus Stock Exchange (CSE) commenced operations in 1996. A number of markets operate within the CSE (e.g. Main Market, Parallel Market, Investment Companies Market, etc.) and different listing requirements apply to each market. Restrictions apply in all markets in relation to the free float and the shares controlled directly or indirectly by any one shareholder, which ensures that the interests of small shareholders are protected. On the Main Market, for instance, no shareholder is allowed to control, either directly or indirectly, more than 75% of the share capital and at least 25% of the share capital must be satisfactorily dispersed to the public at large.[32] In addition, there are requirements in respect of transparency and disclosure of information in relation to important decisions by listed companies and at least semi-annual accounts must be published.

7.8.5   Taxation

Cyprus-resident funds are subject to a tax rate of 12.5% in respect of net taxable income (including income derived from interest), which is one of the lowest tax rates in the EU. Income in the form of distributions received from investments in funds and shares held either directly or via special purposes vehicles is exempt from taxation. There is a 20% CGT due on the disposal of immovable property located in Cyprus and also in respect of gains made from the disposal of titles in unlisted companies which own such property.

7.9   GIBRALTAR

7.9.1   Background

Gibraltar is within the EU but not within the Eurozone. The currency is the Gibraltar pound which has parity with GBP. Gibraltar is a British Overseas Territory and is responsible for its own governance, except in relation to defence, foreign affairs and internal security, which are the responsibility of the British appointed governor, subject – in the case of foreign affairs – to consultation with the Chief Minister of Gibraltar. Gibraltar has a democratically elected parliament. The Gibraltar legal system is based on that of England and Wales and English common law and rules of equity are highly persuasive. As a member of the EU, Gibraltar is also subject to European law.

---

[32] Regulation 3.2.1(b) of the Regulatory Decision of the Council of the CSE on the Stock Exchange Markets (No 326/2009 as amended)

7.9.2   Common structures

The following are the most common structures for setting up Gibraltar alternative investment funds.

(a) Companies

Companies are regulated by the Companies Act 1930. This Act has, however, been subject to various amendments to update the law and to meet the demands of EU legislation. Companies are commonly the vehicle of choice for both private funds and experienced investor funds (G-EIFs) (see below). If a company is authorized as a G-EIF it must have two authorized directors. Corporate funds trading as private companies are able to make offers to the public.

(b) Protected cell companies

Protected cell companies enable the statutory segregation of assets and liabilities into different cells, each of which is ring-fenced from liabilities attaching to the other cells. A PCC is a single legal entity comprising a 'core' and a number of cells. There is no limit to the number of cells that may be created. PCCs are popular and cost-effective structures for umbrella funds, many of which are established as G-EIFs. PCCs are governed by the Protected Cell Companies Act 2001.

(c) Limited partnerships

Gibraltar limited partnerships are governed by the Limited Partnerships Act 1927 and are generally subject to similar rules of equity and common law applicable to partnerships in England. However, unlike English limited partnerships, a Gibraltar limited partnership has a separate legal personality, which makes it an ideal structure for a carried interest vehicle (similar to a Scottish limited partnership). A Gibraltar limited partnership can therefore enter into contracts and hold property in its own name, and most tax authorities, including the UK, accept them as tax transparent. If a limited partnership is authorized as a G-EIF, the general partner must either be, or be controlled by, a corporate entity which has two authorized Gibraltar directors.

(d) Unit trusts

Gibraltar unit trusts are created by a trust deed between the trustee and the manager and are governed by the general principles of trust law. A unit trust does not have a separate legal personality and can take advantage of tax transparency. If a unit trust is authorized as a G-EIF it must have either a corporate trustee with two directors who are authorized Gibraltar directors, or two individual trustees who are authorized in Gibraltar to act in that capacity.

7.9.3   Regulation

(a) Private funds

The Financial Services (Collective Investment Schemes) Regulations 2011 (CIS Regs) provide for the establishment of private funds. A private fund is a collective investment scheme that is not listed on a stock exchange, and its constitutional documents must limit the number of investors to 50. Private funds are unregulated and not subject to any licensing requirements, and they can be established using any of the fund structures mentioned above other than a PCC. There is no requirement for Gibraltar directors, or for any Gibraltar-based service providers under the CIS Regs.[33] A private fund may be self-managed by its directors, or it may appoint an external manager. A private fund must remain private for at least one year following the date of the fund's offering, after which it may be converted into a G-EIF. Private funds are not required to be registered with the Gibraltar Financial Services Commission (FSC) under the CIS Regs.

However, if a private fund is a self-managed AIF and constitutes a small AIFM, pursuant to the AIFMD the private fund will need to register with the FSC pursuant to the Gibraltar Financial Services (Alternative Investment Fund Managers) Regulations 2013 (AIFM Regs) which implement the requirements of the AIFMD into Gibraltar law. If the self-managed private fund is an AIF but does not qualify as a small AIFM it will need to comply with the AIFM Regs in full.

(b) Experienced investor funds

G-EIFs are established under the Financial Services (Experienced Investor Funds) Regulations 2012 (G-EIF Regs). Investors in a G-EIF must be confined to 'experienced investors', which includes (among others) a person whose ordinary business involves investment or advising on investments, an individual with a net worth in excess of EUR 1 million excluding the value of their principal residence and a 'professional client' as defined under MiFID. If a G-EIF is, or is managed by, a fully in-scope AIFM however, the investors will be limited to those who are, or who may be treated as, professional clients under MiFID.

There is no limit on the number of investors in a G-EIF and the fund may be formed using any of the structures described above. The investment manager or adviser may be located in any jurisdiction provided that it complies with the legal requirements of the relevant jurisdiction. A G-EIF is required to have an administrator which may be either an authorized Gibraltar administrator or a foreign administrator approved by the FSC and the Minister with responsibility for Financial Services. Open-ended G-EIFs must also have a depositary which need not be located in Gibraltar unless the fund is, or is managed by, a fully in-scope AIFM, in which case from July 2017 the depositary must be located in Gibraltar.

A feature of G-EIFs that is unique within the EU is that, once the fund meets the requirements of the G-EIF Regs, no regulatory approval is required before the fund can raise capital and commence its investment activities provided that a filing supported by a legal opinion (see below) is made with the FSC within 10 business days following the launch. The G-EIF Regs require the administrator to file certain documents within 10 business days after the fund's launch. The fund will be deemed authorized as of the launch date.

Alternatively, a G-EIF may elect to have a pre-launch registration when the requisite documents are filed with the FSC at least 10 days prior to the launch. If the FSC does not issue a notice within 10 days following the filing then the fund will be deemed to be authorized as of the launch date. This procedure permits a timely launch with no regulatory uncertainty.

---

[33] If a private fund is self-managed and constitutes a fully in-scope AIFM, or it is an AIF managed by a fully in-scope AIFM, however, it will be required to have a Gibraltar depositary from July 2017 pursuant to the AIFMD

In the context of the AIFM regime, an AIF established as a G-EIF can be launched and commence trading on the basis of the pre-authorization launch, since it will be deemed to be authorized as of the launch date under the G-EIF regime. The AIFM's marketing notification can be submitted to the home regulator on the launch date, which means that passporting can commence within 20 days.

(c) UCITS funds

The relevant EU legislation has been enacted into Gibraltar law through the Financial Services (Collective Investment Schemes) Act 2011 (the CIS Act) and the CIS Regs. A UCITS in Gibraltar may be established as an open-ended company, a unit trust or a contractual fund. A unit trust and a contractual fund are both tax transparent. The Financial Services (Collective Investment Schemes) (Corporate Restructuring) Regulations 2011 provide for the merger of UCITS and the establishment of UCITS master/feeder structures. A Gibraltar UCITS will benefit from the marketing passport which allows its units/shares to be marketed in other EU jurisdictions.

(d) Non-UCITS retail funds

The CIS Act provides for the establishment of a non-UCITS retail fund, which can be marketed to the public.

7.9.4   Stock exchange

There is currently no stock exchange in Gibraltar, although an application has been lodged for the establishment of such a firm.

7.9.5   Taxation

A fund can apply to the Commissioner of Income Tax for a certificate confirming that the fund will be exempt from income tax in Gibraltar.

In Gibraltar there is no capital gains tax or withholding tax, and no tax on interest or investment income. In addition, there is no taxation on dividends and interest paid by a Gibraltar fund to a non-resident investor. Gibraltar operates a territorial basis of taxation and income tax is payable only on income which accrues in or is derived from Gibraltar.

Since many Gibraltar funds are fully taxable entities (despite the fact that their Gibraltar tax liability is minimal as they typically derive no income from activities in Gibraltar) they are able to take advantage of the EU Parent & Subsidiary Directive[34] which allows dividends to be paid by a subsidiary of the fund in many other EU member states to a Gibraltar parent company without the imposition of withholding taxes. This ability provides excellent opportunities for private equity and property funds established in Gibraltar to set up tax efficient EU structures with subsidiaries in other EU member states.

---

[34] Directive 90/435/EEC

(C)   REST OF EUROPE

7.10   THE NETHERLANDS

7.10.1 Background

The Netherlands is a member state of the EU and a constituent country of the Kingdom of the Netherlands. Geographically, it is bordered by both Belgium and Germany. The Netherlands is a constitutional monarchy with King Willem-Alexander as the head of state. The monarch's role is limited under the country's constitution. The Netherlands is a civil law jurisdiction whereby the laws of the country are set out in written codes (the opposite being a common law jurisdiction whereby legal precedents are set by previous judicial decisions).

7.10.2 Common structures

The following are examples of the most common structures for Netherlands-based investment funds.

(a) Limited liability company

The two types of limited liability company in the Netherlands are the 'naamloze vennootschap' (NV) and the 'besloten vennootschap met beperkte aansprakelijkheid' (BV). The former is a public limited company and the latter is a private limited company. Most limited liability companies are incorporated as a BV, and should a decision be made to list the company on NYSE Euronext, it may subsequently be converted into an NV.

(b) Cooperative (coop)

A cooperative (coop) is a legal entity which shares some characteristics with a partnership in that it has no minimum capital requirements. All distributions may be made exempt from withholding tax.

(c) Limited partnership

A 'commanditaire vennootschap' (CV) is a contractual arrangement between one or more limited partners and at least one general partner undertaking in activities with a view to a profit. The general partner will usually be a management company, while investors are usually the limited partners. The general partner has unlimited liability to the CV while the investors are liable only to the extent of their investment in the CV.

(d) Fund for joint account

A unique and popular fund vehicle in the Netherlands for the structuring of an investment fund is through a 'fonds voor gemene rekening' (FGR). It does not have the status of a legal entity; rather it is created by a contractual agreement, generally between the fund manager, the investors and a depositary. The fund manager must, under the contractual agreement, invest and manage the assets of the joint account, with the depositary holding the legal ownership of the assets.

7.10.3 Regulation

(a) Undertakings in collective investments in transferable securities

The Netherlands incorporated the European UCITS IV Directive of 2009 to its domestic legislation under the Financial Supervision Act. Funds which fulfil the criteria set down under the directive obtain a European passport and are thereby permitted to market the fund in other EU member states. A UCITS fund will, however, be required to comply with certain Dutch regulations when marketing to Dutch investors.

(b) Non-UCITS funds

The Netherlands implemented the provisions of the AIFMD (see Chapter 12, section 12.6) by the deadline of 22 July 2013. Managers of funds which do not qualify under the UCITS regime require a licence to market funds in the Netherlands although managers may be able to make use of exemptions or the lighter regulatory regime. The compliance requirements for obtaining a licence include regulatory minimum capital, organization and conduct of business principles. There are also ongoing requirements relating to conflicts of interest, leverage, delegation, depositaries, risk management, remuneration and others.

A manager of a fund established in Guernsey, Jersey or the United States (if, for the US-established fund, it is regulated by the SEC), and which is adequately supervised in that country, may market the fund in the Netherlands without a licence, including to non-qualified investors. The fund managers need to comply with certain information disclosure requirements.

7.10.4 Stock exchange

The Amsterdam Stock Exchange is believed to be the world's oldest stock exchange, having been established in 1602. It merged in 2000 with the Brussels Stock Exchange and the Paris Bourse to form the Euronext N.V., which subsequently merged with NYSE Group, Inc. to form NYSE Euronext, an international exchange operator representing one-third of the equities trading worldwide. Its activities include setting common market rules, reviewing applications for listings and publishing information relating to market trading and prices.

7.10.5 Taxation

NVs and BVs are both subject to corporation tax, with the amount payable dependent upon the taxable amount which is calculated by deducting losses from profits. If the company's taxable amount is less than EUR 200,000 the tax rate is 20%. If the taxable amount is EUR 200,000 or more the tax rate is 25%.[35] In relation to a CV and an FGR, any income is apportioned to the investors as though they had invested in the assets themselves. Therefore the CV and the FGR are not subject to income or withholding tax, provided that several conditions with respect to the transfer of participations are fulfilled.

---

[35] Government of the Netherlands website: http://www.government.nl/issues/taxation/corporation-tax: last accessed 28 November 2012

7.11 SWITZERLAND

7.11.1 Background

Switzerland (or the Swiss Confederation) is a landlocked federal parliamentary republic in Central Europe. Switzerland has a long history of armed neutrality. The historic confederation was largely superseded by the constitution of 1848 (amended in 1874) which established the modern federal state consisting of 26 cantons. The legal system is a civil law structure where the judiciary has the authority to review legislative acts. Switzerland's economy is led by the financial services sector, life sciences and high tech manufacturing and although it is not a member of the EU, a large part of its economic activities and regulations is integrated with those of the EU.

7.11.2 Common structures

(a) Open-ended funds

A large amount of assets are held in open-ended funds which are registered in Switzerland. As of 2011, over CHF 615 billion of assets were held, with CHF 439 billion representing the holdings of institutional (or 'qualified') investors and the remaining CHF 176 billion is that of retail investors. In 2011 only 1412 of 7501 registered schemes were domiciled in Switzerland, with the remainder largely Luxembourg or Ireland domiciled as a UCITS scheme. Those which are domiciled in Switzerland are structured as either a contractual fund (equivalent to an FCP) or an investment company with variable capital (ICVC) (equivalent to a SICAV). These structures are largely similar to those described for Luxembourg (see section 7.6.2 of this chapter).

(b) Closed-ended funds

Swiss closed-ended retail funds which can be structured as an equivalent to a French SICAF may only be offered to investors (if they are not listed) with authorization from the Swiss Financial Market Supervisory Authority (FINMA). Alternatively a closed-ended retail fund can be listed on SIX Swiss Exchange as a share company and avoid regulation by FINMA. Another alternative is to structure non-retail closed-ended funds as a limited partnership for collective investment under the Collective Investment Schemes Act but so far only a few funds have been established as such.

7.11.3 Regulation

Both open-ended and closed-ended retail funds are regulated by the Collective Investment Schemes Act, whether local or foreign domiciled. The Act sets out the principles and framework onto which detailed regulation is built. All local funds are required to obtain authorization from FINMA but foreign funds will require it only where interests are publicly offered and distributed in or from Switzerland. Any party managing a local fund, whether open-ended or closed-ended, must be authorized by FINMA and so must any custodian of the fund's assets. A foreign fund can only be offered to the public in Switzerland where a Swiss-licensed representative has been appointed, with a Swiss bank as paying agent in Switzerland and where the fund has received documentary approval from FINMA. Only funds which are domiciled in the US, the EEA, or Jersey and Guernsey have so far been approved in line with the requirement that they are subject to adequate prudential supervision in their home domicile. Foreign funds must meet equivalent regulatory standards for matters such as the rights of investors and the funds in domiciles such as the above are the only ones which currently meet that standard and so such funds benefit from an easier (but not guaranteed) approval process.

7.11.4 Stock exchange

The SIX Swiss Exchange is the primary stock exchange in Switzerland. It was founded from the merger in 2008 of the SWX Group (based in Zurich), the Telekurs Group and the SIS Group. A national regulatory framework was set up by the Stock Exchanges and Securities Trading Act of 1995 under which three implementing ordinances have been passed at the federal level. Local exchanges have their own regulations and rules which are compliant with the more senior rules. SIX Swiss Exchange rules govern admissions of securities to trading, organization of trading, clearing and settlement and oversight and monitoring.

7.11.5 Taxation

An open-ended fund or a closed-ended fund, which is not structured as a SICAF, is not subject to corporate income tax. Such funds do pay a reduced rate of corporation tax from real estate income, but that is the exception. A SICAF typically pays corporation tax at a rate of between 12% and 22%. All funds are subject to 'capital tax' levied by the individual canton in which they are based (which is a tax on the equity or the liabilities which function as equity of a corporate body).

(D)   CARIBBEAN AND ATLANTIC
7.12   THE CAYMAN ISLANDS

7.12.1 Background

The Cayman Islands comprise a territory located in the western Caribbean Sea consisting of three islands: Grand Cayman, Cayman Brac and Little Cayman. The largest of the islands is Grand Cayman which has an area of only 76 square miles. The first documented recording of Cayman Brac and Little Cayman was by Christopher Columbus on his fourth voyage to what is now known as Central America. Being inhabited by many tortoises, the islands were known as 'Las Tortugas'. The Cayman Islands are a parliamentary democracy, having a judiciary, executive and elected legislature. They are a British Overseas Territory, and the governor (who presides over the executive and appoints members of the judiciary) is appointed by the British monarch. Unsurprisingly the legal system of the islands is based on English common law, with the Privy Council in London being the final court of appeal. It is estimated that at least 80% of the world's hedge funds are domiciled in Cayman.

7.12.2 Common structures

There are a number of common investment fund structures which are used in the Cayman Islands.

(a) Exempted company

Under the Companies Law (as revised) of the Cayman Islands, an exempted company is one whose business is mainly carried on outside of the Cayman Islands. Distinct features include that the names of the shareholders of an exempt company are not public and cannot be registered at the Registrar of Companies, there need only be one shareholder, and the requirements to file annual reports are minimal. All exempted companies must have a registered office in the Cayman Islands.

(b) Exempted limited partnership

Limited partnerships of offshore business can be formed in the Cayman Islands in the same way as companies. An exempted limited partnership must be formed with one or more general partners who will be liable for all the debts and obligations of the partnership, and the general partner(s) must be a Cayman person (company, partnership or individual) or registered in Cayman as an overseas company or partnership. Investors are admitted as limited partners and are given statutory protection with regard to the debts of the fund. As with exempted companies, an exempted limited partnership must have a registered office in the Cayman Islands.

(c) Exempted unit trust

A unit trust may also be used as a fund vehicle and may register for offshore business in the same manner as an exempted company and an exempted limited partnership, through registration with the Registrar of Trusts.

7.12.3 Regulation

Closed-ended funds are not subject to regulation. Open-ended funds may be regulated under the Mutual Funds Law unless they fall within the definition of an 'exempted' fund. The Mutual Funds Law defines a mutual fund as:

> 'a company, unit trust or partnership that issues equity interests, the purpose or effect of which is the pooling of investor funds with the aim of spreading investment risks and enabling investors in the mutual fund to receive profits or gains from the acquisition, holding, management or disposal of investments'.[36]

There are three types of regulation for open-ended funds under the Mutual Funds Law.

(a) Registered mutual funds

These are funds which require a minimum initial subscription of USD 100,000 per investor, or whose equity interests have been listed on a Cayman recognized stock exchange. Registration for such a fund is straightforward and quick and CIMA does not have to approve the offering document.

---

[36] Mutual Funds Law (2009 Revision); Part I Introductory; para 2

(b) Licensed mutual funds

A mutual fund may apply to CIMA for a licence. There is no minimum investment requirement. This type of fund is attractive to reputable institutions aiming to launch a fund in cases where the manager does not intend to appoint a Cayman-based administrator.

(c) Administered mutual fund

Funds may, as an alternative, appoint a Cayman Islands licensed fund administrator to provide the fund's principal office. In this case, the fund does not have to separately apply for a mutual fund licence.

Registered, licensed or administered funds must, before the fund is offered to investors, file with CIMA a current offering document, which describes the equity interests of the fund in all material respects, and contains any other relevant information necessary to allow a prospective investor to make an informed decision as to whether or not to invest.

The following are further points relating to Cayman Islands funds:

- master funds must register with CIMA if their feeder fund(s) is obliged to register. This is the case even if there is only one feeder fund
- closed-ended funds are not subject to specific regulation under the Mutual Funds Law
- funds with fewer than 15 investors (the majority in number of whom have the power to appoint/remove the operators of the fund) do not fall to be regulated under the Mutual Funds Law, and are treated as 'exempted'. The 'operators of a fund' are the directors in the case of a company, the general partner in the case of an exempted limited partnership and the trustee in the case of a unit trust
- investment managers and investment advisers will be regulated under the Securities Investment Business Law (as revised) and must apply for either a licence or for exemption from licensing.

7.12.4 Stock exchange

The Cayman Stock Exchange (CSX) was established under the Cayman Islands Stock Exchange Company Law 1996. The CSX is regulated by the Stock Exchange Authority, which is chaired by the Financial Secretary of the Cayman Islands government. In 2004 the CSX was granted, by HMRC, the status of a 'recognised stock exchange' under s. 841 of the Income and Corporation Taxes Act 1988. The following securities may be listed on the CSX: mutual funds, specialist debt securities, Eurobonds, derivative warrants and depositary receipts. There are applicable rules in respect of each of the securities. A mutual fund seeking a listing must appoint a listing agent, approved by the CSX, to assist with the application for listing, as must a company applying to list its own shares. All other applicants for a listing do not have to appoint a listing agent, but may do so. The documentation to accompany the application for listing includes a listing document, though there is no restriction upon the documents the Stock Exchange Authority may request from the applicant.

7.12.5 Taxation

There is no income tax, corporation tax or CGT, estate duty, inheritance tax, gift tax or with-holding tax in the Cayman Islands. The Cayman Islands are not party to a double taxation treaty with any country. Nominal amounts of stamp duty may apply to documents executed in or brought into the Cayman Islands (but significant stamp duty does apply to transfers of interests in real estate in the Cayman Islands).

A corporate fund may apply to the Governor-in-Cabinet of the Cayman Islands for an undertaking that, in accordance with section 6 of the Tax Concessions Law (as revised) of the Cayman Islands, for a period of 20 years from the date of the undertaking, no law which is enacted in the Cayman Islands imposing any tax to be levied on profits, income, gains or appreciations shall apply to the fund or its operations and, in addition, that no tax to be levied on profits, income, gains or appreciations or which is in the nature of estate duty or inheritance tax shall be payable. Partnerships and trusts may also apply for an undertaking in similar terms, although the period of such undertaking is for a longer maximum period (being 50 years).

7.13   THE BRITISH VIRGIN ISLANDS

7.13.1 Background

The BVI consists of 60 islands based in the Caribbean, having a land area of 150 square kilo-metres. The BVI is a self-governing colony, although the British Crown remains responsible for appointment of the governor, who in turn oversees defence, internal security, and courts and finance among other matters. The BVI is a parliamentary representative democracy, and the governor also exercises executive power on behalf of the British monarch, while the leg-islative chamber comprises 15 members in total, made up of 13 elected representative mem-bers, the Attorney General and a Speaker. The judicial system is based on English common law, and there is a final right of appeal to the Privy Council in London. The BVI-FSC is the financial regulator within the BVI and regulates those funds either registered or recognized under the Securities and Investment Business Act (SIBA).

7.13.2 Common structures

The majority of hedge funds domiciled in the BVI are incorporated as BVI business com-panies under the BVI Business Companies Act 2004, although it is also possible to use an alternative vehicle such as a partnership or unit trust.

(a) BVI Business Company

A BVI Business Company will most commonly be structured to issue redeemable shares. The number of shares which can be issued and the attributes of such shares, including the rights attaching thereto, will be governed by the company's Memorandum of Association and Articles of Association which are filed with the Registrar of Corporate Affairs upon in-corporation. These documents will also set out whether the shares are redeemable and if so, redeemable shares will be offered and issued on specified periods with the option to redeem also set at regular intervals. A BVI Business Company must have at least one member and, as noted above, mutual funds must have at least two directors. While a public fund must have directors who are individuals, a professional or private fund will be permitted to have corporate directors provided that it has at least one individual director.

(b) International Limited Partnership

The formation of a BVI partnership is governed under the Partnership Act 1996 (the PA). However the operational affairs of the partnership will be determined by the partnership agreement, save that where the agreement is silent on a matter covered by the PA, the provisions of the PA will apply. It is important to note that an International Limited Partnership cannot carry on business with BVI residents. At least two partners are required to form a partnership, one of whom in a limited partnership must be a general partner who will be liable for the debts of the partnership. The other partners will usually be limited partners, and their liability will be limited to the amount of their committed capital.

(c) Unit trust

Under a BVI unit trust a trust deed will be entered into between the trustee and often a fund manager. The trust assets are held by the trustee for the benefit of beneficiaries. The trust deed will divide the beneficial ownership of the unit trust into shares (known as units) which are often freely transferable and redeemable. Quite often the trustee will be a trust company and it is necessary for the same to be licensed under the Banks and Trust Companies Act 1990. The fund manager will usually be granted the express power under the trust deed to manage the trust's day to day operations.

7.13.3 Regulation

As set out above, SIBA requires that any investment fund which falls under its definition of a 'mutual fund' or 'fund' be recognized by or registered with the BVI-FSC. Mutual fund or fund is defined in SIBA as 'a company or any other body, a partnership or a unit trust that is incorporated, formed or organised, whether under the laws of the Virgin Islands or the laws of any other country, which (a) collects and pools investor funds for the purpose of collective investment, and (b) issues fund interests that entitle the holder to receive on demand or within a specified period after demand an amount computed by reference to the value of a proportionate interest in the whole or in a part of the net assets of the company or other body, partnership or unit trust, as the case may be'. The definition extends to open-ended funds but does not extend to closed-ended funds.

SIBA also requires that any person who carries on an 'investment business' within the Virgin Islands must hold a licence authorizing them to carry on such a business. Investment managers and advisers are within the ambit of this definition.

7.13.4 Taxation

Funds which are established in the BVI are exempt from BVI income tax, as are those persons and entities that perform functions on behalf of the fund.

7.14   BERMUDA

7.14.1 Background

Bermuda is a group of 181 islands with a combined area of 53.3 square kilometres located in the Atlantic Ocean to the north of the Caribbean. It is a self-governing Overseas Territory, with a governor appointed by the British Crown. Bermuda has a bicameral legislature consisting of the House of Assembly with 36 elected members and the Senate with 11 members selected by the Governor. The head of the democratically elected government is given the title of Premier and the country operates under a judicial system derived from English common law, with final right of appeal to the Privy Council in London. Open-ended investment funds are regulated by the Bermuda Monetary Authority (BMA), with most forms of these funds, unless exempted, being subject to the Investment Funds Act 2006 (IF Act).

7.14.2 Common structures

The IF Act deals with the three most common investment fund types in Bermuda.

(a) Limited partnerships

The Limited Partnership Act 1883 defines a limited partnership as consisting of one or more general partners authorized to transact business with the use of funds provided by one or more limited partners. A limited partnership must meet the conditions of the Limited Partnership Act 1883 as well as the Partnership Act 1902. As most limited partnerships in Bermuda are closed-ended, they fall outside of the ambit of the IF Act. They are fiscally transparent and may elect to assume a legal personality. The liability of the limited partners is restricted to the amount that each has agreed to contribute, provided that they do not take part in the general partner's management of the partnership, as participation in the management of the partnership will undermine this limitation on liability. The minimum capital investment for a limited partnership is USD 1.00 (or a fraction thereof).

(b) Mutual fund companies

A mutual fund is defined by the Companies Act 1981 as 'a company limited by shares, or other company having a share capital and incorporated for the purpose of investing the money of its members for their mutual benefit and having the power to redeem for purchase or purchase for cancellation its shares without reducing its authorized share capital and stating in its memorandum that it is a mutual fund'. A mutual fund will usually issue both manager shares without participation rights and investor shares with participating rights. Both classes of shares are subject to the provisions of the Companies Act 1981, with the investor shares being eligible for redemption at a price based on the fund's then current net asset value per share. They may later be reissued to new subscribers. There is no minimum share capital requirement for a mutual fund company in Bermuda.

(c) Unit trusts

A unit trust is similar to a mutual fund company, but it is not a company or separate entity. A unit trust is a contractual agreement embodied in a trust deed or instrument. It is a declaration of trust that is either executed by the trustee only or entered into by the trustee and the manager. The concept of a unit trust is that investors contribute funds to the trustee to hold such funds in trust as trustee while they are managed by the manager for their benefit. Each investor is effectively a beneficial owner (and is possibly also a settlor) of a proportion of the assets held by the trustee. Practically, however, it does operate internally in many of the same ways as a company. Unit trusts that are open-ended funds are required to be authorized under the IF Act.

7.14.3 Regulation

Open-ended funds that fall within the scope of the IF Act are authorized by the BMA, and the BMA authorizes funds into three main categories.

(a) Institutional fund

Institutional funds require an officer, trustee or representative resident of Bermuda, who has access to the books and records of the investment fund. They require each investing participant to invest a minimum of USD 100,000 into the fund or be a 'qualified participant'. Someone would be classed as a 'qualified participant' if their personal income and/or net worth or investment experience are of a sufficiently high level.

(b) Administered fund

Administered fund classification is given to funds which require a minimum fund investment of USD 50,000 per participant or which are registered on a BMA recognized stock exchange. Administered funds also require an administrator licensed by the IF Act.

(c) Standard fund

This classification is given to a fund that does not fall within any other class of fund. Standard funds have a particular set of rules, called 'Fund Rules', which are applicable. They specify that unless the administrator is carrying on fund business in Bermuda, the custodian of the fund must be licensed by the BMA. The operator of the fund is responsible for retaining readily available copies of the fund's constitution and preparing financial reports containing audited financial statements.

7.14.4 Ongoing reporting

An investment fund must make provision for the preparation and distribution of an annual report to investors including copies of its audited financial statements. Financial statements and other financial information distributed to investors and financial information used in the determination of net asset value must be prepared in accordance with GAAP which may be those of a jurisdiction other than Bermuda.

Service providers to an investment fund are required to report specific matters of concern to the BMA. Where a service provider to an investment fund becomes aware that the assets of such investment fund have not been invested in accordance with the constitution or that the general management of the investment fund is not materially in accordance with the provisions of its constitution, such service provider must:

(i) immediately advise the BMA of the occurrence of any such event and the circumstances applicable thereto and

(ii) make a report in writing of such event to the investment fund's administrator.

Such report is required to be included in the investment fund's next annual report and, in addition, in its next periodic report if such next periodic report is to be distributed before the next annual report.

An authorized investment fund is required to submit to the BMA:

(i) within six months after its financial year end, a statement confirming that such investment fund has at all times during the preceding financial year been in compliance with the Act and fund and prospectus rules applicable to it, or, in the circumstances where the investment fund has not been in compliance, the statement shall specify the particulars of such non-compliance and

(ii) when required, a report on such activities of such investment fund as the BMA may reasonably require.

7.14.5 Funds outside regulation

(a) Closed-ended funds (including private equity funds) operate outside the scope of the IF Act.

(b) Private funds of less than 20 participants which do not promote to the public are excluded from authorization under the IF Act.

(c) An investment fund may apply to the BMA to be exempted from the IF Act. A fund qualifies for exemption if it is only open to 'qualified participants'; its fund administrator falls within a class of persons recognized by the BMA; it has appointed an investment manager, registrar, custodian and/or prime broker, as well as an auditor; and it has an officer, trustee or representative resident in Bermuda who has access to the books and records of the scheme.

A new class of 'registration only' investment funds is currently being considered in circumstances where a fund's investment manager is regulated by a competent regulatory authority. This is a direct result of discussions held with market participants and while the details of this are still to be finalized, this is intended to provide a significant development to Bermuda's range of fund products.

7.14.6 Segregated Accounts Companies

Bermuda mutual fund companies and other companies structured to pool investors' investments are permitted to be registered as segregated accounts companies (SACs) pursuant to the Segregated Accounts Companies Act (SACA). However, investment funds established as unit trusts or partnerships are currently not able to take advantage of this legislation. An SAC is permitted to create segregated accounts in order to segregate the assets and liabilities attributable to a particular class or series of shares of the SAC from the assets and liabilities attributable to each other class or series of shares of the SAC, and from the SAC's general assets and liabilities. Any asset or liability linked to a particular segregated account of an SAC is deemed to be held as a separate fund which is not part of the other assets of the SAC and is held exclusively for the benefit or burden of the account owners of that account and any counterparty to a transaction linked to that segregated account. SACs can therefore contract with a creditor or shareholder so that the assets injected by that person are held by the SAC in a segregated account and insulated from any claims of the creditors of other segregated accounts and of the general creditors of the company.

An SAC is required to appoint a segregated account representative (SAR) approved by the Minister of Finance. The administrator, or an appropriate person provided by the administrator or the manager, would normally be acceptable. The purpose of the SAR is to act like an internal watchdog, with the statutory duty to make a written report to the Registrar of Companies within 30 days after (a) the SAR reaching the view that there is a reasonable likelihood of a segregated account or the general account of the SAC becoming insolvent, or (b) it coming to the SAR's knowledge or his or her having reason to believe that certain failures to comply with SACA have occurred or that the SAC has become involved in any criminal proceedings in Bermuda or elsewhere.

7.14.7 Stock market

The Bermuda Stock Exchange (BSX) was established in 1971. It is a recognized member of the World Federation of Exchanges and is committed to meeting and exceeding international securities market standards. The US Securities Exchange Commission recognizes the BSX as a 'Designated Offshore Securities Exchange' and the UK Financial Services Authority recognizes the BSX as a 'Designated Investment Exchange'. BSX is the world's largest offshore securities market and offers listings for international and domestic issuers of equity, debt, depositary, receipts, insurance securitization and derivative warrants. BSX is tailored to provide for its many niche offshore funds in a number of ways, for example with the introduction of the 'mezzanine market': an access point through which development stage companies may list on the exchange without a full initial public offering.

7.14.8 Taxation

There is currently no income, corporation or profits tax, withholding tax, CGT, capital transfer tax, estate duty or inheritance tax payable by a mutual fund company, a closed-ended fund, a unit trust, a limited partnership or their shareholders, unit holders or limited partners, other than shareholders, or unit holders or limited partners ordinarily resident in Bermuda.

A mutual fund company may apply for and is likely to receive from the Minister of Finance of Bermuda under the Exempted Undertakings Tax Protection Act 1966 an assurance that, in the event of there being enacted in Bermuda any legislation imposing tax computed on profits or income, or computed on any capital assets, gain or appreciation, or any tax in the nature of estate duty or inheritance tax, such tax shall not until 31 March 2035 be applicable to such company or to any of its operations or to the shares, debentures or other obligations of such company except in so far as such tax applies to persons ordinarily resident in Bermuda and holding such shares, debentures or other obligations of the company or to any land leased or let to the company. A similar assurance may be obtained by a unit trust or a limited partnership.

(E)   ASIA

7.15   HONG KONG

7.15.1 Background

Hong Kong is located on the south coast of mainland China. It was a British colony from the mid-19th century until 1997 when sovereignty was returned to China. It is governed under what is known as the 'one country, two systems' policy, and it has a high degree of autonomy, with the exception of foreign affairs and defence, responsibility for which is retained by China. It is known as a Special Administrative Region of the Chinese state. While mainland China follows a civil law system, it is no surprise that the legal system of Hong Kong is based on the English common law.

7.15.2 Common structures

Most investment funds offered in Hong Kong are domiciled offshore, with the exception of funds established under Hong Kong's mandatory retirement schemes regulatory framework. Of the funds domiciled offshore, those which are structured as retail UCITS funds are usually domiciled in Europe (commonly Luxembourg, Ireland or the UK) and those which are hedge funds offered to professional and institutional investors are commonly domiciled in the Cayman Islands, Bermuda or the BVI.

A domestic fund structure is currently either a unit trust or a limited partnership, with the latter rarely used. In 2013, the government of Hong Kong announced it was considering regulatory changes which would allow the introduction of a domestic open-ended investment company structure – currently variable capital companies cannot be incorporated in Hong Kong.

The investment fund structures commonly offered in Hong Kong comprise the following.

(a) Unit trusts

Unit trusts are the structure of choice for domestic open-ended retail funds. A unit trust is established under deed between the trustee and the manager of the fund. The trustee holds the assets of the trust on behalf of the investors.

(b) Company

It is typical that an investment company be incorporated in one of the offshore tax neutral locations such as the Cayman Islands. Company structures can include a private limited company, a public company limited by shares and a public company limited by guarantee, in which the company will have no share capital, but the shareholders undertake to contribute to the liabilities of the company in the event of winding up.

(c) Limited partnership

A Hong Kong limited partnership is governed under the Limited Partnership Ordinance. Under section 5(1) a limited partner must not take part in the management of the partnership business, nor have the power to bind the firm, if they are to avoid liability for the debts and obligations arising in relation to the management of the firm. There must be at least one general partner whose liability in respect of the liabilities and obligations of the partnership is unlimited.

It is a requirement that a limited partnership obtains a business registration under the Business Registration Ordinance and also registers as a limited partnership with the Registrar of Companies, and the rights and obligation of the partnership are set out under the partnership agreement, in tandem with the Limited Partnership Ordinance where the partnership agreement is silent in respect of an issue.

7.15.3 Regulation

The Securities and Futures Commission (HKSFC) regulates the offering of securities in Hong Kong. The principal legislation governing the offering of securities is the Securities and Futures Ordinance (SFO), and this is supplemented by subordinate legislation and guidelines issued by the HKSFC. Retail fund offerings in Hong Kong require the authorization of the HKSFC. In the absence of such authorization, a fund may only be offered to non-retail investors by an exemption under the SFO, most notably as an offer to professional investors or by way of private placement.

Both open-ended and closed-ended funds may be listed on the Hong Kong Stock Exchange.

7.15.4 Stock exchange

The Hong Kong Stock Exchange (HKEx) was listed in June 2000. In many respects it is a commercial gateway to mainland China, but it is now more than that, fighting globally for issuers. It is still however the most popular choice for Chinese companies seeking a listing on an international market. Nearly half of the companies listed on the HKEx are from the Chinese mainland and it is the second largest stock exchange by market capitalization in Asia after the Tokyo Stock Exchange.

The Hong Kong securities and futures markets are regulated by HKSFC. Hong Kong's asset management industry is one of the largest in Asia. At the end of 2012 the combined value of the management industry was USD 1 trillion in around 1800 funds.[37] These open-ended funds cannot be structured as a company (unless domiciled offshore) and so cannot be listed unless an offshore company is used. Closed-ended funds such as REITs are also among the largest and most pioneering in Asia; the first renminbi denominated REIT in the world was listed in Hong Kong in 2011. Closed-ended funds are authorized by the HKSFC only if they are also (or will be) listed.

7.15.5 Taxation

Funds authorized by the HKSFC are exempt from Hong Kong profits tax.

Offshore funds which have not been authorized by the HKSFC may also be exempted from Hong Kong profits tax where certain conditions are met under the Revenue (Profits Tax Exemption for Offshore Funds) Ordinance. In order to qualify for the exemption, the offshore fund would, among other things, need to be able to demonstrate that its central management and control is not located or undertaken in or from Hong Kong.

---

[37] http://www.citibank.com/transactionservices/home/about_us/articles/docs/hk_luxembourg.pdf

7.16   SINGAPORE

7.16.1 Background

Singapore is situated in South-East Asia and geographically located in close proximity to emerging markets such as Indonesia and also established markets such as China. It is a sovereign republic, which has a legal system that is based on the English common law,[38] an unsurprising fact given that the country was established as a British colony by Sir Stamford Raffles in 1819. However, unlike Britain, Singapore has a written codified constitution which sets out the organization and structure of the legislative branches – the legislature, executive and judiciary. Legislation enacted must be in compliance with the Articles of the Constitution, and are void to the extent that they are non-compliant.

7.16.2 Common structures

Common Singapore structures for investment funds include both companies and limited liability partnerships.

(a) Company

Singapore companies are governed under the Singapore Companies Act, Chapter 50. Under the Act there are three types of company:

- a company limited by shares
- a company limited by guarantee
- an unlimited company.[39]

All companies must be registered or incorporated with the Accounting and Corporate Regulatory Authority (ACRA). There must be at least one member,[40] and the minimum share value must be at least Singapore Dollar (SGD) 1. At least one director of the company must be either a citizen or a permanent resident of Singapore.

(b) Limited liability partnership

A limited liability partnership combines both the advantages of a company, in that the extent of the partner's liabilities is limited, while it has the administrative advantages akin to a partnership. For legal purposes it is an entity separate from its members and can sue or be sued in its own name.

Every LLP must have at least two partners,[41] and there is no maximum number of partners. An LLP must also have at least one manager who must be a Singapore-resident individual. All limited liability partnerships must be registered with the ACRA.[42]

---

[38] Government of Singapore website: http://www.gov.sg/government/web/content/govsg/classic/about_us: last accessed 6 December 2012

[39] Companies Act, Chapter 50; part III, section 17(2)

[40] Companies Act, Chapter 50; part III, section 20A

[41] Limited Liability Partnerships Act, Chapter 163A; section 22(1)

[42] Limited Liability Partnerships Act, Chapter 163A; section 23(1)

7.16.3 Regulation

In relation to fund management companies, under the Securities and Futures Act (Cap 289) (SFA), a company carrying on fund management activities may elect to be licensed or registered. The activities carried on which require a licence as set out under the SFA include: dealing in securities, trading in futures contracts and fund management.[43] Such companies dealing in these activities either require a Capital Markets Services Licence or they must be registered with the Monetary Authority of Singapore as a registered fund management company. In relation to licensed fund management companies, a retail fund is permitted to carry on business with all types of investors, while alternative investment funds are permitted to carry on business with qualified investors only. Regulated funds may only carry on business with 30 or fewer qualified investors and the total value of the assets managed must not exceed SGD 250 million.

7.16.4 Stock exchange

Companies may be listed upon the Singapore Exchange (SGX) either on the Mainboard or the Catalist, which is aimed towards the listing of local and international growth companies. In order to list a company on the Mainboard, the IPO shares must be at least SGD 0.50 and one of the following requirements must be met:

- have a market capitalization at IPO of not less than SGD 150 million if they are profitable in the last financial year and have an operating track record of at least three years
- have a market capitalization at IPO of not less than SGD 300 million if they only have operating revenue in the latest completed financial year and
- have minimum consolidated pre-tax profit of at least SGD 30 million for the latest financial year and have an operating track record of at least three years.[44]

In relation to companies to be listed on the Catalist, such companies must be sponsored by an approved sponsor, and the decision to list will be based upon the sponsor's determination of whether or not that company is suitable to be listed. Examples of active sponsors include JP Morgan (SEA) Limited and Morgan Stanley Asia (Singapore) Pte.

7.16.5 Taxation

Generally, Singapore-resident companies are subject to a flat tax rate of 17% in respect of both income arising in Singapore and foreign income remitted to Singapore. However, the Inland Revenue Authority of Singapore can grant an exemption to the fund if it is satisfied that the fund is a designated unit trust, and it will be therefore be granted favourable tax treatment. Such treatment includes that gains or profits from Singapore or foreign sources on the disposal of securities will not be taxed.

---

[43] Securities and Futures Act (Cap 289), Second Schedule, Part I
[44] SGX Singapore Exchange website: http://www.sgx.com/wps/portal/sgxweb/home/listings: last accessed 28 November 2012

7.17   DUBAI

7.17.1 Background

Dubai is one of the constituent emirates of the United Arab Emirates (UAE), situated on the south-eastern coastline of the Persian Gulf. It is the largest emirate by population and the second largest by area. The UAE is a federation of seven emirates, each with its own ruler. Despite its history as a British protectorate, the UAE is a civil law jurisdiction. Under the constitution of the UAE, legislation is enacted at both the federal level and in the individual emirates. Dubai has experienced rapid economic growth in recent years, driven primarily by tourism and real estate development. The economy has diversified into financial services and there is a growing commercial sector, acting as a bridge to the Middle East, Asia and Africa.

7.17.2 Common structures

Sponsors seeking to establish a mutual fund (otherwise known as an investment fund) in Dubai must do so by the incorporation of a company under the UAE Commercial Companies Law, and by obtaining a licence for establishment or by obtaining approval of the promotion within the UAE of a foreign mutual fund.[45] Such a company must, by its constitution, be established solely for the purpose of raising and operating mutual funds, and any activities associated with that purpose.

7.17.3 Regulation

Under the Investment Funds Regulation, the licensing and marketing of funds (whether domestic or foreign) is overseen by the UAE Securities and Commodities Authority (UAE-SCA).[46] Domestic funds are subject to the regulation of the UAE-SCA, and a fund can only be established with its approval. Foreign funds must be marketed through a locally registered placement agent.

In the UAE, only UAE joint stock companies or a UAE branch of a foreign company may establish an investment fund. The sponsor company must hold a minimum capital of UAE dirham 10 million,[47] and the sponsor must contribute at least 3% of the capital of each local fund that it establishes and operates. If the fund is an open-ended fund or a publicly traded closed-ended fund, the maximum contribution of the sponsor or any affiliates of the sponsor is 49% of the fund's capital.[48]

Funds are licensed by the UAE-SCA following receipt of an application form and the documents required by the form or any further documentation required by the UAE-SCA.[49] The UAE-SCA must inform the applicant of its decision within 30 business days of the completion of the application.[50]

Funds which are established within a free zone within the UAE are treated as foreign funds and so are regulated accordingly.[51]

---

[45] Article 4(1) of Board Decision No (37) of 2012 of the SCA, 'the Decision'
[46] Article 3 of the Decision
[47] Article 4(2) of the Decision
[48] Article 4(4) of the Decision
[49] Article 5(1) of the Decision
[50] Article 5(3) of the Decision
[51] Article 2(2) of the Decision

7.17.4 Stock exchange

There were two stock exchanges in Dubai: the Dubai Financial Market (DFM) and the NAS-DAQ Dubai. As with the funds industry in general in the UAE, the DFM is regulated by the UAE-SCA which both issues regulations and enforces them. Domestic funds must be approved by the UAE Central Bank prior to obtaining approval for listing from the DFM.

Foreign companies may list securities on either market subject to meeting standards equivalent to those of the UAE-SCA in their home country. They must demonstrate to the DFM that they are financially sound and comply with international accounting standards. Any information memorandum published by the fund or its manager must be made available in both Arabic and English. All foreign applicants with the UAE-SCA must demonstrate two financial years of audited accounts together with interim financial statements and copies of the company's constitutional documents which are attested by the home country of the company and the UAE embassy to that country.

A fund must publish its annual audited accounts within 120 days of the end of the financial year, along with semi-annual and quarterly reports published within 45 days of the end of those periods. Such reports are to be accompanied by a management report which includes details of the fund's investment activities and changes to its portfolio for that relevant period, together with the net asset value of the fund. A listed fund is also under a continuing obligation to disclose information that is likely to affect the price of its units and the decisions made by investors.

7.17.5 Taxation

There is no general corporation tax in Dubai or the UAE as a whole. The only exception is a tax on foreign banks within the UAE, which may be relevant where such a bank sponsors or manages a fund which is listed and based within the UAE.

7.18 MAURITIUS

7.18.1 Background

Mauritius is an island based in the Indian Ocean, off the coast of the African continent. Famed for being home to the now-extinct dodo, the country has become a popular destination for funds, particularly with the growth of investments in Sub Saharan Africa and Asia in the last few years. In addition to a wide network of double taxation agreements, Mauritius offers to prospective investors a whole range of advantages such as its proximity to Africa and Asia and its convenient time zone which enables it to conduct business with Asia in the morning, Europe in the afternoon and the US at closing. The attractiveness of Mauritius is further consolidated by a solid reputation as a well-regulated financial centre with a sound judicial system.

7.18.2 Common structures

Investment funds in Mauritius may be structured as collective investment schemes or closed-end funds. Those involved in global business, that is, those funds whose business is conducted principally outside Mauritius, may be set up as a Category 1 global business company (GBC1) or as a limited partnership.

Both the GBC1 and the limited partnership will normally be resident in Mauritius for tax purposes. Accordingly, their management and control will have to be effected from Mauritius to enable them to benefit from the advantages of the Mauritius network of double taxation agreements.

7.18.3 Regulation

Mauritius-based investment funds are governed by the Securities Act 2005 and a number of rules and regulations under the aforesaid Act. The Financial Services Commission (MFSC) regulates the compliance of investment funds with the legislative requirements.

(a) Collective investment schemes

CISs can be constituted as a company, trust, limited partnership or other such entity approved by the MFSC.

The key features of the CIS are:

- the sole purpose of the entity is the collective investment of funds in a portfolio of securities or other financial assets, real property or non-financial assets approved by the MFSC
- the operation of the entity must be based on the principle of the diversification of risk
- the investors must be entitled to redeem their interests and
- the investors do not have day to day control over the operations of the entity.

CISs operate within one of five main categories below:

(i) the fully regulated CISs which are mainly retail funds offered to the public. Those funds have to comply with full disclosure requirements and do not benefit from certain exemptions which are available to other types of funds
(ii) the regulated global CIS which hold a Category 1 Global Business Licence and may or may not be regulated in another jurisdiction
(iii) the professional CISs which are CISs that offer their shares to sophisticated investors or as a private placement
(iv) the specialized CISs which are CISs that invest in real estate, derivatives, commodities or other products authorized by the MFSC or
(v) the expert fund, which is open to expert investors only. Expert investors are, for the purposes of Mauritius law, investors who make a minimum initial investment for their own account in an amount of not less than USD 100,000 or sophisticated investors.

(b) Closed-ended funds

The Mauritius closed-ended fund (MCEF) is an arrangement or scheme, other than a CIS, constituted in such legal form as approved by the MFSC, whose object is to invest funds collected either from subscribers during an offering to the public, or from sophisticated investors in securities, financial or non-financial assets, or real property. An MCEF may be listed on the Mauritius Stock Exchange and its investors are allowed to freely buy and sell their shares on the market.

The distinguishing feature of the MCEF from the CIS is that an investor in an MCEF is not entitled to redeem its investment.

7.18.4 Stock exchange

Mauritius funds, including domestic funds and funds holding a global business licence, can be listed on the Stock Exchange of Mauritius (SEM). The SEM has attracted a significant number of wealthy and sophisticated investors since its acknowledgement by (among others) HMRC as a 'recognized stock exchange' as UK pension schemes, for example, are now allowed to hold securities traded on the SEM.

7.18.5 Taxation

Funds incorporated in Mauritius are subject to a flat corporate income tax rate of 15% in respect of business income. However, an entity holding a global business licence is entitled to a deemed foreign tax credit of 80%, so that the effective tax rate in Mauritius on the fund's chargeable income would be 3%.

7.19   SOME CONCLUSIONS

This chapter has provided an overview of jurisdictions typically regarded as offshore. These jurisdictions benefit from a form of momentum following each country's decision to 'invest' in upgrading their legal and tax climate to facilitate capital inflows and asset management. In addition, many of these jurisdictions have built up significant administrative and financial infrastructure to facilitate funds. However, in my view, this distinction is becoming increasingly irrelevant as onshore jurisdictions implement reforms which break down these lines. There are notable exceptions, such as the implementation of AIFMD (see Chapter 12, section 12.6 for more detail), where onshore regulation has toughened up following the financial crisis. Some offshore jurisdictions will maintain one advantage: those which can offer a gateway to a particular market or region, such as Hong Kong, Singapore, Dubai or Mauritius.

8

Principal 'Onshore' Fund Locations

8.1 INTRODUCTION

Following on from Chapter 7, this chapter addresses the incorporation of investment funds in a number of the principal onshore fund locations. The term 'onshore' has been traditionally used to refer to a reputable jurisdiction under which funds will comply with stringent legal and regulatory requirements; however, as previously discussed in Chapter 7, I believe that the distinction between onshore and offshore jurisdictions is becoming redundant, as there are numerous examples of onshore jurisdictions beginning to relax their own fund rules and taxation policies and offshore jurisdictions tightening governance rules. For further commentary please refer to Chapter 13, section 13.7.3.

I have included the jurisdictions in this chapter by reason that they include some of the world's largest and fastest growing economies. The jurisdictions below include the 'BRIC' nations (Brazil, Russia, India and China), a term coined by Goldman Sachs in 2001.[1] I have grouped the jurisdictions by continent, with the exception of Islamic investment funds, which are not jurisdiction-specific. I have commenced the analysis in part (A) with a review of the high gross domestic product (GDP) jurisdictions within Asia of China, Japan and India. An analysis of the Americas is provided in part (B), relating to Canada and Brazil, and I have reviewed a number of onshore European jurisdictions, being Russia, Germany and France, in part (C). I have included an analysis of investment funds within the continent of Australia in part (D). I have also included a section within this chapter relating to religious-themed investment funds by reviewing Islamic investment funds within part (E). I have included Islamic investment funds due to the breadth of jurisdictions that such funds span, and the growing popularity of the same within the investment industry.

This chapter does not include an overview of US or UK investment funds, as information relating to structures and regulation of the same are included in detail throughout the various other chapters of this book. While I recognize the growing presence of the emerging markets of Africa and South America, I have not provided summaries of the same (with the exception of Brazil), nor have I provided an analysis of Middle Eastern funds, with the exception of Sharia'a investment funds, as this book does not purport to provide a comprehensive overview of all fund locations.

---

[1] 'Building Better Global Economic BRICs', Global Economics Paper No 66; 30 November 2001

(A) ASIA

8.2 PEOPLE'S REPUBLIC OF CHINA

8.2.1 Background

The People's Republic of China is situated in East Asia, and it is the world's largest country by population, numbered at approximately 1.3 billion,[2] and is also one of the world's largest countries by land area. The People's Republic of China was founded in 1949, and has been ruled by the Communist Party of China (CPC) since then. The famous Chinese leader Mao Zedong was the Chairman of the CPC for 33 years until his death in 1976. The role of Chairman has now been superseded by a General Secretary of the Central Committee, and the current incumbent is Xi Jinping, being the present highest ranking official of the CPC. Under Article 1 of the Constitution of the People's Republic of China (the constitution), the country is to be governed as 'a socialist state under the people's democratic dictatorship'.[3] The CPC's position as the leader of the country is set out under the Constitution. The Chinese legal system is based on a form of civil law, with the Constitution setting out the rights and also duties of the citizens of China. However, unlike in many western European systems, there is no separation of powers between the judiciary and the other branches of government.

8.2.2 Common structures

The most popular structures for investment funds in China include the following.

(a) Wholly foreign owned enterprise (WFOE)

A WFOE may be structured as a company limited by shares or a partnership, but it will most commonly take the form of a limited liability company. WFOEs structured as limited liability companies are limited to having 50 investors and the liability of investors is limited to the amount of their respective registered capital, as WFOEs do not issue shares. An advantage of a WFOE is that control of the structure may remain with the investors, in addition to all of the investment profits. There are however certain areas of business in which such an investment vehicle may not invest, and the lack of a Chinese partner may prove a hindrance to tapping into an essentially unknown market. Registration of a WFOE may be made at provincial level (e.g. Shanghai Municipality, or Beijing Municipality) where for example the WFOE has total investments of less than USD 300 million in an encouraged industry or in a permitted industry as set out under the Catalogue Guiding Foreign Investments. However, if the proposed total investments exceed USD 300 million or exceed a certain investment scope, then an application at a central level must be made.

(b) Equity joint venture (EJV)

An EJV is structured generally as a limited liability company with at least one foreign investor and at least one Chinese-resident investor holding joint ownership of the same. The

---

[2] United Nations Statistics Division: 'Population, latest available census and estimates, latest available data': last accessed 14 January 2013

[3] Constitution of the People's Republic of China; accessed from http://english.people.com.cn/constitution/constitution.html on 11 January 2013

proportion of the registered share capital held by foreign investors is generally 25% or above, though investments of less than 25% may still be authorized by the Ministry of Commerce. The profits and losses of the company are shared between the investors as per their respective capital contributions. An EJV has a distinct advantage over a WFOE as the Chinese investors in an EJV may assist in providing insights into the Chinese market and may also be able to assist in attaining an exit of the fund. Another advantage of an EJV is that it is the only structure that may be used to invest in a number of industries, which are restricted to a fund being at least 50% owned by Chinese investors, such as telecommunication[4] and life insurance companies.[5]

(c) Cooperative joint venture (CJV)

A CJV is similar to an EJV in that it consists of both foreign and Chinese-resident investors. However, unlike an EJV it is not required to be a separate legal entity and it may be either incorporated or unincorporated. In an incorporated CJV the liability of investors is limited to their capital contribution, while the investors in an unincorporated CJV have unlimited liability. In relation to an EJV, while the profits and losses are shared between the investors as per their respective capital contributions, under a CJV the same may be divided according to negotiated terms between the parties.

(d) Foreign investment company limited by shares (FICLS)

An FICLS is structured as an incorporated company and its members' liability is limited by shares. To be incorporated, a minimum share capital of Chinese yuan (CNY) 30 million divided into equal shares is required,[6] and foreign investors must hold at least 25% of the share capital. An FICLS requires a minimum of two promoters, with half of the promoters required to be Chinese resident and at least one foreign. As an FICLS has a share capital it may list upon the Shenzhen Stock Exchange (SZSE) or the Shanghai Stock Exchange (SSE), or alternatively may list upon a foreign stock exchange. An FICLS may also issue shares to the public.

(e) Chinese holding company (CHC)

A CHC shall be a limited liability company and may be structured as an EJV or a WFOE, and its purpose is usually to invest in other foreign invested enterprises (FIEs). The minimum share capital of a CHC is USD 30 million. To establish a CHC both the foreign and Chinese investors must be of good financial standing, and in addition a foreign investor must have either:

---

[4] Catalogue of Industries for Guiding Foreign Investment (Revised 2011); Catalogue of Restricted Foreign Investment Industries; part V: Transportation, Warehouse Management, and Postal Service; No 7. In case of 'basic telecommunication', a fund being at least 51% shall be owned by Chinese investors

[5] Catalogue of Industries for Guiding Foreign Investment (Revised 2011); Catalogue of Restricted Foreign Investment Industries; part VII: Finance Industry; No 2

[6] According to Provisional Regulations on the Establishment of Foreign-Funded Joint Stock Companies Limited (1995), Article 7, the minimum share capital shall be CNY 30 million; according to Company Law of the People's Republic of China (Revised 2005), Article 81, the minimum share capital shall be CNY 5 million

- a total asset value of a minimum of USD 400 million and a record of having established one or more FIEs with total registered capital of a minimum of USD 10 million or
- have more than 10 existing Chinese-based FIEs with a total share capital of a minimum of USD 30 million.

There are certain requirements that a CHC must meet under Chinese laws including that a CHC must invest at least USD 30 million in Chinese-based FIEs and research and development.

8.2.3   Regulation

The regulatory framework in respect of Chinese funds is set out under the 'Law of the People's Republic of China on Funds for Investment in Securities' (FIS Law)[7] and a number of administrative regulations have been made pursuant to the same. The China Securities Regulatory Commission (CSRC) is responsible for the regulation of both open and closed-ended retail funds, and fund supervision is conducted by a branch of the CSRC known as the Department of Fund Supervision (DFS). The DFS has a number of responsibilities, including the following:

- examining securities investment funds, the establishment of securities investment fund management companies and supervising the business activities of the same
- reviewing the qualifications of the senior officers appointed to fund management companies
- verifying the branch established by a foreign fund management company and
- supervising the sales and the operations of investment fund management companies.

Further to requirements set out under the FIS Law, fund management companies are subject to requirements under 'The Measures for the Administration of Securities Investment Fund Management Companies', with these further requirements including that:

- the registered capital is not less than CNY 100 million[8]
- a shareholder with 5% or more of the registered share capital of the fund management company must have capital and net assets of more than CNY 100 million, and have sound corporate governance and internal monitoring rules[9]
- in relation to major shareholders with more than 25% of the registered share capital of the fund management company, major shareholders must have a registered capital of more than CNY 300 million and have a good business performance track record[10] and
- a fund management company may not be dissolved until the CSRC has cancelled its fund management qualification.[11]

---

[7] Law of the People's Republic of China on Funds for Investment in Securities (Order of the President No 9, Revised 2012)

[8] The Measures for the Administration of Securities Investment Fund Management Companies; Article 6(3)

[9] The Measures for the Administration of Securities Investment Fund Management Companies; Articles 7(1) & (2)

[10] The Measures for the Administration of Securities Investment Fund Management Companies; Articles 8(2) & (3)

[11] The Measures for the Administration of Securities Investment Fund Management Companies; Article 28

8.2.4   Stock exchange

Mainland China has two stock exchanges, the Shenzhen Stock Exchange and the Shanghai Stock Exchange.

(a) Shenzhen Stock Exchange

The SZSE was established on 1 December 1990 and is regulated by the CSRC. Within the main board of the SZSE, there are a number of other boards including the SME Board and the ChiNext market. The SME Board was established in May 2004 and its purpose is for the listing of SMEs with well-defined core business, growth potential and hi-tech contents. Companies involved in manufacturing account for 75% of all companies listed on the SME and as such the SME Board is seen as a barometer of China's manufacturing sector.[12] The ChiNext market was established in October 2009 and its purpose is the promotion and development of innovative enterprises and other growing start-ups, and is reflective of the intention to encourage entrepreneurship and also to promote innovative business models.[13]

In relation to the listing criteria for the SZSE, companies seeking to be listed upon the Main Board or the SME Board must meet certain criteria set out under the 'Securities Law of the People's Republic of China', the 'Company Law of the People's Republic of China', the 'Measures for the Administration of Initial Public Offering and Listing of Stocks'[14] and 'Rules Governing Listing of Stocks on SZSE'.[15] These include:

- that the company must have a profit of over CNY 30 million for the latest three accounting years[16]
- the total share capital before the issuance must be not less than CNY 30 million[17] and must be not less than CNY 50 million before the listing[18]
- the shares to be issued to the public must equate to 25% or more of the total company shares, though for a company with a share capital exceeding CNY 400 million, the shares issued to the public are permitted to equate to 10% or more of the total company shares
- there must be no falsification of financial reports in the most recent three reporting periods[19] and
- the company must have no uncovered losses in the latest reporting period.[20]

---

[12] Shenzhen Stock Exchange website: http://www.szse.cn/main/en/ListingatSZSE/ListingQA/: last accessed 24 July 2013

[13] Shenzhen Stock Exchange website: http://www.szse.cn/main/en/ListingatSZSE/ListingQA/: last accessed 24 July 2013

[14] Measures for the Administration of Initial Public Offering and Listing of Stocks, Order of China Securities Regulatory Commission

[15] Rules Governing Listing of Stocks on Shenzhen Stock Exchange (Revised 2012)

[16] Measures for the Administration of Initial Public Offering and Listing of Stocks, Order of China Securities Regulatory Commission (No 32); Article 33(1)

[17] Measures for the Administration of Initial Public Offering and Listing of Stocks, Order of China Securities Regulatory Commission (No 32); Article 33(3)

[18] Rules Governing Listing of Stocks on Shenzhen Stock Exchange (Revised 2012); Article 5.1.1(2)

[19] Rules Governing Listing of Stocks on Shenzhen Stock Exchange (Revised 2012); Articles 5.1.1(3) & (4)

[20] Measures for the Administration of Initial Public Offering and Listing of Stocks, Order of China Securities Regulatory Commission (No 32); Article 33(5)

In relation to listing upon the ChiNext market, a company must meet certain criteria set out under the 'Rules Governing Listing of Stocks on SZSE' and the 'Interim Measures on the Administration of Initial Public Offerings and Listings of Shares on the Chinext'. These include that the company must have been profitable in the previous two years, with profits of no less than CNY 10 million and in steady growth, or the issuer that applies for an IPO must have been profitable in the most recent year with net profits of no less than CNY 5 million and revenues of no less than CNY 50 million, and its revenue growth rate for either of the most recent two years must have been no less than 30%.

(b) Shanghai Stock Exchange

The SSE was founded and established on 26 November 1990 and is regulated by the CSRC. It is the largest stock exchange in mainland China in terms of listed companies, total market value and stock turnover.[21] In relation to listing upon the SSE, companies seeking to be listed upon the same must meet certain criteria as set out under the 'Securities Law of the People's Republic of China', the 'Company Law of the People's Republic of China', 'Measures for the Administration of Initial Public Offering and Listing of Stocks' and 'Rules Governing Listing of Stocks on SSE'.[22] The specific criteria are very similar to the criteria for the companies seeking to be listed upon the Main Board or the SME Board of the SZSE.

8.3   JAPAN

8.3.1   Background

The State of Japan is an archipelago nation in East Asia, situated in the Pacific Ocean off the coast of the continental mainland. Japan's constitution and legal system reflect a western civil law model, and Japan is one of the largest economies in the world by many measures (nominal GDP, purchasing power parity, and imports and exports). The head of state is the Emperor, who retains a ceremonial role, with executive power vested in the Prime Minister, who is drawn from the 'Diet', or parliament.

8.3.2   Common structures

Investment funds in Japan structured as investment trusts or investment corporations are formed under the Investment Trusts and Investment Corporations Act (ITICA).

(a) Investment trusts

A contract to establish an investment trust which is managed under the instruction of the settlor must be concluded between a registered financial instruments business operator acting as settlor and a trust company or an authorized financial institution engaged in trust business to act as trustee. An investment trust managed without instruction from the settlor only requires a trust company or an authorized financial institution engaged in trust business to act as the trustee but cannot primarily invest in securities. Investment trusts must disclose to the

---

[21] Shanghai Stock Exchange website: http://english.sse.com.cn/aboutsse/sseoverview/brief/: last accessed 24 July 2013

[22] Rules Governing Listing of Stocks on Shanghai Stock Exchange (Revised 2012)

Financial Services Agency of Japan (FSAJ) the terms and conditions of the trust in advance of the contract being executed. Investment trusts do not have to hold unit holder meetings and have lower running costs than investment corporations.

(b) Investment corporation

An investment corporation has a separate legal personality and cannot engage in any business other than the asset investment business. An investment corporation cannot, in principle, invest on establishment more than its equity issued at establishment which must be at least 100 million yen. The organizer of an investment corporation must carry out its duties with 'due loyalty' to the same and execute business with the 'due care of a prudent manager'. Investment corporation structures are commonly used for domestic closed-ended REITs, and their securities will usually be listed. As a corporate structure, many features such as regular shareholder meetings are carried over and provide familiarity for investors. They are more expensive to run than investment trusts and will in most circumstances attract higher rates of tax.

Both investment trusts and investment corporations are restricted in how their portfolios are structured and in their overall strategies. Borrowing and short selling are limited and there are regulations which force the holding of a diverse portfolio with low concentrations of shareholding in single portfolio companies. Investing in funds of funds is restricted too. A fund that is marketed as a REIT typically structures its portfolio with real estate.

8.3.3   Regulation

Alongside the provisions of the ITICA and other associated regulations, the registration and supervision of an investment trust company is conducted by the FSAJ and the promotion of units or shares is regulated by the Financial Instruments and Exchange Law. For funds which are listed, they must also be regulated by the Japan Securities Dealers' Association. Open-ended domestic retail trusts are also regulated by the Investment Trusts Association of Japan, a self-regulating industry body.

Where a fund issues units (if a trust) or shares (if a corporation) to the public, the necessary regulatory disclosures must be made to the Local Finance Bureau of the region of Japan in which the fund is based. For funds based in or around Tokyo, and all foreign funds, this will be the Kanto Local Finance Bureau.

The entities responsible for management of domestic funds, including the settlor and trustee of a trust, or the manager engaged by an investment corporation, must be registered with the relevant local finance bureau.

The ITICA has recently been reviewed by the FSAJ and a bill revising various provisions was passed by the Diet in June 2013. The amendment law, broadly speaking, seeks to bring elements of the operation of funds in line with their international counterparts. Some concern the governance of the funds, such as the need for written resolutions for reserved matters (for example a change to the trust deed) which the amendment law seeks to ease. In other respects, certain regulatory requirements for investment trusts have been enhanced as there is an initiative to restrict the proportions of riskier investments in investment portfolios and to force more comprehensible disclosure through management reports of such investments to retail investors.

8.3.4   Stock exchange

The Tokyo Stock Exchange is the third largest stock exchange in the world and the largest in Asia by market capitalization. It was founded in 1878 during the Meiji Restoration, a period of westernization and industrialization which brought Japan into the modern era. The exchange was reconstituted in its present form in 1949. A merger with the Osaka Securities Exchange was approved in August 2012 in order to compete better with international exchanges and in particular with the regional competition from China.

The Tokyo Stock Exchange consists primarily of the following four markets:

- the First Section for large companies
- the Second Section for medium-sized companies
- Mothers and
- JASDAQ (which, together with Mothers, are markets of the high growth and emerging stocks).

Other Japanese exchanges are the Nagoya Stock Exchange (Japan's third largest after the Tokyo and Osaka exchanges) and the Fukuoka Stock Exchange.

Open-ended funds in Japan are typically structured as contractual investment funds and are managed by authorized external investment managers. The offer and sale of units in these funds are regulated by the Financial Instruments and Exchange Law which governs both domestic and foreign funds seeking to sell their units in Japan. Domestic open-ended funds are generally not permitted to be listed, but foreign open-ended funds with share capital may obtain a secondary listing.

Closed-ended funds often take the form of ETFs and REITs. Like open-ended funds, they must be managed by an authorized investment manager. Domestic closed-ended funds may be listed on stock exchanges alongside foreign funds.

8.4   INDIA

8.4.1   Background

The Republic of India is situated in South Asia and borders six countries including Pakistan and China.[23] It is a sovereign socialist secular democratic republic with a parliamentary system of government as set out under the Constitution of India 1949. Under the constitution, the system of government is federal in structure. The Indian Parliament consists of the President and two houses known as the Council of States and the House of the People.[24] The Indian legal system is largely based on English common law. However, it is important to distinguish that the Indian legal system incorporates a common law system along with statutory law and regulatory law.[25]

8.4.2   Common structures

Investment funds in India may be set up either as a trust under the Indian Trusts Act 1882 (Trusts Act), and registered as a mutual fund with the Securities and Exchange Board of India

---

[23] National Portal of India: http://india.gov.in/india-glance/profile: last accessed 8 February 2013

[24] Constitution of India 1949; Article 79

[25] Society of Indian Law Firms website: http://www.silf.org.in/16/Indian-Judicial-System.htm: last accessed 8 February 2013

(SEBI), or as a trust, company, body corporate or limited liability partnership and registered with SEBI as an alternative investment fund (IAIF – not to be confused with a European AIF). Pools of investment in India which do not qualify as mutual funds or IAIFs may be categorized as collective investment schemes (InCISs – not to be confused with a UK CIS). InCISs are regulated under the Securities and Exchange Board of India (Collective Investment Schemes) Regulations 1999. Having said that, the preferred route of setting up investment funds in India is either as a mutual fund or as an IAIF.

Under the Trusts Act, a trust is valid only if declared by a trust instrument in writing,[26] and the author of the trust must indicate: an intention to create a trust; the purpose of the trust; the identity of the beneficiaries; and describe the trust property. It is compulsory to register the instrument of trust under the Indian Registration Act 1908.

Trusts which are registered with SEBI as mutual funds are governed under the Securities and Exchange Board of India (Mutual Funds) Regulations 1996 (MFR). Under the MFR a trust must have a sponsor, a trustee and an asset management company (AMC). The sponsor is a person who establishes the fund and appoints the trustee and the AMC. The trustee is the person who holds the property of the fund on trust for the beneficiaries (who are unit holders in the trust). The AMC manages the fund and operates its schemes.

Entities which are registered with SEBI as IAIFs are governed under the Securities and Exchange Board of India (Alternative Investment Funds) Regulations 2012 (IAIFR). In India, while there is no specific recognition of hedge funds, the IAIFR allow for registration of an open-ended IAIF which is similar in nature to hedge funds.

8.4.3   Regulation

SEBI regulates mutual funds, IAIFs and InCISs in India.

All mutual funds, including those promoted by foreign entities, are governed by the MFR, and must be registered with the SEBI.[27] The AMC must be approved by the SEBI to enable it to manage the fund and make investments.

The sponsor of the fund must submit an application to sponsor the fund, and the SEBI must be satisfied that the sponsor meets certain financial criteria, among other requirements. Following approval from the SEBI, formalities of setting up the fund can be carried out, such as executing the instrument of trust. However, the fund will require further SEBI approval to launch a scheme. Permitted schemes include open- and closed-ended schemes. For this submission to the SEBI, the consent of the fund's trustee must be sought, and filed together with a copy of the fund's offering document.

AIFs fall into three categories: (i) Category I IAIF which invests in start-up, early stage ventures or ventures the government or regulator consider as socially or economically desirable; (ii) Category II IAIF which does not fall under Category I or Category III and which does not undertake leverage or borrowing other than to meet day to day operational requirements; and (iii) Category III IAIF which employs diverse or complex trading strategies and may employ leverage including through investment in listed or unlisted derivatives. Depending on the category, different restrictions and compliance requirements are prescribed for IAIFs under the IAIF regulations.

The entity seeking to be registered as an IAIF must make an application to SEBI for registration. Among other things, the experience of the key investment team of the manager and

---

[26] Indian Trusts Act, 1882, section 5

[27] Securities and Exchange Board of India website: http://www.sebi.gov.in/sebiweb/home/list/4/37/21/0/Mutual-Funds

infrastructure of the manager and sponsor of the IAIF will be considered by SEBI in granting registration to the entity. IAIFs are required to submit a placement memorandum of their schemes with SEBI prior to launch and incorporate any comments SEBI may have in such documents.

8.4.4   Stock exchange

There are two main stock exchanges in India, with the National Stock Exchange (NSE) and the Bombay Stock Exchange (BSE) being the country's largest. Many large Indian-based companies are listed on both of these exchanges.

(a) National Stock Exchange

The NSE is located in Mumbai and is one of the world's largest stock exchanges. It commenced trading in 1994, and there are approximately 1400 Indian-based companies listed on the NSE, which provides such companies with a liquid market and access to equity capital. It offers the options of trading in capital markets, derivatives market and currency derivatives segments including equities, and ETFs. An index used by the NSE to measure performance is the S&P CNX Nifty, which comprises 50 of the NSE's largest stocks composed of companies across 22 sectors of the economy.[28]

(b) Bombay Stock Exchange

The BSE was established in 1875 and was the first stock exchange in Asia. There are over 5000 companies listed on the BSE, and it is the 11th largest stock exchange by market capitalization. The performance of the BSE is measured by the S&P BSE SENSEX, which is an index of 30 of the BSE's largest stocks composed of financially sound companies across a wide variety of industry sectors.[29]

(B)   THE AMERICAS

8.5   CANADA

8.5.1   Background

Situated in North America, Canada is the second largest country in the world, has a population of just over 35 million and is rich in natural resources. In particular, Canada holds significant oil and gas reserves and as such is a net energy exporter. Canada is a democratic constitutional monarchy, with the Queen as head of state and an elected Prime Minister as head of government. Canada is composed of ten provinces and three territories. The country has a federal system of parliamentary government with responsibilities and functions shared between federal and provincial/territorial governments.

---

[28] National Stock Exchange website: http://www.nseindia.com/products/content/equities/indices/cnx_nifty.htm: last accessed 11 June 2013

[29] Bombay Stock Exchange website: http://www.bseindia.com/indices/DispIndex.aspx?iname=BSE30&se nsid=30&type=sens&graphpath=/applet/images/graf_appSENSEX.gif&page=B16FEF6B-3A5C-45B8-89F9-C79E884CC716: last accessed 11 June 2013

8.5.2   Common structures

The most common forms of investment funds in Canada include the following.

(a) Open-ended retail funds

Canada has a well-developed mutual funds industry that is accessible to individuals and small businesses as well as large institutional investors. Open-ended mutual funds account for 30% of the Canadian public's financial wealth and as at March 2013, Canadian mutual funds had assets under management of over Canadian dollar (CAD) 900 billion. The legal entities favoured by open-ended retail funds are trusts (for tax and flexibility) and corporations (desirable for taxable investors who make frequent trades, as transfers between classes or funds do not trigger capital gains at the shareholder level).

(b) Closed-ended retail funds

Closed-ended funds may not be as popular an investment structure as open-ended retail funds; however, a number of closed-ended funds are converted into open-ended funds. Further, in Canada, the closed-ended fund structure remains a viable option for investors and mergers of closed-ended funds are often carried out in order to produce larger entities. In fact, Northwater, one of Canada's largest fund of funds companies, first entered the retail market by listing closed-ended funds on the Toronto Stock Exchange (the TSX). Listing of securities of a closed-ended fund so as to provide investors with liquidity is a common feature of such funds.

(c) Hedge funds

The Canadian hedge fund market holds investments of around CAD 40 billion and is predominantly focused on long/short fund models. Management fees typically follow the '2 and 20' model; however, funds increasingly offer investors more attractive incentives such as lower fees or multiple classes if investors are willing to provide more flexible investment. This might include early seed investment, long-term lock-in and/or high levels of minimum investment. In addition, some of the country's largest institutions, such as the Ontario Teachers' Pension Plan, have established their own hedge fund portfolios. Hedge funds in Canada are typically formed as trusts or limited partnerships, and less frequently as corporations, with tax considerations being the most significant factor when determining a legal structure.

(d) Private equity funds

Canada has a well-developed private equity sector, although the United States, European and other private equity funds regularly fund-raise in Canada and pursue acquisitions of Canadian-based enterprises. The limited partnership is the typical fund structure. Each province/territory has its own limited partnerships act. Generally, funds are formed under the act of the home province of the sponsor, although this is not required. A Manitoba-formed limited partnership is often used as Manitoba offers a slightly more favourable regime to preserve limited liability of limited partners who also participate in the management of the fund. For tax purposes, it is important that the limited partnership is not treated as a 'SIFT' partnership (i.e. one whose units are listed or traded on a public market or other organized trading facility) so that the partnership maintains its flow-through status. In addition, many fund groups segregate investors so that Canadian residents invest through one limited partnership and non-residents invest through a separate limited partnership. This permits planning for any acquisition to meet the objectives of different investors, and also allows the Canadian limited partnership to benefit from certain roll-over provisions that may apply on acquisitions or re-organizations.

8.5.3 Regulation

Together with National Instruments of the Canadian Securities Administrators, each Canadian province and territory has its own securities regulatory authority to regulate the distribution and sale of mutual fund securities and other securities in its jurisdiction (although the National Instruments seek to nationally harmonize registration regimes through the country). The largest authority is the Ontario Securities Commission. With both open-ended and closed-ended retail funds, fund managers must generally be registered as 'investment fund managers' in the province/territory where the fund is formed and managers must comply with various proficiency, insurance, capital and other requirements.

Regulation of the mutual fund industry has undergone significant reform with the introduction in 2009 of National Instrument 31–103. Under this instrument, investment fund managers, advisers and dealers are subject to registration requirements (in certain circumstances, including those operating outside of Canada who actively solicit their funds in Canada), and there is also direct regulation at the product level. The regulatory environment for investment funds continues to evolve as specific areas (such as the 'best interest' standard for dealers and advisers, disclosure requirements and other aspects of investor protection) are subject to ongoing analysis and consideration.

Canadian regulators apply several investment restrictions to open-ended funds in an effort to ensure that they remain stable and liquid. For example, a maximum of 10% of net assets can be held in a single security of an issuer and mutual funds are prohibited from borrowing or providing a security interest except where strictly limited by time and asset value.

There are no regulatory restrictions on the investments that can be made by closed-ended and hedge funds (although typically such funds will have investment restrictions contained in their offering documents). As private funds, reporting and other requirements applicable to public open-ended funds are significantly less onerous. However, the direction of regulation of closed-ended funds is to more closely align the requirements with those which apply to open-ended funds. Closed-ended funds generally list their securities on the TSX, provided that they satisfy the exchange's original listing requirements and, as listed issuers, are subject to additional regulatory requirements.

Hedge fund products sold as principal-protected notes are subject to federal banking legislation. In Canada, short selling is regulated by the Investment Industry Regulatory Organization and by the various Canadian stock exchanges.

Funds are offered in Canada pursuant to either a prospectus or an exemption from the prospectus requirements. The most often used exemption is for accredited investors which are sophisticated and wealthy investors which satisfy one or more enumerated criteria. If, as is typically the case for an exempt offering, the investors receive information about the fund that is more fulsome than a term sheet, an offering memorandum containing a contractual right of action for damages or rescission must be provided.

If a dealer is involved in the trade of securities in Canada, that dealer must be registered under provincial/territorial securities laws where the securities are sold or an exemption from the registration requirements must be available. The international dealer exemption is available for a trade in a security to a 'permitted client' in Canada by a foreign registered dealer who has filed a submission to the jurisdiction, appointed a local agent for service and provided a specified notice to the Canadian investor.

There are many Canadian incorporated issuers whose principal (or sole) assets comprise interests in foreign natural resources. Recent tax changes in Canada, and the enactment of the foreign affiliate dumping rules, create additional tax constraints for certain issuers.

8.5.4   Stock exchange

The largest stock exchange in Canada is the TSX, which is owned and operated by TMX Group Ltd. A broad range of businesses from Canada, the US, Europe and the rest of the world are represented on the TSX. In addition to conventional securities, the exchange lists the securities of various exchange traded funds, split share corporations, income trusts and investment funds.

Interestingly, more mining and oil and gas companies are listed on the TSX than on any other exchange in the world: a fact that reflects Canada's position as one of the major holders of natural resources, the expertise in Canada's resource-related capital markets community and the sophistication of the disclosure requirements that apply to resource issuers which attract resource issuers from around the world to raise capital in Canada and list on the TSX.

8.6   THE FEDERATIVE REPUBLIC OF BRAZIL

8.6.1   Background

Brazil is the largest country in South America, with almost 7500 km of Atlantic coastline, high levels of biodiversity and a population of over 196 million. The country was previously a colony of Portugal until gaining independence in 1822, hence the national language is Portuguese. It is a federative republic comprising states, municipalities and a federal district.[30] The country is governed by a democratically elected President who acts as both head of state and head of government.[31] Brazil is a civil law jurisdiction, with a new civil law code that was enacted in 2002[32] and a Federal Constitution that is central to the national legislative system. This Federal Constitution defines the spheres governed by the judiciary as well as the elected executive and legislative branches of government. Brazil is grouped with China, India and Russia as one of the leading emerging market economies in the world.

8.6.2   Common structures

The most common structures of investment funds in Brazil include the following.

---

[30] Constitution of the Federative Republic of Brazil, 1988; Article 1 (translation by www.v-brazil.com: last accessed 10 June 2013)

[31] Government of Brazil website: http://www.brasil.gov.br/sobre/brazil/president-of-the-republic/presidential-duties: last accessed 10 June 2013

[32] CIA World Factbook online: https://www.cia.gov/library/publications/the-world-factbook/fields/2100.html: last accessed 10 June 2013

(a) Corporations

According to Corporations Law 1976, a corporation, or SA,[33] in Brazil may be either publicly held, if its securities are accepted by the Brazilian Securities Commission (CVM) for trading in the securities market,[34] or closely held, if it obtains capital from private subscribers or shareholders. Though optional for closely held corporations, publicly held corporations are required to have a board of directors. SAs must have at least two officers, who shall be Brazilian resident. At the discretion of shareholders, SAs may also have a permanent audit committee composed of a group of between three and five delegates elected in the general meeting.

(b) Limited liability company

A Sociedade Limitada (LTDA) is a limited liability company, defined and provided for in Article 1052 to 1087 of the Brazilian Civil Code.[35] Partners in an LTDA are jointly liable for the payment of quotas in the corporate capital and the responsibility of each individual partner is limited to the value of their quotas. An LTDA is governed under its articles of association, which form the company's constitution in establishing the terms of management, auditing and company ownership. The articles of association also govern quota holders' meetings and rules regarding payment of dividends, as well as matters related to dispute resolution.

8.6.3   Regulation

The financial markets of Brazil are supervised by three regulatory institutions, each of which seeks to uphold the parameters defined by the Securities Law 1976[36] and the Corporations Law 1976.[37] The Central Monetary Council issues regulations applicable to all participants within the Brazilian financial system and is also responsible for the coordination of credit, budget, fiscal, debt and monetary policies. These monetary policies are executed by the Brazilian Central Bank (BCB), an institution that ensures 'the stability of the currency's purchasing power and a solid and efficient financial system'[38] and which is also responsible for the control of foreign capital flow and the credit risk of the markets. The CVM engages in securities, derivatives and investment fund regulation, and has additional duties which involve supervision of the stock exchange. The Council of Appeals of the National Financial System is an appellate body which reviews decisions of both the BCB and the CVM.

8.6.4   Stock exchange

The BM&FBOVESPA is a self-regulated stock exchange based in Sao Paulo, which is supervised by the CVM, and it is the 14th largest stock exchange by market capitalization. It is the product of a 2008 merger of Bolsa de Valores de Sao Paulo (Bovespa) and the Brazilian

---

[33] The Portuguese equivalent of *Société anonyme*, being Sociedade Anônima

[34] Law 6.404 of December 15, 1976 (Article 4) (translation by the Securities and Exchange Commission of Brazil online: http://www.cvm.gov.br/ingl/regu/law6404r.ASP: last accessed 10 June 2013)

[35] Law 10.406, 2002

[36] Securities Law 1976 (6.385/76)

[37] Securities and Exchange Commission website: http://www.cvm.gov.br/ingl/regu/Regu.asp#Legal: last accessed 11 June 2013

[38] Banco Central do Brasil website: http://www.bcb.gov.br/?english: last accessed 11 June 2013

Mercantile and Futures Exchange (BM&F), and has a history of similar mergers stretching back to 1890. BM&FBOVESPA introduced additional special listings in 2000 with the aim of enhancing the rights of shareholders and improving the quality of information customarily released by public companies. Within these listings, companies can voluntarily adhere to varying levels of special corporate governance practices, which supplement those required by applicable Brazilian legislation.[39] There are currently four special listing segments: the New Market, the Market of Shares of SAs, and Corporate Governance Levels 1 and 2. The New Market has the highest level of corporate governance requirements but is also the most popular of the four listings. Examples of such requirements are given below:

- the company must have a board of at least five directors, 20% of which are independent
- companies must produce a calendar of annual corporate events
- a company's capital may be represented only by voting shares and
- voting shares representing at least 25% of the company's capital must be kept in circulation at all times.

(C)   ONSHORE EUROPEAN JURISDICTIONS

8.7   RUSSIAN FEDERATION

8.7.1   Background

Russia is a civil law jurisdiction subject to civil and criminal codes, although court decisions are beginning to have more influence. Russia has a population of over 140 million and is the ninth largest economy in the world, just behind India. Mineral products accounted for 71% of total Russian exports in 2012 while 50% of total imports were machinery, equipment and means of transport. The EU is Russia's leading trading partner, accounting for almost 50% of trade turnover, followed by APEC countries with 24%, of which 10.5% is with China. CIS countries account for 14.1%. The country's GDP growth in 2012 was 3.4%.

8.7.2   Common structures

The available structures for foreign direct investment by foreign legal entities into Russia are as follows.

(a) Investment partnership (IP)

This form was introduced in 2012 and is designed for companies involved in innovative activities (including providing venture capital). This vehicle, which does not have a separate tax status, is quite similar to an English limited partnership and constitutes a significant improvement over the previously available structures for fund vehicles in Russia. The introduction of this new law intends to provide foreign fund managers with an opportunity to bring offshore fund structures to Russia. An IP does not have a separate legal entity and does not require any registration or any licence. The types of activities permitted to be performed by an IP are prescribed by law and include: the acquisition and (or) sale of non-publicly traded

---

[39] BM&FBOVESPA Corporate Governance Guidelines 2000 (translation provided by BM&FBOVESPA website: http://ir.bmfbovespa.com.br/fck_temp/26_2//CA-28-Annex1_CG_Guidelines.pdf: last accessed 11 June 2013)

shares (participatory interests), of corporate and partnership bonds, financial instruments of forward transactions and participatory interests in the capital of partnerships.

The constitutional document of an IP is the partnership agreement concluded by its investing partners. A partnership can be created by two or more persons (both individuals and corporates). Generally, there are two types of participants in an IP: (i) managing partners and (ii) limited partners. A partner that is not a managing partner cannot act in relation to the management of the partnership, and foreign corporations with no permanent establishment in Russia cannot act as managing partners.

A limited partner's liability is limited to its share in the IP. Where a limited partner's share does not satisfy a claim then the managing partner bears unlimited liability. An IP must have a term not exceeding 15 years.

(b) Limited liability company (LLC)

Foreign legal entities often choose the LLC to conduct wholly owned business in Russia. Investors in an LLC are called participants and the interests in the LLC are referred to as participatory interests, not shares. The LLC can be an inefficient structure from a tax point of view as both the LLC and its participants are taxed. The LLC articles may restrict the transfer of its participatory interests to third parties. An LLC participant may at any time withdraw from the LLC, only if this right is prescribed by the LLC articles, and require the LLC (or remaining participants) to provide to it a portion of the LLC's net assets.

(c) Joint stock company (JSC)

The closed JSC is probably closest to the US/UK limited liability structure. A JSC may be either 'open' or 'closed', meaning publicly held or privately held. A JSC issues shares to generate capital for its activities.

(d) Representative office (RO)/branch

A foreign legal entity may also choose to establish a presence in Russia through an RO, or through a branch. An RO or branch is not a Russian legal entity but is a legal part of the foreign legal entity and therefore the foreign legal entity bears full liability for the operations of the RO/branch. An RO/branch needs to be accredited in Russia by State Registration Chamber. An RO is typically authorized to conduct only certain preparatory or auxiliary activities for its respective head office. A branch, meanwhile, is able to conduct all activities that the head office of the foreign legal entity itself could perform, including execution of contracts.

A shareholder in a JSC, and a participant in an LLC, is not generally liable for the activities of the relevant company and its losses are limited to the value of the shares/participatory interests it holds. The maximum number of investors in an LLC, closed JSC or IP is in each case 50 persons; the number of investors in an open JSC is not limited. A closed JSC or LLC with more than 50 investors must be re-organized into an open JSC.

8.7.3   Regulation

Typically, an investment related to Russian assets will be required to comply with the competition law. Competition law in Russia, as well as seeking to prevent non-competitive market practice, is acknowledged to have a secondary function; namely to allow the Russian authorities to scrutinize acquisitions above a threshold value.

The 'Law on Foreign Investment in Strategic Companies' restricts foreign investment activity in areas such as geophysical processes, nuclear technology, weapons, space technology, telecommunications, media and the extraction of mineral resources. Foreign companies are generally prohibited from gaining a controlling stake in strategic enterprises. A foreign company may acquire 25–50% of the charter capital of a strategic company (different thresholds are set for different types of strategic companies) provided that it obtains state approval.

Corporate governance in the two main corporate forms of investment vehicle, namely the LLC or JSC, has many similarities with UK/US limited liability companies. There is, however, one crucial distinction. The general director (i.e. the CEO) is the key person authorized by the company's shareholders/participants to represent the company and not its board of directors.

8.7.4   Stock exchange

The Moscow Exchange, MICEX-RTS, is the largest exchange in Russia and Eastern Europe. It was created in December 2011 after the merger of the country's two leading exchanges, MICEX and RTS. The Moscow Exchange ranks among the world's top 20 exchanges by value of securities traded and market capitalization. It is also the ninth largest exchange worldwide by derivatives trading.

Trading on the Moscow Exchange's securities market is held in the following sectors: T+2, Main Market, Standard and Classica. Futures and options are traded on the derivatives market FORTS. Foreign currencies (FX Market) are traded in the electronic trading system which combines regional technical centres within the Unified Trading Session (UTS). The Money Market includes two sections: government securities repo and money market instruments as well as repo in equities and bonds. The Moscow Exchange implements projects on organizing and promoting on-exchange commodities markets via the National Mercantile Exchange.

8.8   GERMANY

8.8.1   Background

Germany is the largest country in the EU by population, with approximately 82.5 million people,[40] and also by GDP. Germany is a democratic parliamentary federal republic. Federal legislative power is conferred upon the Bundestag, which is the federal parliament of Germany, and in specific matters as well upon the Bundesrat, which is the representative body of the 16 federal states. The head of the German federal government is the Chancellor, who is elected for terms of four years by the members of the Bundestag. Germany is a civil

---

[40] United Nations Statistics Division: 'Population, latest available census and estimates, latest available data': last accessed 24 January 2013

law jurisdiction, with its legal system based upon codified statutes, with the Constitution of Germany being the highest source of law.[41]

8.8.2   Common structures

The Capital Investment Code (*Kapitalanlagegesetzbuch* – KAGB) provides for 'Sonderver-mögen' and investment stock corporations with variable capital as possible fund vehicles for investment funds within the meaning of the UCITS Directive as well as for German open-ended retail alternative investment funds (AIFs). For German open-ended special AIFs, the KAGB further provides for the legal form of an open investment limited partnership with variable capital.

For closed-ended funds, the KAGB mandates the investment stock corporation with fixed capital and the closed investment limited partnership as fund vehicles.

Limited partnerships are governed by the German Commercial Code (*Handelsgesetzbuch* – HGB). Under the HGB and much like an English limited partnership (see Chapter 2, section 2.2), a limited partnership is a legal entity consisting of at least two partners, at least one of whom must be a limited partner and at least one of whom must be a general partner whose liability is unlimited.

A limited partnership can also be structured as a limited partnership where the general partner is a limited liability company. It is a requirement that the minimum share capital of the limited liability company is EUR 25,000.

A German limited partnership (in either form described above) has advantages similar to its English counterpart; namely that the liability of limited partners is limited to their capital contribution (or registered liability with the commercial register) and that the partnership entity is tax transparent – the income and capital gains are taxed at the level of partner.

However, if under German tax law the fund is qualified as 'business active', the partnership will be subject to trade tax. Trade tax is levied by the local municipality with varying tax rates which are usually between 7% and 17.15%. It can be credited against German investors' tax liabilities at investor level, but not those of non-German investors, which increases the costs and reduces the distributable profit for non-German investors.

The status of a German or non-German private equity fund as non-business active requires that:

- the fund does not qualify as business active pursuant to the legal structure which can be avoided by allocating managing authority to a limited partner
- the fund does not invest in other German or non-German partnerships which qualify as business active, causing the infection of the fund's entire income as business income and
- the fund does not carry out activities which qualify as exceeding administration of assets or asset management.

8.8.3   Regulation

The German implementation of the Alternative Investment Fund Managers Directive (AIFMD) (for more information see Chapter 12, section 12.6) introduced the new KAGB, which superseded the Investment Act (*Investmentgesetz* – InvG), previously in effect.

---

[41] Constitution of Germany adopted 23 May 1949

The KAGB distinguishes between open-ended and closed-ended funds. For the purposes of the KAGB, open-ended funds are those that provide the possibility of redeeming the units at least once yearly. All other funds are closed-ended funds. Open-ended funds are structured as UCITS or open-ended AIFs. Closed-ended funds are always closed-ended AIFs.

AIFs, both open-ended and closed-ended, appear both as:

- retail AIFs – in which (also) retail investors may invest
- special AIFs – in which only professional investors or semi-professional investors may invest.

The term 'professional investor' is to be understood in the sense of the term 'professional client' within the meaning of the Markets in Financial Instruments Directive[42] (MiFID). The term 'semi-professional investor' will include the management team of a fund, any investor committing to invest at least EUR 200,000 (but this is subject to various checks about the investor's being sophisticated as an investor) and investors committing to invest at least EUR 10 million (in this case without the need for any checks).

(a) Open-ended retail AIFs

Open-ended retail AIFs include the following types of funds:

- mixed funds (Gemischte Sondervermögen)
- other funds (Sonstige Sondervermögen)
- funds of hedge funds (Dach-Hedgefonds)
- real-estate funds (Immobilien-Sondervermögen).

Mixed funds and other funds are not permitted to invest in real estate funds and mixed funds cannot invest in hedge funds. In addition, other funds are now entirely forbidden from directly investing in company shares due to the illiquidity of these assets. Infrastructure funds can only be structured as closed-ended funds.

Authorized asset management companies are permitted to launch both single hedge funds and funds of hedge funds. Units in single hedge funds may be held exclusively by professional and semi-professional investors (see above). Regulations in respect of funds of hedge funds state that no more than 20% of a fund of hedge funds may be invested in a single target fund and that leverage and short selling may not be carried out.

(b) Open-ended special AIFs

Open-ended special AIFs include 'general' open-ended special AIFs. They are permitted to invest in all assets the market value of which can be determined. Units in single hedge funds may be held only by professional and semi-professional investors.

Special funds (*Spezialfonds*) formed under the InvG continue to exist as open-ended special AIFs with fixed investment rules. For these funds the provisions for open-ended retail AIFs apply with regard to fund assets and investment limits with the proviso that the relevant rules can be deviated from subject to compliance with certain minimum requirements.

---

[42] 2004/39/EC

(c) Closed-ended retail AIFs

Closed-ended AIFs include closed-ended retail AIFs. In the KAGB they are treated almost in the same manner as open-ended funds.

A conclusive catalogue of assets in which closed-ended retail AIFs may invest applies. The use of debt financing is restricted to 60% of the value of the AIF. In addition, the KAGB intends to make blind-pool funds more transparent by a prescriptive description of the investment strategy. The KAGB contains provisions on fund rules, sales prospectuses and key investor information.

Units in closed-ended retail AIFs which invest in only one or two assets may only be held by investors committing to invest at least EUR 20,000 and who fulfil the criteria of a semi-professional investor, provided that these AIFs do not invest in private equity.

(d) Closed-ended special AIFs

Closed-ended special AIFs form a second group of closed-ended AIFs accessible only to professional and semi-professional investors. They can invest in any asset which can be given a market value.

Under the KAGB, each investment fund must have one capital management company (or *Kapitalverwaltungsgesellschaft* – KVG). In accordance with the AIFMD, a fund may have an external manager or be managed internally. An external KVG may only be structured as a limited liability company (*Gesellschaft mit beschränkter Haftung*), a stock corporation (*Aktiengesellschaft*) or a GmbH & Co. KG.

KVGs are required to obtain a licence from the German Federal Financial Supervisory Authority (BaFin) and will be subject to the ongoing supervision of BaFin thereafter, unless one of the limited exceptions of the KAGB applies. KVGs that manage funds that are considered small for the purposes of AIFMD (see Chapter 12, section 12.6) are required to register with BaFin, rather than obtain a licence, but this still triggers certain ongoing disclosure obligations.

(e) Marketing provisions

The KAGB contains comprehensive provisions on marketing of investment funds. The marketing provisions for AIFs go far beyond the requirements of the AIFMD to regulate marketing to retail investors or semi-professional investors. Marketing to any class of investor, including professional investors, will be permitted only where the alternative investment fund manager (AIFM) notifies BaFin, or in the case of investors other than professional investors, complies with the necessary registration requirements. This has abolished the old private placement regime, with a grandfathering exception for funds marketed prior to 22 July 2013.

(f) Marketing of special AIFs

With regard to the marketing of special AIFs, i.e. AIFs for professional and semi-professional investors only, the KAGB implements the corresponding provisions of the AIFMD for professional investors.

With regard to the marketing of AIFs involving a 'third country element', during the two-year transition period, the KAGB requires that several conditions are met by the manager of a non-EU AIF or a non-EU manager of an AIF.

(g) Marketing of retail AIFs

With regard to the marketing of retail AIFs, the Bundestag has imposed stricter national regulations than the AIFMD requires, especially concerning private placements, investor information and the requirement for a representative within Germany for a fund domiciled outside of Germany.

8.8.4   Stock exchange

The Frankfurt Stock Exchange (FWB) is one of the world's largest stock exchanges. It is Germany's largest stock exchange with a share turnover accounting for more than 90% of turnover in the German market.[43] The origins of the FWB can be traced back to the 14th century when fairs held in Frankfurt became an important centre for commercial and monetary transactions.[44] It is now owned and operated by Deutsche Börse. The Official Market, Regulated Market and Regulated Unofficial Market of the FWB provide the legal frameworks for a number of segments, each with different transparency levels: (i) Prime Standard, (ii) General Standard and (iii) Entry Standard.[45] The Entry Standard is part of the Regulated Unofficial Market (Open Market) and it is the segment with the least stringent reporting requirements. It is therefore aimed towards small to mid-sized companies seeking access to the capital market.[46] The Entry Standard is regulated by the FWB and is not an EU-regulated market.

The General Standard and the Prime Standard are part of the Exchange Regulated Market. They are EU-regulated markets and have enhanced regulation in comparison with the Open Market, with stringent requirements including the disclosure of events which might materially affect shares prices, and disclosure of directors' dealings. When companies are listing to the Regulated Market, they are automatically admitted to the General Standard. Companies listed on the General Standard are therefore subject to those transparency requirements applicable to the Regulated Market, including ad hoc disclosure and publication of interim reports.[47] Due to the fact that it is EU-regulated, the Prime Standard is aimed at international investors. However, companies listed on the Prime Standard are subject to stringent regulation including the requirement for quarterly reporting and the use of international accounting standards (IFRS/IAS or US-GAAP).[48] More about German stock exchanges in a European context is available in Chapter 6, section 6.5.1.

---

[43] Deutsche Börse Group website: http://deutsche-boerse.com/dbg/dispatch/en/kir/dbg_nav/about_us/20_FWB_Frankfurt_Stock_Exchange: last accessed 30 January 2013

[44] Deutsche Börse Group website: http://deutsche-boerse.com/dbg/dispatch/en/kir/dbg_nav/about_us/20_FWB_Frankfurt_Stock_Exchange/70_History_of_the_FWB: last accessed 30 January 2013

[45] Deutsche Börse Group website: http://www.boerse-frankfurt.de/en/basics+overview/market+segments/market+segments+and+transparency: last accessed 31 January 2013

[46] Deutsche Börse Group website: http://www.boerse-frankfurt.de/en/basics+overview/market+segments/entry+standard: last accessed 31 January 2013

[47] Deutsche Börse Group website: http://www.boerse-frankfurt.de/en/basics+overview/market+segments/general+standard: last accessed 31 January 2013

[48] Deutsche Börse Group website: http://www.boerse-frankfurt.de/en/basics+overview/market+segments/prime+standard: last accessed 31 January 2013

8.9   FRANCE

8.9.1   Background

Geographically, France is the EU's largest country by total area, and also has the second largest population in the EU, estimated to be 61.4 million.[49] It is bordered by Belgium, Luxembourg, Germany, Switzerland, Italy, Monaco, Spain and Andorra. France is a republic as set out under the Constitution of the Fifth Republic.[50] The President is elected for five-year terms, and is permitted to retain office for a maximum of two consecutive terms.[51] The President appoints the Prime Minister and the other members of government, with the government of the day responsible for proposing new legislation. The French legal system is based on civil law, with the cornerstone of the legal system being the Napoleonic Code, which among other things laid out the rights and obligations of French citizens.

8.9.2   Common structures

Since the transposition in France of the AIFMD in July 2013, the French monetary and financial code distinguishes three types of collective investment schemes: (i) *Organismes de Placement Collectif en Valeurs Mobilières* (OPCVM), which are collective investment undertakings that comply with the UCITS IV Directive, (ii) AIFs and (iii) other collective investment schemes.

The most common French investment structures are as follows.

(a)   General investment structures

(i)   SICAV

As discussed in Chapter 7, a SICAV is an investment company with variable capital. In France they are regulated under the rules governing French limited liability companies (SAs). Also a SICAV may be managed by a board, but it is more generally managed by a regulated investment management company.

(ii)   FCP

The FCP is the most often used form of funds. It is a co-ownership of financial instruments. An FCP is not a separate legal entity and is legally represented by its regulated investment management company, which manages the assets on behalf of the fund.

(iii) SICAF

The SICAF is another form of closed-ended fund existing under the French regulation. However, this structure is not commonly used. The SICAF must be incorporated as an SA; they are therefore subject to the requirements of the code regulating SAs albeit with a few exceptions. One exception is that a SICAF can increase its capital at any time, unless it is offering shares at a discount to the NAV, in which case the existing shareholders have a right of priority. An increase in capital is the only way in which a SICAF can issue new shares following the initial subscription period. A SICAF must engage a regulated investment management company to run the fund.

---

[49] United Nations Statistics Division: 'Population, latest available census and estimates, latest available data': last accessed 21 January 2013
[50] Constitution of October 4, 1958
[51] Article 6, Constitution of October 4, 1958

All of the above structures may be used for retail funds and non-retail funds.

(b) Specific private equity investment vehicles

Private equity funds are divided into three main types of retail funds: FCPR, FCPI and FIP, which are co-ownerships of financial instruments and must obtain a licence from the *Autorité des Marchés Financiers* (AMF), like a standard FCP, and have the following main characteristics.

(i) FCPR
Assets of the FCPR shall be composed of at least 50% of participating securities or securities of unlisted companies.

(ii) FCPI
Assets of the FCPI shall be composed of at least 60% of participating securities or securities of companies qualified as 'innovative company' (as defined in the French monetary and financial code[52]) whose activities are located in a specific geographic area.

(iii) FIP
Assets of the FIP shall be composed of at least 60% of participating securities or securities of small-cap and mid-cap companies (as such terms are defined by the EU regulation[53]) whose activities are located in a specific geographic area.

Private equity funds also include two main types of non-retail funds (*fonds professionels spécialisés* and *fonds professionnels de capital investissement*), which are not subject to AMF approval and shall only file with the AMF, however their subscription is restricted to qualified investors. Both such funds are co-ownerships of financial instruments and have to be managed by a regulated investment management company. The implementation of AIFMD will not greatly affect the obligations of these two types of fund, which were already obliged to have their assets under the control of a custodian and had reporting obligations to the AMF. The scope of the reporting obligations may change with the detailed AIFMD implementation regulations, especially if the AIFM is not a small AIFM (see Chapter 12, section 12.6 for more information on the AIFMD).

8.9.3   Regulation

The regulations governing funds include:

- the French monetary and financial code
- the General Regulations of the AMF together with instructions/recommendations issued by the AMF and
- the business rules issued from time to time by the *Association Française de la Gestion financière*, the *Association Française des Investisseurs pour la Croissance* and the *Association Française des Sociétés de Placement Immobilier*.

---

[52] Article L. 214–30 of the French monetary and financial code
[53] Commission regulation (EC) No 800/2008 of 6 August 2008 Annex I

The AMF is an independent public body, with legal personality and financial autonomy, and it regulates both OPCVMs and AIFs. The AMF has jurisdiction over:

- regulation of corporate finance activities and disclosures by listed companies
- licensing of regulated investment management companies
- authorization for the creation of open-ended and closed-end retail funds
- setting the principles and operation applicable to market operators, such as the Euronext Paris
- setting conduct of business rules and other requirements in respect of professionals authorized to provide investment services. It has the power to investigate and also impose penalties and sanctions in respect of any rules or regulations.[54]

8.9.4   Stock exchange

The Euronext Paris, formerly known as the Paris Stock Exchange, was created in 1724 by an order of the Royal Council of State. It merged with the Amsterdam Stock Exchange and the Brussels Stock Exchange in 2000 to form the Euronext N.V. in September 2000 and the Euronext group merged with the New York Stock Exchange in 2007 to form the actual NYSE Euronext (see Chapter 6 for more information).

(D)   COMMONWEALTH OF AUSTRALIA

8.10.1 Background

Australia is situated between the Indian, Southern and Pacific oceans, and is neighboured by countries including Indonesia, Timor-Leste and Papua New Guinea to the north and New Zealand to the east. It is the world's sixth largest country by land area[55] and has a population of approximately 22.9 million people.[56] Australia is a constitutional monarchy, having a written constitution which sets out the powers of the government of the Commonwealth of Australia. The Australian head of state is the current British monarch, represented by a Governor-General appointed on recommendation of the Australian Prime Minister. Australian law has its early origin in the English common law system, supplemented by an extensive body of local legislation, with the High Court of Australia being the highest appellate court. The Commonwealth was born in its current form in 1901 with the agreement of six British colonies to form together under the Australian Constitution. The Commonwealth follows a Westminster system of government with the Commonwealth Parliament consisting of two main political parties and a number of smaller parties. The six states of New South Wales, Queensland, South Australia, Tasmania, Victoria and Western Australia each retain the power to make their own laws over matters not controlled by the Commonwealth, and have their own constitutions as well as their own structure of legislative, executive and judicial branches.

---

[54] Autorité des marchés financiers website: http://www.amf-france.org/en_US/: last accessed 10 January 2014

[55] Australian Government website: http://australia.gov.au/about-australia/our-country: last accessed 14 January 2013

[56] United Nations Statistics Division: 'Population, latest available census and estimates, latest available data': last accessed 14 January 2013

8.10.2 Common structures

Investment funds are infrequently structured as companies because they are not tax transparent. The most popular structures in respect of Australian investment funds include unit trusts and to a lesser extent partnerships.

(a) Fixed unit trust

A fixed unit trust is a contractual relationship made between the unit holders, being the investors or the beneficiaries, and a trustee who is the legal holder of the property. The trustee may also act as the trust manager, or appoint a manager as its delegate. A fixed trust provides the unit holders with fixed entitlements to income and capital derived from the trust. Unless the contract to the trust states otherwise, or the circumstances of the trust are such that the unit holders are involved in the trust's management, the liability of the unit holders will generally be restricted to the amount unpaid in respect of their units. Provided that the trustee distributes all the annual trust net income, the trustee of a unit trust is not generally subject to income tax at the fund level (though beneficiaries/investors will be subject to income tax).

(b) Limited partnership

A limited partnership formed in Australia must consist of at least one or more general partners (who will be liable for all the debts and obligations of the firm) and one or more limited partners, although in general a limited partnership must not consist of more than 20 persons. In relation to limited partnerships, there are a number of incentives introduced by the Australian government including the Venture Capital Limited Partnerships (VCLP) programme and the Early Stage Venture Capital Limited Partnerships (ESVCLP) programme.

(i) VCLP

To be eligible, the limited partnership must be a new venture capital fund, the general partner must be Australian resident or a resident in a country which has a double tax agreement with Australia, and the fund must be registered with Innovation Australia and have capital commitments of at least Australian dollar (AUD) 10 million from its investors. The benefit of a VCLP is that it receives flow-through tax treatment, and foreign limited partners are exempt from their share of profits provided that the profits arise in respect of eligible investments. Eligible investments include shares, convertible notes, units or options in Australian businesses whose assets are less than AUD 250 million, although it may not invest in certain businesses including those which predominantly deal with property development and construction. A VCLP has ongoing quarterly reporting obligations on its eligible investment activities, and must provide an annual report on its structure and portfolio.[57]

(ii) ESVCLP

To be eligible, the limited partnership must be a new venture capital fund, the general partner must be Australian resident or a resident in a country which has a double tax agreement with

---

[57] AusIndustry website (AusIndustry is a division within the Department of Industry, Innovation, Science, Research and Tertiary Education); 'Venture Capital Limited Partnerships (VCLP) program and Early Stage Venture Capital Limited Partnerships (ESVCLP) program': 'http://www.ausindustry.gov.au/programs/venture-capital/esvclp/Documents/ComparisonofVCLP-ESVCLPprograms.pdf

Australia, and the fund must have capital commitments of at least AUD 10 million and no more than AUD 100 million from its investors. An ESVCLP must be registered by, and have an investment plan (that focuses on early stage venture capital investments) approved by, Innovation Australia. The benefit of an ESVCLP is that it receives flow-through tax treatment, and partners (both Australian resident and foreign resident) are exempt from tax on their share of profits made on eligible investments. Eligible investments include new shares, convertible notes, new units or options in Australian businesses whose assets are less than AUD 50 million, although it may not invest in certain businesses including those which predominantly deal with property developing and construction. In addition, ESVCLPs must divest once an investee has grown to AUD 250 million in assets. An ESVCLP has reporting obligations similar to those applying to a VCLP, with the added annual report requirement to report on progress in implementing its approved investment plan.[58]

8.10.3 Regulation

In Australia the regulations and regulatory bodies relating to investment funds apply to both open-ended and closed-ended retail funds, and to a lesser extent to funds restricted to wholesale investors. The Corporations Act 2001 sets out a number of requirements in respect of the retail funds. A managed investment scheme must be registered with the Australian Securities and Investments Commission (ASIC) if it has more than 20 members, or if it is promoted by a person whose business involves the promotion of managed investment schemes, or as otherwise determined by the ASIC.[59] In addition, the trustee of such schemes is referred to as a 'responsible entity' and must hold an Australian financial services licence that authorizes the entity to operate the fund. A manager (if one is appointed by the responsible entity) may also need to be licensed to deal in fund assets and to provide financial product advice to the beneficiaries/investors. The Act further imposes obligations upon entities, and the relevant officers responsible for the management investment scheme, whereby they are under a duty to exercise care and diligence, and act in the best interests of the members of the fund.[60]

Where funds are restricted to investment by wholesale investors, the fund registration requirement does not apply. Wholesale investors include persons investing more than AUD 500,000, persons controlling more than AUD 10 million for investment in funds (including through trusts or by associates) and other types of professional or sophisticated investors. The trustee, however, may still require an Australian financial services licence unless they are exempted, or authorized as a representative under another person's licence to provide the financial services in respect of the fund.

ASIC is an independent Commonwealth governmental body. It is empowered to regulate under the Australian Securities and Investments Commission Act, and oversees the compliance with the Corporations Act 2001. Regulation by the ASIC extends to Australian companies, financial services organizations and professionals who deal and advise in investments, and trustees who operate retail funds, or provide custodial or depositary services for a fund.

---

[58] AusIndustry website (AusIndustry is a division within the Department of Industry, Innovation, Science, Research and Tertiary Education); 'Venture Capital Limited Partnerships (VCLP) program and Early Stage Venture Capital Limited Partnerships (ESVCLP) program': 'http://www.ausindustry.gov.au/programs/venture-capital/esvclp/Documents/ComparisonofVCLP-ESVCLPprograms.pdf

[59] Corporations Act 2001; Section 601ED

[60] Corporations Act 2001; Section 601FC

The powers of the ASIC include registration of companies and managed investment schemes, and the granting of Australian financial services and credit licences.[61]

8.10.4 Stock exchange

The Australian Securities Exchange (ASX) is Australia's largest stock exchange. It was created in July 2006 through a merger of the Australian Stock Exchange and the Sydney Futures Exchange.[62] In listing an entity upon the ASX, there are certain categories of admission:

- general admission
- foreign exempt listing and
- debt listing.

In relation to General Admission Listing, a significant number of listed retail investment property trusts (A-REITs) are listed on ASX as well as public companies. There are certain requirements for listing units of an A-REIT that apply to the responsible entity and the fund. Each A-REIT is a retail fund. Units in an A-REIT are tradable at a market price on the securities market of ASX, rather than redeemed from the fund assets at the net asset value as calculated by the trustee.

In relation to an ASX Debt Listing, there are certain requirements in respect of the same including that the entity must be either a private company limited by shares, a government borrowing authority, a public authority, or a person approved by the ASX; and the entity must appoint a person to be responsible for communication with the ASX in relation to listing rule matters. The issuer must itself have net tangible assets of at least AUD 10 million, or its parent entity must meet this net tangible assets requirement and unconditionally and irrevocably guarantee repayment of the debt securities for the period of quotation.[63] In relation to the listing of a Foreign Exempt Listing, there are certain requirements in respect of the same including: that the entity must be a foreign entity and must have as its overseas home exchange a stock exchange or market which is a member of the World Federation of Exchanges (formerly Fédération Internationale des Bourses de Valeurs); it must be subject to and compliant with the listing rules of its overseas home exchange; and it must satisfy a profit or asset test akin to a general admission.[64]

(E)   ISLAMIC INVESTMENT FUNDS

8.11.1 Background

Since the re-emergence of Islamic banking in the mid 1960s, Islamic financial institutions have developed a range of sophisticated financial products in a Sharia'a compliant manner. In recent years there has been a gradual increase in interest for Sharia'a compliant products

---

[61] Australian Securities and Investments Commission website: http://www.asic.gov.au/asic/ASIC.NSF/byHeadline/Our%20role: last accessed 23 January 2013

[62] Australian Securities Exchange website: http://www.asxgroup.com.au/our-organisation.htm: last accessed 14 January 2013

[63] Australian Securities Exchange website: http://www.asx.com.au/professionals/regulatory_requirements_in_listing_retail_debt_securities.htm: last accessed 24 July 2013

[64] ASX Listing Rules *Guidance Note 4 – Foreign Entities listing on ASX*

due, in part, to constraints on the availability of loan finance from conventional banks and to an increase in the desire of individual Muslim investors and Middle East companies/wealth funds to conduct their financial affairs in accordance with Islam.

The development of the Islamic investment funds industry was initiated as a result of a ruling by the Fiqh Academy of the Organisation of Islamic Countries. This ruling defined the shares of a company as an 'undivided portion of the company's assets', thereby removing the uncertainty in relation to whether fund investment in shares was permissible under Sharia'a law. Investment funds have been defined by the Accounting and Auditing Organisation of Islamic Financial Institutions (AAOIFI) as follows:

> 'Funds are investment vehicles which are financially independent of the institutions that establish them … Investment funds are permissible by Sharia'a.'

8.11.2 Key principles of Sharia'a law

Sharia'a is a set of principles that provides guidance on a variety of issues (including religious, family, business and financial affairs) for Muslims. The primary sources of the Sharia'a are the Qur'an (the holy book of Islam) and the Sunna (the sayings and the actions of the Prophet Mohammed (PBUH) during his lifetime).

Sharia'a requires the parties to a transaction to be just, fair and ethical in their dealings with one another. Sharia'a actively encourages trade and requires any profit realized to be the result of lawful trade. In Islam, for profit to be lawful, it must be linked to the performance of a real asset or investment and involve the financier assuming some risk for the success or failure of the commercial venture being financed.

The key Sharia'a principles when engaging in financial transactions include the following.

(a) Prohibition on riba

Riba is often understood to mean 'interest', but its literal meaning is 'excess' and refers to any excess compensation without due consideration. For the purposes of investment funds it is required that any returns on capital should be linked to any gains made as a result of a business risk.

(b) Avoidance of haram (forbidden) commodities and activities

Muslims are not permitted to consume alcohol, pork or substances such as prohibited narcotics. Consequently, the fund manager must ensure that haram commodities or activities do not form part of the portfolio of a fund. Similarly, if a company is dealing in unethical or other activities which are frowned upon by Sharia'a (such as pornography, prostitution, gossip magazines, weapons trading and so on), then such a company would not be suitable for investment.

Due to events outside of the control of the management, for example a merger of a portfolio company, many investment funds may unavoidably be linked in some form to a prohibited activity during the fund lifetime. However, there are means by which this can be remedied. The earnings of such a fund may be 'purified' by deducting those earnings derived from prohibited investments and distributed at the direction of the fund's Sharia'a and fatwa board.

(c) Avoidance of gharar (uncertainty)

This refers to the prohibition on unnecessary uncertainty or ambiguity in commercial dealings, as this could inadvertently lead to deceit, as well as outright fraud. Therefore, there is a general prohibition on the sale of items whose existence or characteristics are not certain and upon contractual terms that are ambiguous or unclear (for example, if the price is unknown or the payment terms are unspecified).

(d) Prohibition on qimar (gambling) and maisir (speculation)

Gambling and speculation are strictly prohibited as Sharia'a forbids excessive risk in transactions and activities. This prohibition extends further by analogy to certain financial transactions that constitute purely speculative trades, with no certainty of outcome or success, such as dealings in futures and options (to the extent that they are speculative).

8.11.3 Common structures for Sharia'a compliant funds

Islamic funds exist in a range of forms from fixed-income funds to hedge funds. Generally, the relationship between the investor and the fund is governed by either a Mudaraba (partnership) or a Wakala (agency) agreement in which the investor appoints the fund manager to invest his funds with the objective of generating a profit. The fund manager receives a fee for his services and the investor is liable for losses incurred, providing that the fund manager has acted professionally and in line with the terms of the management services contract that governs his duty.

Fixed-income funds typically invest in ijara (see section 8.11.4(d) below) and use cash and cash equivalent instruments to ensure they can meet their liquidity requirements. The allocation of assets between liquid instruments and yielding instruments such as Sukuk (asset-backed Islamic bond) and ijara (lease) depends on the risk-return characteristics of the fund. In addition, the creditworthiness (see section 8.11.4 below) of the yielding assets has an impact on the risk levels, transaction costs and costs associated with having to maintain the required liquidity in the fund.

Fixed-income funds can invest in any combination of the following instruments to generate a return on liquid assets (including commodity Murabaha, Sukuk and ijara).

(a) Islamic equity funds

Investment in public (listed) and private equity is permitted by Sharia'a. In relation to equity funds, on a strict interpretation, investment in companies may be at odds with Sharia'a law; for example, with respect to the principle of riba, where a company uses interest-bearing accounts to invest its surplus capital. A modern interpretation of investments in companies may reconcile such concerns, by introducing the idea that as investors have no responsibility in respect of investments, they will not be deemed under Sharia'a law to have permitted an investment in a company whose business activities are not exclusively halal (permissible). In order to identify potentially Sharia'a compliant equity investment opportunities, a screening process is applied to identify equity that will not contravene Sharia'a rules, thus enabling it to become a part of the investment fund's portfolio. Alternatively, the investment fund may invest in equity that can be tracked on an Islamic index (see section 8.11.5 below).

Private equity funds also create problems where they use leverage to invest in the controlling shares of a company (as they must finance the acquisition through Sharia'a approved mechanisms) or if they invest in leveraged companies. In relation to leveraged companies there are differing views on this subject from Sharia'a scholars including: (i) that the acquisition of a company is permitted if the interest-bearing debt to equity ratio is 33% or less and (ii) that the acquisition of a company is permitted if a controlling stake in a leveraged company is purchased and a fixed period of time, usually three years, is afforded to repay the company debt or convert the same into a Sharia'a compliant form of debt.

(b) Commodity funds

A commodity fund invests in a range of eligible commodities with a view to forward sales of the same. Such funds may be at odds with Sharia'a as it forbids short selling. The below forms of contract may be used by an investment fund to comply with Sharia'a.

(c) Istisna'a (procurement) funds

Istisna'a is a deferred delivery and payment arrangement under which the delivery of an asset is deferred until a later date. Istisna'a structures are generally used to provide advance funding of the construction/development of an asset. A specification of the descriptive nature and quality of the asset must be provided to the buyer. The purchase price for the asset may be paid in a lump sum in advance (generally on the date of the Istisna'a agreement), or progressively in accordance with the progress of the construction/development of the asset.

(d) Ijara (leasing) funds

Similar to lease financing and hire purchase arrangements, the ijara structure involves a fund purchasing an asset (usually at the request of a party), and then leasing it (usually to the party that requested the financial institution to purchase the asset) for a fixed lease term. Ijara funds typically invest in finance leases and therefore do not run the residual risk of the asset, since the asset is sold to the lessee at the end of the lease term. The assets remain the property of the ijara fund, while responsibility for the assets remains with the fund manager.

(e) Murabaha funds

A Murabaha fund entails the purchase of an asset by the Murabaha fund, which it will subsequently sell to a third party at the cost of the asset plus a fixed profit which will be agreed in advance between the fund and a third party.

8.11.4 Parties to an Islamic investment fund

(a) Investors

The shareholders of an Islamic fund are issued with only one class of share, as under Sharia'a law it is a requirement that all shareholders be treated equally. Muslim investors who are subject to zakat (an obligatory social/religious payment which is calculated in accordance with an individual's personal wealth) will generally be required to calculate and pay their respective payment in relation to any gains in respect of capital invested in the fund.

(b) Sharia'a and fatwa board

The role of a Sharia'a and fatwa board will vary between funds, though standard duties will include:

- providing advice to the fund manager and setting compliance parameters in relation to the allocation of the fund's assets
- setting out criteria which potential investments must meet to be acceptable under Sharia'a law
- once the fund is launched, the Sharia'a and fatwa board must meet with the fund manager on a quarterly basis, or as otherwise agreed, to discuss issues relating to the ongoing Sharia'a endorsement of the fund
- annually publish its written fatwa (legal opinion) covering the reporting period, confirming compliance with the Sharia'a stipulations and guidelines to which the fund must adhere and
- advising on any deductions to be made in respect of purification required as a result of non-Sharia'a compliant investments.

All of the fund's potential investments must be reviewed by the Sharia'a and fatwa board and its rulings in relation to the same are binding upon the fund manager.

(c) Fund manager

The fund manager will select a draft list of potential investments for the fund, which they believe meet the investment criteria, and they will present this list to the Sharia'a and fatwa board and request a ruling. In accordance with the rulings provided by the Sharia'a and fatwa board the fund manager will then select the investments of the fund. The rulings of the Sharia'a and fatwa board are binding upon the decisions of the fund manager. A fund manager may be remunerated either via a fixed-fee arrangement or by taking a share of the profits produced by the fund.

8.11.5 Stock exchange

Sharia'a compliant index series are offered by Dow Jones, FTSE, S&P, MSC1 and Russell-Jadwa, each of which largely apply AAOIFI Sharia'a standard to determine eligibility of the investments. There are, however, some differences in the way the different index series apply the industry and financial screens as determined by the index's Sharia'a board. Fund managers generally prefer to use Sharia'a compliant indices as indicators, or references, for the performance of their portfolios and funds. There are, however, also managers that prefer to compare their portfolios to mainstream benchmarks as they consider that they are more relevant to the investment objectives of their clients or their own investment style. Some of the above exchanges are discussed in further detail below.

(a) Dow Jones Islamic Market Index

The Dow Jones Islamic Market Index (DJIM) was the first index created specifically for investment in companies compliant with Sharia'a law. Companies wishing to be listed upon the DJIM are subject to a two-stage screening process. First, companies are screened to ensure that their income does not exceed 5% of revenue in respect of impure sources, namely alcohol, tobacco, pork-related products, conventional financial services (i.e. banking and insurance), weapons and defence, and entertainment. Second, a company is subject to a financial ratio filter, whereby all of the below must total less than 33% to be approved:

- total debt divided by trailing 24-month average market capitalization
- the sum of a company's cash and interest-bearing securities divided by trailing 24-month average market capitalization and
- accounts receivables divided by trailing 24-month average market capitalization.

Companies which are approved on the basis of this two-stage test are permitted to be listed on the Dow Jones Islamic Market World Index.

(b) FTSE SGX Asia Shariah 100 index

In response to the growth for investment in companies compliant with Sharia'a law, the FTSE Group and the SGX launched the FTSE SGX Asia Shariah 100 Index. Similar to the DJIM, there is a two-stage criterion which a company must meet to be admitted to the index. First companies will not be deemed to be Sharia'a compliant where they engage in any of the following non-exhaustive list of business activities: conventional finance, entertainment, pork-related products, alcohol, tobacco. Second, financial ratio screening of the company must be undertaken, and the company must meet the following criteria to be considered Sharia'a compliant:

- debt is less than 33.333% of total assets
- cash and interest-bearing items are less than 33.333% of total assets
- accounts receivable and cash are less than 50% of total assets and
- total interest and non-compliant activities income should not exceed 5% of total revenue.

Not all Islamic funds that are currently established have performed well, but some have achieved performance in line with, or better than, both international and Islamic benchmarks. Those with more diversified investment strategies have often fared better. Performance swings have frequently been more acute in narrowly focused products. The exclusion of non-permissible industries reduces the prospective investment universe, although the global investment universe remains substantial.

Although the number of funds as well as the aggregate assets under management is still relatively small, the market is growing and fees are generally starting to come into line with those of conventional funds as investor demand drives it.

This chapter has addressed jurisdictions that are both the most significant sources of capital and the main recipients of that capital investment. The breakdown of the distinction between onshore and offshore is addressed in Chapter 13, section 13.7.3.

9

Sovereign Wealth Funds, State-sponsored Funds, Pension and Superannuation Schemes and Charities

9.1 INTRODUCTION

This chapter describes a sample of the various funds created and operated by the state either alone or in conjunction with the private sector. These funds are enormous investors in direct fund (and indeed fund of funds) managers' sponsored funds. With the exception of some of the sovereign wealth funds, most funds are operated exclusively in the public interest and so are frequently subjected to public and state review and scrutiny. Many of the state pension systems are vast in scale, in terms of assets managed or distributed and the number of people served by the schemes. Private pension funds are among the largest investors by asset value and play a key role in various markets. They are all significant operators in the global investment scene and for most fund managers they are likely to be investors with specific demands and restrictions.

9.2 SOVEREIGN WEALTH FUNDS (SWFS)

9.2.1 Definition of sovereign wealth fund

An SWF is a special purpose investment fund or arrangement owned and managed (directly or indirectly) by a government, created for macroeconomic purposes. An SWF is commonly established out of balance of payments surpluses, official foreign currency operations, the proceeds of privatizations, fiscal surpluses and/or receipts resulting from commodity exports. SWFs are created to hold, manage or administer assets to achieve financial objectives.

SWFs have existed for decades but are emerging as a potential large source of capital. SWFs have substantial resources and assets of high liquidity, and have grown significantly. These attributes of SWFs have seen them become an important investor group during the economic downturn/slowdown.

The first sovereign wealth fund named as such was the Kuwait Investment Authority established in 1953 to invest in excess oil revenues. Since this date the number and size of SWFs have increased dramatically: there are now more than 50 SWFs established with a combined assets under management (AUM) total of around USD 8.8 trillion.[1]

---

[1] http://www.swfinstitute.org/fund-rankings/

9.2.2   Source of sovereign wealth funds

There is a variety of sources from which SWFs are formed but in general they are the result of current account surpluses from a country's exports of commodities (commonly oil) and manufactured goods, fiscal surpluses, public savings or privatization receipts.

SWFs are usually sourced from two categories.

(a) Commodity funds

Commodity SWFs are predominantly funded from oil revenue, although other natural resources such as gas and minerals provide a not insignificant source of revenue. The main objectives of commodity-focused SWFs are to insure against the risk of volatile commodity markets, maintain economic stability and provide an income source for future generations.

(b) Non-commodity funds

Non-commodity SWFs are funded by the transfer of assets directly from official foreign exchange reserves, budget surpluses and privatization revenue.

9.2.3   Types of SWF investment vehicles

These are numerous, but commonly include the following.

(a) Stabilization funds

Stabilization funds are often set up in countries which have rich supplies of natural resources to safeguard the economy from the effects of volatile commodity markets. A stabilization fund is therefore established to help mitigate volatility by stabilizing fiscal revenues and sterilizing capital inflows. This is often achieved by building up a fund during times of favourable commodity prices and drawing on a fund when commodity prices or reserves fall low.

The investment strategy of a stabilization fund is conservative, focusing on fixed-income rather than equity investments; this helps the fund achieve its purpose.

(b) Saving funds

Saving funds are intended to share wealth across generations. For countries rich in natural resources (in particular those countries which have non-renewable natural resources), a savings fund allows the benefit of that resource to be shared with future generations. This is achieved by converting that source into a diversified portfolio of international financial assets which will be able to provide for future generations and other long-term objectives.

Given the long-term nature and investment horizon of a saving fund, the fund tends to invest in a broad range of assets and forms of alternative investments such as real estate, private equity, hedge funds and commodities.

(c) Reserve investment corporations funds

Reserve investment corporations funds are established for one of two reasons, either to reduce the opportunity cost of holding excess foreign reserves or to pursue investment policies with higher returns. These types of fund seek high returns and use leverage in their investments.

(d) Development funds

A development fund utilizes returns to further develop a country's economic and development goals such as improving its infrastructure.

(e) Pension reserve funds

Sovereign pension reserve funds are investment vehicles funded by a portion of assets set aside to prepare for the future needs and obligations owed to an aging society. The objective behind the fund is to accumulate assets in the now to offset predicted higher liability in the future in order to sustain future pensions and social welfare. A number of countries such as New Zealand, France and Ireland have established this type of fund.

9.2.4   SWF investment strategies

The investment strategies of SWFs vary according to several factors along with the state of the markets at the time and the investment outlook. The type of the sovereign wealth fund (see section 9.2.3 above) can influence the strategy – a reserve investment fund will for example seek liquid investments to mitigate the risk of balance of payment repercussions. The source of the wealth can also influence the investment strategy.

(a) Commodity SWFs

SWFs that derive their wealth primarily from commodities often have a long-term approach to investment decisions and a preference for investments which do not correlate strongly to the pricing of the commodities markets. Around four-fifths of funds derived from oil wealth are invested in overseas assets. Equity investments account for close to a half of their overseas investments, followed by fixed-income and bank deposits. This trend has shifted away from equities following the financial crisis of 2008.

(b) Non-commodity SWFs

Non-commodity SWFs are typically financed by capital resources built up from fiscal policies such as foreign currency reserves (in particular the US dollar) and often invested in US assets, particularly US government bonds. These SWFs have been an important source of liquidity on global capital markets. In recent years the poor performance of foreign currency denominated holdings has led to non-commodity SWFs diversifying their holdings. Asian central banks held the largest stock of US Treasury securities in 2012, with China and Japan each accounting for more than a fifth of foreign holdings.

(c) Diversification

SWFs are gradually creating more diversified investment portfolios with several SWFs embracing alternative asset classes such as real estate, infrastructure, hedge funds and private equity. The general reasoning behind a diversified portfolio is to reduce risk and mitigate loss, as investments are spread across a variety of asset classes and therefore the losses of one particular class have less effect.

9.2.5   Taxation of SWFs

The distinction between SWFs and the many other funds owned or managed by governments is unclear. As a consequence, it is not surprising that SWFs generally are taxed in the same fashion as the other government owned or controlled funds. The taxation systems applicable to SWFs and other governmental funds fall into three categories that are defined by their underlying policies. The three categories are described below.

(a) Unilateral exemptions

In the first category are countries that provide unilateral exemptions for SWFs on their investment income. The exemption is granted as an extension of the doctrine of sovereign immunity. Because of the widespread adoption of the **restrictive** theory of sovereign immunity (with immunity no longer applying to commercial activities of foreign government enterprises), the unilateral tax exemptions typically apply only to passive investment income and do not apply to income from commercial activities. The United States, Australia and the UK are in the first category.

The United States grants a unilateral exemption to foreign governments.[2] So long as the SWFs are either an integral part of a foreign government or an entity controlled by the foreign government, SWFs enjoy the benefit of a tax exemption.

The UK exemption for foreign governments also is done administratively. The UK government has said that where an SWF is an integral part of a foreign government it will benefit from the exemption from UK taxes. Because the UK recognizes the principle of sovereign immunity under which one state does not attempt to tax the activities of another state, the current practice of the UK government is to treat all passive income and gains beneficially owned by a foreign government as immune from direct taxes.[3]

(b) Reciprocal exemptions

The second category consists of governments that exempt foreign governments and their SWFs only where the foreign governments extend a comparable exemption. The reciprocal exemption is accomplished either domestically or through inclusion in bilateral double taxation treaties.

Even though it provides a unilateral tax exemption for foreign governments and their agencies, the United States has obtained exemptions for its government funds, including sub-national SWFs, such as the Alaska Permanent Fund, and US sub-national government investment funds that are not SWFs, such as CalPERS and SWIB.

(c) No special exemptions

In the third category are countries that have no special provisions for SWFs and other government owned and controlled entities. Presumably the dominant policy underpinning this category is the notion of taxpayer equity. Under this policy, as all foreign investors – irrespective

---

[2] US Internal Revenue Code of 1986 (as amended) Section 892

[3] HM Revenue and Customs, INTM155010 – *Sovereign and Crown Immunity*: http://www.hmrc.gov.uk/manuals/intmanual/INTM155010.htm: last accessed 17 July 2008. Joint at A-49

of their ownership or the source of their funds – obtain benefits from the host country's infrastructure and the investment opportunities it offers, they should all be subject to the same level of taxation.

9.2.6   Transparency of an SWF

(a) Introduction

There is a varying degree of transparency among SWFs. Some SWFs, such as Norway's Government Pension Fund Global, are very transparent – publicly disclosing the details of their fund including asset size, investment portfolio and returns – whereas other funds (in particular those in the Middle East) can be opaque.

(b) The Linaburg–Maduell Transparency Index

The Linaburg–Maduell Transparency Index was developed by the Sovereign Wealth Fund Institute (SWFI) and is used to rate the transparency of an SWF. The index uses a base of 10 essential principles, with each principle followed adding one point of transparency to the index rating. The SWFI recommends that a fund aims to achieve a minimum index rating of 8 in order to claim adequate transparency.

Table 9.1   The 10 essential principles of the Linaburg–Maduell Transparency Index

No	Principle
1	Fund provides history including reason for creation, origins of wealth and government ownership structure
2	Fund provides up-to-date independently audited annual reports
3	Fund provides ownership percentage of company holdings and geographic locations of holdings
4	Fund provides total portfolio market value, returns and management compensation
5	Fund provides guidelines in reference to ethical standards, investment policies and enforcer of guidelines
6	Fund provides clear strategies and objectives
7	If applicable, the fund clearly identifies subsidiaries and contact information
8	If applicable, the fund identifies external managers
9	Fund manages its own website
10	Fund provides main office location address and contact information such as telephone and fax

(c) Generally accepted principles and practices – Santiago Principles

The emergence of SWFs as powerful players in global financial markets, the considerable number of financial assets held in SWFs and the lack of transparency caused a degree of unease across advanced economies. The International Monetary and Financial Committee expressed the need to identify best practices among SWFs, highlighting the position of SWFs as recognized and well-established institutional investors and important participants in the international monetary and financial system. As a result of the above, the International Working Group of Sovereign Wealth Funds (IWG) was formed consisting of 26 International IMF member countries all realizing the need to demonstrate and communicate clearly the constructive role of SWFs in the world economy.

In October 2008 the IWG, assisted by the IMF, agreed a set of 24 'Generally Accepted Principles and Practices' (GAPP), known as the 'Santiago Principles', covering transparency and governance arrangements. The principles aim to provide guidance to help ensure that SWFs' investment decisions are based on economic and financial risk considerations and not political motive. The reasoning behind the principles stemmed from the recognition of SWFs as both beneficial and critical to international markets, and the need to demonstrate on an international level the economic and financial basis of the investments made to help maintain an open and non-discriminatory cross-border investment regime.

The principles are voluntary in their nature. The implementation of the principles is left to the individual SWFs and each principle is subject to the applicable 'home country laws' of each SWF.

(d) International Forum of Sovereign Wealth Funds

The International Forum of Sovereign Wealth Funds continues the work of the IWG. It remains a voluntary group of SWFs, which meet, exchange views on issues of common interest and facilitate an understanding of the Santiago Principles and SWF activities.

9.2.7 Key regulation

Concerns about the influence of SWF investment overseas have prompted calls to regulate or restrict the access of SWFs to domestic investment opportunities. The causes for concern include investments in industries which are of political and economic strategic importance and investments in currency reserves that are then used to manipulate exchange rates in order to aid the exports of the SWF's nation. These calls have generally been resisted on several grounds: such restrictions would be protectionist and could lead to retaliatory enactments; SWFs are an increasing source of finance and as a result can provide necessary capital where it is harder to raise locally; and there is a lack of evidence that such investments are made for political or economic strategic gain.

In the UK, governmental policy has been welcoming of SWF investment and few deals are obstructed. The Enterprise Act 2002 restricted the capacity for ministers to refer potential acquisitions to the Competition Commission, except on grounds of national security, financial stability or media pluralism. The scope for restriction is further limited by the provisions of EU law, as set out below.

Investments made by SWFs in assets within the EU are subject to the same rules and controls imposed on any other type of investment. SWFs are therefore subject to EU legislation governing the free movement of capital and the rules on both merger control and state aid. The EU has traditionally pledged itself to be open to foreign investments and favourable to the liberalization of transnational movement of capital. To this end, the Treaty on the Functioning of the EU (TFEU) prohibits not only restrictions to free movement of capital and payments between member states, but also between member states and third countries (Article 63 TFEU). Although Articles 64–66 TFEU provide some limitations to the principle laid down in Article 63, especially with respect to capital from third countries, the EU has not produced any specific restriction on the activities of SWFs. The European Commission issued a communiqué titled 'A Common European Approach to Sovereign Wealth Funds' which repeated these concepts, which declares that 'the commitment to openness to investments and free movement of capital has been a long standing principle of the EU and is key to success in an increasingly globalized international system'.[4]

In the US, investments made by SWFs have been a major political issue over the last two decades. The protectionist arguments and concerns about national security (including economic) are given greater weight in the public debates about such investment. Foreign equity investment is overseen by the Committee on Foreign Investment in the United States, chaired by the Treasury Department. Notifying the Committee is voluntary and it is under no obligation to investigate a referral. Only where there is credible evidence of a security risk and there is no other avenue to mitigate the risk will the Committee be permitted to prohibit the investment. The powers of the Committee have been strengthened by the Foreign Investment and National Security Act, requiring investigation of foreign government investment activity and broadening the scope of national security to include economic security and infrastructure.

9.3   STATE-SPONSORED FUNDS

9.3.1   Introduction

State funds are pools of capital provided by various governments to be invested in line with public policy. They are distinguished from SWFs typically by their commitment to smaller-scale investments (which primarily focus on stimulating economic activity within the state in question at particular times in the economic cycle), rather than investing surplus government income or capital in assets either domestic or international (usually with the sole intent of providing a direct economic return on investment). Many state funds have been established following the recent economic crisis in an effort to fill the commercial void with respect to lending to higher risk small enterprises. This void has been created by new regulation and changing attitudes within banking.

9.3.2   UK

(a)   Project Merlin

The government and the UK's four biggest banks, HSBC, Barclays, Royal Bank of Scotland and Lloyds Banking Group, came to an agreement in 2011 in which the banks committed to lending more money, in particular to small businesses.

---

[4] Communication from the Commission to the European Parliament, the Council, the European Economic and Social Committee and the Committee of the Regions, 'A Common European Approach to Sovereign Wealth Funds', COM(2008), 27 February 2008, p 1

As part of the agreement the four banks (and Santander) stated both their capacity and commitment to lending GBP 190 billion of new credit available to businesses. GBP 76 billion of the lending commitment is allocated to small and medium-sized enterprises. In addition, an extra GBP 1 billion of equity capital over a three-year period will be given to the Business Growth Fund and GBP 200 million to David Cameron's Big Society Bank which helps small businesses in disadvantaged parts of the UK.

(b) Funding for Lending Scheme

The Bank of England and HM Treasury launched the Funding for Lending Scheme in July 2012 with the aim of increasing the incentive for banks and building societies to lend to households and businesses within the UK.

The scheme is established with the view to reducing funding costs for banks and building societies so that consequently banks are able to make cheaper and more easily available loans.

This will be achieved by allowing banks and building societies to borrow from the Bank of England, in the form of UK Treasury Bills, for up to four years, for a fee. The scheme provides an 18-month period in which banks and building societies may borrow from the Bank of England; this is known as the drawdown period.

As security against the loan banks will provide collateral in the form of assets such as business or mortgage loans to the Bank of England. Once the loans mature the collateral will be swapped back to the relevant bank or building society. This structure will ensure that the risk from the loans will remain on the lender banks and building societies.

(c) Business Growth Fund

The Business Growth Fund (BGF) was established in 2011 following recommendations of the Business Finance Taskforce (the BFT), set up by the British Bankers' Association to consider what could be done to help the UK return to sustainable growth. It has been dubbed by private equity investors the 'new 3i', a reference to the founding of 3i, or Investors in Industry.

The BGF provides long-term capital for medium-sized British companies. In order to get the scheme off the ground and to help the BGF invest in businesses, the sponsoring BFT banks provided an initial GBP 2.5 billion. The initial criteria stated that the fund would invest between GBP 2 million and GBP 10 million into businesses in return for a minority stake, ranging from around 10% to 40%, and each portfolio business having an annual turnover of between GBP 5 million and GBP 100 million.

(d) The Innovation Investment Fund (IIF)

The IIF was established in 2009 as part of an initiative to encourage investment in private sector companies specializing in clean energy and hi-tech industry. It aimed to use public funds as seed capital and to raise a projected GBP 1 billion for investment. Of the two funds set up under the initiative only GBP 5 million of third party capital was raised between them. The government was to commit GBP 50 million to one fund and GBP 100 million to another, and the respective managers were to commit GBP 75 million and GBP 100 million.

The failure of the funds to achieve what the government later described as an 'aspirational target' appears to have been in part due to their structure and the requirements for investing were much more restrictive than those of equivalent privately run funds plus (as is often the case with these schemes), a suspicion on the part of private investors that government money comes with non-economic strings.

9.3.3   Europe

(a)   The European Central Bank (ECB)

The ECB, established in 1998, is a key part of the infrastructure of the Economic and Monetary Union (EMU) and the Eurozone, but it is also an institution of the EU more generally – the central banks of the 27 member states of the EU (including those 17 states that have adopted the euro) together with the ECB form the European System of Central Banks (ESCB). The ESCB does not take part in discussions or decisions concerning the monetary policy of the euro. Instead, this is reserved to those 17 central banks of the Eurozone and the ECB, together forming the Eurosystem. This abundance of bodies and acronyms makes policy discussions and reporting a potential source of great confusion.

The main objective of the ESCB and by extension the ECB is to support the general economic policies of the EU without prejudice to 'price stability', set out in the TFEU, Article 127(1). It is left to the ECB to define 'price stability'. It has been interpreted as low inflation. The ECB's monetary policy aims to restrict inflation to a maximum of an annual increase of 2% in the Harmonised Index of Consumer Prices, and to avoid deflation. The ECB is also the sole issuer of euro banknotes, and regulates the minting of coins.

The ECB operates two investment funds: one is of its foreign currency holdings (the 'foreign reserves portfolio') and the other is euro-denominated (the 'own funds portfolio'). The foreign reserves portfolio is managed to provide liquidity, security and return on investment in order for the ECB to have sufficient reserves of the key foreign currencies (such as the US dollar and the yen). The own funds portfolio consists of the ECB's reserve capital and paid-up capital with the aim of providing income to cover operating expenses. Neither fund is put to direct use in line with the ECB's objective of price stability.

(b)   The European Financial Stability Facility (EFSF) and the European Stability Mechanism (ESM)

The EFSF is a temporary fund set up in 2010 in the wake of the financial crisis to safeguard financial stability within the Eurozone. It is funded by issuing bonds and other debt securities on the capital markets and then in turn lends to member states of the Eurozone. It also undertakes an interventionist role in the capital markets to promote its objectives. The maximum that the EFSF was allowed to borrow was EUR 440 billion. A request for support is a formal procedure: the Eurozone state must request assistance and negotiate with the European Commission and the IMF a support package, which must be approved by the other Eurozone states unanimously. The need for support is tied to the cost of borrowing reaching an unacceptably high rate.

The EFSF has been formally replaced by the permanent ESM. The EFSF will continue to run the rescue programmes of Greece, Ireland and Portugal, while responsibility for the recapitalization of the Spanish banking sector has been turned over to the ESM. The EFSF will remain in operation until the last obligations are fully repaid.

The ESM is the permanent 'firewall' for the Eurozone. It is funded in part by paid-in capital (EUR 80 billion) and the remaining EUR 620 billion of its authorized capital will be raised by debt issuances as and when they are needed. The Eurozone states will back the total of EUR 700 billion in proportion to their economic capacity to support the programme. Germany is the biggest contributor, Malta the smallest. The total amount of bailout loans cannot exceed EUR 500 billion and the remaining EUR 200 billion is a reserve amount to guarantee the highest credit rating for the debt instruments issued. This has not proved entirely successful as the credit rating for debt issues was downgraded by Moody's in November 2012.

A request for assistance is made to the ESM and assessed for its potential impact on the Eurozone and the sustainability of the applicant's public debt by the so-called troika: the European Commission, the ECB and the IMF. A Memorandum of Understanding is drawn up which sets out the conditions attached to lending along with a facility agreement. The troika is responsible for monitoring compliance with the conditions attached to the facility.

Investors acquire the debt securities issued by the ESM in much the same way as other state debt is invested in. Although the Eurozone states are contributors to the pooled funds, the securities issued are not attributable to the individual states. That has made little difference to the market's perception of such securities; Moody's downgraded the debt securities issued by the ESM in November 2012 in part motivated by concerns about the ability of France to fulfil its capital commitments.

(c) The European Investment Bank (EIB)

The EIB is a long-standing institution which pre-dates the EMU by several decades, being established in 1958. It is a bank owned by the member states of the EU (rather than the Eurozone states) and invests to bring about 'European integration and social cohesion'. The member state shareholders set the broad policy goals of the EIB and also oversee the decision-making bodies – the Board of Governors and the Board of Directors. The bank is financed by the member states and by raising money on the capital markets. The EIB does not loan exclusively to or within EU member states; about 10% of its lending was to or within over 150 'partner countries'. Its debt is priced at a similar level to prime sovereign debt and carries an AAA rating.

The investment policy is currently directed towards four areas: innovation and skills, access to finance for smaller companies, resource efficiency and strategic infrastructure. One of the EIB's divisions is the European Investment Fund (EIF) which is a venture capital provider investing in small and medium enterprises.

(d) The European Investment Fund (EIF)

The EIF was established in 1994 and is an entity formed by the EU to provide finance to small and medium-sized enterprises. It is owned by the EIB, the EU through the European Commission and several private European financial institutions. It does not lend directly to these enterprises, instead it finances them through private banks and funds. It is reported to be the largest LP in European venture capital funds.

9.3.4   The US

The US Small Business Jobs Act 2010 (SBJ Act) created a number of initiatives and funds to support small businesses and manufacturers. These initiatives are administered by the US Small Business Administration (SBA). This federal government agency is part of the US Department of the Treasury. The SBA has numerous programmes that are designed to assist small businesses including educational programmes and a variety of loan programmes. Two major creations from the SBJ Act were the State Small Business Credit Initiative and the Small Business Lending Fund.

The JOBS Act 2012 is much heralded in the US and aims to provide further support to small business and start-up funding by reducing federal regulation. Although the fund-raising platform known as 'crowdfunding' pre-dates the passage of the JOBS Act by several years, the passing of the legislation has seen an increase in the number of small investors using crowdfunding platforms to provide capital to start-ups and small businesses. The JOBS Act 2012 allows a business to raise up to USD 1 million a year from small investors who otherwise could not be approached without stricter regulatory approval or a public offering registered under the Securities Act of 1933. A potential investor who earns less than USD 100,000 a year may invest up to USD 2000 or 5% of their annual income (whichever is greater), and for those with greater income, a maximum of 10% of their annual income. The company must sell equity to investors through an SEC-registered broker but can offer non-equity rewards to investors without further registration (rewards such as discounted products or services once the business is established).

9.4   PENSIONS

9.4.1   What is a pension?

A pension is a way of saving for retirement. Money is paid into a pension fund (to a pension provider) that then invests the money with the aim of increasing the value of the fund over a long period of time in order to provide an income on retirement – a pension.

A simple definition of a pension for an individual is a regular payment paid to a person on their retirement so that the individual can remain economically active in the absence of work. Pensions are also referred to as 'superannuation funds', which in some countries carries a specific meaning (see below) or is a broader term encompassing company pension plans or certain public sector plans.

9.4.2   UK pensions

(a)   History

The first UK pension began life in 1670 for Royal Navy officers. It was not until 1908 that the Old Age Pensions Act introduced the first general old age pension on a means-tested basis. In 1925 the Contributory Pensions Act established a contributory state scheme for manual workers and others earning up to GBP 250 a year. It was in 1946, following Sir William Beveridge's published paper titled 'Social Insurance and Allied Services' containing proposals for state welfare reform, that the National Insurance Act 1946 introduced a contributory state pension for all.

(b)   The state pension

There are two parts to a state pension: a basic state pension and a state second pension. Individuals who have made a sufficient amount of National Insurance contributions or accrued National Insurance credits during their lifetime will be eligible for the basic state pension.

The state second pension, previously known as the State Earnings Related Pension Scheme (SERPS), provides additional money on top of the basic state pension. An individual may contract out of a state second pension and choose to join a private pension scheme instead. However, contracting out of SERPS has been a minor scandal and some people have contracted back.

(c) Public sector pensions

Individuals working for the public sector are generally entitled to join a public sector pension scheme such as the National Health Service (NHS) scheme for England and Wales or the teachers' scheme for England and Wales. The incentive of such schemes is to provide a more generous pension provision than the private sector schemes; however, in recent years due to government changes the benefits of public sector pensions have been heavily disputed.

(d) The private pension

Private pensions can be established on an individual basis or through an employer's scheme. There are two main types of private pensions: occupational pension schemes and individual arrangements.

Occupational pension schemes are set up by an employer for the benefit of employees. The scheme is administered by a trustee together with the employer with ultimate liability for administering the scheme and providing benefits under it.

A personal pension scheme is created through a contract between a pension scheme provider and an individual, and an employer may if they wish pay into an employee's personal pension.

(e) Types of benefit provisions/arrangements

The type of arrangement to which a pension scheme belongs is an important factor as this determines how the pension fund is taxed and withdrawn. There can be a number of arrangements to any one scheme. There are four types of arrangements.

(i) Money purchase arrangements or defined contribution scheme

In this type of scheme the contributions payable to a member are of a specified level (defined) but the final benefit of the scheme remains unknown until retirement. This is because the benefit the individual receives on retirement will be based on the total contributions made into the scheme, the level of investment returns on those contributions (which are dependent on the stock market) and the available rates for buying into an annuity that will provide the pension.

(ii) Defined benefit arrangements

Under this type of arrangement the amount of pension received on retirement is fixed and is not dependent upon the size of the pension fund at the date of retirement. These schemes have become less popular over the years given the risk posed to the pension provider in making up any shortfall between the investment return on the contributions and the amount promised, which in some cases creates a slow decline in the main operating business.

(iii) Cash balance arrangements

In a cash balance arrangement all or part of the member's pot is promised or guaranteed without direct reference to payments made by the member. The amount that is paid by the member (either actually or notionally) is fixed, meaning that there can be a shortfall, the risk of which is placed on the employer or the fund rather than the member. This promise or guarantee breaks the connection between the amounts going into the scheme and the pot that will eventually be made available to provide benefits, making these cash balance arrangements.

(iv) Hybrid arrangements

Hybrid arrangements are private pension schemes which are neither pure defined benefit nor defined contribution arrangements. One example of how such a scheme may work is that an individual would be allowed to accrue benefits on a defined contribution basis until a certain age at which benefits would then accrue on a defined benefit basis.

(f) Structure of pension schemes

A pension scheme may be set up in various ways as for example by a trust, a contract, a board's resolution or a deed poll. The most common structure used is that of a trust. A pension scheme trust is usually created with one or more trustees, who become the legal owners of the pension scheme assets. The governing document of a pension trust will be the trust deed and rules which not only create the trust but contain specific provisions and rules in relation to key elements of the scheme such as administration and management.

The trustees' power to invest is often wide ranging, with legislation conferring power upon the trustees as if they were the outright owners of the assets. The trust deed will give trustees a number of powers, importantly: the powers to accept contributions into the scheme, to decide the investment strategy of the scheme, to invest the scheme's assets and often detailed powers as to particular investments which they may make.

9.4.3 European pensions

There is no consistent pension scheme across Europe. Pension rules, such as taxation and regulatory requirements, vary significantly across all member states. In order to bring a more homogenized system across Europe, the IORP Directive (Directive 2003/41/EC on the activities and supervision of institutions for occupational retirement provisions) was enacted in June 2003. The Directive has made a step towards harmonizing the pension provisions across Europe. The provisions in the Directive recognize the fact that an internal market for financial services was needed for economic growth and job creation. Thus, company pension plans play a key role in ensuring the integration, efficiency and liquidity of financial markets. The Directive is trying to provide a harmonized Community legislative framework for occupational pension funds to fully benefit from the advantages of the internal market.

One important feature of the IORP Directive is the establishment of a regulatory mechanism supporting the operation of cross-border occupational pension schemes. These rules apply only to funded pension schemes, and do not apply to state or personal pension schemes.

The Directive enables the establishment of pan-European pension funds that manage the pension schemes of employees in different member states. The Directive states that the pension funds should:

- have sufficient assets to cover pension commitments
- possess professionally qualified bodies, sound administrative procedures and adequate internal control mechanisms and
- be transparent towards plan members by clearly communicating the target level of benefits, risk exposure and investment management costs.

(a) Establishing a cross-border pension fund

Under the Directive, cross-border assets and liabilities of a pension fund can be combined within a single legal entity.

(b) Barriers against establishing a cross-border pension fund

Problem areas appeared due to the different interpretation and implementation of the IORP Directive. Member states have 'definitional differences' and clarification is required in four areas: cross-border activity, subordinated loans, ring-fencing and investment regulations. There is also reluctance from member states to see pension capital drift away from domestic markets.

However, some of the biggest hurdles faced by the multinationals have been discriminatory tax treatments in EU member states, although these barriers have recently started to break down. Others include complying with the social and labour laws of each country. As long as these laws are not harmonized within the EU, occupational pension products will be subject to different requirements in the various EU countries, which makes it very complex to administer cross-border schemes.

The European Commission is currently carrying out a review of the IORP Directive and has received advice from the European Insurance and Occupational Pensions Authority on the drafting of a new, IORP II Directive. The European Commission plans to publish the revised directive in the near future.

9.4.4   France

The pension system in France is formed by a three-pillar system. Beyond the three pillars, all employees can enrol into a private retirement saving scheme.

(a) Public pension system

This is primarily funded by social tax imposed on income from estates and investments, surplus sums from the French National Old Age Fund and the proceeds from the sale of certain state-owned assets. The statutory pension insurance scheme is a compulsory basic social security system, which provides earnings-related benefits for employees in the private sector.

(b) Private pension schemes

These can be either defined contribution or defined benefit plans. Private pension plans are not mandatory, however all employees must be enrolled in the basic and supplementary pension schemes. Therefore, all employees are subscribed to the first and second pillar pension plans, and can choose to enrol in a third pillar scheme operated by an insurance company. The third pillar pension schemes are administered by an insurance company authorized to do so by the French authorities.

9.4.5   Germany

The German pension system was one of the earliest universal national pension systems. It has been the model for many other social security systems across the world. The current system is mainly influenced by the 1972 reform which made the German pension system one of the most generous in the world.

(a) Statutory pension scheme

Participation in the statutory pension scheme is mandatory for all employees. The statutory pension scheme provides for old age pensions (normal retirement age: 67), reduced earnings capacity pensions and widow's and orphan's pension. The monthly contributions calculated on the basis of the employee's individual salary are borne by the employer, who can claim half of the contributions from the employee by deducting them from the monthly salary. Hence, the contribution rate is equally shared between the employee and the employer. As a pay-as-you-go-system the statutory pension scheme is barely protected against the demographic change.

(b) Company and private pension schemes

As a consequence of the decreasing capability of the statutory pension scheme due to demographic change, the co-existing company and private pension schemes are of growing importance.

There are five different ways to carry out a company pension promise, as follows.

(i) Direct pension promise ('Direktzusage')
The employer contractually promises to grant the employee or his/her survivors pension benefits financed out of its own equity.

(ii) Direct insurance ('Direktversicherung')
The employer enters into a contract in favour of the employee with a life insurance provider carrying out the contractual pension promise between the employer and its employee. The employer has to bear the insurance contributions and the employee is entitled to the insurance benefits.

(iii) Company pension fund ('Pensionskasse')
Company pension funds are a special type of life insurance provider in the field of company pension schemes. As in the case of a direct insurance, the employer generally enters into a contract with the company pension fund for the benefit of the employee in order to carry out the contractual pension promise between the employer and its employee. The employer has to bear the insurance contributions and the employee is entitled to the insurance benefits.

(iv) Pension fund ('Pensionsfonds')
The contractual structure between the employer, the employee and the pension fund equals the contractual structure in cases of a direct insurance. Pension funds – as life insurance providers and company pension funds – are subject to the German Insurance Supervisory Authority, but are able to act more freely in their investment policy. In case of a shortfall the employer has an obligation to make additional contributions.

(v) Pension relief fund ('Unterstützungskasse')

Pension relief funds serve one company or several companies at once and are financed by allowances of the employer(s).

Company pension plans can be financed by the employee, the employer or both. The employer always has to promise a certain or at least determinable amount of pension benefits. As a result, independent of the type of financing or the way of carrying out the pension promise, the employer is always liable for the promised pension benefits. This even applies if the employer involves an external pension provider (e.g. direct insurance or company pension fund) to carry out the pension promise and if the promise is solely financed by conversion of employees' earnings.

9.4.6   US pensions

(a) General

Employee benefit plan investors are generally subject to the fiduciary responsibility provisions of Title I, Part 4 of ERISA. These provisions impose standards of conduct on each individual or entity which has discretionary authority or control over the investment of employee benefit plan assets, or which is otherwise treated as a fiduciary with respect to a plan under ERISA. These rules require, among other things, that each fiduciary discharge its duties prudently and for the exclusive purpose of providing benefits to plan participants and beneficiaries. Fiduciaries are required to diversify plan investments so as to minimize the risk of loss and to invest the assets of a plan as a whole, in a manner that is consistent with the purposes of the plan, the terms of the plan insofar as they comply with ERISA, and the cash flow requirements and funding objectives of the plan. ERISA and related provisions of the IRC also prohibit certain specified transactions (or 'prohibited transactions') between a plan and a 'party in interest' (or related party to the plan) unless a statutory or administrative exemption applies.

Before proceeding to invest a portion of an employee benefit plan's assets in a fund, the fiduciary, taking into account the particular facts and circumstances of such employee benefit plan, should consider all applicable fiduciary standards, any prohibited transaction concerns, and the permissibility of such investment under the documents and procedures governing the administration of the plan. The fiduciary should give special attention to:

(i)   the Department of Labor's regulations defining 'plan assets' (the 'Plan Asset Regulations'), and the impact of such regulations upon the fiduciary's decision to invest in a fund, and

(ii) the prudence of an investment in a fund, taking into account the other investments made with the assets of the plan and the diversification thereof, whether an investment of plan assets in a fund is consistent with the cash flow requirements and funding objectives of the plan and all other facts and circumstances of the investment which the fiduciary knows or should know are relevant to the investment in a fund.

A fiduciary can be personally liable for:

- losses incurred by an employee benefit plan resulting from a breach of fiduciary duties
- a civil penalty, which may be imposed by the Department of Labor, of as much as 20% of the amount recovered by the employee benefit plan and
- prohibited transaction excise taxes described below.

(b) Plan Asset Regulations

The Plan Asset Regulations set forth guidelines to determine when an employee benefit plan's equity investment in an entity, such as a fund, that is neither publicly offered securities nor securities of an investment company registered under the ICA, will cause the underlying assets of that entity to be treated as assets of the plan for purposes of the fiduciary responsibility provisions of ERISA and the prohibited transaction provisions of ERISA and the IRC ('Plan Assets').

The Plan Asset Regulations impose a 'look-through rule' based on the premise that, with certain exceptions, when a plan indirectly retains investment management services by investing in non-publicly traded equity securities of a pooled investment vehicle, the assets of the vehicle should be viewed as plan assets and managed according to the fiduciary responsibility provisions of ERISA. The Plan Asset Regulations distinguish pooled investment vehicles, which are subject to the look-through rule, from operating companies, which are not. Because venture capital companies may have characteristics of both pooled investment vehicles and operating companies, specific venture capital operating company (VCOC) and real estate operating company (REOC) definitions are included in the regulations, to provide guidance in determining when the operating company exception is available for a venture capital operating company or real estate operating company. The Plan Asset Regulations generally provide that the assets of an entity will not be regarded as plan assets if, among other conditions, the entity is a VCOC or REOC or if equity participation in the entity by 'benefit plan investors' is not 'significant'.

For the purposes of the Plan Asset Regulations, equity participation in an entity by benefit plan investors will not be significant if they hold, in the aggregate, less than 25% of the value of any class of such entity's equity, excluding equity interests held by persons (other than a benefit plan investor) with discretionary authority or control over the assets of the entity or who provide investment advice for a fee (direct or indirect) with respect to such assets, and any affiliates thereof. In this event, the entity's underlying assets would not be considered to be plan assets under ERISA or the Code. For purposes of this 25% test, 'benefit plan investors' include all employee benefits plans that are subject to ERISA or the Code, including 'Keogh' plans, individual retirement agreements (IRAs) and any entity whose underlying assets are deemed to include plan assets under the Plan Asset Regulations (e.g. an entity of which 25% or more of the value of any class of equity interests is held by employee benefit plans or other benefit plan investors and which does not satisfy another exception under the Plan Asset Regulations), but only to the extent of benefit plan investors invested in such entity. Foreign pension plans, government plans and church plans are not considered to be benefit plan investors. Private equity and hedge funds will typically seek to limit investments in the fund so that equity participation in the fund by benefit plan investors is not significant.

(c) Plan asset consequences

If the assets of a fund were to be deemed to be plan assets under ERISA, this would result, among other things, in the application of the prudence and other fiduciary responsibility standards of ERISA to investments made by the fund, and the possibility that certain transactions in which the fund might seek to engage could constitute 'prohibited transactions' under ERISA and the Code. If a prohibited transaction occurs for which no exemption is available, the general partner and any other fiduciary that has engaged in the prohibited transaction could be required to restore to a plan any profit realized on the transactions and to reimburse the plan for any losses suffered by the plan as a result of the investment. In addition, each disqualified person (within the meaning of IRC Section 4975) involved could be subject to an excise tax equal to 15% of the amount involved in the prohibited transaction for each year the transaction continues and, unless the transaction is corrected within statutorily required periods, to an additional tax of 100%. Plan fiduciaries who decide to invest in a fund could, under certain circumstances, be liable for prohibited transactions or other violations as a result of their investment in the fund or as co-fiduciaries for actions taken by or on behalf of the fund. With respect to an IRA that invests in a fund, the occurrence of a prohibited transaction involving the individual who established the IRA, or his or her beneficiaries, would cause the IRA to lose its tax exempt status.

(d) Additional fiduciary responsibilities

Regardless of whether or not the assets of a fund are treated as plan assets, the purchase and retention of any interests in a fund by an employee benefit plan will be subject to fiduciary standards of conduct and the prohibited transaction rules that are otherwise applicable to employee benefit plans under ERISA and the IRC. For example, interests in a fund should not be purchased by an employee benefit plan if the general partner, the investment manager or any of their affiliates:

(i)   is a party in interest with respect to the employee benefit plan, or
(ii) either
    (A) has investment discretion with respect to the investment of such employee benefit plan's assets, or
    (B) regularly gives investment advice with respect to such employee benefit plan's assets for a fee, pursuant to an understanding that such advice will serve as a primary basis for investment decisions with respect to such employee benefit plan's assets and that such advice will be based on the particular investment needs of the employee benefit plan, if, as a result of exercising such discretion or giving such advice, the employee benefit plan invests in the fund.

Also, a prohibited transaction may still occur under ERISA or the IRC where there are circumstances indicating that:

(i)   the investment in the fund is made or retained for the purpose of avoiding application of the fiduciary standards of ERISA
(ii) the investment in the fund constitutes an arrangement under which it is expected that the fund will engage in transactions which would otherwise be prohibited if entered into directly by the employee benefit plan investing in the fund
(iii) the investing employee benefit plan, by itself, has the authority or influence to cause the fund to engage in such transactions or
(iv) the person who is prohibited from transacting with the investing employee benefit plan may, but only with the aid of certain of its affiliates and the investing employee benefit plan, cause the fund to engage in such transactions with such person.

(e) Government pension plans

It should be noted that ERISA generally does not cover pension plans established and maintained by government entities. The laws and regulations of the jurisdiction governing the government pension plans should be consulted to determine the fiduciary rules and any other issues that may need to be considered when a government plan invests in a fund.

9.4.7   Australia

In Australia the general term used synonymously with pension is 'superannuation', and for this section (9.4.7), all references to 'superannuation' are used in this context. Australian superannuation schemes are increasingly investing offshore in European, US and Asian markets and funds and have become (although not as much as US plans of course) a major investor in private equity worldwide.

Superannuation normally takes the form of a fund held on trust and invested for the members of the fund until they retire or reach their set preservation age, at which time the money invested in the fund can be withdrawn as a pension or (subject to certain requirements) as a lump sum.

(a) How is a superannuation fund formed?

A superannuation fund is formed by a trustee creating a trust and irrevocably electing treatment as a complying superannuation fund under applicable laws. Over time the fund is built up through compulsory contributions made by an individual's employer, voluntary contributions by the individual and government co-contributions.

Employer contributions are paid at a rate determined by the employer/employee agreement (which may be enterprise or industry wide or an individual contract). From 1 July 2013 the minimum rate is 9.25% of an employee's annual ordinary times earnings, otherwise the employer incurs a superannuation guarantee charge (effectively a tax impost on the employer non-deductible for income tax purposes).

(b) Types of superannuation funds

There are many different types of funds which individuals can choose to contribute into if they meet the appropriate eligibility criteria.

The six basic types of funds are:

(i)   Retail funds – available to the public, are run by financial institutions that offer products on a commercial basis and the trustees of the fund are usually part of a financial conglomerate
(ii) Industry funds – large industry funds are available to the public, in general others are restricted for those working in a particular industry
(iii) Self-managed superannuation funds (or SMSFs) – private funds set up and managed by up to four members, who either act as individual trustee(s) or establish a proprietary company to act as trustee where each member must be a director of the company
(iv) Public sector funds – are available for the benefit of government employees or are schemes established by a Commonwealth, State or Territory law

(v) Corporate funds – available for the benefit of individuals working for a particular employer or corporation and

(vi) Small Australian Prudential Regulatory Authority (APRA) funds – these offer the flexibility of an SMSF; however, associated trustee responsibility and risk of compliance breaches are performed by a professional licensed trustee.

The above funds will be structured in one of the following two forms.

(i)   Accumulation (or defined contribution) benefit
Overwhelmingly, this structure is the most common form of fund.

(ii) Defined benefit
It is no longer possible to establish new defined benefit funds, as a result of changes to the law, so members with these benefit types belong to funds already in existence prior to the change in law.

(c) Superannuation investment structures

(i)   The general structure
All superannuation funds operate as trusts. The trustee, however, will usually delegate their investment management responsibilities to one or more external fund managers through an investment management agreement.

(i)   Implemented consulting
Under this structure, an asset consultant will provide both the advice to the fund trustee on the selection of investment managers and the investment vehicle that will administer investments of differing super funds.

(ii) Corporate master trust
Funds operating as a corporate master trust pass on the entire governance of the scheme as well as the trusteeship to an external service provider which will act on a commercial basis. The main purpose of the fund is to pool money to enable access to larger and more varied markets to produce higher returns.

(iii) Self-managed superannuation fund
SMSFs form the largest superannuation sector by number of funds and asset size. Within an SMSF, members of the fund can manage all of the affairs of their SMSF but most engage a service provider (e.g. their accountant or a package supplier) to perform a substantial number of the tasks of running a fund.

(d) Regulation

(i)   Superannuation Industry (Supervision) Act
The Superannuation Industry (Supervision) Act 1993 is the legislation which governs the majority of superannuation funds and is the statutory basis for all superannuation funds. The legislation has been significantly enhanced in the decade to 2013, with new and stronger requirements being imposed in such areas as fund registration and licensing of trustees.

(ii) APRA

The APRA is the prudential regulator of the Australian financial services industry, responsible for prudential supervision of banks, insurers and superannuation fund trustees. Its oversight applies to all registrable superannuation funds and entities (excluding SMSFs, which are regulated by the Commissioner of Taxation).

(ii) ASIC

The ASIC is responsible for the enforcement of the Corporations Act 2001 which regulates the conduct and disclosure obligations of financial services providers.

The ASIC also provides policy guidance outlining their expectations in relation to certain requirements in the legislation.

9.4.8   Pension funds as an investor

Pension funds are the largest class of institutional investors worldwide. There are trillions of dollars under management across the main markets such as the US, the UK, France, Germany, the Netherlands, Japan and Australia. It is important for any fund manager to appreciate the strategies and concerns of pension fund managers as they become increasingly significant investors in alternative asset classes. So for example when US ERISA pension funds invest in private equity partnership funds, they sometimes require their own rules or structures in separate ERISA governed parallel partnerships.

Pension funds were historically very conservative in their investment strategies, investing in government bonds or life insurance annuities – seeking low risk long-term investment with a fixed rate of return. Inflation and other socio-economic pressures have led to pension funds needing to invest with strategies which led to greater returns, both to counter inflation and because pensioners live longer. To overcome these pressures, funds increasingly turned to other traditional investment classes such as equities or bonds in order to obtain a higher return and lower the eventual cost of pension plans. Further to this, pension funds have turned to alternative assets in order to seek ever greater returns; these investments include venture capital and private equity, hedge funds and debt finance.

Regulations surrounding the area of pension fund investments have historically varied between continental Europe on one hand, and the UK and the US on the other hand. In continental Europe quantitative restrictions were generally applied to institutional investors' investments. By contrast, in the common law tradition of the Anglo-Saxon countries, fund managers as trustees were under an obligation to invest as a prudent person would, with focus on their conduct and status (such as potential or actual conflict of interest) and a free choice of investment strategy so long as it is prudent and contains diversification, subject to any terms of the pension fund trust documents.

The interpretation by the courts of the prudential manager has frequently been narrow with the result that only investments such as government issued securities would be upheld as prudent. In the UK more flexibility was given to fund managers in 1961[5] and investment policy and trustee restrictions were rewritten completely in 1995.[6] Trustees are free to (unless otherwise restricted) invest the fund's assets as if they owned those assets themselves. The trustees are obligated to draw up and maintain a written statement of principles governing investment decisions and addressing matters such as the investment assets to be held, the balance between different types and the risk profile of the portfolio.

---

[5] Trustee Investments Act 1961

[6] Pensions Act 1995

The US has provided flexibility to pension funds since 1974. While the UK and the US were the first ones to lift these restrictions, continental Europe remained concerned about high risk investments and gave priority to financial stability over higher returns. Over time, however, regulations have been liberalized in all countries. The IORP Directive required all member states to adopt prudent person rules for pension funds. The assets shall be invested in the best interests of the beneficiaries and members of the fund and in a manner as to ensure the security, quality, liquidity and profitability of the portfolio as a whole. Member states are still allowed to impose some quantitative restrictions on investment management although these are heavily qualified.

The liabilities of a pension scheme are long term, and it is important that the scheme is able to meet its liabilities when they fall due. To ensure that liabilities can be met as they fall, the funding level, existing investments and new contributions all need to be monitored along with the age of the members. It is generally the trustee who decides and is responsible for the investment strategy of the fund. A trustee will often take decisions on the investment strategy of a scheme following the professional advice of the scheme's advisers such as an investment consultant.

A number of factors will be taken into consideration when deciding upon the investment strategy of the fund, in particular: any limitations on investments contained in the trust deed and rules; any legal requirements such as the fiduciary duty to choose investments which are in the members' best financial interests and not for ethical or political purposes; the suitability of an asset class to meet the scheme's needs; the possible risks and returns in different types of investment; and ensuring diversification of the scheme's asset so as not to rely upon one particular asset class.

Once an investment strategy is established the trustee will draw up a written statement of investment principles which sets out principles as to how investments should and must be made. The statement will govern factors such as the choice and types of investments, risk management and the rights to be attached to investments. The statement will be reviewed every three years (or sooner if there is a significant change in investment policy).

9.5 CHARITIES

9.5.1 What is a charity?

Charities are commonly defined as not-for-profit organizations established and run with a philanthropic goal. In the UK, charities must be established for exclusively charitable purposes, be set up for the benefit of the public or community and must use any profits generated for the purpose of the charity. It is important to note that charity is a status and not a legal form or structure. Various different kinds of organizations can qualify as a charity, whether they are companies, trusts or bodies set up by specific legislation. Regardless, all charities in England and Wales are regulated by the Charity Commission and are subject to the general principles of charity law.[7]

Although the definition may vary from country to country depending on regulation and legislation, what is clear is that endowed charitable institutions are a significant investor group which should not be overlooked. Given that many charities derive a significant proportion of their income from investment returns, it is true to say that charities share certain characteristics with pension funds and private trusts.[8]

---

[7] The Charity Commission, *The Essential Trustee: What you need to know*, March 2012, section B1.

[8] Jenkins R, *The Governance and Financial Management of Endowed Charitable Foundations*, Association of Charitable Foundations, London, 2012.

9.5.2   UK history

The practice of charitable giving has been common for centuries, with wealthy benefactors providing funds for the less fortunate as well as for the benefit of religious and learning institutions. Charity is a cornerstone of the Christian faith and before the advent of the welfare state, charity developed alongside society. However, early charity tended to be direct and disorganized with little forward planning. The industrial revolution saw the rise of great industrialists and bankers of the Victorian era and this coincided with a period of great hardship for the working poor. This in turn spawned charities such as the Peabody Trust for social housing, and the establishment of religious charities such as the Salvation Army. Consequently, this period saw the development of charities into something more similar to the sector we see today. The US too has a great tradition of philanthropy epitomized by the Rockefeller Foundation and the thousands of libraries and other public buildings funded by Andrew Carnegie.

As charities have grown and the organizations have acquired greater supplies of funds, so their reach has expanded and greater organizational complexity is the result. Today, the largest charities must function as businesses in order to guarantee efficiency and secure their long-term future. As such, charities must use their resources wisely and guarantee the availability of stable streams of cash flow. Like many other large businesses with similar demands, investing assets into funds is a way for charities to manage their resources and engage in long-term financial planning. With charities now investing into funds, the products themselves must be tailored to the needs of the charity. Often, charities may not wish to have their assets invested (even indirectly) into industries which they do not support. This so-called 'moral' investment strategy can result in funds that do not invest in areas such as tobacco, pharmaceuticals, defence, oil and gas.

Historically, charities were prohibited from making investments that carried any significant degree of risk. UK legislation such as the Trustee Investments Act 1961 and the Trustee Act 2000 have brought changes which allow charities to manage their investments in order to focus on greater returns despite the increased level of risk associated with a high-yield strategy. The focus for trustees is to balance the opportunity of securing good investment while avoiding any undue risk.[9] As such, a foundation's investment strategy should be in line with its charitable objectives. Specifically, a charity will try to make investments that will produce levels of returns sufficient to provide it with income and capital appreciation that will cover all the foundation's costs (including investment management fees) and, of course, facilitate its charitable objectives.

Under the UK Trustee Act 2000, trustees of unincorporated charities are permitted to delegate various aspects including:

(a) carrying out a decision that the trustees have taken
(b) the investment of assets or
(c) raising funds for the trust other than by the profits of trade which is integral to carrying out the trust's charitable purposes.[10]

This means that UK charities are permitted to delegate their investment duties to professional investment managers and therefore gives the charity better access to the wider fund and investment market.

---

[9] *Ibid.*
[10] s11(3) The Trustee Act 2000

9.5.3   Investment strategies

Similar to the various approaches taken by different investment portfolios such as hedge funds and pension funds, the goals and strategies of different charities occupy the full spectrum of the investment market. A charity will seek to adopt a strategy that serves to meet its operational objectives.

A charity's investment strategy will usually be driven by either the terms of the endowments themselves or by strategic management decisions taken by the trustees.

9.5.4   Taxation

There is a variety of different tax reliefs available to charities. For example, provided a donation is used for charitable purposes only, a charity may apply for an exemption to corporation or income tax which would otherwise be payable on receipt of such a donation. Business rates relief can be applied in order to assist charities with their overheads and is applied to property occupied by a charity.

There are various tax incentives to encourage businesses and individuals to make charitable donations such as relief from corporation and income tax.

Although charities typically enjoy favourable tax treatment, this will not usually extend to income or capital generated by financial investments. The tax exemptions applied to charities are normally restricted to charitable donations, trading in the charity's primary purpose (such as a religious charity selling holy books) or else trading mainly carried out by the charity's beneficiaries. Any non-charitable trading undertaken in order to raise funds to be applied for charitable purposes, such as financial investments, is taxable subject to small trading exemptions.

9.5.5   Charities as investors

In the UK, investments made by charities are dwarfed by those made by pension funds. However, certain organizations such as university colleges and religious orders are relatively major players in the British investment scene.

One explanation for investment success for charitable foundations is that, unlike some hedge funds and pension funds, the foundations are able to focus on long-term investment strategies and do not have such severe restrictions in terms of the needs for liquidity and short-term returns.

In the US, charitable endowments operate on a larger scale and as such investments into funds are also more common. The largest US investment portfolio is that of the Bill & Melinda Gates Foundation (the Gates Foundation). Indeed, with around USD 36.4 billion of assets under trust, the Gates Foundation is the largest charitable foundation in the world.[11] The Gates Foundation is unusual in its relatively aggressive approach to its investment strategy. The Gates Foundation effectively operates the 'spending out' model and as such will aim to spend all its resources within a finite period following the death of its founders. The Gates Foundation has been credited with developing the strategy of 'philanthrocapitalism' which includes using leverage to maximize investments.

---

[11] www.gatesfoundation.org

This hybrid of philanthropy and capitalism is rapidly developing and there is fluid evolution of the charity fund model. For example, the Google Foundation, which is part of software giant Google's commercial arm, mixes for-profit and non-profit investments in order to maximize its impact.[12] Also, see the development of social impact funds in Chapter 5, section 5.10.

9.6   SOME CONCLUSIONS

The requirement to bridge a culture gap is frequently commented on when working between different entities involved in fund structures. The gap is sometimes thought of as being widest during commercial negotiations between actors in the public and private sectors. It is certainly useful to bear the cultural issue in mind when considering the behaviour and objectives of the organizations reviewed in this chapter. SWFs, state-sponsored funding bodies and banks, pension funds and charities represent different investment classes but they are habitual sources of investment funding as well as being significant market players. Arguably, they hold a unique position sitting at the junction between private and public sectors. Each of these organizations will have their own cultures which may be compared to greater or lesser degrees with the objectives of the solely private investor. Anyone who has worked alongside institutions from this sector will know that understanding where they come from and what drives them is critical to facilitating an investment.

Pension funds are of course the single largest sector source of this funding. Although some pension funds have, historically, kept clear of what they view as the high management charges of private equity and hedge managers, in recent years many other pension funds have adopted more aggressive investment positions, in some cases using the higher returns of private equity to offset the damage caused to pension funds by the financial crisis and the consequent low interest rates and stock market volatility.

> 'Since the 1980s, pensions' investment in private equity funds has grown ... pension funds have been the largest contributor of capital in private equity investments in the US during 2001–2011... Pension funds make up 43% of capital invested, of which public pension funds comprise almost 30%.'[13]

SWFs are also a substantial source of funds. Middle Eastern state-backed funds, for instance, are thought to invest up to one-third of their new investment into private equity. SWFs focused more on the long-term wealth preservation model (e.g. the Abu Dhabi Investment Authority or Kuwait Investment Authority) tend to favour co-investment models, whereby they invest alongside a private equity fund manager that they already back through a fund. In contrast, SWF funds attached to the development model tend to build in-house teams to conduct their own deals.

Each of the potential investors reviewed in this chapter needs to be carefully assessed, understood and accommodated. They each represent different opportunities along a wide spectrum of investment models. The long-term view of an institution such as a pension fund, an SWF or a charity (the latter often being the most prescribed in their investment objectives) in some ways makes these institutions ideally positioned to engage with the long-term investment horizon and the limited liquidity of private equity and other alternative asset strategies.

---

[12] *The Economist*, 'The Birth of Philanthrocapitalism', February 2006

[13] Private Equity Growth Capital Council (April 2013)

10

Investment Manager Structures

10.1 INTRODUCTION

The manager is retained by the fund to invest and divest on behalf of the fund and to provide overall control of the operation of the portfolio assets. It is staffed by a team of executives with investment experience and sufficient track records to attract investors to a fund. The legal structure of the manager will depend on commercial and regulatory considerations but has recently been a limited liability partnership or a limited liability company.

If the fund is domiciled offshore, the manager might also be domiciled offshore, and advised by a regulated investment adviser onshore, or based where the principals or team are located. This chapter assumes that the manager is located in the UK, the US or within the EU.

10.2 GENERAL PARTNER IN LIMITED PARTNERSHIP STRUCTURES

In a typical limited partnership structure there is only one general partner, which is often an entity controlled by the manager. The general partner has responsibility for the decisions of the fund, can make legally binding obligations and has unlimited liability for the debts and obligations of the fund. The limited partners will seek to avoid intervening in the operation of the fund in order to avoid accidentally attaining general partnership status and therefore assuming unlimited liability for the debts of the fund.

The general partner will usually be a subsidiary organization of the fund adviser or manager. It will have a legal structure (such as a limited liability company) which limits the liability of its owner(s) – including the authorized adviser/manager entity (regulated in the UK by the FCA), and any seed or other investors who have taken a share in the ownership of the general partner – shielding them from liability in the event that the fund incurs losses or liabilities. The private equity executives are usually directors or employees of either the general partner or the manager (or both) and will also have ownership of either or both of these entities alongside any seed or other investors.

While a general partner could, in theory, obtain the necessary authorization from the FCA, if a fund manager manages multiple funds each with its own general partner, this would necessitate obtaining multiple FCA authorizations. In addition, unlimited liabilities can be trapped at the general partner level.

The manager is appointed by the partnership to act as its manager and operator. Therefore, the manager takes all the day to day decisions related to the operation and management of the partnership including the acquisition, management and disposal of investments. The role of the general partner is limited to monitoring and supervising the manager and a small number of more formal matters.

The manager in a UK structure is most often now an LLP. The use of an LLP has a number of benefits, namely:

(a) providing its members with limited liability
(b) a flexible vehicle with some corporate-like elements
(c) tax transparency
(d) the principals of the business that are members of the LLP are taxed (including in respect of National Insurance contributions) as if they were self-employed rather than as employees. Note however that the UK HMRC is looking further at these treatments, following the April 2013 Budget. This might impact significantly on the use of LLPs as management vehicles.

In a corporate structure, where the fund will often be a limited liability company or a company limited by shares, there is no requirement for a general partner, and the fund entity itself will enjoy limited liability status. The liability of the manager of the fund, which itself will often be a corporate entity, is limited to the amount which is unpaid on its shares in the fund and itself.

10.3   REGULATION OF INVESTMENT MANAGERS

10.3.1 The UK Financial Conduct Authority

Within the UK, promoters, fund managers and investment advisers must be authorized by the FCA where they perform 'Regulated Activities'.[1] Any employees or officers of authorized firms who carry out key functions in that firm must be authorized as individuals by the FCA as well. There are several activities that a fund manager is likely to undertake which require authorization. These include:

- establishing or operating a CIS
- arranging deals in investments
- managing investments
- providing investment advice or
- communicating an invitation or inducement to participate in a fund.

A UK private equity fund manager performs regulated activities where it operates a CIS (which includes most funds structured as an English or Scottish limited partnership) within or from the UK. Using an authorized entity as a general partner is unattractive as it exposes such entity to unlimited liability and potential difficulties with future authorizations where a fund defaults on its obligations. Instead, a limited liability vehicle (such as a company) will commonly be created to act as the general partner of the fund. This vehicle will then engage the FCA authorized manager to operate the fund on its behalf. Certain overseas limited partnerships such as Delaware limited partnerships can benefit from an exemption to holding CIS status, avoiding the requirement for an authorized manager in relation to that particular Regulated Activity.

---

[1] As defined/set out under Schedule 2 of the Financial Services and Markets Act 2000

As defined under Schedule 2 of FSMA 2000, arranging deals in investments is another Regulated Activity. This potentially has a broad scope, and often covers a wide range of marketing activities as well as more mechanistic forms of deal making. It also will likely cover an investment adviser. The 'overseas person exemption'[2] reduces the need for authorization in respect of certain (but not all) 'arranging' activities where a person carries on regulated activities in the UK but not from an established place of business in the UK. As it is only a partial exemption it is not a particularly worthwhile exercise to seek to base the manager offshore to avoid authorization, as the activities not covered by the exemption will require an authorized person to conduct them in any event. For a manager who is not based in the UK, it is common to engage an authorized person in the UK to act on its behalf in these respects.

Unauthorized persons must not communicate invitations or inducements to participate in the fund. Such communications must be issued by an authorized person or approved by an authorized person. There is a wide range of exemptions applicable to this restriction. If the fund is not a CIS, the restriction on financial promotions is narrower and so communications approved by an authorized person can often be circulated to a wider range of persons.

10.3.2 The US Securities Exchange Commission

In the US, the primary regulator of the financial sector is the SEC. Certain regulatory authority is also exercised at the state level, generally by the state attorney general. For more details about its background, structure and remit see Chapter 12, section 12.5.1. Private equity funds in the US are subject to a wide range of legislation but in many instances may be able to rely on exceptions from the provisions of those pieces of legislation.

The ICA regulates funds and other entities that engage primarily in investing and trading in securities and whose own securities are offered in public offerings. The manager of a fund will have to ensure the fund complies with this legislation. Unless an exception applies, under the ICA a fund will have to register with the SEC as an investment company. Typically, a fund will seek to qualify under two specified exemptions: ICA Section 3(c)(1) which requires that the fund securities are beneficially owned by not more than 100 persons; and ICA Section 3(c)(7) which requires that the fund's investors are exclusively institutional investors (known as 'qualified purchasers', who generally speaking are those who own as an individual at least USD 5 million worth of investments or as an entity at least USD 25 million worth of investments) and knowledgeable executives. If the fund solicits investments through general advertisements or general solicitations, then certain additional rules are applicable. These rules have fairly complex anti-avoidance provisions which look-through those investors that are corporates or other legal entities to their ultimate beneficial owners.

The Investment Advisers Act of 1940 (the IAA) regulates the manager or adviser of a fund (if separate entities) by requiring them to register as an investment adviser with the SEC unless an exception applies, or the applicable state. The historical exception, known as the 'private adviser exemption', was for an investment adviser which had fewer than 15 clients (and each fund advised was a separate client). Therefore it was a fairly simple matter for most advisers and sponsors: advise fewer than 15 funds. However, the provisions of the Dodd–Frank Act (see more in section 10.3.3 below) have eliminated this particular exception.

Under the IAA an investment adviser is subject to a number of provisions determining whether or not it is required to register with the SEC. It owes a fiduciary duty to the fund and

---

[2] Article 72 of the Regulated Activities Order 2001

is prohibited from any action that is fraudulent, deceptive or manipulative with respect to the fund.

Offerings and sales of securities in the US (including interests in private equity funds) must be made in compliance with the Securities Act of 1933, which requires a registration statement filed with and approved by the SEC unless an exemption is applicable. A registered offering (i.e. a public offering) is both time-consuming and expensive and many will subject the fund and its operations to the obligations under the Securities Exchange Act of 1934. Consequently, private equity funds are structured and marketed to avoid these requirements. The exception used most frequently is provided under Section 4(2) of the Securities Act 1933. This is a fact-sensitive exemption. Factors that are often present in an offering that does not involve a public offering under Section 4(2) include a limited number of offerees and purchasers, no general marketing and solicitation of the fund.

The Securities Act regulations provide a 'safe harbour' known as Regulation D. This regulation generally permits sales to accredited investors and requires the filing of a form with limited information with the SEC. An additional benefit of using Regulation D to solicit and sell securities is that part of the regulation – Rule 506 which is the most commonly used part of Regulation D – generally exempts the offeror (fund) from state securities law filings, other than notice filings, the payment of a fee, anti-fraud provisions and certain other provisions of state law. Recent changes in Regulation D that were adopted by the SEC on 10 July 2013 permit an offering under this safe harbour to include general solicitations and advertisements (factors that were not permitted prior to this change) as long as each of the purchasers is an 'accredited investor' as defined under the SEC regulations. This is a significant change and allows placement agents and issuers to widely solicit investment. Advertisements can be in any form, ranging from electronic means such as websites and Twitter accounts to outdoor advertising (billboards). An SEC report on examination regarding Netflix clarified the SEC position on social media. Effectively, the content provided through social media messaging such as Twitter will be evaluated in a manner similar to content distributed through traditional media (e.g. a private placement memorandum).

10.3.3 Dodd–Frank Wall Street Reform and Consumer Protection Act

The Dodd–Frank Act expands provisions of previous legislation such as the IAA to broaden the range of sponsors and advisers who must register with the SEC. Foreign investment managers/advisers are required (as of 31 March 2012) to register with the SEC. The previously relied upon 'private adviser exemption' under the IAA has been removed by the Dodd–Frank Act. The new exemptions to the requirement to register with the SEC are extremely narrow and are summarized below:

- 'Private Fund Adviser Exemption' – applies to those that solely advise private funds with less than USD 150 million in private fund assets under management in the US. Only assets managed from within the US can count towards the threshold and the exemption is not available to any adviser that manages any separate accounts for a US client.
- 'Foreign Private Adviser Exemption' – to obtain this exemption the adviser must (i) not have a 'place of business' in the US (an office or location in or at which it regularly provides advisory services, solicits, meets with or communicates with clients); (ii) have fewer than 15 US advisory clients and investors in private funds; (iii) have fewer than USD 25

million under management with US clients and investors in private funds; and (iv) not offer advisory services to the US public or advise a US registered fund.

The requirement to register with the SEC brings a significantly increased regulatory oversight. In addition to requiring the adviser be registered, the IAA requires compliance with Rule 206 – referred to commonly as the Custody Rule. This requires the adviser to comply with detailed procedures that are designed to keep the investor informed about the location and person that maintains the custody of their assets. This includes performing 'surprise' inspections or (in lieu of certain procedures) ensuring that their external auditors are also registered with and subject to monitoring by the Public Company Accounting Oversight Board and that the assets are subject to the audit. External auditors must also comply with the SEC's independence rules. Additionally, financial statements must be produced in accordance with US GAAP[3] and enhanced anti-affiliate rules that strengthen the reporting and custodial procedures. These rules are generally in response to the Madoff scandal where an affiliate of the investment adviser purported to hold the assets of the investment adviser while in fact facilitating a massive fraud.

Under the Dodd–Frank Act the IAA is amended to require an investment adviser with assets under management of between USD 25 million and USD 100 million (or if the SEC requires, a higher amount) to register with the US state of its principal office and place of business only if it is subject to a requirement to register within that state in question. This is subject to any applicable exceptions within those states as well.

10.3.4 The EU Alternative Investment Fund Managers Directive

The AIFMD was implemented by member states of the EU on 22 July 2013. The provisions of the AIFMD are extensive and require careful consideration in planning a fund and consultation with compliance experts. The AIFMD seeks to create a harmonized legislative framework for alternative asset managers that operate within the EU, whether they are established within the EU or not and regardless of where the fund under management is established. Managers who are within the scope of the AIFMD are AIFMs – those individuals or legal persons whose regular business is the management of (one or more) AIFs which, broadly speaking, includes all non-UCITS funds together with some joint venture arrangements and managed accounts. More information in relation to AIFs can be found in Chapter 12, section 12.6.

All EU-based AIFMs are required to be authorized and subject to supervision in their home state, although the definition of who is the AIFM may lead, in certain fund structures, to only certain 'onshore' managers being the AIFM. The home regulator may qualify any authorization granted by limiting its scope such as by placing restrictions on the investment strategy.

An AIF can have only one AIFM and it must have one. In applying for authorization, the AIFM must provide both information relating to the AIFM and information relating to each AIF it intends to manage. The information required includes the credentials of the people conducting the AIFM's business, shareholders with 10% of the voting rights or with an ability to exert 'significant influence' over the management of the AIFM, the organizational structure of the AIFM, a plan on how it intends to comply with the AIFMD, the remuneration regime of the AIFM and arrangements regarding delegation.

---

[3] 'Generally Accepted Accounting Principles'

Where the AIF is internally managed it will need to be authorized as the AIFM and in other circumstances (including the typical limited partnership structure of a private equity fund) the AIFM can be an external party. Managing the AIF includes providing portfolio management and risk management services. The provision of risk management services is not frequently referred to in private equity fund agreements and this may result in a fund being deemed to be self-managing in the absence of express reference to risk management. Some managers will also need to consider the wording of the agreements vesting managerial responsibility on them by the general partner. If the manager is a delegate of the person in whom managerial responsibility is vested, then it will not be the AIFM. Only the person directly appointed by or on behalf of the AIF will be the AIFM.

There is a partial exemption for the manager from the requirements of the AIFMD if it manages (across all AIFs for which it is the manager) small AIFs with either:

- assets under management of less than EUR 500 million, provided that there is no leverage and investors do not have redemption rights for the first five years or
- assets under management of less than EUR 100 million including assets acquired by leverage.

The partial nature of the exemption means that if an AIFM managing small AIFs wishes to take advantage of the management or marketing passporting provisions it will require full compliance with the AIFMD. In any event, a small AIFM must register as such with its local regulator (e.g. the FCA).

The regulatory requirements of the AIFMD are described in more detail in Chapter 12, section 12.6.

10.4   STRUCTURES OF MANAGEMENT VEHICLES

10.4.1 UK LLP

In the UK, incorporation of an LLP as manager of the fund has been the common structure. The ability to use LLPs in the UK is relatively recent, having come into effect under the Limited Liability Partnerships Act 2000. Unlike limited partnerships, LLPs have a legal personality, bearing traits of both companies and partnerships. The advantages of using an LLP as a management vehicle are that: it is tax transparent; the constitution of the entity is governed by an LLP deed which can be drafted to the members' requirements, and amended without the need for filings at Companies House; and establishment costs are relatively inexpensive, with future administrative and secretarial costs being quite low. However, there are some disadvantages to using an LLP in that: the LLP deed must be drafted with care to ensure that any unwanted legal presumptions relating to, for example, partnerships are rebutted; returns to the LLP are treated as direct returns to members who may therefore face a tax liability before any of the returns are distributed; and an LLP cannot be converted into a limited company should this become relevant (and see further section 10.2 (d) of this chapter).

10.4.2 US Limited Liability Company

Similar to LLPs in the UK, an LLC is a hybrid vehicle which is permitted by US state statute, with similar traits of both partnerships and companies. Like a company, the members of the

LLC benefit from limited liability, while at the same time it is treated as tax transparent. Members of LLCs can be individuals, companies or other LLCs. There is no maximum number of members and states permit single member LLCs.[4] An LLC also provides significant flexibility to the members or members of the executive team in establishing their relationships, including finance, governance and equity-based incentives.

10.4.3 Company

The manager may be established as a limited company. The management team of the manager will be shareholders in the company, and also directors. This will have tax implications, as a company is not tax transparent, and the management team will therefore receive a salary and potentially bonuses or dividends.

10.4.4 GP as an LP structure

In a 'GP as an LP' structure, the general partner will be a limited partnership and therefore will not be a separate legal entity. The GP will itself have a separate general partner, often a company. These structures are more common in US closed-ended funds, and the GP in such a structure will usually receive the carried interest. The management fees can flow through the GP, but more typically in the US direct to a separate LLC manager (see Chapters 2 and 3).

The formation of limited partnerships is governed under state and federal law. The majority of US limited partnerships are formed as 'Delaware LPs', under the Delaware Revised Uniform Limited Partnership Act. An advantage is that a Delaware LP is not required to reveal the identity of its partners. In addition there is an established body of case law regarding the governance of Delaware LPs.

10.5   INVESTMENT MANAGER FEES

10.5.1 Closed-ended funds

(a) During the investment period

The management fee is generally calculated during the investment period as a percentage of the fund's total commitments. It is typically between 1% and 2% depending on a number of factors including the fund's size and investment strategy. The management fee will be lower for a secondaries fund or a fund of funds, reflecting the fact that making investments into other funds is less costly than making investments into underlying assets such as portfolio companies, and also in recognition of the fact that the underlying funds will also charge management fees.

Investors will often take the view that the purpose of the management fee is simply to provide the manager with sufficient funds to allow it to manage the fund, not to allow the manager to generate a profit. Therefore, investors may wish to compare the management fee against a specimen budget for the manager in order to ensure that the management fee is not significantly in excess of what is required to meet the day to day expenses of the manager. This approach has hardened from investors during the recent financial crisis.

---

[4] Internal Revenue Service: http://www.irs.gov/Businesses/Small-Businesses-&-Self-Employed/Limited-Liability-Company-(LLC): last accessed 7 June 2013

(b) After the investment period

The management fee is typically calculated as a percentage of the acquisition costs of the investments that the fund continues to hold after the investment period (for this purpose an investment that has been written off is treated as having been disposed of so no management fee is payable in respect of it). Alternatively the management fee 'steps down' to a reduced percentage of total commitments to the fund.

Investors may want the management fee to take into account any write-downs in investments (that is, if an investment has been written down below its acquisition cost, the amount of the write-down is taken into account in calculating the management fee). If this approach is taken the manager will typically request that the test be applied only on a portfolio basis so that any write-ups can be offset against any write-downs to determine whether there has been any overall write-down of the investment portfolio. This approach should only result in the management fee being reduced and not result in it being increased as a result of an overall increase in the value of the fund's investments.

As discussed in Chapter 2, instead of being a fee payable directly by the fund to the manager, in the UK and the US, the management fee is typically structured as a priority profit share which is paid by the fund to the general partner and then by the general partner to the manager. Further information is set out in Chapter 2.

10.5.2 Open-ended funds

(a) Management fee

The management fee is designed to cover the manager's operating costs and is typically set at 2% per annum (but can vary between 1% and 4% depending on the fund manager and strategy) and is charged on the NAV of the fund's assets. While represented as an annual charge, the management fees are often paid monthly or quarterly.

(b) Redemption fees

An additional layer of fees also deals with where an investor seeks to withdraw its funds. In such circumstances the investor may be charged a fee to withdraw, which generally operates to charge investors a redemption fee if they withdraw money within say a 12- or 18-month period. Redemption fees may also be applicable where an investor seeks to withdraw a large amount from the fund, as they may be limited to withdrawing a fixed amount or percentage at any given time.

10.5.3 Transactional or monitoring fees

Managers may receive certain additional fees, including:

- transactional fees from investors, such as entry and exit fees
- monitoring fees from portfolio companies
- directors' fees from portfolio companies
- consulting or other fees from portfolio companies.

However, these fees are not very popular with fund investors, and are therefore either fully or partly refundable to the fund (or often set against managements fees).

10.6   PERFORMANCE FEES AND CARRIED INTEREST

10.6.1 Closed-ended funds

(a) Distributions/carried interest

As a limited partnership fund typically operates on a drawdown/distribution model, the fund will typically distribute any income or capital gains which it receives to investors periodically in the case of income (often quarterly) and as soon as possible in the case of capital gains.

The profits which are available for distribution are split between the investors and the carry vehicle held by the executives of the manager and others, on pre-agreed terms. The amount paid to the carry vehicle is called carried interest and is the performance-based remuneration which the management team is eligible to receive. The provisions in the partnership agreement which deals with the calculation of these distributions are commonly referred to as 'the waterfall'.

There are a number of different ways in which the waterfall can work. Further details are set out in Chapter 2, but the principal concept is to motivate the investment team to make profits. Once investors have received their money back, plus a 'hurdle', then the investment team of the manager receives a carried interest (often 20%) of the fund's profits.

The hurdle in a closed-ended fund can be structured in a number of ways, but a private equity hurdle is often just that – a hurdle – and once cleared, the profits taken by the carry vehicle constitute all the profits of the fund, whereas in real estate or infrastructure, the hurdle is more like a fixed coupon. Again, more information is contained in Chapter 2.

(b) Carried interest, escrow and clawback

With most waterfalls, it is possible that too much carried interest could be distributed or, more precisely, that the amount of carried interest distributed may exceed the amount that would have been distributed had all the distributions been at the same time on a consolidated basis.

Upon termination of the fund, the carry limited partner will be required to repay any distributions it received in respect of its carried interest (the 'clawback') to the extent that such distributions exceed 20% of the fund's cumulative net portfolio gain. A further protection for limited partners on carried interest overpayment is holding part of the carried interest in escrow until the fund's investment returns are known. In investment bank-sponsored funds, the escrow is often held by the bank. The escrow also has the effect of protecting the partners of the carry vehicle (known as carry holders) from overspending by other carry holders of the carry returns.

(c) Carried interest vehicle

The partners of the carry vehicle are the principals of the fund manager, together with any cornerstone or seed investors that have negotiated a share of the carried interest. The carry vehicle is often structured in line with the Memorandum of Understanding between HMRC and the British Private Equity & Venture Capital Association (BVCA), which allows for carried interest to be treated as capital by the executives for tax purposes rather than income (for further detail see Chapter 11, section 11.5.3). The carry deed governs the terms of the principals' returns with the manager, such as share of income, joiners and leavers, consents, etc.

(d) Underlying control of the carry vehicle

Invariably the main principals of the manager or investment adviser 'control' the carry vehicle and operate a form of carry 'board' or adjudication committee that regulates the carry vehicle. The carry vehicle, if it is a partnership, is bound by general laws of partnerships, such as fair dealing, and confidentiality. If a carry partner leaves the manager or investment adviser, then he will be treated as a 'leaver' and his carry might be cancelled in whole or in part. The carry documentation will contain rules about leavers, often defining them 'good' or 'bad', and further penalizes the leaver if he competes post-leaving (hence why many individual managers 'retire' for a year or two between investment houses).

10.6.2 Open-ended funds

(a) Performance fee

The second principal level of fees for open-ended funds is the performance fee, which is designed to be an incentive for the manager and reward stellar performance. A typical 'performance fee' will often be set at 20%; however, this can range from as little as 10% to as much as 50%.

(b) Hurdle rate

Often built into the performance fee mechanism is what is known as 'hurdle rate' (historically often set at 8%), which is a rate of return that must be paid to investors before the manager can claim its entitlement to the performance fee. The hurdle rate can also either be soft or hard, 'soft hurdle' being that after the hurdle is cleared a catch-up mechanism applies so that the performance return is calculated on all returns once cleared, while alternatively the 'hard hurdle' only allows the performance fee to be calculated on the returns above the hurdle.

(c) High water mark

Most performance fees also include a 'high water mark', which essentially works to carry forward any losses from the manager to ensure that the manager only receives a performance fee over its highest performance level. Effectively, this means that any previous losses must first be recovered. The high water mark 'issue' is often a reason only open-ended funds are later liquidated by the manager, if the fund's returns start to decline.

10.7   INTERNAL ECONOMICS

The internal economics of the manager predominantly concern how the senior investment executives are remunerated. The management team as a whole will want to ensure that everyone is equally motivated by the success of the manager and the pay and reward structure will aim to reflect this. That said, investment houses established by dominant founders can have structures skewed against the majority of the team, with founders also expecting to pick up more carry (in a closed-ended fund) as the fund matures, and team members leave.

10.7.1 Salary and fixed draws

The remuneration of the investment team depends in part on the legal vehicle chosen for the structuring of the manager. Whether it is a corporate or a partnership vehicle, the team and other staff will be paid a base of some description. The senior members of the team will also participate in a profit share. In a partnership structure this is achieved by permitting fixed and variable drawings by the partners of the firm. For a corporate structure, the senior members can also hold either ordinary shares or a secondary class of shares that pay out dividends. In both cases the payments of fixed amounts of remuneration can be linked to milestones. Since 22 July 2013 the policies underlying remuneration in the form of both salaries and fixed drawings are required to be in line with the provisions of the AIFMD (for further information, see Chapter 12, section 12.6) which may require a change in policy depending on the manager in question.

10.7.2 Bonuses

Bonuses are typically awarded on a discretionary basis and in order to incentivize the team these are fixed to certain milestones. Again, since 22 July 2013 the award of bonuses has been subject to the provisions of the AIFMD.

10.7.3 Share and option ownership of investment company

Share option plans may exist in relation to a listed company or a private company. The success of the manager is aligned with the investment team that participates in the rewards through the increase in share price (more significant with a listed company) and by any payment of dividends. If the manager is structured as a partnership, then such a scheme would still be possible where a corporate entity is established as a partner of the manager, through which the payments of dividends are made and options granted.

10.7.4 Performance fee share and carried interest

This is discussed in section 10.6 above and is designed to both motivate and retain key staff. Investors expect managers to be aligned to them by principally being interested in the performance elements of fees, and not be mere management fee 'gatherers'.

10.7.5 Co-investment

Individual members of the investment team may also be permitted to co-invest alongside the fund on a deal-by-deal basis, an arrangement which is not entirely favourable to the investors of the fund as a whole, unless it is fixed to every investment. Alternatively if it is a deal-by-deal co-investment arrangement then it can be fairer to investors if it invests where the fund does not have the firepower to invest the full amount of an investment. Banks have in the past also allowed their in-house team access to bank leverage to allow individual members to invest into deals.

10.7.6 Fund investment or the GP commitment

The investment team may be incentivized by investing fully alongside the investors in the fund. The investors of the fund will indeed commonly expect a commitment to be made by the investment team in the whole fund (known as the 'GP commitment' in a closed-ended fund) in order to ensure its commitment is aligned with the success of its investments. These commitments are often expressed as a percentage of the investors' commitments or as a hard cap. Historically this requirement was set at 1% of a fund for certain US tax purposes. However, especially during the recent financial crisis, investors have been expecting up to 10% GP commitment, or 10% of all fund commitments. There are banks that will lend to executives of the GP or the GP itself to make this investment.

10.8   EXTERNAL OWNERSHIP OF INVESTMENT MANAGER GROUPS

Newly formed investment managers are increasingly seeking external investment in order to raise the level of seed capital required to establish the manager. Cornerstone or seed investors invest in newly established managers. This practice can lead to a situation where the cornerstone investor will receive profits from later funds in which they do not participate. An alternative arrangement is for the cornerstone investors to take a share in the ownership of the general partner of the fund in which it invests, which is ultimately a fee rebate. Depending on the level of the cornerstone investors' equity shareholding, they will obtain a degree of influence over the internal management of the manager. Equity investment will carry voting rights and if the investment is significant, board representation and other rights such as enhanced co-investment may be granted to the cornerstone investors.

An alternative for a newly established manager is to find a strategic partner that is willing to invest in the manager (or group) and provide financial or other support such as assistance in promoting a fund. Such an external owner may also insist on a share of the carried interest, performance fees, management fees or a combination of some or all of these, and may also invest in the first fund-raise.

In situations where investment manager groups have received external investment, the challenge for the manager is to balance the benefits of extra capital with the financial and corporate burdens, as well as an inference (to other fund investors) that such investors are a higher class of citizen than a straight fund investor.

10.9   LISTING OF INVESTMENT MANAGER GROUPS

Some larger investment managers seek a flotation on a stock exchange. Examples of such listed alternative asset managers are 3i and Man Group (listed on the London Stock Exchange), and Blackstone Group, KKR and Apollo Global Management (all listed in New York).

Investment managers will typically list in order to raise extra working capital or to expand their funds under management and to bulk up their balance sheets to cornerstone their own funds. Indeed, KKR acquired its own listed feeder fund before listing. In recent years, because investors have increasingly been moving out of traditional index-linked investments towards alternative investment seeking returns, and because alternative asset managers are under less government scrutiny and regulators' influence, this has led in my view to a major shift in the balance of power in the financial world. Investment banks and insurance companies were once the domain of the 'masters of the universe';[5] however, it is now the large investment managers that are becoming the key players in global finance.

Unburdened by some of the bureaucracy and inefficiencies that have restricted the activities of banks and other more traditional financial companies, and because investment managers have secured consistent returns for investors, their assets under management have greatly increased. Where banks and other traditional institutions have been forced (due to political, regulatory and shareholder pressure) to scale back lending activities perceived as risky, alternative asset groups have been able to fill the vacuum. In Europe and the US, the 'shadow banking' sector (see Chapter 5, section 5.6) has developed rapidly in recent years, in part because investment management groups do not have the capital requirements demanded by banks.

Listed investment managers (and their funds) are now positioned to use the flexibility of their structures and availability of capital in order to replace banks as the predominant lenders to businesses.

Listed investment managers are valued on a blend of:

- management fees
- transactional fees
- carried interest and performance fees (typically shared across the listed company and the team members)
- fund returns – from their own fund investing and
- other investments.

10.10 BOARDS AND COMMITTEES OF AN INVESTMENT MANAGER

10.10.1 Board

A manager will be operated by its board of investors, members or partners, depending on its legal structure. Like any other company, it will have a Chairman, CEO, CFO, etc., although the role of CIO (Chief Investment Officer) is critical.

10.10.2 Non-executives

Larger managers will have significant non-executive representation of relevant persons.

10.10.3 Executive committee

The executive committee oversees the management of the firm as a whole. It will guide the investment strategy and recruitment policy and will take overall responsibility for its compliance obligations and finances. It is often chaired by the chief operating officer or the chief risk officer.

---

[5] *The Bonfire of the Vanities* by Tom Wolfe; first published 1987

10.10.4 Investment committee

The investment committee makes the investment and divestment decisions, signing off the proposals of those members of the management team that are responsible for the sourcing of deals. Such proposals will be detailed with analysis and projections. This committee will be chaired by the chief investment officer, joined by the chief risk officer and other key senior members of the team.

10.10.5 Industrialists

Private equity groups will have industrialists and recent CEOs on tap to advise and indeed to later manage portfolio companies. Venture capital groups will have entrepreneurs in residence for similar roles.

10.11   MANAGER OR ADVISER

10.11.1 Permanent establishment rules

Under the rules of permanent establishment, a business entity may be liable for taxation where it conducts revenue-generating activities within the jurisdiction in question. As discussed in Chapter 11, section 11.2.4 (b), there is UK regulation providing an exemption for investment managers that operate within the UK. The exemption requires a number of tests to be satisfied for it to apply, and if it does not, the income and gains of the offshore fund attributable to the activities of the UK-based investment managers would be liable to taxation – undermining the taxation drivers which led to establishing the fund offshore in the first instance.

An alternative would be to reduce the functions of the onshore investment managers to that of an onshore 'adviser' with the managerial functions being undertaken offshore, or to bulk out the board of the offshore fund. Determining whether or not an agent or branch of the main business (in this case the fund manager) is resident in the UK will be a somewhat grey area. In effect the adviser having the ability to make binding decisions could in itself be enough to bring activities onshore, although if all transactions were subject to approval of the offshore manager this might mitigate that finding. This in itself would be impractical for a hedge fund relying on frequent trading as part of the investment strategy.

10.11.2 Other drivers

In some instances it may be necessary for the manager to be based in the offshore jurisdiction where the fund is located. An example is discussed in more detail in Chapter 3, section 3.5.2. Although the manager is offshore, it is not always preferable for investment decisions to be made there. This is partly because a substantial body of investment experts is based in onshore jurisdictions and locations such as London and New York, so it may be necessary for an advisory entity to be established onshore to take advantage of this pool of talent despite the regulatory requirement in the offshore jurisdictions or the overall fund tax requirements. This arrangement will usually be effected by an advisory agreement between the offshore manager and the onshore advisory (usually related entities). The onshore adviser will typically be regulated by that jurisdiction's main regulatory body (such as the FCA in the UK) even though it is carrying on a reduced role than that of a manager. For the regulatory requirements in the UK and the US, see Chapter 12.

10.12   FAMILY OFFICES

Family offices in many ways behave like a fund manager or investment adviser for that family's money. Many family offices have a significant percentage (say 30%) of their 'non-core' business invested in private equity, real estate and other alternative strategies. A family office is a private company that manages investments and trusts either for a single wealthy family or for several families.

Many family offices start within family companies where a wealthy individual will delegate certain personal matters to an assistant. However, the direct correlation between wealth and the volume of affairs such an assistant is tasked with dealing with will almost inevitably lead to the point where technical expertise is required.

Family offices may expand beyond the original family which they were founded to support. These multi-family offices will then charge fees to other families who are seeking similar solutions. These operations may then eventually begin to fund-raise to support their investment activities – in which case it will need to become a regulated entity, and it begins to take on a character much like wealth managers. One such example is Rockefeller & Co., which expanded from the family office dedicated to the Rockefeller family to a regulated wealth manager with a wide range of clients.

Some family offices may be established in a reverse of the pattern described above. An example would be a successful hedge fund manager which moves away from fund-raising from outside investors and begins to actively manage the wealth of its management team. This in effect is a multi-family office which has developed in order to cope with its own success and fund management.

10.13   SOME CONCLUSIONS

This chapter has looked at how the manager entities are structured. There are several competing factors which influence how the structure is fixed: the taxation of the principals, the regulatory environment, the domicile of the fund and the cost of operating more complex offshore structures. Managers are also shifting towards leaner models, family offices being one example, as regulatory constrictions come into force.

11

Taxation Principles in Funds

11.1   INTRODUCTION

This chapter will consider taxation in terms of the fund, the investors, investment manager companies and investment manager principals in the UK, the US and the EU generally. This chapter is very much an overview of a subject matter that frankly warrants a separate book (or books). However, understanding the basic issues is helpful and enables further reading around the core issues set out in this chapter.

11.2   TAXATION OF FUNDS

11.2.1 UK

(a) Limited partnerships

A limited partnership structure for a fund is fiscally transparent. Capital gains which arise in the course of the partnership's business are assessed and taxed to each partner separately in proportion to their interest in the capital of the fund.[1] The profits of the business of the partnership are not treated as the proceeds of a separate entity in respect of income[2] or corporation tax.[3] They are apportioned to each partner in accordance with the partnership agreement and taxed as income in their hands.

(b) AUTs and OEICs

These are treated in similar ways and will be considered together. The investments of an AUT or an OEIC are held by the trustees (for more details about the structure of these funds, see Chapter 4, section 4.11 and Chapter 6, section 6.3.3(c), respectively). Any capital gains arising in the hands of the trustees from the disposal of any of those assets are treated as tax exempt.[4] If the AUT is an umbrella fund, then each sub-fund is treated as a separate AUT, and the trustees are still exempt from paying tax on the chargeable gains arising from the disposal of assets.[5] If the gains are treated by HMRC as profits from trading activity then the gain will be treated as income and taxed accordingly.

The income from the assets of the AUT which comes into the hands of the trustees is taxed as if it is the income of a UK-resident company but is taxed at the basic rate of income tax for the tax year in question.[6] An OEIC is a corporate vehicle subject to corporation tax but

---

[1] Section 59 TCGA 1992
[2] Section 848 ITTOIA 2005
[3] Section 1258 COTA 2009
[4] Section 100(1) TCGA 1992
[5] Section 99A TCGA 1992 as inserted by Section 118 Finance Act 2004
[6] Sections 617 and 618 COTA 2010

it too is taxed at the basic rate of income tax.[7] As AUTs and OEICs qualify as investment companies,[8] relief is available for the management expenses, which are deducted from the calculation of total profits. Dividend income paid out from investee companies is exempt from the charge to corporation tax, whether the income is from within the UK or overseas.[9]

(c) UUT

A UUT is a UK-based unit trust which has not sought approval from the FCA (see Chapter 4, section 4.11) and so is subject to the 'normal' rules on taxation, coupled with decreased regulation. For the purposes of the taxation of chargeable gains, a UK-resident UUT is treated as a corporate body and the investors as shareholders. The trustees are subject to CGT for the chargeable gains arising out of the trust and are not subject to corporation tax.[10] This is not the case however where the entirety of the investor base is made up of UK resident bodies which are exempt from CGT, such as UK-registered pension funds, in which case the trustees are exempt.[11]

The income of a UUT is treated as the income of the trustee.[12] The income is taxed at the basic rate regardless of the source of income,[13] subject to a few exceptions. Any dividend income received does not come with a tax credit.[14] The taxable income of the fund cannot be reduced by the deduction of management expenses, but how it is treated can be important for investors. The management expense can be deducted before the total amount available for distribution is calculated or recovered from the investors once the distribution amount is known. If an institutional investor is able to claim relief from its own income for the management expenses, then it will prefer that management expenses are treated as recovered from the investors, which increases the taxable income and the amount which can be recovered as a result.

(d) Investment trusts

Investment trusts require annual approval from HMRC in order to qualify for the tax exemption regime. An investment trust is a corporate body but once authorized any capital gains from its investment portfolio are tax exempt.[15] HMRC will treat gains arising from the portfolio as income instead if it is apparent from the fund's activities that it earns income from the frequent trading of investment products. The fund can avoid this by creating a subsidiary which deals frequently in assets. There is a tax inefficiency where the income of the fund (but not allowable dividends) is taxed and then the later distributions to the investors are taxed as dividends. There are regulations in place which allow an investment trust to elect to have its corporation tax bill reduced by the amount taxed when it makes a distribution to the investors, and this distribution is treated as interest income in the hands of the investor.[16]

---

[7] Section 614 COTA 2010
[8] Section 1219 COTA 2009
[9] Part 9A COTA 2009 as inserted by Section 34 and Schedule 14 to the Finance Act 2009
[10] Section 99(1) TCGA 1992
[11] Section 100(2) TCGA 1992
[12] Section 504(2) ITA 2007
[13] Section 504(3) ITA 2007
[14] Section 504(4) ITA 2007
[15] Section 100(1) TCGA 1992
[16] SI 2009/2034 as amended by SI 2011/2951

11.2.2 US

(a) Partnerships

Entities classified as partnerships (whether created under law in the US or not) for US federal income tax purposes are fiscally transparent. All income, gains, losses, deductions and credits realized by a partnership are effectively 'passed through' and treated as if they were realized directly by the partners in accordance with the allocation regime provided in the partnership agreement and under the IRC, which requires that the allocation regime have 'substantial economic effect', as defined under IRS regulations. The pass-through of these tax attributes to the partners does not depend on the distribution of cash or property by the partnership. The characterization of an item of the partnership's income, gain, loss, deduction or credit will generally be determined at the partnership (rather than at the investor or partner) level.

A private equity investment fund organized as a limited partnership under Delaware law (most common) or the laws of any other state within the US (less common) will be fiscally transparent for US federal income tax purposes, assuming that the fund does not make a special election (referred to as 'check the box') to be taxed as a corporation. It would be unlikely that a private equity investment fund would 'check the box' to be treated as a corporation. Private equity funds that are not a US person under the IRC can ensure partnership classification by 'checking the box' to be classified as a partnership.

A significant risk to an investor in a private equity investment fund that is classified as a partnership for US federal income taxes is that the investor may be allocated income (and be required to pay taxes on such income) without receiving a distribution from the fund sufficient to pay such tax liability. Accordingly, investors will often require assurances from the fund that is classified as a partnership, under the terms and provisions of the partnership agreement or a side letter, that the fund will make payments that are sufficient to pay the tax liability on the allocated net income and gains determined on the basis of a deemed tax rate. Such payments are typically deemed advances that are repaid from subsequent distributions. A partnership that makes such assurances should consider such obligations in its investment strategy and financing of investments and will likely, to the extent possible, make the distributions under the partnership agreement rather than such tax advances so that the investors receive amounts that are credited to their priority return (amounts that must be distributed prior to the carried interest).

(b) Publicly traded partnerships

If the fund is classified as a 'publicly traded partnership' it will be subject to entity-level tax and treated as a corporation. Subject to certain limited exceptions, a publicly traded partnership is any partnership where the equity interests are regularly traded on an established securities market or readily tradable on a secondary market (or the substantial equivalent thereof), regardless of the number of its partners. In general, the private equity fund will be structured to not be treated as a publicly traded partnership by qualifying under an exemption which includes not having its interests publicly traded or focusing and, subject to certain provisions, limiting its investment strategy to have 90% or more of its gross income in 'qualifying income' as defined by the IRC, generally, passive income such as interest, dividends and rents.

(c) Non-US partnerships

Although non-US partnerships are not subject to US tax at the entity level, any amounts that they receive from sources within the US may be subject to withholding taxes. Certain withholding taxes will be reduced to the extent that the partners of the non-US partnership demonstrate that they are either (i) US persons, or (ii) entitled to treaty benefits or certain other exemptions.

A non-US fund classified as a corporation for US federal income tax purposes will be subject to the US tax rules applicable to non-US persons. The non-US owners of the fund will not be required to pay tax on, or report to the US IRS, the income of such a corporation. For this reason, non-US persons sometimes use corporations organized in tax haven jurisdictions to hold their US investments; although this may increase the overall tax liability attributable to such investments, it should shield such non-US persons from tax filing obligations in the US. However, the non-US corporation will be subject to the payment of US federal income tax or have payments from US taxpayers subject to withholding obligations. Additionally, a non-US entity may be subject to the branch profits tax.

Certain US taxpayers are subject to reporting to the IRS certain information regarding their holding financial assets that are held outside the United States under FATCA (see Chapter 12, section 12.5.4). In addition, FATCA requires foreign financial institutions (FFIs) to report directly to the IRS certain information about financial accounts held by US taxpayers, or by foreign entities in which US taxpayers hold a substantial ownership interest. Non-compliance with FATCA by a US taxpayer results in fines and underpayments of tax attributable to non-disclosed foreign financial assets will be subject to an additional substantial understatement penalty of 40%.

(d) State and local taxes

The tax regime in the US includes the federal tax regime under the IRC and each state and local tax regime (i.e. the municipal level of government such as New York City). Most states and a few municipal governments assert taxes on the basis of income. These taxes can be significant. State and local laws often differ from federal income tax laws with respect to the treatment of specific items of income, gain, loss, deduction and credit. An investor's distributive share of a fund's income, gain, loss, deduction and credit generally will be required to be included in determining its reportable income for state and local tax purposes in the jurisdiction in which he or she is a resident, and in each state and locality in which the fund invests. For example, in New York City, the entity that receives the carry interest or the management fee will be subject to an income tax and each resident that is a resident of New York City is subject to an income tax. Investors in a fund that is fiscally transparent may also have an obligation to file state and local tax returns. In some states and localities, the fund may have the ability to, and elect to pay state and local income taxes on behalf of the investors attributable to the gains and income received in a state or locality. Nevertheless, even in states and localities where such an opportunity is available to the fund, the fund makes no assurances that it will take advantage of such opportunities in each case. In addition, it is possible that, in some states, the sale or transfer of an interest in the fund may be subject to state and/or local transfer tax.

11.2.3 EU

Across the EU there is a wide range of tax rates, set in accordance with the laws of the individual member states that remain responsible for taxation in a majority of cases. The application of these tax rates and laws in the applicable member states will commonly be dependent upon the structure which the fund takes. Some details of taxation applied in respect of popular EU fund jurisdictions are contained within Chapters 7 and 8.

However, within the EU there has been support among some member states and individuals in the European Parliament for enhanced cooperation and harmonization in the form of a financial transaction tax. On 28 September 2011 the European Commission tabled a proposal for a Council Directive on a common system of financial transaction tax (FTT).[17] The main objectives of the proposal were:

1. Harmonizing legislation concerning indirect taxation on financial transactions
2. Ensuring that financial institutions make a fair and substantial contribution to covering the costs of the post-2007 financial crises and creating a level playing field with other sectors from a taxation point of view
3. Creating appropriate disincentives for transactions that do not enhance the efficiency of financial markets, thereby complementing regulatory measures to avoid future crises.

Following discussion of the proposal it became evident to the European Commission that the proposal could not be agreed within a reasonable time period by the EU as a whole. However, following requests from 11 member states for a legislative proposal based on the above, the European Commission adopted a proposal for a Council Directive[18] on 14 February 2013 with the intention of creating a common system of financial transaction taxation among as large a number of member states as possible. This is because some member states believe there is a fragmentation of the tax treatment in the internal market for financial services and there are possibilities of distortions of competition between financial instruments, actors and market places across the EU.

The key elements which the proposal would seek to implement are the:

1. Imposition of a tax of 0.1% in relation to financial transactions, where the taxable amount is proposed to be everything which constitutes consideration paid or owed, in return for the transfer, from the counterparty or a third party and
2. Imposition of a tax of 0.01% in respect of derivative contracts, where the taxable amount of the FTT would be the notional amount referred to in the derivatives contract at the time of the financial transaction.

At the time of writing the above Council Directive is being discussed, with all member states permitted to contribute their views. However, only those 11 member states participating in enhanced cooperation (the UK is not one of those 11) are entitled to vote in respect of the same.

11.2.4 Permanent establishment rules

(a) A permanent establishment

A permanent establishment is a fixed place of business which is in a jurisdiction other than where the business is ordinarily resident. Generally speaking, a significant part or the whole

---

[17] 'Proposal for a Council Directive on a common system of financial transaction tax and amending Directive 2008/7/EC' (COM (2011) 594 final)

[18] 'Proposal for a Council Directive implementing Proposal for a Council Directive implementing enhanced cooperation in the area of financial transaction tax' (COM (2013) 71 final)

of the business needs to be carried on in the place of establishment, whether that is as a branch or the place of management. If a trade is conducted in the UK by an agent or branch on behalf of non-residents there is a charge to income tax. If an overseas company has a permanent establishment in the UK the profits and chargeable gains which are attributable to that establishment are subject to UK corporation tax.[19]

(b) The investment managers' exemption

(i) Overview

The investment managers' exemption was developed in the UK to avoid (for example) UK-resident managers of overseas hedge funds being taxed on the income of the fund and to avoid overseas investors in those funds being subject to UK tax as a result of the manager conducting transactions on behalf of the funds. The UK rules are similar to those of other countries, and for this section I have focused on the UK.

(ii) Eligibility

To be eligible for the exemption a number of tests have to be met, but there is a chance to prove to UK HMRC that the relationship between the manager and the fund is in line with the principles of the restriction and to convince the Revenue that the exemption should apply. Regardless of the applicability of the exemption, some sources of income which go through an investment manager to an overseas fund are exempt from UK tax, and a double taxation treaty may apply in any event in favour of the fund.

For example, for the UK exemption to apply the non-resident fund must be trading in the UK, and the transactions carried on by the investment manager must be in the ordinary course of the fund's trade. The UK-resident manager must itself be in the business of investment management and the transactions it conducts for the fund must also be in the ordinary course of its trade.

The investment manager of the fund must be independent of the fund to the extent that the legal, financial and commercial characteristics of the relationship reflect a relationship conducted at arm's length. To this end, if the fund is one which is held by a wide range of investors or would be if it were not either newly constituted or in the process of being wound up, then the relationship is considered to be one in which the manager is independent. The fund must show within 18 months (this period may be extended) that it has become widely held. A widely held fund is one where no majority interest is held in the fund by five or fewer investors, or where not one investor holds greater than a 20% interest in the fund. If the fund does not meet either of the above independence criteria, then another test may determine independence. This other test is satisfied where the manager's services to the fund do not represent a substantial part of its business, i.e. no more than 70% of the business.

The manager has 18 months to establish a track record in this regard. In the first 18 months it may exceed the 70% figure as long as for the rest of the period it is consistently below 70%. If it exceeds 70% after the 18-month period but the reasons for this are beyond the manager's control, the exemption may still apply but the manager will have to prove to a high standard that it was beyond its control and that it took all reasonable steps to avoid and rectify the breach. If the test still is not met, then the manager may yet convince HMRC that the relationship is one of independence and is conducted at arm's length.

---

[19] Sections 5(3) and 19 COTA 2009

A further requirement is that the investment manager must not receive remuneration for its role at less than the customary market rate, which is typically 2%. Where other fee structures are used, HMRC will look at the market and the transaction as a whole to see whether or not the structure in place is one which is negotiated at arm's length.

(iii) The 20% test

The final test for the exemption to apply is known as the '20% test'. The rule is that the investment manager or any connected persons of the investment manager are not beneficially entitled to more than 20% of the taxable profits of the fund which derive from the transactions conducted by the investment manager. This 20% figure is established over the 'qualifying period': a period of five years which is made up of no more than two complete accounting periods (including the one in which the transaction occurred) where the figure exceeds 20%, and the average figure over that five-year period does not exceed 20%. Management and performance fees are not included in the chargeable profit figure (which is the basis of the 20% calculation) as long as they would be allowable in the calculation of profit if the fund was UK resident. Where the manager's entitlement to the fund exceeds 20%, then that whole share is liable to assessment for tax.

11.3   INVESTORS

11.3.1 UK

(a) The fund is a partnership

A fund structured as a limited partnership is tax transparent for the purposes of income and capital gains. As a result it is the investors, as partners, who are subject to direct taxation. If the fund is not involved in trading as part of its business, any returns received from the sale of investments are treated as capital. The dealings by the partnership are treated as dealings by the partners themselves for the purpose of CGT and as such any gain or loss is a gain or loss of the partner in question.[20] The tax legislation does not accommodate the subtle shifts in position that an investment agreement can produce, so HMRC has issued a statement of practice.[21] When calculating the amount to be assessed (whether a gain or a loss) the entitlement to profit is used to apportion the acquisition cost of the asset and the proceeds of disposal.

When the fund receives income, it is taxable in the hands of the investors and the amount is determined by the method of apportionment above. If there is a blend of individual and corporate investors, the partnership must produce two sets of accounts. The first set is for the benefit of the non-corporate investors and treats the profits and losses of the partnership as those of a UK-resident individual (or if applicable, a non-UK-resident individual), and those are then allocated to each individual investor.[22] The second set deems the profits and losses of the partnership to be those of a company and the corporate investor is charged to its share in the partnership, as if the business were its own.[23]

A charge to tax can also arise where there is a change in the ownership of the partnership, either where a new partner joins, reducing every investor's share, or where a partner leaves.

---

[20] Section 59 TCGA 1992
[21] SP D12
[22] Part 9 ITTOIA 2005
[23] Part 17 COTA 2009

When a new partner joins, the incumbent investors are treated as making a disposal of their share in the partnership assets as their own interest is reduced. If the assets of the partnership are not revalued before this change, the disposal is treated as being for consideration equal to the same fraction of the assets acquired on entering the partnership (or at the last acquisition) and so there is no gain or loss.[24] When a new partner joins and the assets are revalued before the change in ownership ratio, a chargeable gain may arise if there is an increase in the value of the partnership assets (on revaluation) and the partner's share is then reduced by the deemed disposal. When a partner disposes of their interest by selling to a third party, the consideration received less the base cost attributable to their share is the basis of the calculation of any capital gain or loss. If the disposing partner is a UK CGT payer the consideration received will have to be attributed to each asset of the partnership to calculate the charge for the disposal of his share in each asset.

(b) Other fund structures

AUTs and OEICs are treated in largely the same way when it comes to the taxation of investors and will be considered together. Any interest which is distributed by a bond fund or a tax-elected fund is treated as yearly interest and is subject to a withholding tax at the basic rate.[25] There are exemptions where the recipient is a company, the trustees of a unit trust, a 'reputable intermediary' or the recipient satisfies the 'residence condition'.[26] Any withholding tax is returned where the investor is a non-taxpayer. A reputable intermediary is one who receives the distribution on behalf of a company which is not ordinarily resident in the UK (or the trustees reasonably believe that is the case) and the company is resident in a jurisdiction where there are sufficient anti-money laundering regulations. The residence condition is met by a valid declaration that the investor is not ordinarily resident in the UK.

A dividend distribution to an investor by an equity fund (one which is not paying out interest payments) is treated by HMRC as a UK company dividend.[27] As a result, the distribution carries a tax credit for the amount deducted on distribution at the ordinary rate for dividend income.

When a UK-resident investor disposes of his interest in the AUT or OEIC he will be liable for CGT for any increase in the value of the shares or units. An investor may be eligible for entrepreneurs' relief to reduce the charge to tax, and any shares or units held in an ISA (individual savings account) will be exempt from the charge to CGT. A UK-resident corporate investor will be charged on disposal for any gains arising, subject to losses and the effect of the indexation allowance. Non-resident investors are generally not liable to pay UK CGT.

The trustees in a UUT are treated as if they have paid to the investors distributable income annually at the basic rate of income tax (regardless of whether or not the income was distributed),[28] in order to prevent the UUT accumulating income for distribution later as capital. UK-resident taxpayers will receive a tax credit for the deemed income received. When disposing of his units, an investor is treated as a shareholder in a company[29] and is charged for any capital gains that arise on disposal.

---

[24] SP D12
[25] Section 874 ITA 2007
[26] Regulation 26, SI 2006/964
[27] Regulation 22 SI 2006/964
[28] Sections 941–943 ITA 2007 for income tax and sections 971–973 COTA 2009 for corporation tax
[29] Section 99(1)(b) TCGA 1992

11.3.2 US

(a) Taxable US persons

US persons (other than tax exempt organizations such as charities, pension funds and states or municipalities) are subject to US federal income tax on their allocated amount of income of a fund (US or non-US) whether or not such amounts are distributed, if the fund is a partnership, or on the amount of dividends received, if the fund is a corporation. US corporations are subject to tax at the corporate tax rate, currently 35% on all income.

As noted above, a fund that is classified as a partnership under the IRC will 'pass through' the amount and the character of income and gains realized by the partnership. US individuals are generally subject to tax at the applicable tax rate. Currently, long-term capital gains (assets held for more than one year) are subject to tax at a maximum rate of 20%. Short-term capital gains (assets held for one year or less) are currently subject to tax at a maximum rate equal to 39.6%. In addition, as discussed below, individuals classified as high-income taxpayers are subject to Unearned Income Medicare Contribution Tax equal to 3.8% that is applied to their capital gains and other net investment income.

Investors are subject to US tax on the sale or taxable disposition of their investment interest in the fund based on the amount that is realized less their adjusted tax basis in the investment. Any gain or loss recognized with respect to such sale or other disposition will generally be treated as capital gain or loss and will be short term, long term or some combination of both, depending upon the investor's holding period in the interest. Certain exceptions apply, including the recharacterization as ordinary income of gain (which results in a larger applicable tax rate) attributable to certain 'hot assets', such as unrealized receivables, equity interests in controlled foreign corporations (CFCs) and passive foreign investment companies (PFIC). In addition, a redemption-in-kind may or may not result in a taxable disposition, depending on the composition of the assets distributed or retained by the fund, and the manner of the redemption.

An investor's adjusted tax basis in their investment in a fund will, generally, be equal to their capital contributions, plus their allocable share of items of the fund's income and gain, plus the increase in liabilities of the fund, if any, allocated to, or actually or deemed assumed by the investor.

There are also limitations under the IRC on the ability to deduct certain expenses of the fund. Interest expenses that are currently deductible after applying the relevant limitations, to the extent that a non-corporate US investor has interest expenses in connection with its investment in the fund or if the fund has interest expenses that are allocated to a non-corporate US investor, are likely subject to the 'investment interest expense' limitations. The deduction for investment interest expenses is limited to net investment income, i.e. the excess of investment income over investment expenses. Excess investment interest expenses that are disallowed are not lost permanently but may be carried forward to succeeding years.

The carry interest payable by the fund will generally be intended to be treated as an allocable share of the fund's earnings and not a fee. This treatment is a position that is often taken but no assurance can be given, however, that the IRS would not successfully assert that the carry is actually (and should be recharacterized and treated as) a fee for services, in which case the US investors could be subject to the limitations on deductibility relating to miscellaneous itemized deductions and certain other itemized deductions of high-income individuals described above.

A fund may invest, directly or indirectly, in non-US corporations that may be classified as PFICs. A foreign corporation is classified as a PFIC for any given year if 75% or more of its gross income for such year is 'passive income' (the 'income test'), or 50% or more of the average percentage of its assets for such year consists of assets that produce or are held for the production of 'passive income' (the 'asset test'). Under certain circumstances, rental income and gain from the sale of real property may be characterized as 'passive income'.

If a fund makes a direct or indirect equity investment in a foreign corporation that is classified as a PFIC, a US investor may be subject to adverse income tax consequences, unless the fund makes a 'qualified electing fund' (QEF) election with respect to such investment for the first year in which the fund owns shares (directly or indirectly) of the PFIC. If a QEF election is made by the fund with respect to a PFIC, a US investor must include in income its allocable share of the fund's pro rata share of the ordinary earnings and capital gains of the foreign corporation for each year such corporation meets the income test or the asset test regardless of whether any distributions are made. The tax basis of a US investor in its interests will generally be increased to reflect such QEF income inclusions. No portion of any such ordinary earnings inclusions will be eligible for the reduced long-term capital gain tax rate applicable to 'qualified dividends'.

A QEF election will be possible only if the PFIC furnishes the fund with an annual statement, including in it the fund's share of the PFIC's ordinary earnings and net capital gain. It is possible that a PFIC may not provide such information, and therefore a QEF election may not be available with respect to every foreign corporation that is a PFIC. If the fund does not make a timely QEF election with respect to a PFIC, US investors in the fund will be taxed at maximum ordinary income tax rates (currently 39.6%), and must also pay an interest charge on deferred tax liability, on any 'excess distributions' made by a PFIC that are allocable to such investor, even if the foreign corporation no longer meets the income test or the asset test for PFIC status in the year the distributions are made. An excess distribution for any year generally equals the aggregate of distributions to the fund from the PFIC with respect to the fund's PFIC stock during the year that is in excess of 125% of the average of annual distributions from the PFIC during the three preceding years. Gain realized on the sale or redemption of a PFIC interest for which a QEF election is not in effect will also be treated as excess distribution. A tax exempt organization generally is not subject to the special tax rules applicable to shareholders of PFICs unless it would be taxed on a dividend from the foreign corporation. Another election generally available with respect to publicly traded PFICs, the 'mark-to-market' election, may not be available with respect to PFICs in which the fund is likely to invest.

A fund may also invest, directly or indirectly, in stock of a CFC for US federal income tax purposes. In general, a non-US corporation will constitute a CFC if more than 50% of its outstanding stock (measured by vote or value) is owned either directly or indirectly through certain attribution rules by US persons each owning 10% or more of such non-US corporation's total voting power ('US shareholder'). In general, any US shareholder is required to include currently as ordinary income its allocable share of certain items of income (e.g. dividends, interest) earned by the CFC (known as the 'subpart F income') whether or not such income is actually distributed to such shareholder. Thus, the US investors may be required to include currently their allocable shares of the fund's share of subpart F income earned by the CFC. In addition, if the fund holds a CFC stock for more than a threshold period, a portion of any gain from the disposition of the CFC stock may be treated as dividend rather than gain from the sale or exchange of such stock.

In addition to possible investments in PFICs and CFCs, a fund may make an investment outside the US that may be subject to one or more other special rules under the IRC, which may affect the amount, character and timing of income allocable to the US investors.

A fund may incur taxes in foreign jurisdictions in connection with its activities outside the US. Such non-US taxes may be creditable by the US investors towards their US federal income tax liability, or deductible in computing their taxable income, subject to applicable limitations under the IRC on the utilization of foreign tax as credits or deductions.

(b) Tax-exempt US persons

An investor that is a tax exempt organization for US federal income tax purposes and, therefore, generally exempt from US federal income taxation may nevertheless be subject to 'unrelated business taxable income' (UBTI) to the extent, if any, that its allocable share of a fund's income consists of UBTI. A tax exempt partner of a partnership that engages in a trade or business that is unrelated to the exempt function of the tax exempt partner must include its pro rata share (whether or not distributed) of such partnership's gross income derived from such unrelated trade or business in computing its UBTI. Moreover, a tax exempt partner of a partnership could be treated as earning UBTI to the extent such partnership derives income from 'debt-financed property'. Debt-financed property means property held to produce income with respect to which there is 'acquisition indebtedness' (generally indebtedness incurred in acquiring or holding property). A tax exempt investor could be treated as earning UBTI to the extent that the acquisition of its interest in the fund itself is debt financed, or if the fund finances its activities or investments with borrowed funds.

A fund may, directly or indirectly, borrow to make investments, which may give rise to UBTI from 'debt-financed property' including borrowing to acquire and/or operate one or more portfolio companies that constitute corporations for US federal income tax purposes or blocker corporations. The fund may also, from time to time, make certain investments directly or indirectly that will give rise to UBTI from engaging in a trade or business. Therefore, it is expected that a significant portion of the income of the fund allocable to investors will be treated as UBTI. Tax exempt investors should consider requesting and then investing in a Cayman entity, which does not borrow.

(c) PFICs and CFCs

As an anti-avoidance measure, special rules apply to US persons that invest (directly or indirectly through a partnership) in non-US companies that are classified as PFICs or CFCs.

A non-US corporation will be a PFIC if 75% or more of its gross income is income such as interest, dividends, royalties and gain from the disposition of property that generates such income, or 50% or more of its assets produce (or are held for the production of) such income. A non-US corporation generally will be a CFC if US persons (excluding those persons who can exercise less than 10% of the voting power of the corporation's stock) collectively exercise more than 50% of the total combined voting power or total value of the corporation's stock.

Investments in PFICs and CFCs generally result in higher effective tax rates for US persons and/or current taxation of income held offshore. In addition, such investments may result in special filing obligations.

(d) FATCA

Tax exempt US persons are not considered US account holders for the purposes of the FATCA regulations. The result of this is that any investment made by a tax exempt US person into a private equity fund which is treated as an FFI is not subject to the reporting and other information requirements of FATCA. Any 'pass-through payments' which are ordinarily subject to withholding will not be so where the recipient is not deemed a US account holder for the purposes of FATCA, so payments made to tax exempt US persons will not be subject to the 30% levy. Any US-sourced income which is not treated as a pass-through payment may still be subject to the withholding tax where the FFI is non-participating and so tax exempt US persons will need to consider any investments in offshore funds carefully for their compliance with FATCA. The definition of a pass-through payment is yet to be fully detailed as the IRS and the Treasury have reserved certain definitions for further guidance. The withholding charge for pass-through payments will not be phased in until January 2017 in any case so the regulatory position may not be settled for some time.

(e) Non-US investors in US private equity investment funds

There are certain rules in place regarding the income of non-US persons, which includes those who invest in US private equity funds.

The US federal taxation of a non-US investor will depend on whether the non-US investor holds its interest in the private equity fund in connection with the conduct of a US trade or business (USTB), as determined under the IRC. For this purpose, the activities of a fund that is classified as a partnership under the IRC will be attributed to the non-US investor. A non-US investor holding an interest in a private equity fund should typically expect to be attributed USTB from that fund as private equity funds are typically engaged in a USTB. Certain structures that use corporations could effectively shield the non-US investor from USTB. These structures include the use of a parallel fund that is a corporation or invests in corporations or a separate class of partnership interests held by the non-US investor that invests in businesses that are corporations or held by the fund indirectly through a corporation. If the corporate blockers or shields are not used and the fund invests in businesses 'pass-through' entities such as a limited liability company, the non-US investor is likely to be subject to US federal taxation on a net basis (in a manner similar to the tax on US investors) on its allocable share of the private equity fund's income and gain that are 'effectively connected' with the USTB (ECI), in whole or in part, and may also be subject to state and local level income taxation within the US. In addition, a corporate non-US investor will be subject to the 'branch profits tax' on its after-income tax amount. The current branch profits tax is generally taxable at the rate of 30%.

Generally, a private equity fund will, on a periodic basis, withhold and pay over to the IRS amounts representing a percentage of the estimated taxable income and gain of the private equity fund allocable to the non-US investor, which the non-US investor will credit towards its US federal net income tax liability. To the extent that such amounts withheld exceed the investor's actual tax liability, the investor can seek a refund upon its US federal tax return filed for the same year.

Tax treaties that are applicable will not reduce or eliminate the net income tax applicable to the non-US investor but may reduce the branch profits tax applicable to that non-US investor.

A non-US investor that participates in private equity fund investments directly or indirectly through a corporation would, generally, not be expected to hold the interest in connection with any USTB. As such, the non-US investor's distributive share of the private equity fund's income and gain will not be subject to US federal income taxes on the basis of net income or the branch profits tax. However, the non-US investor would be subject to US federal withholding taxes on some of its income, including fixed or determinable annual or periodical income, such as dividend income, considered to be from US sources. To the extent that a private equity fund allocates any income or gain that is not taxed as ECI, such amounts generally will be taxed in a similar manner. The US federal withholding tax is generally imposed at a rate of 30% of the US-sourced income, without the offset for any loss or deduction. In addition, or as an alternative, to the withholding tax, even if the private equity fund is not engaged in a USTB, dividends from US mutual funds (investing in real estate-related securities) or US real estate investment trusts attributable to the gain from the sale of US real property interests will likely be subject to US federal income tax on a net basis (i.e. after offsetting for allowable losses and deductions), as well as the branch profits tax.

Generally, capital gains and qualified interest, such as portfolio interest (as defined in section 871(h) of the IRC and, generally, is US-source interest on a registered debt obligation where the recipient owns less than a 10% interest in the company and certain other requirements are satisfied) and interest on bank deposits, are not subject to the US federal withholding tax. Individual non-US investors present in the US for greater than one hundred and eighty-three (183) days in any specific year, however, may be subject to a US federal withholding tax of 30% on gain from, or with respect to, their investment during such year. In addition, gain from the sale of certain securities classified as US real property interests within the meaning of section 897 of the IRC will be subject to US income and withholding taxes. For example, if the private equity fund owns greater than 5% of the stock in US corporations which own significant US real property interests, sales of such stock may be subject to US income and/or withholding tax. Applicable income tax treaties may reduce or eliminate the US federal withholding tax.

(f) Tax shelter provisions

In certain circumstances, an investor who disposes of an interest in a transaction resulting in the recognition by such investor of significant losses in excess of certain threshold amounts may be obligated to disclose its participation in such transaction (a 'reportable transaction') in accordance with Treasury regulations governing tax shelters and other potentially tax-motivated transactions. In addition, an investment in a fund may be considered a 'reportable transaction' if, for example, the fund recognizes certain significant losses in the future. Failure to comply with these and other reporting requirements could result in the imposition of significant penalties. Investors may be required to make various tax filings with respect to their investments in a fund, including as a result of investing directly or indirectly in non-US entities. Significant penalties are imposed for failure to file such forms. Prospective investors are urged to consult their tax advisers regarding their tax filing requirements with respect to an investment in the fund.

Under recently enacted legislation, a tax return preparer may not sign a return without itself incurring a penalty unless either in its view each position taken on the return is more likely than not to be sustained if challenged by the IRS or such position is separately disclosed on the return. A fund may adopt positions that require such disclosure, which may increase the likelihood the IRS will examine the fund's tax returns, or may forego otherwise valid reporting positions to avoid such disclosure, which may increase the tax payable by an investor.

11.4   INVESTMENT MANAGER COMPANIES

11.4.1 Closed-ended funds

(a) UK

(i) Management fees

Management fees are currently subject to VAT in the UK as they constitute a service provided in the course of the management company's business. The fund can be structured in a tax efficient manner which reduces the charge to VAT. If the general partner of a limited partnership receives priority profit shares, then there should be no charge to VAT. How it is taxed once it is received by the general partner will depend on the structure used by the manager itself. If it is a partnership, then the partners themselves will be charged to income tax and capital gains where applicable. If the manager is constituted as a corporate body it will be subject to corporation tax on income and capital gains, and the executives and employees will be subject to income tax on their salary and bonuses.

(ii) Fees for services

Income for monitoring, transaction or other services provided by the manager are treated in much the same way as management fees, as above.

(b) US

(i) Management fees

US private equity investment funds often pay the management fee to a management company that is separate from the general partner entity for reasons as described in Chapter 10, section 10.2. Alternatively, the management fee is paid by the fund to the general partner entity, which typically pays the fee (net of expenses) to the management company. The management fee is normally taxed as ordinary income. Another alternative often used to achieve a more favourable tax position is to receive a lower management fee and instead receive a larger carry interest. This position may be subject to change. The US tax laws are promulgated by the US Congress. All legislative action originates in the US House of Representatives Ways and Means Committee. This committee has visited and may revisit the character of the income of the carry interest and require that it be recognized as ordinary income. In addition, the IRS has the authority to require that the substance of the transaction and not the mere form control the recognition and character of the income. One alternative that is often used by private equity funds and hedge funds is to not charge a management fee by the investment amount contributed by the management team. This prevents a circular cash flow that would result in the recognition of income (the management fee).

If the management company is organized as a fiscally transparent vehicle (such as a limited liability company or a 'subchapter S corporation'), the management fee, along with any expenses of the management company (including salaries), will be allocated to the owners of the management company and included in the calculation of their taxable income.

If the management company is organized as a corporation which is not fiscally transparent the management company will be taxed on the receipt of the management fees. Generally, this fee income, net of any expenses of the management company, will be paid to the managers as compensation which the managers must include in their taxable income at ordinary income rates. Double taxation may be avoided where the compensation payments to the managers remain at a reasonable level because the corporation should receive a tax deduction for these compensation payments. The use of a non-fiscally transparent corporation where the deduction is unavailable is not tax efficient. The IRC and the applicable regulations include certain rules regarding the appropriate or reasonableness of compensation. It is unlikely that a corporation can merely 'wash' the income through compensation and such structure would merely result in structure that is substantially equivalent to using a fiscally transparent vehicle. Using a corporate structure could be useful, at least in the near term, if the amount of the fees is expected to be re-invested in the fund, for example due to a clawback, or used to support other businesses.

The structure should also consider state and local tax regimes.

(ii) Fees for services

Where a private equity fund receives fee income such as directors' fees, consulting fees, monitoring fees, or any other fees for services provided, such income likely would constitute ECI. It is common for such fee income when paid by investee companies of a private equity investment fund to be received by the managers of the fund and not by the fund directly to avoid this treatment, and to reflect the reality that the management of the fund is providing these services. Funds may provide for a reduction of the management fee to a specified extent that such fees are received.

11.4.2 Open-ended funds

(a) UK

In the UK, open-ended funds generally take the form of unit trusts or OEICs. The management of a unit trust acts in two relevant capacities. It runs the fund by buying and selling the underlying investments, and it deals with the investors directly when issuing or redeeming investment units in the fund. The manager receives an annual management fee in relation to the underlying investments, which is exempt from the charge to VAT if the unit trust is authorized.[30] Where a unit trust is unauthorized the management fees are not exempt from VAT. When the manager issues or redeems the units in the trust (whether authorized or unauthorized), the income derived from those dealings (the entry fee or the redemption fee as applicable) is exempt from VAT.[31]

HMRC has drafted regulations which will amend the VAT legislation to exempt from the charge to VAT the fees the fund pays to the management of certain CIS.[32] The Treasury has yet to publish a commencement date for these regulations.

Where the authorized corporate director of an OEIC deals in the underlying assets and receives a management fee, or deals with the investors by issuing or redeeming shares for a fee, those fees are exempt from the charge to VAT.[33] If the management functions of both OEICs and AUTs are subcontracted to third parties, the third party is also exempt from the charge to VAT with respect to any management function except for acting as a depositary.[34]

Management fees to hedge fund managers are treated as income and taxed depending on the hedge fund and the fund manager structure.

---

[30] Item 9 of Group 5 of Schedule 9 to the Value Added Tax Act (VATA) 1994
[31] Item 6 of Group 5 of Schedule 9 to VATA 1994
[32] The Value Added Tax Finance Order 2012
[33] Items 6 and 9 of Group 5 of Schedule 9 to VATA 1994
[34] HMRC Business Brief 07/06

(b) US

In the US open-ended funds are typically structured as mutual funds (which themselves are not exclusively open-ended). The fee structure of a mutual fund is typically divided in two: fees which are owed by the investors to the fund and the fees owed by the fund to the investment manager. The latter fees are indirectly owed by the investors but the distinction is important in its tax implications for the manager.

The fund typically pays the manager management fees out of the pooled assets of the fund on an annualized basis to cover the cost of providing portfolio management and other related services. This income is taxed as ordinary business income and the person who bears the tax liability depends on the structure used; if it is a company that is not fiscally transparent it is corporation tax and if it is a partnership it is borne by the individual members.

Other fees paid by the fund to the manager include those that cover expenses such as legal and accounting costs, and as they are directly attributable to those expenditures, there is a small likelihood that such fees will generate profit that is taxable.

11.5   PRINCIPALS OF AN INVESTMENT MANAGER

11.5.1   Equity ownership of investment manager and the fund

Senior principals of the manager entity are usually the key partners or equity owners of the entity, as they are typically the founders and drivers of the business. They may be owners of the management group alongside key cornerstone investors or other strategic partners. For further details of the ownership structures of the manager, see Chapter 10. As owners of the management group, they will often pay tax on receipt of income or capital through a tax transparent UK LLP or US LLC, or income tax from a corporate vehicle, received by way of dividend or a fee. The principals will likely own the management group. If they sell shares, gains should be subject to CGT. In the UK, entrepreneur's relief of 10% can apply.

Principals of the manager entity are usually required by the commercial terms of a fund to invest in the fund itself in order to demonstrate to investors that they are sufficiently committed to its success; this is commonly referred to as the 'GP commitment' for a closed-ended fund, or 'skin in the game'.

(a) UK

The tax treatment for the equity ownership by management principals of an interest in the fund is the same as described for investors above in section 11.3.1 of this chapter. Those who own an equity interest in the manager will be taxed in accordance with the structure of the entity. If it is a partnership there is a single charge to CGT to the principal on disposal of the interest. Alternatively, if it is a corporate entity, the principal will also be charged to CGT on the disposal of his or her interest where there is a gain, following any tax paid by the corporate entity on income profits it receives.

(b) US

In the US equity ownership of the manager and the fund by the principals is treated much the same as for the investors in the fund as described above in section 11.3.2 of this chapter: the increase in value of equity ownership of the manager and/or the fund is typically treated as long-term capital gains and is taxed at a rate of up to 20%. If the manager entity distributes any profits by way of dividend (if a corporate structure) then the income (if qualifying dividend income) is taxed at a maximum rate, currently 20%. Other income is treated in the usual way.

11.5.2 Management fees

(a) UK

Where the fund manager is structured as a partnership or a UK LLP or US LLC, tax transparency should apply and the income and expenses of the management firm are assessed to determine the profits and losses of the partners.[35] The management fees for a fund are typically set low as they are (in the view of investors) to cover the cost of running the fund rather than to make a profit for the managers. When the assessment of taxable profit is made, deductions may be made for expenditure that was wholly for the purpose of the trade of the partnership. This will not allow for any deductions for the salaries of the partners, or any deductions for a rebate made to the partners in respect of their investment in the fund.[36] The allocation of the profits or losses (as the case may be) is done in accordance with the profit sharing agreement, which forms part of the partnership agreement.

(b) US

Income received by a management principal from management fees is taxed as ordinary income (currently, up to 39.6% plus Medicaid and state liabilities). It is sometimes the practice of private equity fund managers to channel a principal's share of the management fees into the fund to contribute towards their required investment, known as the management fee waiver. This converts the tax liability from that of ordinary income to long-term capital gains. Recent investigations begun by the IRS and state prosecutors into this practice suggest that it could be in question and its effectiveness could be wiped out in a test case or regulatory decision.

11.5.3 Carried interest

(a) UK

When a principal receives carried interest, as long as he is an employee of the manager or the general partner he will receive a tax benefit.[37] There is a Memorandum of Understanding between the BVCA and HMRC to the effect that where its terms are followed, no income tax charge will arise on the acquisition or disposal of the partnership interest. This charge would have potentially arisen when the restrictions on the interest in the partnership (such as compulsory transfer on dismissal) depressed the value of the interest when it was acquired or disposed of as part of the Income Tax (Earnings and Pensions) Act 2003 regime. Instead, where the conditions of the Memorandum of Understanding are met, the employee is treated as being within an exception and there is no charge to income tax, but to capital gains instead.

---

[35] Section 848 of the Income Tax (Trading and Other Income) Act (ITTOIA) 2005
[36] HMRC v Lansdowne Partners Limited Partnership [2011] EWCA Civ 1578
[37] Part 7 of the Income Tax (Earnings and Pensions) Act 2003

(b) US

The carried interest paid by US private equity investment funds is normally structured as an allocation of fund profits to the general partner of the fund. The general partner (normally a partnership or a limited liability company) then allocates the carried interest among its members, the fund managers. To the extent that such profits represent long-term capital gains realized by the fund, those profits will be taxed at preferential capital gain rates when allocated to the managers (provided that the managers are treated as 'partners' of the general partner entity for US federal income tax purposes). As noted in section 11.4.1 of this chapter, in the US a change to the tax treatment of carried interest is possible in the near future.

(c) The future

There is much debate around the capital treatment of carried interest. This was especially highlighted during the campaign of Mitt Romney for the US Presidency in 2012. It was clear that the treatment of his earnings was politically divisive, and the reaction was magnified by the state of the economy at the time.

11.5.4 Performance fees

Broadly speaking, performance fees for hedge fund managers are charged to tax as income. Hedge side pockets have the opportunity to create capital.

11.6   SOME CONCLUSIONS

This chapter has been a high level overview of the taxation of investors, managers and the funds in the UK and the US. Some of the taxation policies, such as the UK Memorandum of Understanding, are designed to protect an industry by eliminating frictional costs. These policies are not too dissimilar from offshore jurisdictions, but the levels of corporation tax are currently not at the levels seen offshore due in part to fiscal policy and political viability.

12

Regulatory Environment

12.1 INTRODUCTION

12.1.1 US, UK and EU regulatory environment

This chapter provides an introduction to the overlapping regulatory regimes that are relevant to investment managers, placement agents and other advisers to asset managers. I include an overview of the following:

- UK regulatory environment (FCA, PRA and FSMA)
- US regulatory environment (SEC, Dodd–Frank Act and FATCA)
- EU regulatory environment (AIFMD).

12.1.2 Other regulatory environments

The contents of this chapter are restricted to summaries of the US, UK and EU regulatory environments. Summaries of further regulatory environments in relation to other popular fund locations are contained within Chapters 7 and 8.

12.2 UK REGULATORY ENVIRONMENT

Prior to 1 April 2013, the Financial Services Authority (FSA) was responsible for the regulation of the financial services industry in the UK. However, the FSA has now become two separate regulatory authorities known as the FCA and the Prudential Regulatory Authority (PRA). The PRA and the FCA work together forming a 'twin peaks' regulatory structure in the UK.

The PRA is now part of the Bank of England and is responsible for the prudential regulation and supervision of banks, building societies and various other institutions presently totalling 1700 financial firms.[1]

The FCA is a quasi-governmental body which is responsible for the regulation of the financial services industry in the UK.[2] The FCA is now responsible for conducting the regulation of all UK-based retail and financial services firms. In addition the FCA is the regulator of the UKLA. The statutory powers to regulate the financial services industry were conferred on the FCA by the FSMA as amended by the Financial Services Act 2012. The FCA is accountable to the Treasury, including the Chancellor of the Exchequer, as the Treasury appoints the board of the FCA.[3] However, the FCA does not receive any government funding. Instead it is

---

[1] Bank of England website: http://www.bankofengland.co.uk/pra/Pages/default.aspx: last accessed 5 September 2013
[2] Financial Conduct Authority website: http://www.fca.org.uk/about/governance/who: last accessed 5 September 2013
[3] Financial Conduct Authority website: http://www.fca.org.uk/about/governance/who: last accessed 5 September 2013

funded by charging fees to the firms which it regulates and to other bodies such as investment exchanges.[4] At the time of writing, the FCA supervises the conduct of 26,000 financial firms.[5]

12.3   FINANCIAL CONDUCT AUTHORITY

12.3.1 Statutory objectives

The FCA has three statutory objectives under FSMA:

- to protect consumers
- to enhance the integrity of the UK financial system
- to help maintain competitive markets and promote effective competition in the interests of consumers.

12.3.2 Regulation

Under FSMA, any person who carries on a 'regulated activity' must either be authorized by the FCA or come within one of the statutory exemptions.[6] The RAO (The Financial Services and Markets Act 2000 (Regulated Activities) Order 2001)[7] prescribes the 'regulated activities', which include (for our purposes):

- dealing in investments as principal or as agent. Both activities include buying, selling, subscribing for or underwriting securities or investments
- arranging deals in investments for another person, whether as principal or agent
- managing investments or assets belonging to another person whereby a degree of discretion is involved
- safeguarding and administering investments
- establishing, operating or winding up a CIS, or acting as trustee of an AUT scheme, or acting as the depositary or sole director of an open-ended investment company
- advising on investments.[8]

For each regulated activity, an applicant for FCA authorization must identify which investment types their activities concern. The RAO describes these as:

- shares
- instruments creating or acknowledging indebtedness
- government and public securities
- instruments giving entitlements to investments
- certificates representing certain securities

---

[4] Financial Conduct Authority website: http://www.fca.org.uk/about/how-we-are-funded: last accessed 5 September 2013

[5] Financial Conduct Authority website: http://www.fca.org.uk/about/what/regulating: last accessed 5 September 2013

[6] FSMA; section 19(1)

[7] The Financial Services and Markets Act 2000 (Regulated Activities) Order 2001

[8] The Financial Services and Markets Act 2000 (Regulated Activities) Order 2001; Articles 5, 14, 21, 25, 37, 40 & 51–53

- options to acquire or dispose of a security or contractually based investment.[9]

12.3.3 Exemptions

Persons exempt from FCA authorization include:

- professional firms such as solicitors and accountants that carry on certain of the above listed activities that are incidental to their main business[10]
- local authorities or housing bodies which carry on insurance mediation or mortgage activities.[11]

12.3.4 Financial promotions

A person must be FCA authorized, or the content of the 'promotion' being made to would-be investors must be approved by an 'authorized' person. A 'promotion' is generally regarded as communicating an invitation or inducement to engage in investment activity.[12] Under the FSMA, engaging in investment activity is defined as:

> 'entering or offering to enter into an agreement, the making or performance of which by either party constitutes a controlled activity; or exercising any rights conferred by a controlled investment to acquire, dispose of, underwrite or convert a controlled investment.'[13]

12.3.5 Supervision of firms

The FCA monitors and regulates firms according to the risks they present. For this purpose, the FCA places firms into four different categories. The first category applies to the largest firms with the most customers and those firms are subject to continuous assessment over rolling two-year periods. The assessments in the other three categories are less stringent, as these firms will have fewer customers and/or pose fewer risks. Firms in the fourth category are subject to FCA assessment every four years.

12.3.6 Supervision of individuals

An 'approved person' is an individual that has been approved by the FCA to perform one or more 'controlled functions' on behalf of an authorized firm. Under FSMA, in order to obtain approval, the FCA must be satisfied that the candidate is 'fit and proper' to perform the relevant controlled functions.

When determining fitness and propriety, the FCA considers honesty, integrity, reputation, competence, capability and financial prudence. The supervision of individuals performing controlled functions integrates with the FCA's regulation of the authorized firm for which

---

[9] RAO; Articles 76–80 & 83

[10] Financial Conduct Authority website: http://www.fca.org.uk/firms/about-authorisation/do-i-need-to-be-authorised: last accessed 2 June 2013

[11] Financial Conduct Authority website: http://www.fca.org.uk/firms/about-authorisation/do-i-need-to-be-authorised: last accessed 2 June 2013

[12] RAO; Article 21(1) & (2)

[13] RAO; Article 21(8)

the approved person acts. An individual cannot be approved before the firm is authorized but both applications can be performed simultaneously.[14]

12.4   PRUDENTIAL REGULATION AUTHORITY

12.4.1 Statutory objectives

The PRA has two statutory objectives:

- to promote the safety and soundness of those firms it regulates
- in relation to insurers, to ensure there is an appropriate degree of protection for policyholders.[15]

12.4.2 Regulation

Firms are required to apply for authorization to carry on the following PRA-regulated activities:

- accepting deposits
- electing or carrying out contracts of insurance
- managing the underwriting capacity of a Lloyd's syndicate as a managing agent of Lloyd's.[16]

As such, there is no definition of a bank under the PRA, although it lists those banks that are regulated by PRA as:

- banks incorporated in the UK
- banks incorporated outside the EEA authorized to accept deposits through a branch in the UK
- banks incorporated in the EEA entitled to accept deposits through a branch in the UK.

Firms that seek to carry on activities other than those listed above need to apply to the FCA for authorization (see 12.3.2 above). To carry on one of the above activities without authorization from the PRA may constitute a criminal offence.[17]

12.4.3 Supervision of firms

As in the case of the FCA, the frequency and intensity of supervision which the PRA applies to firms it supervises is decided through the division of firms into specified categories. Category 1 is subject to the most frequent and intense supervision, while category 5 is subject to the least supervision:

---

[14] Financial Conduct Authority website: http://www.fca.org.uk/firms/being-regulated/approved/approved-persons: last accessed 2 June 2013

[15] Bank of England website: http://www.bankofengland.co.uk/pra/Pages/about/default.aspx: last accessed 2 June 2013

[16] Bank of England website: http://www.bankofengland.co.uk/pra/Pages/authorisations/newfirm/default.aspx: last accessed 2 June 2013

[17] Bank of England website: http://www.bankofengland.co.uk/pra/Pages/authorisations/newfirm/default.aspx: last accessed 2 June 2013

- Category 1 – significant deposit-takers, designated investment firms or insurers with the potential to cause very significant disruption to the UK financial system; and insurers with a certain type of business with the potential to cause significant disruption to the interests of a substantial number of policyholders
- Category 2 – significant deposit-takers, designated investment firms or insurers with the potential to cause some disruption to the UK financial system; and insurers with a certain type of business with the potential to cause some disruption to the interests of a substantial number of policyholders
- Category 3 – deposit-takers, designated investment firms or insurers with the capacity to cause minor disruption to the UK financial system, in the event difficulties across the whole financial sector arise; and insurers with a certain type of business with a minor capacity to cause disruption to the interests of a substantial number of policyholders
- Category 4 – deposit-takers, designated investment firms or insurers with very little capacity to cause disruption to the UK financial system, but which have the potential to generate disruption in the event difficulties across the whole financial sector arise; and insurers with a certain type of business with very little capacity to cause disruption to the interests of a substantial number of policyholders
- Category 5 – deposit-takers, designated investment firms or insurers, with almost no capacity to cause disruption to the UK financial system, but which may cause some disruption in the event difficulties across the whole financial sector arise; and insurers with a certain type of business with no capacity to cause disruption to the interests of a substantial number of policyholders.[18]

12.4.4 Supervision of Individuals

Under section 59 of the FSMA, individuals who are to carry out 'controlled functions' on behalf of a firm must be approved by the PRA. An individual cannot be approved before the relevant firm is authorized, but the applications can be formed simultaneously. 'Controlled functions' includes all directors, CEO and partners.

Individuals who apply to carry out a controlled function are assessed by the PRA in respect of their reputation and financial soundness, and in addition they must be deemed to be competent and capable to carry out the role. However, it is also the responsibility of the relevant firm to ensure that the individual is fit and proper to take up a controlled function.[19]

12.5   US REGULATORY ENVIRONMENT

12.5.1 The United States Securities and Exchange Commission

(a) Introduction

The SEC was established in response to the Great Depression and stock market crash of 1929 by the Securities Exchange Act (1934) which along with the Securities Act (1933), set out to restore market confidence by providing more reliable information and setting out clear rules for legitimate dealing. The SEC's primary role is to protect investors, which it

---

[18] The Prudential Regulation Authority's approach to banking supervision (April 2013), p.16: accessed via http://www.bankofengland.co.uk/publications/Documents/praapproach/bankingappr1304.pdf

[19] Bank of England website: http://www.bankofengland.co.uk/pra/Pages/authorisations/approvedpersons/default.aspx: last accessed 2 June 2013

does in essence by requiring companies that publicly offer securities or have more than 2000 shareholders (or at least 500 that are not accredited investors) and have total assets in excess of USD 10 million to register the applicable class of stock under the Securities and Exchange Act and be open and honest about their business, any securities being offered and the risks involved; and by obliging those that sell and trade securities (brokers, dealers and exchanges) to treat investors fairly and honestly, putting investors' interests first.

The SEC's remit also encompasses the maintenance of the markets as well as facilitating capital formation with a view to macroeconomic growth.

In the US the rules governing the securities industry derive from one mantra: full and fair disclosure of all material facts to all investors. In light of this, the SEC obliges public companies to disclose to the public, financial and other information. Based on this publicly available information investors can make an informed judgement on their investment; whether to buy, sell or hold the same.

As a regulator, the SEC constantly samples the opinions of market participants in order to gauge concern and learn from their experiences in an attempt to maintain this information flow. Aside from the investors themselves, which the SEC is charged with protecting, it regulates the major participants in the market such as exchanges, brokers, dealers, investment advisers and mutual funds. The SEC's dealing with such entities is dual in so much as it tries to aid the market by promoting the disclosure of information while protecting investors through the policing of such bodies.

In its role as an enforcement authority, the SEC can and does bring civil actions against those (whether individuals or companies) in violation of the securities laws. Typical causes of action include insider trading, fraudulent accounting and providing false or misleading information about securities and the companies that issue them. The SEC relies heavily on investors providing information in order to bring actions. Moreover the SEC is responsible for maintaining the database of disclosures that public companies are required to file.

The SEC is part of a wider regulatory network in the US and while its primary responsibility relates to securities, it works closely with other bodies and institutions. Furthermore, the Chairman of the SEC serves on the President's Working Group on Financial Markets along with other institutional heads such as the Chairman of the Federal Reserve and the Secretary of the Treasury.

(b) Structure

The SEC is headed by five presidentially appointed commissioners of which one is appointed Chairman. In order to maintain impartiality and prevent tribalism, no more than three of the commissioners may belong to one political party.

The SEC has approximately 3500 staff, who are responsible for: interpreting federal securities laws; issuing and amending rules; overseeing inspection of securities firms, brokers, investment advisers and ratings agencies; overseeing private regulatory organizations in the securities, accounting and auditing sectors; and coordinating US securities regulation with federal, state and foreign authorities (such as the FCA).

The SEC is divided into five divisions, each responsible for a different area of the securities industry.

(c) Division of Corporation Finance

The Division of Corporation Finance is responsible for overseeing the provision of obligatory information to public investors. Public companies are compelled to disclose information that must be made when stock is initially sold and then on a continuing and periodic basis. The information disclosed is reviewed on an ongoing basis. The division also supports companies by providing guidance on the rules and regulations. By extension, it recommends rules to the SEC for adoption.

(d) Division of Trading and Markets

The Division of Trading and Markets is charged with maintaining an efficient market. It provides oversight of the major market participants. The division also oversees the Securities Investor Protection Corporation, which is a private, non-profit corporation that provides insurance to member firms for the securities and cash in customer accounts against the failure of those firms (such insurance does not extend to market decline or fraud).

(e) Division of Investment Management

The Division of Investment Management protects investors and promotes capital formation by overseeing and regulating the investment management industry in the US. This important part of the market includes mutual funds, professional fund managers, analysts and advisers to individual customers. As this division's remit involves a high concentration of individual investors, the division focuses on ensuring that disclosures are useful to retail customers and that the regulatory costs borne by consumers are not excessive.

(f) Division of Enforcement

The Division of Enforcement recommends the instigation of investigations and the bringing of civil actions, and prosecutes any such cases on behalf of the SEC. The division works closely with law enforcement agencies in the US and around the world to bring criminal cases when appropriate.

(g) Division of Risk, Strategy, and Financial Innovation

The Division of Risk, Strategy, and Financial Innovation was established in September 2009 to analyse and identify emerging risks and growing trends in the market. The division then makes recommendations as to how any developments or trends affect the regulation of the markets. This division also provides support to the other divisions by way of research, analysis and training.

12.5.2 The Commodity Futures Trading Commission

The other significant regulator is the CFTC. Congress created the CFTC in 1974 as an independent agency with exclusive jurisdiction over futures trading in all commodities. Similar to the SEC, the CFTC has the mission to protect investors. The regulatory scope of the CFTC has expanded significantly as certain swaps are now under the regulatory authority of the CFTC.

There are five commissioners of the CFTC which are appointed by the President of the United States, with the advice and consent of the US Senate. The commissioners serve staggered five-year terms. The CFTC has several divisions that oversee and enforce the regulations.

The Division of Market Oversight (DMO) oversees trade execution facilities and data repositories, conducts surveillance, reviews new exchange applications and examines existing exchanges to ensure compliance with applicable core principles. The DMO also evaluates new products to ensure they are not susceptible to manipulation as well as rule filings by exchanges to ensure compliance with core principles.

The Swap Dealer and Intermediary Oversight (DSIO) division oversees the registration and compliance of intermediaries and futures industry self-regulatory organizations, including US derivatives exchanges and the National Futures Association. The DSIO is also responsible for developing and monitoring compliance with regulations addressing registration, business conduct standards, capital adequacy and margin requirements for swap dealers and major swap participants.

The Clearing and Risk (DCR) division oversees derivatives clearing organizations (DCOs) and other market participants in the clearing process, including futures commission merchants, swap dealers, major swap participants and large traders. The DCR also monitors the clearing of futures, options on futures and swaps by DCOs, assesses DCO compliance with CFTC regulations, and conducts risk assessment and surveillance. The DCR makes recommendations on DCO applications and eligibility, rule submissions and which types of swaps should be cleared.

The Division of Enforcement investigates and prosecutes alleged violations of the Commodity Exchange Act and CFTC regulations. Potential violations include fraud, manipulation and other abuses concerning commodity derivatives and swaps that threaten market integrity, market participants and the general public.

12.5.3 The Dodd–Frank Wall Street Reform and Consumer Protection Act

The Dodd–Frank Act (for the purposes of this section, referred to as the Act) was signed into US federal law by President Barack Obama on 21 July 2010 and was passed as a response to the recession of the late 2000s. The Act brought significant changes to financial regulation in the United States that affect all federal financial regulatory agencies and almost every part of the US financial services industry and is a consideration for all fund managers who deal with (or may deal with) US investors.

Named after the House of Representatives Financial Services Committee Chairman Barney Frank and Senate Banking Committee Chairman Senator Christopher J. Dodd, the Act restricts the types of trading activities that certain financial institutions (such as banks) are allowed to practise, increases the registration requirements of financial institutions in the private equity and hedge fund industries and increases the oversight and supervision responsibilities of the SEC and the CFTC, in particular in the swaps and derivative markets. The 2008 market crash was in part fuelled by the bursting of the housing bubble in the US. In an attempt to prevent this in the future, the Act includes provisions to protect borrowers against predatory lending and to prevent abusive mortgage practices. The Act aims to achieve this by establishing US government agencies to monitor banking practices and oversee financial institutions.

The Act created the Financial Stability Oversight Council (FSOC) to oversee financial institutions and fill the regulatory gaps created by the numerous agencies responsible for regulating the various corners of the financial markets.[20] In a broad sense, the FSOC identifies and responds to risks to stability and promotes discipline by reducing bailout expectations. While creating this and other new agencies, the Act introduced a swathe of reforms to the mandates and procedures of existing agencies such as the SEC and the Federal Reserve.

(a) Securitization

Under the Act, the rules regarding credit risk retention were tightened, obliging an increased retention of risk including a prohibition on the transfer of the same.[21] The disclosure requirements in this area have also been strengthened, including an obligation on the securitizer to perform due diligence on products and provide this to investors.

(b) Derivatives

While the substantive law dealing with this element of the Act will be developed by other agencies such as the CFTC and the SEC, the Act does provide a set of objectives. A key development is that no federal government assistance (subject to conditions) will be provided to non-bank institutions engaging in 'swaps'. Moreover the proposed regime includes provisions for the regulation of those participating in the derivatives market such as swap dealers.[22]

(c) Investment adviser registration

What the financial crisis following 2008 revealed was a broad lack of investor knowledge with regard to the complex financial products in which they were investing. With respect to this, the Act proposes greater investor protection through imposing fiduciary duties on those providing investment and related advisory services to investors. Moreover, the prevention of malpractice has been partly addressed by proactively offering rewards to whistle-blowers.[23] For more detail, see Chapter 11, section 11.3.2.

(d) Credit rating agencies

The Act seeks to build on the reforms introduced by the Credit Rating Agency Reform Act (2006). The Act attempts to achieve reforms in this area by extending the liabilities and penalties similar to those applicable to accountancy firms as well as increasing the burden of proof on the agencies by requiring them to demonstrate quantitative and qualitative reasoning for their publications. Moreover certain activities are now restricted or prohibited, such as the requirement to separate rating activities from sales and marketing activities and that each agency must establish an effective internal control structure for which it is accountable to the SEC.[24]

---

[20] Title I, The Dodd–Frank Wall Street Reform and Consumer Protection Act
[21] Section 941, Dodd–Frank Act
[22] Title VII, Dodd–Frank Act
[23] Title IX, Dodd–Frank Act
[24] Title IX, Subtitle C, Dodd–Frank Act

(e) The 'Volcker Rules'

Introduced by Title VI of the Act, the 'Volcker Rules' relate to certain speculative trading activities. Important distinctions are made between activities that may be conducted by banking entities and by non-bank financial companies supervised by the Federal Reserve. The rules set out explicitly permitted activities and services as well as capital requirements and restrictions on transactions with affiliates. The prohibitions specifically apply to 'banking entities' which include insured depositary institutions, the controlling company and any foreign bank with operations in the US including parents, affiliates and subsidiaries of the foreign bank.

The Volcker Rules prohibit a banking entity from: engaging in 'proprietary trading'; acquiring or retaining any equity, partnership or other ownership interest in a hedge or private equity fund; and sponsoring a hedge or private equity fund. These prohibitions apply to US banking entities, regardless of where the trading or activities are conducted. For non-US organizations, the rules will only apply if the trading or activities take place in the US or if they involve the offering of securities to a US resident.

The Act defines 'proprietary trading' as engaging as a principal for the trading account of a banking organization or supervised non-bank financial company in any transaction to purchase or sell, or otherwise acquire or dispose of any security, derivative, futures contract, option on any such security, derivative or contract or any other financial instrument so determined by the regulators.[25] A trading account is defined as any account used for acquiring or taking positions in the proprietary trading of securities and instruments principally for the purpose of selling in the near term, and other accounts as determined by the regulators.

Conversely, the Volcker Rules also explicitly permit certain types of trading, such as in government securities and on behalf of customers. The rules also permit certain hedging that is undertaken to mitigate risk, investments in small business investment companies and public welfare.

As mentioned above, banking entities are prohibited from having ownership interests in a fund. This prohibition is subject to an exception for seed investment. In order to take advantage, the organization must comply with the same conditions allowing 'sponsorship' in certain cases and that within a year of the fund having been established, the banking organization's interest must be no more than 3% of the total ownership interests. Moreover, where the seed investment amounts to more than 3% of the ownership interests in the fund; the banking entity cannot dilute its interest by divesting interests to an affiliated organization. Additionally, the aggregate of all such interests may not exceed 3% of the banking entity's Tier 1 capital.

In relation to 'sponsoring' of hedge and private equity funds, it should be noted that this has not been taken to mean simply advising. The Act defines 'sponsoring' as serving as general or managing partner or trustee of a fund; selecting or controlling a majority of the directors, trustees or management of a fund; or sharing the same name of the banking organization or any affiliate or a similar name with the fund.[26] However, subject to certain conditions, in certain circumstances, banking entities may be able to organize and offer a hedge or private equity fund.

---

[25] Section 619, Dodd–Frank Act
[26] Section 619, Dodd–Frank Act

The Federal Reserve issued a ruling on 19 April 2012, stating that banks would have two years to bring their activities in line with the Volcker Rules, before regulations would be enforced.[27]

(f) Corporate governance

A particularly topical item on the Act's agenda deals with corporate governance[28] and executive remuneration. Shareholders now get a non-binding vote on the compensation of executive committee members. A new set of standards promoting independence have also been applied to compensation committees. Moreover, executive compensation must now be linked to financial performance. Companies are now obliged to operate policies designed to recuperate any compensation that falls out of line with a restatement of accounts. In addition the Act imposes much tighter regulatory capital requirements on financial institutions.

12.5.4 The Foreign Account Tax Compliance Act (FATCA)

Under FATCA, the relevant withholding agent may be required to withhold 30% of any interest, dividends and other fixed or determinable annual or periodical gains, profits and income from sources within the US or gross proceeds from the sale of any property of a type which can produce interest or dividends from sources within the US paid after 31 December 2013 (or 31 December 2014 in the case of payments of gross proceeds), to:

(i) a foreign financial institution unless such foreign financial institution agrees to verify, report and disclose its US accountholders and meets certain other specified requirements or
(ii) a non-financial foreign entity that is a beneficial owner of the payment unless such entity certifies that it does not have any substantial US owners or provides the name, address and taxpayer identification number of each substantial US owner and such entity meets certain other specified requirements.

Thus, non-US investors could be subject to the FATCA withholding tax if they do not provide information to the private equity fund in which they invest so that the private equity fund is able to comply with the FATCA information reporting rules. In such case, the partnership agreement of the private equity fund will often require the investors whose failure to provide information resulted in the FATCA withholding tax, to indemnify the private equity fund for the tax and associated costs, treat the FATCA withholding as an amount deemed distributed to such investors for purposes of calculating the carried interest threshold and/or seek other remedies.

12.5.5 FBAR reporting requirements

A US person (including a US tax exempt investor) is required to file with the IRS, the Report of Foreign Bank and Financial Accounts (FBAR), with respect to their financial interest in or

---

[27] Alternative Investment Management Association website: http://www.aima.org/en/regulation/asset-management-regulation/volcker-rule.cfm: last accessed 11 March 2013
[28] Title IX, Subtitle G, Dodd–Frank Act

signature authority over certain classes of foreign financial accounts for each calendar year when their aggregate value exceeds USD 10,000 at any time during the year. The FBAR reporting requirement generally does not apply to a US person's ownership of an equity investment in an offshore hedge fund. The FBAR reporting requirement, however, applies to:

(i)   any foreign financial account of an offshore hedge fund if the US person owns, directly or indirectly, more than 50% of the value or voting power (or, if partnership, profits or capital) of all classes of equity investments in the fund and

(ii) any foreign financial account of any corporation, partnership, other entity or trust (other than the fund) if the US person, directly or indirectly (including through the investment in the offshore hedge fund), owns more than 50% of the value or voting power (or, if partnership, profits or capital) of equity investments in such entity or trust.

12.6   EU REGULATORY ENVIRONMENT – THE ALTERNATIVE INVESTMENT FUND MANAGERS DIRECTIVE

12.6.1 Background

The AIFMD provides a framework for the regulation of Alternative Investment Fund Managers (AIFM). It was due to be transposed by member states by 22 July 2013, which the UK and 11 other member states achieved on that date.[29] This section will take a look at both the AIFMD-level requirements and the transposed provisions of the UK.

For the purposes of this legislation, an AIF is broadly a structure which falls within the following description, i.e.:

'collective investment undertakings, including investment compartments thereof, which:

(i)   raise capital from a number of investors with a view to investing it in accordance with a defined investment policy, for the benefit of those investors; and

(ii) which do not require authorization pursuant to [the UCITS Directive].'[30]

Certain structures fall outside of this definition, such as managed accounts (see Chapter 4) but regardless of this, the definition of an AIF is wide. It includes, for example, closed-ended company structures that have not been subject to fund regulation in the UK before implementation of the Directive.

The legislation is largely indiscriminate towards the asset classes or structure of a fund and therefore applies to the managers of any AIF. The AIFMD defines an AIFM, for the purposes of the Directive, as a legal person (i.e. a company or other legal entity, distinct from a natural person) whose regular business is the management of one or more AIFs.[31] For further clarity, this has been defined as performing at least portfolio or risk management functions.[32] There-

---

[29] Austria, Croatia, Cyprus, Denmark, Germany, Ireland, Latvia, Luxembourg, Malta, the Netherlands and Sweden
[30] Art 4, 1(a), The Alternative Investment Fund Managers Directive 2011/61/EU
[31] Art 4, 1(b), 2011/61/EU
[32] Art 4.1(w) and Annex 1 2011/61/EU

fore advisers providing only advice to an AIFMD are not within the remit of the legislation.[33] An AIF must have a single AIFM which is responsible for compliance with the Directive.[34]

Where an AIFM does fall within the scope of the AIFMD, the applicable regulator is that in its home state which for EU AIFMs means where it has its registered office[35] (e.g. the FCA for AIFMs whose registered office is in the UK). Areas covered by the AIFMD include:

- an obligation to appoint a depositary
- conditions relating to being an AIFM and authorization
- regulatory capital and financial resources requirements
- general conditions relating to investors including conflicts of interest, fair treatment and risk and liquidity management
- requirements pertaining to the organization of the AIFMD including internal governance
- requirements for independent valuation of assets
- restrictions on the ability to delegate functions to third parties
- remuneration requirements for senior executives
- reporting requirements such as annual reports, disclosure to investors and regulatory reporting
- special rules relating to listed and unlisted companies in the portfolio including 'asset stripping' restrictions on dividend payments and other actions after acquiring stakes.

These requirements do not, however, apply universally to all AIFMs and are in particular relaxed for small AIFMs.

12.6.2 Authorization requirements for AIFMs

An AIFM will need to obtain authorization from its home regulator, unless it is subject to one of the exemptions. In the UK this is known as 'Part 4A Authorization' in reference to FSMA 2000. In applying for authorization, the AIFM must provide information relating to the AIFM as well as information relating to each AIF it intends to manage.

The information required includes the credentials of the people conducting the AIFM's business; shareholders with 10% of the voting rights or with an ability to exert 'significant influence' over the management of the AIFM; the organizational structure of the AIFM; a plan on how it intends to comply with the AIFMD; the remuneration regime of the AIFM; and arrangements regarding delegation.

In terms of the AIF, the AIFM is required to provide information about investment strategies, information about the master fund (where the AIF is a feeder AIF), the fund's governance documents, the AIFM's plan for appointing a depositary and the proposed information that is to be disclosed to investors investing in the AIF (as prescribed by the AIFMD).

It should be noted that the home regulator may qualify any authorization granted by limiting its scope such as by placing restrictions on the investment strategy.

---

[33] Appendix 3, Alternative Investment Fund Managers Directive COM (2009) 20
[34] Art 5.1 2011/61/EU
[35] Art 5, 7, 2011/61/EU

12.6.3 Authorization requirements for small AIFMs

A 'small AIFM' is a manager that operates one or more AIFs with aggregate assets under management below one of two thresholds.[36] The relevant threshold depends on whether the fund uses leverage or not to acquire its assets; note that this does not include the portfolio assets (e.g. shares in unlisted portfolio companies) of private equity funds where the fund is not exposed to the borrowing of such portfolio assets.[37] The thresholds are:

- assets under management across all AIFs managed of no more than EUR 100 million including any assets acquired through the use of leverage[38]
- assets under management across all AIFs managed of no more than EUR 500 million when the assets acquired by the fund(s) are unleveraged and the AIFs have no redemption rights exercisable during a period of five years following the date of initial investment in each AIF.[39]

A small AIFM complies with a lighter regime than other 'full-scope' AIFMs – although it will not be entitled to the EEA marketing passport available to full-scope AIFMs. This includes an option for member states to introduce a registration regime for small AIFMs – which is less onerous than requiring full authorization. The AIFMD requires that a small AIFM at least:

- registers with the competent authority of its home member state
- identifies the AIFs that it manages to such authority at the time of registration
- provides information about the investment strategies of the AIFs that it manages to the competent authority at the time of registration
- regularly provides information to the competent authority relating to instruments in which it trades and the most important concentrations of the AIFs managed in order to allow effective monitoring of systemic risk by the such authority and
- notifies the competent authority where it no longer meets the conditions for being a small AIF.[40]

A small AIFM can also opt in to the full-scope compliance requirements of the AIFMD in order to obtain the rights granted therein (i.e. the right to passport the fund across the EU without relying on the private placement regimes).[41]

In the UK, a distinction is drawn between 'small authorized AIFMs' and 'small registered AIFMs'. A small authorized AIFM is a small UK AIFM (i.e. it has its registered office in the UK) which meets the threshold test and has not opted into the full-scope regime.[42] A small registered AIFM is a small UK AIFM which meets the threshold test and is:

- the internal AIFM of an AIF which is a body corporate and not a CIS under existing UK law or

---

[36] Art 3(2), 2011/61 EU and regulation 9 SI 2013/1773

[37] Art 6(3), Commission Delegated Regulation (EU) No 231/2013

[38] Art 3(2(a) 2011/61 EU and reg 9(1)(b) SI 2013/1773

[39] Art 3(2(b) 2011/61 EU and reg 9(1)(a) SI 2013/1773

[40] Art 3(3) 2011/61/EU

[41] Art 3(4) 2011/61/EU

[42] Reg 2(1) SI 2013/1773

- the external AIFM of AIFs which are CISs under pre-existing UK law (and not an AUT, an OEIC or an authorized contractual scheme) and hold the majority of their assets as land provided that the AIFs are established or operated by a firm which has regulatory permission for this activity under pre-existing UK law or
- it has applied for registration as a European Social Enterprise Fund Manager or a European Venture Capital Manager and meets the necessary criteria.[43]

Small AIFMs which are not eligible for registration must obtain authorization from FCA.

An internal AIFM is an AIF with a legal structure that permits the management of its assets by its governing body or other internal body. In such a case, the fund is both the AIF and the AIFM. An external AIFM is a separate legal person from the AIF that has been appointed to manage the AIF.

Both small authorized AIFMs and small registered AIFMs may be subject to pre-existing UK requirements (including in effect those applicable to CISs under pre-existing UK requirements).

12.6.4 Marketing of AIFMs

Marketing is defined by the AIFMD as 'a direct or indirect offering or placement at the initiative of the AIFM of units or shares of an AIF it manages to or with investors domiciled or with a registered office' in an EEA state.[44] As with the definitions of AIF and AIFM, the definition is wide; however in this case it will capture third parties such as placement agents. The marketing restrictions do not apply to an offering or placement of units or shares made at the initiative of the investor in question.[45]

In general, full-scope AIFMs must obtain regulatory consent to market specific EU AIFs in their home member state.

Where a full-scope AIFM with its registered office in an EEA state is authorized to provide its services in one member state, it may provide and market EU AIFs throughout the EU under a passport (on a similar basis under the UCITS regime). The passport for EEA AIFMs to market non-EEA AIFs will not be available until late 2015 and presently such funds can only be marketed (if at all) in accordance with national private placement regimes. The concept of the passport means that an authorized AIFM can market to non-retail investors in other member states without having to comply with local regimes regarding private placement. The AIFMD also regulates non-EU managers that, for example, manage an EU AIF or market a non-EU AIF within the EU.

The marketing passport is provided by the home state regulator once satisfied that the AIFMD has been complied with. It only allows direct marketing to 'professional' investors,[46] i.e. those who are 'professional clients' for the purposes of MiFID, which includes credit institutions, investment firms and pension funds. It is worth noting that 'professional' may not include high net worth individuals or family offices, even if they are sophisticated investors, although individual member states may permit this in accordance with their own rules. The AIFMD does allow for retail marketing under certain circumstances but this is separate to the passport and local private placement rules would apply.

---

[43] Reg 10(3), (4), (5) SI 2013/1773
[44] Art 4, 1(x), 2011/61/EU
[45] Reg 47 SI 2013/1773
[46] Art 40, 17, 2011/31/EU

12.6.5 National private placement

The private placement regime permits member states to allow the marketing of AIFs to professional investors within an EU member state without a passport, but in limited circumstances, and at the discretion of the member state in question. In the UK the private placement regime in place allows for:

- the marketing of a non-EEA AIF by a UK or EEA full-scope AIFM
- the marketing of a UK or EEA AIF managed by a UK or EEA full-scope AIFM that is a feeder vehicle in a master/feeder structure (see Chapter 2, section 2.2.7) where the master vehicle is either an EEA AIF managed by a non-EEA manager or a non-EEA AIF
- the marketing of a UK, EEA or non-EEA AIF by a non-EEA AIFM (small or not).[47]

An EU AIFM wishing to market under the private placement regime is required to notify the FCA that it will comply with the directive (with certain exceptions), that there are sufficient cooperation arrangements for the exchange of information between the UK and the relevant country or countries, and that any relevant non-EEA state is not listed as a Non-Cooperative Country and Territory by the Financial Action Task Force.[48]

A small non-EEA AIFM wishing to market will be required to comply with certain information requirements with the FCA.[49] A non-EEA AIFM which is not a small AIFM wishing to market must give a written notification to the FCA confirming that:

- the non-EEA AIFM in question is responsible for compliance with the FCA's rules
- the AIFM complies with the directive in respect of reporting obligations, managing leveraged AIFs and the acquisition of control of non-listed companies and issuers (and the FCA rules relating to implementation of the same)
- there are sufficient cooperation arrangements for the exchange of information between the UK and the relevant country or countries, and that any relevant non-EEA state is not listed as a Non-Cooperative Country and Territory by the Financial Action Task Force[50] and
- certain other requirements apply (in particular, if there is no depositary information must be provided as to appropriate custodial arrangements).

The European Commission will review the operation of the passport after two years under the AIFMD,[51] and it may recommend that it be extended to non-EEA AIFMs. If the passport is extended to such managers, they will then have to be subject to the full provisions of the AIFMD in order to obtain the right to do so.

12.6.6 Delegation

The delegation provisions[52] will have an impact on an EU AIFM's ability to delegate functions to third parties or group companies, particularly with reference to those outside the EU and where investment management responsibilities are delegated. It should be noted that seeking advice without providing any discretion to said adviser is unlikely to amount to delegation.

---

[47] Reg 50, SI 2013/1773
[48] Reg 57(4)(a) SI 2013/1773
[49] Reg 58(2) and (3) SI 2013/1773
[50] Reg 59(2) SI 2013/1773 see also FCA Handbook FUND 3.10 for detailed rules
[51] Recital (2), 2011/61/EU
[52] Art 20, 2011/31/EU

A full-scope UK AIFM may not delegate its functions of portfolio or risk management for an AIF to an undertaking (or an undertaking may not sub-delegate, etc.) unless that undertaking is authorized or registered for the purpose of asset management and is subject to supervision in respect of that asset management function.[53]

The specific provisions provide that:

- advance notification to the relevant regulator is required
- delegation must be justified with reasoning
- authorization or registration will be required in the delegated jurisdiction where the delegation involves portfolio or risk management
- liability to the fund will not be affected by the delegation[54]
- the delegation cannot be so extensive that the result is that the entity to which the functions have been delegated has become the de facto manager.

12.6.7 Depositaries

The AIFMD requires the AIFM to appoint, in writing, a single independent depositary. Under the AIFMD, the depositary must be appointed to perform certain functions including overseeing the fund's cash flows, holding the fund's financial instruments in custody, verifying the ownership interests in any assets of the fund and various overseeing functions in relation to the units and shares in the AIF.[55] Marketing of non-EEA AIFs under national private placement regimes is subject to broad equivalence requirements in respect of depositaries.

For example, in the UK, authorization of the marketing of any third-country AIFM requires, among other things, that where a depositary is not appointed, a custodian is appointed to carry out certain functions of a depositary. Use of a depositary is not a formal pre-condition to marketing of any AIF by a third-country AIFM, although a level of compliance with the directive is still required. Consistent with the lighter touch regime for small AIFMs, small third-country AIFMs seeking to market AIFs in the UK are subject to more limited notification requirements with no formal requirement for a depositary or custodian.

12.6.8 Capital requirements

There are various minimum capital allowances depending on the manager's relationship to the AIF. The manager of an internally managed AIF is required to have minimum initial capital of EUR 300,000. External managers are required to have initial capital of EUR 125,000 as well as an 'own funds' requirement equal to the higher of:

- one-quarter of fixed annual overheads and
- 0.02% of the amount by which the total value of assets under management exceeds EUR 250 million, subject to a cap of EUR 10 million.

However, if so permitted by member states, the percentage of funds under management requirement can be reduced by up to 50% if the AIFM is guaranteed by a bank or insurer.[56]

---

[53] Reg 26 SI 2013/1773
[54] Reg 28 SI 2013/1773
[55] Arts 21(2), (7)–(9), 2011/61/EU
[56] Art 9 2011/61/EU; reg 5(3)(c) SI 2013/1773

Notwithstanding the requirements of the AIFMD, the Capital Adequacy Directive may also apply where a firm is subject to its requirements.

AIFMs must also have professional indemnity insurance or sufficient funds to cover professional negligence and that of the third parties (if any) to which any functions have been delegated.

It should be noted that AIFMs authorized under the UCITS Directive need not comply with the capital requirements under the AIFMD.

12.6.9 Code of conduct

In addition to specific rules, the AIFMD contains a wide-ranging set of general principles. These principles include acting in the best interests of the fund and investors as well as obtaining the client's approval before investing all or part of the client's portfolio in units or shares of the AIFs it manages.

As well as following a set of principles regarding conflicts of interest and treating investors fairly, AIFMD requires (subject to issues of proportion and scale) AIFMs to have a permanent risk management function and that risk management is 'functionally and hierarchically' separated from operating units, including the portfolio management function. The principles also call for appropriate liquidity management protocols allowing for the accurate monitoring of the liquidity risk of the fund. The FCA requires a programme of activity to be submitted with the application for permission to manage an AIF which details compliance with these requirements.[57] Additionally, the Commission Delegated Regulation, in force from 22 July 2013, introduces further compliance measures.

12.6.10 Transparency

Certain information must be provided to investors and the regulator during the marketing process and on an ongoing basis. Before investors make an investment, the manager must disclose to the investors information including the investment strategy, the legal implications of the investment contract and the identities of the manager, depositary and other third-party service providers. An audited annual report must be disclosed in respect of each EU AIF within six months of the end of the financial year. AIFMs must also regularly report trading information and information regarding the portfolio to regulators. The frequency upon which such disclosures to regulators must be made is determined by reference to the amount of funds under management.

12.6.11 Leverage and asset stripping

In order to monitor risk, AIFMs are required to report to the regulator the level of leverage employed in a fund, the make-up of the leverage as between borrowed cash and securities and other elements, as well as provide any information requested by the regulator in order to monitor the risk to the fund.

During the first two years of ownership of portfolio companies controlled by an AIFM, there are restrictions on distributions (including dividends and interest on shares), capital

---

[57] Reg 5(8)(c) SI 2013/1773

reductions and share purchases/redemptions.[58] These restrictions apply to both listed and unlisted companies with the definition of control generally held to mean more than 50% of the voting rights for unlisted companies, and for listed companies by reference to the Takeover Directive (in the UK and other member states this is 30% or more). There are also notification requirements to (among others) the FCA and the company's shareholders relating to acquisition or disposal of major holdings in non-listed portfolio companies (with thresholds beginning at 10%).

12.6.12 Remuneration

The AIFMD prescribes certain principles for AIFMs which relate to the remuneration policies for staff who exert influence on the risk profile of the AIFM and/or the AIF under management.[59] Broadly, the rules aim to prevent policies that promote risk taking, avoid conflicts of interests and keep policies and practices in line with the investors' best interests.

12.6.13 Valuation

Under the AIFMD, managers are directed as to who can value the assets of a fund as well as the method for making such a valuation and the manager's liability to investors for valuations. The applicable rules pursuant to the AIFMD will be according to the laws of the member state in which the fund is incorporated and/or has its registered office.[60]

12.7 OTHER EU REGULATION

12.7.1 Basel III

The Basel III framework is the latest in a line of international agreements which regulate the conduct of banks, with particular regard to their capital adequacy. Basel II is currently the framework with legal effect. Capital adequacy is the holding of capital to cover liabilities owed to the bank. Capital adequacy is commonly expressed as a ratio of liquid assets to the sum of liabilities owed to the bank, with different weighting given to various liabilities. The overall purpose of capital adequacy rules is to ensure that banks are sufficiently liquid to reduce the risks of default-inspired contagion spreading through the banking system, by forcing banks to hold sufficient capital to honour their own debt obligations (whether to other lending banks or to retail depositors). The Basel III framework will be implemented by the EU through the Capital Requirements Directive IV, with implementation anticipated for 2014. Many commentators have suggested that due to perceived over-complexity with Basel III, there is a need for a fourth framework with clearer drafting.

The Basel III regulations are widespread and are intended to satisfy capital requirement objectives. One is to reduce leverage in both individual banks and the sector as a whole to where the total on-and-off balance sheet assets of a bank do not exceed the bank's capital by greater than a factor of 33. This measure may lead to reduced lending as banks seek to

---

[58] Art 30, 2011/61/EU

[59] Annex II, 2011/61/EU

[60] Reg 24 SI 2013/1773

increase the amount of assets held. This will be dependent on the ability of banks to raise further capital, both to meet this ratio and to meet other requirements.

Banks are required to also improve the quality of their capital. A greater proportion of capital will be required to be made up of common equity and retained earnings rather than debt instruments (or debt-like instruments, such as convertible loan stock). This may drive the raising of capital but, given the health of the IPO and placing markets and low confidence in the banking sector as a whole, it may prove difficult to raise money by the issue of new shares. The quantity of capital required to be held will increase as well, whereby a bank will need to have a higher proportion of equity to assets. This may lead to increased capital retention (i.e. fewer or lower dividend payments) and, again, further attempts to issue new ordinary equity shares through rights and other issues.

Another measure proposed to increase capital adequacy is to require banks to increase the short-term liquidity coverage of the bank's high-quality liquid assets against expected cash outflows measured over a 30-day period. This is commonly referred to as a 'stress test', examining and proving a bank's ability to meet its obligations during a time of market difficulty. Many banks have publicly failed such tests. The liquidity of assets held is weighted (an issue of some contention) where assets such as government bonds are considered the highest quality assets for a bank to hold when valued in the context of a 'stress test'.

These measures and other ancillary provisions are beginning to affect banking activity in the markets. A lot of banks are now retreating from certain asset classes and instruments, due to either their long-term illiquidity or the risk weighting that they are apportioned for the adequacy ratio and rules. This retreat is giving rise to a shadow banking sector described in more detail in Chapter 5, section 5.6, which is a largely unregulated 'sector' made up of private wealth and hedge funds, seeking greater returns and more diverse portfolios.

12.7.2 Solvency II

The Solvency II directive[61] aims to impose coordinated rules to supervise insurance groups, with the objective of protecting consumers by increasing the chances that insurance payments are made following a claim. The directive comes into effect on 1 January 2014. Most EU insurers are covered by the directive, and only the smallest insurers will be excluded from the scope of the directive.[62]

The directive imposes the following requirements on EU insurers:

- to provide greater information to consumers in relation to their business, including providing details of their group structure, and demonstrating that they have sound financial health
- to demonstrate that they have put in place an effective system of governance to provide for the sound and prudent management of the business[63]
- to fulfil certain 'fit and proper' requirements in respect of key personnel, including ensuring such members have adequate professional qualifications, knowledge and experience, and they must also be of good repute[64]

---

[61] Directive 2009/138/EC of the European Parliament and of the Council of 25 November 2009 on the taking-up and pursuit of the business of Insurance and Reinsurance

[62] Directive 2009/138/EC; Article 4

[63] Directive 2009/138/EC; Article 41

[64] Directive 2009/138/EC; Article 42

- to satisfy minimum capital requirements (MCR) and solvency capital requirements (SCR). The MCR is the minimum level of security below which an insurance company's resources should not fall. The SCR is the solvency margin, which an insurance company must hold to cover the risk that their assets will not meet their liabilities.

Solvency II may have the effect of preventing insurance companies from investing in traditionally illiquid funds, such as infrastructure and private equity funds, because the underlying assets in these types of funds are held for a fixed period of time. This may be contrary to sound and prudent management which requires a certain level of liquid assets to satisfy liabilities.

12.7.3 European Market Infrastructure Regulation (EMIR)[65]

EMIR came into force on 16 August 2012, with the objective of reducing the risk which derivative contracts may pose to the financial system. The regulations came into effect in stages during 2013–14 and impose certain conditions upon entities entering into any form of derivatives contract. The key obligations imposed under the EMIR are:

- certain eligible OTC derivatives are subject to clearing by a CCP
- authorization and supervision of CCPs
- reporting obligations
- imposition of risk management techniques for non-CCP cleared OTC derivatives
- application of organizational, conduct of business and prudential requirements for CCPs.

The EMIR regulations restrict the market in derivatives, often a core element of some alternative asset investment strategies, or part of an underlying strategy in relation to real estate or commodities. Limiting these strategies may affect the gearing strategies of funds and may reduce the amount of capital available for investment. It may also have unforeseen knock-on effects in the market such as funds moving offshore to avoid restrictions if they prove too unworkable.

12.7.4 EU energy infrastructure proposals

There are various pieces of European legislation which address the energy markets and the operation of energy-generating facilities. In the field of investment there is proposed legislation from the European Commission seeking to generate investment in more integrated and productive energy infrastructure across the internal market.[66] The overall purpose of this legislation is to ensure that key energy networks (including access to gas from East Europe – either Russia or elsewhere) and storage facilities are in place by 2020.

The proposed regulation seeks to foster a more attractive investment environment by two approaches: simplification of the authorization and cross-border processes and policy initiatives which are intended to stimulate public and private financing of projects. The proposal

---

[65] Regulation (EU) No 648/2012 of the European Parliament and of the Council of 4 July 2012

[66] Proposal for a Regulation of the European Parliament and of the Council on guidelines for trans-European energy infrastructure and repealing Decision No 1364/2006/EC 2011/0658:

http://eur-lex.europa.eu/LexUriServ/LexUriServ.do?uri=CELEX:52011PC0658:EN:NOT

estimates that the overall funding requirement by 2020 will be EUR 1 trillion, and that private contributions will need to be in the range of EUR 60–80 billion. The proposal states that a more effective, efficient market with higher capacity in itself will encourage future investment in this sector, particularly with respect to energy generation.

The proposal outlines current funding models and the difficulties with them that the regulation will need to address. Currently, returns are generated through the payment of regulated tariff charges by users of energy transmitted. This model does not deal directly with issues such as non-commercial positive externalities (i.e. benefits from investment which are not appreciated by market pricing) which derive from investment in infrastructure and new technologies, with the result that there is little market incentive to provide finance for these (as the tariff prices won't increase to cover this cost, but it is of great social benefit to improve the energy network). It is also difficult to harmonize cross-border developments where tariff setting remains on a national basis and public funding remains focused on national projects.

One approach to improving the investment environment in the proposal is to develop further the EU's relationships with international financial institutions under existing technical assistance directives. The second is a suite of 'tools' to further incentivize private investment, such as equity participation and support to infrastructure funds, specialized facilities for project bonds, risk sharing facilities (with particular focus on new technology) and loan guarantees for public private partnerships.

12.8   REGULATION – SOME CONCLUSIONS FOR ALTERNATIVE ASSET FUND MANAGERS

This chapter broadly covered the principal national and supra-national regulation affecting alternative asset fund managers. It ties in with section 10.3 of Chapter 10, being the chapter on investment manager structures and the specific regulation pertaining to them.

The changes brought in by Dodd–Frank and FATCA will have far-reaching effects on the alternative asset management industry. The provisions of Dodd–Frank significantly reduce the scope for small private fund managers to market in the US to private investors without SEC approval. This will increase costs and time delays for fund managers outside the US who wish to source US investors. FATCA will also increase the burden on alternative asset managers who have accepted US investors into their funds. They will be required to report to the IRS information regarding their US investors in order to avoid a 30% withholding charge on income sourced from the US.

The extensive 1933 Banking Act in the US is often referred to as the Glass–Steagall Act, which over time came to be further condensed in the public imagination to refer to two provisions of that legislation restricting affiliations between commercial banks and securities firms. Starting in the early 1960s, federal banking regulators interpreted provisions of the Glass–Steagall Act to permit commercial bank affiliates to engage in an expanding volume of securities activities. In 1999, the Gramm–Leach–Bliley Act finally repealed these two provisions. The Volcker Rule sought, in part, to re-instate the division between retail and investment banking.

The Volcker Rule is by far the most controversial plank of all the reforms that have emerged from the crisis. It has led to an exodus of top proprietary traders from large banks to form their own hedge funds or join existing hedge funds. Prevailing industry sentiment is that it may prove difficult under this new regime to distinguish banned proprietary trading from its bona fide counterpart: the buying and selling of securities on behalf of clients. Industry participants also contend various unwanted adverse consequences of the rule: that market liquidity will be negatively impacted, that transaction costs will rise, that trading volumes will be driven to other jurisdictions and that the US economy will suffer. They also point out that these effects are likely to be extraterritorial in that, if the analysis is correct, these consequences will extend to overseas funds and bank subsidiaries.

Meanwhile, AIFMD will have a widespread effect on asset managers that are based in or wish to market in Europe. In order to market across borders, managers will have to comply with new capital requirements, information standards, standards of disclosure to regulators, requirements to use certain functionaries such as depositaries, and a plethora of other obligations. There is a euro threshold limit for the 'full scope' of the AIFMD regulations, but the implementation of this threshold varies across member states of the EU. In the UK, for example, asset managers operating under the threshold are still required to seek authorization from the FCA, which entails compliance with a significant proportion (but not a majority) of the new AIFMD rules.

The overarching impact of these rules will be to introduce higher costs to the operation of an investment fund, in terms of both money and time. Such regulation is targeted at Ponzi schemes and other frauds, at reducing systemic risk in the financial markets by limiting the investment activities of fund managers and at the protection of investors. From the industry's point of view, although regulation which protects against Madoff-like fraud is welcome, the new regulatory landscape of the industry is, in my view, out of proportion to what is necessary for the prevention of fraud. To target the asset management industry in this manner for the after-effects of the financial crisis is disproportionate. Not only that, but excluding considerations of fraud, the investors in asset management funds are mostly well advised and savvy enough to understand the risks they take in investing.

As can be seen, since the start of the financial crisis, there has been a considerable amount of reform. Much of this reform is new and untested. It is feasible that the new regulation will be diluted or be more narrowly defined over time. Indeed much of it will be properly understood only by its implementation.

On the broader policy front, asset management firms are recognizing that regulation will lead to a restriction on liquidity available to their clients. We have already seen some direct effects, for example of the Volcker Rules impacting affiliates of US banks, when Citi (and others) announced its withdrawal from alternative asset funds. In general, there has been a tendency for banking institutions to retrench and to re-focus on core activities. We have to recognize that asset management firms are likely to experience the higher costs of debt and equity capital because of this resultant lower liquidity and that this effect must be exacerbated by the sense of greater regulatory uncertainty about the future, as the reforms are yet to be implemented and fully detailed. The effect of this regulatory uncertainty may turn out to be significant, but its magnitude is as yet hard to estimate from the data available.

13

Comparisons and Conclusions

13.1   INTRODUCTION

The focus of this book has not been on investment risk, economic returns or other commercial assessments. Instead, I have sought to explain a range of fund products, the logic behind their establishment and the way they are structured. In doing this, I have reviewed the legal environment and the applicable tax and regulatory regimes in which these funds operate within the broader context of alternative asset management.

This is an industry that moves rapidly and one that is required to be highly responsive to macroeconomic changes. There are many industry constants but what is in vogue one year will more than likely need revisiting the next. The search for the structure and strategy that generate the greatest returns for the lowest risk, within an investor-, tax- and regulator-friendly model, is a constantly evolving one.

13.2   EVOLVING STRUCTURAL DRIVERS

13.2.1 Tax efficiency

Tax planning is one of the constant themes of fund engineering. It is less about tax avoidance (although not if you believe what you read in the newspapers) but more to ensure that the investor is no worse off as a result of investing through a fund structure than if the investment had been made by the investor directly into the underlying asset.

The key objective is to avoid the additional layer of taxation (often referred to as the 'double charge') that may arise where investors invest in a vehicle that in turn invests in an underlying portfolio company. Tax may then occur both on the sale of the interests in the underlying portfolio company and also on the distribution of the realized fund gains to investors or on the sale by investors of their own interests in the fund. In many jurisdictions, the distribution of gains arising from the sale of an asset during the fund's life is treated as a dividend rather than a realization of capital, thereby switching a capital gain into income, which is often unacceptable for investors.

There are broadly two methods to create a tax efficient structure. First, where capital gains made by the fund are not subject to tax at the fund level and where tax crystallizes only on distribution of profits to investors, it then needs to be confirmed that a tax exempt vehicle (i.e. 'approved' by the relevant tax authority) or a vehicle situated in a tax haven or a country providing an exemption from tax on capital gains can be used as the fund vehicle. For the investor to take advantage of this type of arrangement, there will need to be an efficient tax relationship between the tax efficient location of the fund vehicle and the jurisdiction of the investor. If there is no advantageous double tax treaty in place between such jurisdictions then the investor may suffer withholding taxes at the fund level on income and/or capital gains.

The second method involves the use of a transparent fund structure, usually a form of partnership, and it is intended to treat the investor as if they had made a direct investment into the underlying asset. If properly structured, this should have the effect of avoiding the double tax risk while allowing the investor to take advantage of any tax treaty arrangements operating between the country of residence of the investor and the jurisdiction of the underlying portfolio company. The partnership (or its manager) must, however, also avoid creating a permanent establishment in its own jurisdiction.

Investors will want to take advantage of any available preferential treatment, 'approved' regimes and the use of effective tax avoidance structures to make their investment as tax efficient as possible. But tax regimes are moving targets and fund structures need to take into account recent developments and current applicable tax rates. Investors also need to be cognizant of rules that may be extraterritorial in application but which could impact the entire fund structure and management arrangements. Such rules generally emanate from the EU or the US. One example of new rules impacting a range of fund structures is FATCA (see Chapter 12, section 12.5.4). As a result of FATCA, US investors now need to be wary of the disclosure requirements designed primarily to combat offshore tax evasion and recoup US federal tax revenues. This law obligates US nationals to report their financial accounts held overseas and imposes a heavy burden on foreign financial institutions to report to the IRS about their clients. Such new rules not only impact fund design but are also required to be reflected in the fund documentation.

13.2.2 Regulation

The regulation of the funds industry has changed dramatically post-2007 in the aftermath of what the IMF described as 'the largest financial shock since the Great Depression'.[1] A perception by many that the lack of transparency and non-regulation of the funds industry may have contributed to the financial crises has led to a raft of new reforms. Here, in my view, the fund industry's natural shyness and lack of transparency led to a PR own goal.

The big story was that Joe Public does not need to know what hedge funds are, other than that they are run by clever clogs and MBA whizz-kids who must have screwed up the system. The resulting drive to promote financial stability and investor confidence could be argued to be at the expense of unduly hindering fund management and, ultimately, growth.

Here are some examples of regulatory developments:

(a) AIFMD – this seeks to regulate hedge funds, private equity, real estate, infrastructure funds and investment trusts. AIFMD places additional burdens on fund managers, such as the requirement to provide extra information including publicizing its business plan and submitting periodic returns to the FCA (as detailed in Chapter 12, section 12.6). However, it can be argued that this EU directive has in many respects had a

---

[1] *The Guardian* website: http://www.guardian.co.uk/business/2008/apr/10/useconomy.subprimecrisis: last accessed 11 June 2013

positive influence in respect of EU managers, the key reason being that funds which comply with the AIFMD are able to be marketed (passported) to EU professional investors in any EU member state. Conversely, AIFMD creates difficulties for non-EU managers in that it does not afford an 'EU passport' to allow funds to be marketed by non-EU managers across the EU until at least 2015. This drawback is substantiated by a number of reports indicating that several US hedge funds have halted plans to enter the EU, and that non-EU managers will attempt to fund-raise without marketing to EU-investors.[2]

(b) Dodd–Frank – this US legislation was passed in response to the financial crisis and brought significant changes and greater oversight to the financial services industry. The main impacts identified by fund managers were increased costs (management company expenses, recruitment of staff to handle compliance and increased costs in portfolio companies) and potential restrictions in their fund-raising activities.

(c) Volcker Rules – as part of Dodd–Frank, the Volcker Rules set out explicitly permitted activities and services as well as capital requirements and restrictions on transactions with affiliates. The prohibitions specifically apply to 'banking entities' which include insured depositary institutions, the controlling company and any foreign bank with operations in the US including parents, affiliates and subsidiaries of the foreign bank. These rules have significantly impacted on banks' alternative asset strategies with many teams spinning out and funds being shut.

(d) FATCA – there have been reports that FATCA reporting requirements have put US funds at a disadvantage in attracting investors.[3] Experience to date has shown that the imposition of reporting requirements under FATCA has led to some UK and EU managers being discouraged from seeking US investment.

While increased regulation has been viewed by many outside the industry as promoting financial stability, reports have also suggested that this has been at the expense of fund managers struggling to cope with the heavier legislative burden. Indeed, the constant need to re-assess the impact of legislation at its various stages of drafting has proven time-consuming for fund managers. And unfortunately, there is an overlap of regulation across jurisdictions, especially with regards to reporting and transparency.[4]

Increased regulation of the funds industry looks likely to continue with, for example, the EU Economic and Monetary Affairs Committee in March 2013 having backed proposals to cap bonuses of key fund staff to 100% of their salaries under the draft UCITS V Directive. This had caused concern in the industry because capping bonuses is viewed by many in the industry as a major disincentive to the performance of key fund staff. There have been strong indications that this proposal to cap bonuses will be removed from the final UCITS V Directive in the teeth of strong opposition.[5]

---

[2] *The Financial Times* website: 'US hedge funds threaten to flee Europe'; by Madison Marriage: reported 2 June, 2013

[3] *The Financial Times* website: 'US legislation: Industry concerned at extraterritorial tax clampdown plan'; by Kate Burgess: reported 8 May 2012

[4] *The Financial Times* website: 'Regulatory fatigue hits compliance bosses'; by Ruth Sullivan: reported 10 February 2013

[5] *The Financial Times* website: 'EU bonus cap could be scrapped'; by Baptists Aboulian: reported 9 June 2013

As discussed in Chapter 11, section 11.2.3, there has been support from some EU member states for the implementation of a directive that would have the effect of imposing a 0.1% tax on financial transactions, including the trade of shares and bonds, and a 0.01% tax on derivatives contracts. However, the proposal has met with strong opposition from some member states, including the UK, which launched legal proceedings in April 2013[6] following intimations from the financial industry that the proposals would likely harm not only the industry but also wider economic growth.

Overall, it is clear that the consequence of regulatory developments is that fund managers will need to assess the strategic costs and benefits of any required changes to fund structures or their location, along with the attendant tax consequences of any changes. There are suspicions that a portion of these developments is likely to be ineffectual. The implication is that there is a danger of smothering the industry while failing to tackle those that operate outside the rules (think Madoff). Individual governments continue to make significant regulatory moves while, ironically, promoting their jurisdictions as open to business.

13.3 CORE STRUCTURES COMPARED

In seeking to attract inward investment, each jurisdiction provides its own niche fund pooling vehicles, underpinned by applicable regulatory, legal and tax legislation. Due to their longer history of fund manager infrastructure, certain jurisdictions are more developed than others. Broadly speaking, in developed jurisdictions, investors will have more than one possible vehicle when considering an appropriate investment structure. Often, a prolonged investigation period is required by principals and their advisers to confirm and clarify the most favourable investor, fund and management vehicles that will satisfy the often complex requirements of the various parties as well as meeting the requirements of the specified target assets.

13.3.1 Key differences between private equity funds, hedge funds and quoted funds

Table 13.1 compares the three typical types of funds: closed-ended, open-ended and quoted, from an investor's perspective.

---

[6] *The Financial Times* website: 'Britain challenges EU over "Tobin tax"'; by James Fontanella-Khan and Chris Giles: reported 19 April 2013

Table 13.1 Comparison of closed-ended, open-ended and quoted funds from an investor's perspective

Factor	Private equity or other closed-ended funds – invest, drawdown and distribution model	Hedge or other open-ended funds – invest, NAV and redemption model	Quoted funds – invest and trade model
Strategy	Managers use bespoke structures and active management of portfolio companies to generate profits. Although funds have historically had a defined narrow investment focus, investment scope is becoming more broadly defined.	Returns are usually generated by exploiting trading positions (rather than single investment decisions), typically by using indices, arbitrage or market inefficiencies to generate profits. Hedge funds often combine wide-ranging investment strategies seeking superior returns.	Returns are generated by growth in value of investee company shares and income streams.
Fund liquidity	Private equity, real estate and infrastructure investments are illiquid for the period of the investment horizon (anything from 3 to 7 years or much longer for infrastructure funds); for liquidity they rely on a sale of their stake in the portfolio company or asset to achieve a capital gain. There is rarely borrowing within the fund and therefore there is generally no bankruptcy risk. Funds are not publicly traded so are not subject to public market fluctuations.	Investments held are freely tradable on a stock exchange if quoted. Large stakes are less easy to place (sell) than smaller ones. The greater the influence/stake sought by an investor, the less liquidity is available. Hedge funds often have (sometimes very large) borrowings within the fund. They therefore carry a risk of bankruptcy and can suffer a 'run' on the fund (i.e. where investors seek redemptions that cannot be met). Hedge funds can, and do fail dramatically.	Quoted funds can vary the proportion of their investment in any portfolio company. A quoted equity fund has permanent capital in the form of share capital, or units in a unit trust, and investors commit their investment to the fund but can sell shares or units when they want. Funds are provided by new investors and retained earnings. Some also use borrowings at the fund level to increase returns.
Investor liquidity	A limited partner must trade on the illiquid secondaries market or wait for distributions through bespoke transactions.	Investors can redeem at a small discount to NAV, subject to lock-ups or gates.	Investors can buy and sell units or shares on the exchange.
Financing structure	Private equity funds insert leverage within portfolio companies but usually there is no borrowing at the fund level.	Use of derivatives (options, swaps, etc.) to create reward, rather than debt. Common for larger hedge funds to use leverage at the fund level to increase investment activity.	Quoted funds do not usually increase the borrowings of investee companies. Borrowings may occur in the fund structure.

Factor	Private equity or other closed-ended funds – drawdown and distribution model	Hedge or other open-ended funds – invest, NAV and redemption model	Quoted funds – invest and trade model
Due diligence	Managers undertake substantial financial, commercial and legal due diligence before making an investment. In a management buyout, knowledge of incumbent management is critical to the process of assessing risk and reward.	Funds rely on publicly available information. But managers use similar due diligence to private equity managers if investing in unquoted assets, as well as running often secretive trading strategies to gain market advantage.	Quoted company funds have access to and rely only on publicly available information on the companies in which they invest, with private equity analysis of private investee companies.
Control	Private equity funds usually own a substantial or controlling stake in the underlying business(es). Shareholders agreements are used to control and manage rights in portfolio companies.	Investment is typically into quoted companies with little influence except possibly indirectly over a company's board. Sometimes a fund may seek to influence management but typically these are pure trading funds seeking to benefit only from market price movements and sophisticated investment strategy.	Small stakes are acquired which offer no special management rights. As with hedge funds, institutional shareholders may be influential, but have no contractual control. Larger stakes can be acquired, with listed private equity funds.
Monitoring	Monitoring is comprehensive. Private equity managers have rights to obtain sensitive financial and business information, often by way of observer status or actual board representation or by private equity fund managers being actively involved in executive management.	Use of public information to monitor investments. Pure trading funds may only take a 'position' in a company in the anticipation that the company's value will change to their benefit. When investing in private companies, monitoring is more similar to a private equity fund.	Reliance is on official company announcements, management presentations and analysts' research to monitor investments. When investing in private companies, monitoring is more similar to a private equity fund.
Manager's reward	Fund managers invest in the fund they manage and share in any aggregate realized profits of the fund over its whole life through 'carried interest'. Managers are tied by the carry which aligns their interests with investors. Carried interest may be taxed as capital, but it often takes a long time to realize (i.e. the life of the fund). Managers also typically receive annual fee income. Managers usually invest themselves in the fund.	Managers may be rewarded in connection with increase in portfolio value. This might be income (but at least compared with private equity) it can come earlier. They also receive fee income from funds. There is not usually a hurdle rate of return to exceed (as in a private equity waterfall), although there can be high water marks. Managers usually invest themselves in the fund.	Managers receive fee income and may be rewarded for increase in portfolio value. The rewards for management in quoted companies are a matter for the remuneration committee, not the shareholders. Managers are not required to show a financial commitment although they may benefit from capital growth through option schemes.
Fund certainty	Closed-ended funds are long life. For this reason, they weren't so severely impacted at the onset of the credit crisis.	'Shorter' money. Subject to gates and lock-up, units can be redeemed at any time.	Unless it is a closed-ended fund, the fund can be permanent capital (until the arbitrageurs move in).

Table 13.2 Key documents in private equity, public fund and hedge fund models

Document	Description
Offering document (often called a PPM or IM in a private fund)	This contains information on the fund such as its investment objective and strategy, a summary of its terms, background on the management team and its track record together with more technical information such as risk factors, a summary of the tax consequences of investing and details of restrictions on the marketing of the fund.
Limited partnership agreement (for closed-ended)	This is entered into between the general partner and each limited partner. It is the principal document governing the partnership and sets out the fund's terms in detail. Hedge funds may be structured as limited partnerships, but may also take other forms.
Fund structure agreement	These govern the running of the fund and will set out in detail the investment policy and the investors' rights. In a corporate fund structure, normally there will be a shareholders' agreement and articles of association. If a unit trust, then a trust deed.
Investment management agreement	This is entered into between the fund and its manager. It provides, among other matters, for the appointment of the manager and the circumstances in which the manager's appointment can be terminated. The manager is either paid fees by the fund or remunerated by the general partner out of its general partner's priority profit share.
Investment advisory agreement	This is entered into between the manager and the investment adviser. Its content is similar to the investment management agreement. It deals with the adviser's appointment, its termination and its remuneration.
Subscription agreement	Each investor will sign a subscription agreement under which they agree to be bound by the fund constitutional documents. Each investor will also provide information about themselves (contact information, bank account details, etc.) and give representations and warranties about themselves including eligibility to invest in the fund.
Carried interest documentation	Where another limited partnership has been established to act as a carry vehicle, it will require its own limited partnership agreement and management agreement. This is not necessary for a hedge fund, as instead of carried interest the manager receives a performance fee, which is often not paid through a dedicated vehicle.
Side letters	In the course of negotiations, the manager may agree certain matters with individual investors that are consistent with the partnership agreement (for example, specific reporting information that is required by an investor). Such agreements with individual members are set out in side letters with the relevant investors.

13.4   THE PAPERWORK

There are many documents which are common to private equity (or other closed-ended funds, e.g. real estate, infrastructure, energy), public fund and hedge fund models. This section looks at the key documents in each. Unless stated otherwise, the documents listed are common to each type.

13.5   THE ACTORS

The funds market has four main parties: (1) investors, (2) funds or intermediaries, (3) managers of the funds and (4) issuers of securities as investees. Figure 13.1 depicts these four groups and the typical flows that can occur between them.

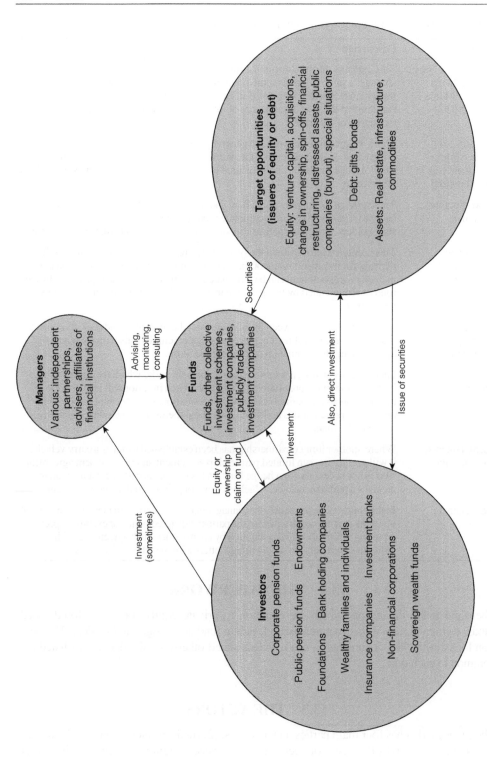

Figure 13.1   The four main groups involved in the funds market and the typical flows that can occur between them.

13.6   THE SUPPORTING ACTORS

Table 13.3 outlines the roles of the main supporting actors.

Table 13.3   The roles of the main supporting actors in the funds market

Actor	Description
Legal counsel	Legal counsel will be based in the jurisdiction of the investment adviser or manager, and will assist the management on selecting the most appropriate structure and jurisdiction of the fund. Legal counsel also liaise with offshore or local legal counsel on the formation of the fund.
Prime broker	A hedge fund's prime broker provides a number of services to the fund, including holding custody of the fund's assets, loaning securities for short sales, providing detailed research and making capital introductions through introducing hedge fund managers to potential investors. In addition, a prime broker may assist the hedge fund to raise capital and market the fund and to select their service providers such as tax and legal advisers and fund administrators. Since the post-2007 market crash, it is common to find that many hedge funds will have two or more prime brokers, with the aim being to spread the assets of the fund to divide exposure and risk across different counterparties.
Administrator	The role of an administrator is to alleviate the administrative burden from the management by participating in the day to day operation of the fund, thereby allowing the manager to focus on the investment decisions of the fund. The administrator's duties will generally include calculating the NAV of interests in the fund (if a hedge fund or another fund with a NAV model); issuing drawdown notices for closed-ended funds; holding and maintaining the fund share register (if there is one); maintaining accounting and financial records; ensuring that the fund is complying with the terms set out under the offering memorandum; and if the fund's shares are listed, the administrator will liaise with management to ensure that the applicable listing and ongoing requirements are complied with. The administrator's role has increased post-Madoff, and will increase further as the new EU and US regulation kicks in.
Custodian	The custodian is referred to as a 'depositary' in the AIFMD. Under the AIFMD, the role of the depositary/custodian encompasses a number of functions; namely, to have safekeeping of the monies and financial instruments belonging to the fund ('custody'), but also to oversee the fund's cash flows and to verify that the fund or manager of the fund has obtained the ownership of all other assets in which the fund invests. The depositary/custodian is a legally separate organization that is appointed and obliged to act independently and solely in the interests of investors. Consequently, under the AIFMD, the fund manager (AIFM) is not permitted to have custody of money or financial instruments and must appoint a custodian. Furthermore, the custodian must be a bank with its registered office in the EU. It is necessary for a UCITS fund to have a custodian and many managed account private equity structures will utilize one too.
Fund auditor	The role of an auditor is to audit the accounting practices of the fund and to review the fund's balance sheets and profit and loss accounts. The auditor will generally coordinate with the administrator in respect of preparing the fund audit. Whether the fund will be required to be audited, and at what frequency, will often be determined based on whether the manager is registered with the relevant financial authority (e.g. FCA/SEC). However, generally, investors will expect a commitment to have the fund audited on at least an annual basis.

Actor	Description
Manager auditor	The auditor will audit the accounting practices of the manager; the profits and loss accounts and balance sheet will be reviewed. Managers are audited in accordance with their regulatory requirements together with any demands placed in their constitutional documents by seed or cornerstone investors who have taken an interest in the fund and the manager.
Placement agents	The role of a placement agent often includes assisting the manager with fund-raising activities, through sourcing and introducing prospective investors to the manager, and assisting with drafting and reviewing the fund's marketing materials and reviewing terms presented to investors in the fund's offering documents. Their fees are principally paid from management fees and performance fees.
Manager consultant(s)	Certain groups assist the manager with conducting due diligence, and advising in relation to compliance and governance of the fund. Other services which are commonly provided by such consultants include advising in relation to the fund and portfolio companies business and marketing strategies.
FCA or SEC umbrellas	Fund managers based in the UK or US are likely to be carrying out regulated financial activities, and will in many cases require FCA or SEC authorization (for more information see Chapter 12). Applications by managers for such authorization can take many months, and clearly managers will be keen to carry out fund-raising activities in the interim. Some entities will offer an FCA or SEC umbrella, whereby the scope of permissions they have received from the relevant regulator permits them to provide an umbrella service to managers who have not sought, or are awaiting authorization, and thereby allows them to carry out regulated financial activities. These umbrellas can continue their role to become outsourced consultants.

13.7   WHAT IS TRENDING?

13.7.1 Internet

The internet almost seems designed for the funds industry. Not just in terms of supporting new transparent, flexible economies suitable for new waves of investment but in terms of altering the business landscape in favour of fund managers. Communications, marketing (with extremely low costs), financial services, information gathering technology, improved business collaboration, the ability of micro managers to compete with larger groups – it all seems made to measure for our industry. Take flattening of markets. In the same way that technology has allowed for collaboration beyond geographical borders, technology has also reduced the barriers to entering different markets around the world. This allows buyers and sellers from around the world to connect and do business. An investment adviser team comprising four persons can now operate effectively from locations as diverse as New York, Sydney, Hong Kong and London with minimal office back-up.

13.7.2 Multi-immediate media

As the internet age is out of its infancy, truly multi-immediate media is a new reality. A country can't even quash a revolution without information about its actions being beamed around the world by the mobile internet, or via immediate media, such as Twitter or Facebook. Multi-immediate media is also a natural marriage partner to increasing transparency within the funds industry.

13.7.3 Onshore/offshore debunked

There has traditionally been a distinction in many people's minds in the industry between 'on' and 'off' shore. A fund is either located within the net of a particular taxpaying or legislative jurisdiction or it sits outside that net and within a non-taxpaying environment. However, that distinction is already becoming blurred.

There is an emerging pattern for jurisdictions to become more homogenized: traditional offshore jurisdictions are tightening up (to avoid being accused of inviting money laundering or helping people avoid paying tax in their home country) while traditional onshore jurisdictions are relaxing their rules, as competition provoked by globalization mounts. Other (traditionally onshore) jurisdictions such as Ireland and The Netherlands are challenging the likes of the Cayman Islands and the Channel Islands. The US and certain powers within the EU are trying to close these 'loopholes';[7] while the former President of France, Nicolas Sarkozy, accused the UK of being an offshore centre during the EU fight over regulation of financial services. The US has managed to almost single-handedly neuter the banking industry in Switzerland. The overall picture is diverse.

There are numerous examples of onshore jurisdictions relaxing their own rules.[8] Certain onshore jurisdictions even seem to emulate their offshore counterparts, for example Delaware and Nevada for shell companies where incorporation is cheap and easy and no client ID is required. Delaware, like the traditional offshore model, charges company fees but takes no sales tax. UK companies can have BVI corporate directors and nominee shareholders. UK LLPs are not required to file tax returns or to have individuals as directors. Tax in traditional onshore jurisdictions is becoming increasingly competitive: Ireland is popular with mutual funds and tax planning companies. The Netherlands is the world's largest venue for tax treaty shopping. Multinationals put foreign investment through Dutch or Luxembourg holding companies to avoid withholding taxes on dividends or interest. Countries are increasingly fighting, like New York hotels, to outpace each other on the headline-grabbing rate of corporation tax over shorter and shorter time-frames. Post the internet age, and as the globalizing world becomes increasingly multi-immediate, each country will have to become specialist and world-beating in a handful of areas.

Global companies are shopping for low tax zones and arrangements to reduce their headline rates of corporation tax. Conversely, there is in some quarters a growing societal concern about capturing revenues and clamping down on so-called aggressive tax avoidance schemes. The jury is still out on just how strong the political will is to engage with these issues. The likely impact of populist vilification of a company such as Starbucks in the UK is unclear. As Starbucks has argued, the amount of 'sub-company' tax they pay is enormous – employee taxes, social security, VAT, property rates, as well as effectively being 'taxed' by spending a lot of money in the country. It may be that offshore centres are a convenient way for onshore regulators, politicians and tax authorities to turn a blind eye to 'evaders' born or based in their own country.

---

[7] March 2013: 'No safe havens: Our offshore evasion strategy 2013 and beyond': http://www.hmrc.gov.uk/budget2013/offshore-strategy.pdf

[8] http://www.economist.com/news/special-report/21571554-some-onshore-jurisdictions-can-be-laxer-offshore-sort-not-palm-tree-sight

13.7.4 Change of focus

The last six years have been a lean period for funds. Funds are still operating today in an uncertain environment. The global financial crisis of the late noughties triggered three main collapses worth repeating here as they have proved critical to the funds industry: a collapse of the banking system resulting in a contraction of bank lending; a collapse in demand as households and firms retrenched; and a collapse in world trade due to the weakness of debt-ridden economies and a downturn in demand for commodities.

These shocks are still being worked through, but how has this impacted the funds industry specifically? Mainly through the difficulties in raising finance in order to execute deals and through the precarious viability of existing portfolio companies. This initially hit fund valuations and threatened the survival of portfolio companies, especially those that were highly leveraged. Otherwise profitable companies became victims of the contraction of lending by banks. There was a negative impact on headline activity such as buyouts, which shrank in both size and number. There was talk of an LBO debt repayment cliff. At an earlier stage of the investment cycle, UK venture capital groups wrote off investments due to a lack of follow-on funding. Downbeat valuations of portfolio companies were further evidence of the effects of the economic downturn.

While the initial adverse effects of the crisis have to some extent flattened out, the current economic situation today, which results from that financial crisis, has overall meant an increased focus on lower risk strategies. Private equity and hedge fund managers are, however, nothing if not adaptable. I have seen far more focus on access to quality deal flow and more management time spent on portfolio assets. Other significant trends appear to me to be:

- **Switch to different alterative investment areas**: such as infrastructure (possibly partly in response to governmental encouragement), real estate (for real asset protection) and debt (for yield and lower risk).
- **Shadow banking**: this has risen in my view to its peak for now. Private funds did replace banks during the crisis. Now the regulators will seek to smash shadow banking.
- **Off balance sheet fund establishment**: often cornerstoned by an industrial major with access to a recession-proof income stream.
- **Switch of institutional investing**: increased pension fund allocation to alternative assets to generate higher returns.
- **Secondary activity**: more activity on the secondary markets and a shift from raising primary funds to secondary funds. Indeed this is now leading to a future crunch where there is not enough primary to be later acquired by secondary without a squirt up in valuations – watch those future premiums to NAV.
- **Reduced financial engineering**: it is more difficult for funds to raise money from banks for new deals. Larger than usual numbers of buyouts have used no leverage. Mezzanine finance has to some extent stepped into this gap. As I finish this chapter, however, the credit markets, especially in the US, are returning with a vengeance to alternative asset investing, debunking the earlier notion that the fall of old redeeming credit was going to destroy the western world!
- **Fees**: Some have questioned whether fees should be temporarily adjusted when deals and returns are hard to come by. It is not so much the performance-related part that is the problem; it is the non-performance-related part that causes concern. LPs have more power now and will expect lower fees. They will also expect more GP commitment to funds.
- **Club deals**: the participation of several different private equity firms otherwise known as a syndicated investment, where the investor group of private equity firms pools assets and makes the acquisition collectively.

- **Portfolio management**: as stated, more management time and energies spent on portfolio management, as well as increased buy-and-build. While early post-credit crisis measures involved managing liquidity and deleverage, attention has turned to creating value through operational improvements and working closely with management teams.
- **Distressed assets**: investors are looking more closely at distressed opportunities, in particular at distressed debt investing and also as a way into acquiring a business.
- **Increased regulation**: such as AIFMD, the new FCA, Dodd–Frank and FATCA.

13.7.5 Masters of the Universe

Allocation to alternative asset investment continues to increase; whether for a thirst for growth, protection or income. It also follows the destruction by the financial crisis of the banking and investment banking industry; first by over-leverage, over-investment, and over-trading (becoming enormous hedge funds in themselves), and now by over-regulation. Out of the debris, the alternative asset manager is the new Master of the Universe. In time those managers with both returns and (perhaps more importantly to investors) scale and a feeling of permanency are attracting increasing firepower and also swallowing up other areas of financial services, such as corporate finance and market making. At the other end of the scale, the financial crisis has seen the rise of the niche financial expert. The middle or undifferentiated are suffering.

13.7.6 Paradigm bashing

As we enter 2014, a number of these impacts of the financial crisis are working themselves out, or are returning to their pre-crisis position.

Following severe market impacts or dramatic up-swells, there can be much talk of paradigm shifts. I loathe this expression! Certainly, banks are becoming more conservative and over-regulated, but conversely, shadow banking has increased, and in turn will become more regulated and tightened. However, as this book goes to print, UK (and especially) US debt markets are enjoying something of a resurgence, yesterday's junk is today's bling, and even the much pilloried CLO is back. Debt was good, then became bad and is now re-invited back to the old parties. Cycles and fundamental human truths don't disappear – ask Mr Columbus.

13.7.7 Book conclusion

Having now finished this book, I remind myself of some essential current truths:

- in historical terms, there is no doubt we are still at the dawn of the alternative assets industry
- market trends are accelerating quicker than they used to
- but trends are still overplaying their hands
- the financial crisis has radically overhauled the regulatory environment
- but that regulatory environment still remains largely untested
- attitudes to taxation are not what they used to be
- countries use economic muscle to control global cash streams
- and this book will need updating very quickly!

Appendix I
Definitions

GLOSSARY TERMS

Acquisition cost	The costs of all aspects of an acquisition, which include legal, accounting and any necessary registration fees or taxation
Advisory committee/ investors committee	A committee or board made up of representatives of certain investors. The role of the advisory committee is limited to being consulted on matters such as conflicts of interest, approving exceptions to the investment restrictions and potentially certain other matters set out in the LPA and discussing the performance and operation of the fund. Their role in the management of a fund structured as a limited partnership is often restricted to avoid becoming a general partner
Alternative assets	A broad term covering potential investments outside of listed equities and bonds
Blind-pool fund	A fund where the investors' capital is committed to be used in any investment. The investor cannot opt out of a specified investment and the fund is 'blind' as it has made no investments at the point of commitment
Carried interest	The private equity equivalent of the hedge performance fee. During the distribution, or 'the waterfall', following the return of capital to the investors and the payment of a preferred return to investors (usually 8% of capital, also known as the 'hurdle rate'), the manager and its executives receive a percentage (usually 20%) of all profits thereafter with catch-up of the hurdle – i.e. the hurdle is a hurdle
Carry deed	The legal contract by which the carry vehicle is established
Carry general partner	As most carry vehicles are established as limited partnerships, at least one general partner is necessary which will have unlimited liability
Carry holder	The manager and the senior members of its team that receive the carried interest
Carry partner	The carry vehicle is a partner in the fund, and is assigned this label in the fund documentation and structure
Carry vehicle	The legal entity which receives the carried interest from the fund and passes it on to the manager and those individuals who are entitled to receive it

Catch-up	During the waterfall, the carry partner is paid a percentage of the preferred return to investors – which will, if the carried interest is 20%, be 25% of the amount paid as a preferred return
Close company	A company which is UK resident and controlled by five or fewer participators who have either control of the company or are entitled to receive a majority of its assets on winding up (s 439 CoTA 2010)
Closed-ended fund	A fund which has a fixed number of investor interests (whether represented by units, shares, etc.) following its final closing, investors cannot cancel (or redeem) interests until the fund is terminated and the fund has a determined life
Closing	The date on which the fund will admit a round of investors. A fund may have only one closing, but often there are multiple rounds
Combo fund	A fund which has both a blind-pool of committed capital and a pledge fund, which invest together
Commitment	The amount that an investor is bound to provide when called upon by the fund manager
Committed capital fund	A fund in which the investors are committed to provide funds when called upon to do so
Companies House	The UK registrar of companies through which all incorporation and filing is processed
Cornerstone investor	An investor that provides a significant early commitment to provide capital to the fund, usually on better terms (for the cornerstone investor) than for later investors. Will also assist in the promotion of the fund
Credit crisis	The crisis of mid to late 2008 which saw the bankruptcy of Lehman Brothers
Development capital	An investment in a business which is beyond the start-up phase but is not considered a mature business, with the aim of funding further expansion
Establishment expenses	The costs of setting up a fund. They vary from legal and administrative fees to marketing costs
Federal Reserve	The Federal Reserve System is the central banking system of the United States. Aside from the provision of finance to the government and key financial institutions, it also has regulatory and supervisory functions and plays an active role in monetary policy
Financial crisis	The period of negative to low growth across many developed economies from 2007 to 2013
First closing	Where a fund has multiple closings, the first is usually the most significant barometer of the likely success of the fund-raising
Founder partner	See 'Carry partner'
Fund-lite	A single portfolio asset fund which is established either as a first-time fund by a new manager or a bridge between large fund-raises by an established manager
General partner	In a limited partnership, there is a requirement that there is at least one general partner whose exposure to the fund's liabilities is unlimited
General partner's commitment	Most investors in a limited partnership structure require the manager (who acts as the general partner) to commit capital to the fund to ensure that they are fully incentivized to manage the fund correctly

Growth capital	A typically minor investment in a mature company for the purpose of funding growth or other expansion
Investment adviser	Some fund structures require the engagement of an investment adviser separate from the manager. This is often an entity associated with the manager. It is often necessary in hedge funds, where the jurisdiction of the fund requires a manager within that territory
Investment club	An informal association of investors that will pool capital on an ad hoc basis to make investments
Investment objective	The strategy of the fund is geared towards the overall investment objective
Investment period	The period of time in which a fund with a fixed lifespan is to make investments. This is usually from first closing to the midway stage of the fund's life
Investor	The provider of capital to the fund
Key person	The management team is as much about individuals as the collective. Investors are often attracted to a fund by the persons involved in running it and will want to ensure that they remain so, and have control over any succession to other persons
LIBOR	The London Inter-Bank Offered Rate. Various LIBOR rates exist for different financial institutions, but it also is a headline figure of the rate at which banks will lend to each other. It is used as a reference point in calculating other payments of interest (e.g. 4% above LIBOR)
Limited partner	In a limited partnership, the limited partner provides equity capital to the fund and has an interest in the profits and capital distributions made by the partnership. A limited partner will not have unlimited exposure to the liabilities of the fund, in contrast with a general partner. A limited partner may become a general partner by taking a role in the management of the fund
Limited partnership	A limited partnership is established under the Limited Partnership Act 1907. Unlike a partnership, where all partners are jointly and severally liable for the liabilities of the fund, a limited partnership allows for certain partners to have liability limited to their capital contributions
Managed accounts	A managed account is an alternative to a fund structure whereby the assets are held by a custodian on behalf of the investor, rather than pooled by a manager into a fund
Management fee	An annualized fee payable to the manager of the fund to cover the operating costs it encounters. It is not intended to act as a source of profit, and some investors will require audited accounts to show that the fee covers no more than costs
Manager	The entity representing the investment team which promotes and manages the fund and makes investments on behalf of the fund
Model Code	The UK Model Code is contained in Annex 1 to Chapter 9 of the UKLA's Listing Rules. It governs the conduct of listed entities and persons discharging managerial responsibility on behalf of such entities
Official List	The UK Official List is maintained by the UKLA. It is a list of all securities which are traded on a regulated market within the UK
Open-ended fund	An investment vehicle which can freely issue and redeem shares or other interests as investors subscribe to and leave the fund

Partnership agreement	A partnership agreement is the constitutional document at the heart of a partnership. It is not necessary for the legal establishment of a partnership, but any well advised person will formally set out the rights and responsibilities of partners together with the procedures necessary for running of the partnership
Pledge fund	A fund in which investors pledge their capital rather than commit. Capital is drawn on an investment-by-investment basis and investors are invited to make a contribution. There are still incentives to commit to each investment as it is proposed, which often take the form of punitive measures (e.g. three strikes and out of the fund).
Private equity	Generally, a term for investments made into companies which are either unlisted private entities or listed entities with the intention of delisting the target company
Real estate	Investment into land and the property developed on it
RIS	An RIS is a regulated information service to the markets. Listed entities are required to make certain announcements through an RIS
RNS	The Regulatory News Service (RNS) is an RIS operated by the London Stock Exchange
Sponsor	The sponsor is usually synonymous with the private equity firm establishing the fund and managing both the fund and the portfolio companies (but not always – especially not with a listed fund, where the sponsor is a separate investment bank or broker)
Tax-elected fund	An authorized investment fund which elects to be exempt from tax on certain investment income in accordance with rules 69Z52 to 69Z75 of the AIF Regulations
Unauthorized unit trust	A unit trust which does not obtain authorization from the FCA which is treated differently for tax purposes
Venture capital	A form of private equity investing which targets early stage and start-up operations with funding requirements and cash flow profiles distinct from other private equity targets, often (but not always) investing in technology-driven businesses

Appendix II
Abbreviations

2004 Law	Luxembourg law of 15 June 2004 on the investment company in risk capital
2007 Law	Luxembourg law of 13 February 2007 on specialized investment funds, as amended
2010 Law	Luxembourg law of 17 December 2010 on undertakings for collective investment, as amended
AAOIFI	Accounting and Auditing Organization of Islamic Financial Institutions
ABS	asset backed securities
ACL	Alternative Companies List
ACRA	Accounting and Corporate Regulatory Authority
AIF	alternative investment fund
AIFM	alternative investment fund manager
AIFMD	Alternative Investment Fund Managers Directive
AIFM Regs	Gibraltar Financial Services (Alternative Investment Fund Managers) Regulations 2013
AIM	Alternative Investment Market
AMC	asset management company
AMF	Autorité des Marches Financiers
APEC	Asia-Pacific Economic Cooperation
APRA	Australian Prudential Regulatory Authority
A-REIT	Australian Retail Investment Property Trusts
ASIC	Australian Securities and Investments Commission
ASX	Australian Stock Exchange
AUD	Australian dollar
AUM	assets under management
AUT	authorized unit trust
BaFin	German Federal Financial Supervisory Authority
BCB	Brazilian Central Bank
BFT	Business Finance Taskforce

BGF	Business Growth Fund
BMA	Bermuda Monetary Authority
BSE	Bombay Stock Exchange
BSX	Bermuda Stock Exchange
BV	Besloten Vennootschap met beperkte aansprakelijkheid
BVCA	British Private Equity & Venture Capital Association
BVI	British Virgin Islands
BVI-FSC	British Virgin Islands Financial Services Commission
BVI-ITA	British Virgin Islands Income Tax Act
CAD	Canadian dollar
CBC	Central Bank of Cyprus
CBI	Central Bank of Ireland
CCF	common contractual fund
CCP	central counterparty
CDO	collateralized debt obligations
CEIF	closed-ended investment fund
CFC	controlled foreign corporation
CFTC	Commodity Futures Trading Commission
CGT	capital gains tax
CHC	Chinese holding company
CIF	collective investment fund
CIF Law	Collective Investment Funds (Jersey) Law 1988
CIMA	Cayman Islands Monetary Authority
CIO	chief investment officer
CIS	collective investment scheme
CIS Act	Financial Services (Collective Investment Schemes) Act 2011
CIS Regs	Financial Services (Collective Investment Schemes) Regulations 2011
CISX	Channel Islands Stock Exchange
CJV	cooperative joint venture
CLO	collateralized loan obligations
CNY	Chinese yuan
COBO	Control of Borrowing (Jersey) Order 1958
COBS	Conduct of Business Sourcebook
COLL	Collective Investment Schemes Handbook
Coop	cooperative
CoTA	Corporation Tax Act
CPC	Communist Party of China
CSE	Cyprus Stock Exchange

CSRC	China Securities Regulatory Commission
CSSF	Commission de Surveillance du Secteur Financier
CSX	Cayman Stock Exchange
CTA	commodities trading advisers
CV	commanditaire vennootschap
CVM	Brazilian Securities Commission
DFM	Dubai Financial Market
DFS	Department of Fund Supervision
DJIM	Dow Jones Islamic Market Index
DRULPA	Delaware Revised Uniform Limited Partnership Act
ECB	European Central Bank
ECI	effectively connected income
EEA	European Economic Area
EFSF	European Financial Stability Facility
EIB	European Investment Bank
EIF	European Investment Fund
EIS	Enterprise Investment Scheme
EJV	equity joint venture
EMIR	European Market Infrastructure Regulation
EMU	Economic and Monetary Union
EPM	efficient portfolio management
ERISA	Employee Retirement Income Security Act
ESCB	European System of Central Banks
ESM	European Stability Mechanism *or* European Securities Market
ESVCLP	Early Stage Venture Capital Limited Partnerships
ETF	exchange traded funds
EU	European Union
EUR	euro
FATCA	Foreign Account Tax Compliance Act
FCA	Financial Conduct Authority
FCP	Fonds Commun de Placement
FFI	foreign financial institution
FGR	fonds voor gemene rekening
FICLS	foreign investment company limited by shares
FIE	foreign invested enterprise
FINMA	Swiss Financial Market Supervisory Authority
FINRA	Financial Industry Regulatory Authority
FIS Law	Law of the People's Republic of China on Funds for Investment in Securities

FS Law	Financial Services Law
FSAJ	Financial Services Agency of Japan
FSB	Financial Stability Board
FSC	Financial Supervision Commission *or* Gibraltar Financial Services Commission
FSMA	Financial Services and Markets Act 2000
FSOC	Financial Stability Oversight Council
FTT	financial transaction tax
FWB	Frankfurt Stock Exchange
FX	Foreign Exchange
GAAP	generally accepted accounting principles
GAPP	generally accepted principles and practices
GBC1	Category 1 global business company
GBP	pound sterling
GDP	gross domestic product
G-EIF	Experienced Investment Fund (Gibraltar)
G-EIF Regs	Financial Services (Experienced Investor Funds) Regulations 2012
GEM	Global Exchange Market
GFSC	Guernsey Financial Services Commission
GIIN	Global Impact Investing Network
GP	general partner
HGB	German Commercial Code
HKEx	Hong Kong Stock Exchange
HKSFC	Hong Kong Securities and Futures Commission
HMRC	Her Majesty's Revenue and Customs
IAA	Investment Advisers Act 1940
IAIF	Indian Alternative Investment Fund
IAIFR	IAIF Regulations
ICA	Investment Company Act 1940
ICC	incorporated cell company
ICIS	International Collective Investment Scheme
IF Act	Investment Funds Act 2006
IIF	Innovation Investment Fund
IM	Information Memorandum
IMF	International Monetary Fund
InCIS	Indian collective investment scheme
INVCO	INVestment Company with fixed share capital
InvG	Investment Act (Germany)
IOM	Isle of Man

IP	investment partnership
IPO	initial public offering
IRA	individual retirement agreement
IRC	Internal Revenue Code
IRR	internal rate of return
IRS	Internal Revenue Service
ITA	Income Tax Act
ITICA	Investment Trusts and Investment Corporations Act
ITTOIA	Income Tax (Trading and Other Income) Act 2005
IWG	International Working Group of Sovereign Wealth Funds
JFSC	Jersey Financial Services Commission
JOBS Act	Jumpstart Our Business Startups Act 2012
JPUT	Jersey property unit trust
JSC	joint stock company
KAGB	German Capital Investment Code
KVG	capital management company
LBO	leveraged buyouts
LLC	limited liability company
LLP	limited liability partnership
LP	limited partner/limited partnership
LPA	Limited Partnership Agreement
LSE	London Stock Exchange
LTDA	Sociedade Limitada
MCEF	Mauritius closed-ended fund
MCR	minimum capital requirement
MFL	Mutual Funds Law
MFR	Securities and Exchange Board of India (Mutual Funds) Regulations 1996
MFSA	Malta Financial Services Authority
MFSC	Mauritius Financial Services Commission
MiFID	Markets in Financial Instruments Directive 2004/39/EC
MSE	Malta Stock Exchange
MSM	Main Securities Market
NAV	net asset value
NHS	National Health Service
NSE	National Stock Exchange
NURS	non-UCITS retail scheme
NV	naamloze vennootschap
NYSE	New York Stock Exchange

OEIC	open-ended investment company
OEICR	OEIC Regulations
OPCVM	Organismes de Placement Collectif en Valeurs Mobilières
OTC derivatives	over-the-counter derivatives
PA	Partnership Act 1996
PCC	protected cell company
PFI	private finance initiative
PFIC	passive foreign investment company
PID	property income distribution
PPM	Private Placement Memorandum
PPP	public–private partnership
PRA	Prudential Regulation Authority
QEF	qualifying electing fund
QIC	qualifying investee company
RAO	Financial Services and Markets Act 2000 (Regulated Activities) Order 2001
REIT	real estate investment trust
RIS	regulated information service
RO	representative office
ROI	Republic of Ireland
SA	Société anonyme
SAC	Segregated Accounts Companies
SACA	Segregated Accounts Companies Act
SAR	segregated accounts representative
Sàrl	Société à Responsabilité Limitée
SBA	Small Business Administration
SBJ Act	US Small Business Jobs Act 2010
SCA	Société en Commandite par Actions
SCR	solvency capital requirements
SCS	Société en commandite simple
SCSp	Société en commandite spéciale
SCX	Singapore Exchange
SEBI	Securities and Exchange Board of India
SEC	US Securities and Exchange Commission
SEM	Stock Exchange of Mauritius
SERPS	State Earnings Related Pension Scheme
SFA	Securities and Futures Act (Cap.289)
SFM	Specialist Fund Market

SFO	Securities and Futures Ordinance
SGD	Singapore dollar
SIBA	Securities and Investment Business Act
SICAF	Société d'Investissement à Capital Fixe
SICAR	Société d'Investissement en Capital à Risque
SICAV	Société d'Investissement à Capital Variable
SIF	Specialized Investment Fund
SIV	structured investment vehicle
SMSF	self-managed superannuation fund
SPACs	special purpose acquisition companies
SPV	Special Purpose Vehicle
SSE	Shanghai Stock Exchange
SWF	sovereign wealth fund
SWFI	Sovereign Wealth Fund Institute
SZSE	Shenzhen Stock Exchange
TCGA	Taxation of Chargeable Gains Act
TEF	tax-elected fund
TFEU	Treaty on the Functioning of the European Union
Trusts Act	Indian Trusts Act 1882
TSX	Toronto Stock Exchange
UAE	United Arab Emirates
UAE-SCA	United Arab Emirates Securities and Commodities Authority
UBTI	unrelated business taxable income
UCI	undertakings for collective investment
UCITS	undertakings for collective investment in transferable securities
UK	United Kingdom
UKLA	UK Listing Authority
US	United States of America
USD	US dollar
USTB	United States trade or business
UUT	UK-based unit trust
VAT	value added tax
VCLP	Venture Capital Limited Partnerships
VCT	venture capital trust
VPUT	very private unit trust
WFOE	wholly foreign owned enterprise

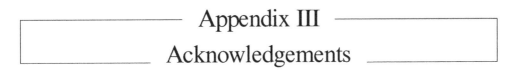

Appendix III
Acknowledgements

THE MJ HUDSON TEAM

Gavan McGuire (Centaur Fund Services) for his comments and suggestions on hedge funds. Richard Jobling (Hedgestart), for his time and dedication in reviewing the manuscript as a whole.

I am grateful to the following lawyers who have kindly provided comments and suggestions for the parts of the book which concern their jurisdictions.

Jurisdiction	Contributing lawyer(s)
AIFMD (EU and UK implementation)	Tony Watts Consultant Solicitor tony.watts@keystonelaw.com Keystone Law 53 Davies Street London W1K 5JH, UK +44 20 7152 6550
Australia	Tony Dhar Partner tony.dhar@minterellison.com +61 3 8608 2916 Charlie Huang Associate Minter Ellison (Melbourne) Level 23, Rialto Towers 525 Collins Street Melbourne 3000 Australia

Jurisdiction	Contributing lawyer(s)
Bermuda	Martin Lane Director martin.lane@conyersdill.com Conyers Dill and Pearman 10 Dominion Street London EC2M 2EE, UK +44 20 7562 0341 Chris Page Counsel chris.page@conyersdill.com Conyers Dill and Pearman Clarendon House Church Street, Hamilton Bermuda +441 295 1422
Brazil	João Paulo de Seixas Maia Krepel joao.krepel@lhm.com.br Fabio Weinberg Crocco fabio.crocco@lhm.com.br Lilla, Huck, Otranto, Camargo Av.Brigadeiro Faria Lima, 1744, 11° andar 01451–910, São Paulo, SP, Brazil
British Virgin Islands	Martin Lane Director martin.lane@conyersdill.com Conyers Dill and Pearman 10 Dominion Street London EC2M 2EE, UK +44 20 7562 0341 Alison Chilcott Associate alison.chilcott@conyersdill.com Conyers Dill & Pearman Commerce House Wickhams Cay Road Town Tortola BVI
Canada	David Matlow Partner dmatlow@goodmans.ca Mitchell Sherman Partner (Tax) msherman@goodmans.ca Avi Greenspoon Partner (Securities) agreenspoon@goodmans.ca Goodmans LLP Bay Adelaide Centre 333 Bay Street, Suite 3400 Toronto, ON M5H 2S7 Canada +1 416 979 2211

Jurisdiction	Contributing lawyer(s)
Cayman Islands	Gavin Lowe Partner gavin.lowe@turners.ky Turners PO Box 2636 Grand Cayman KY1–1102 Cayman Islands +1 345 943 5555
China	Sean Liu Associate sean.liu@mhplawyer.com Martin Hu & Partners 8/F, Kerry Parkside Office 1155 Fang Dian Road, Pudong Shanghai 201204 China +86 21 5010 1666
Cyprus	Galatia Sazeidou Associate gsazeidou@cypruslaw.com.cy Georgiades & Pelides LLC Advocates-Legal Consultants Eagle House, 10th Floor 16 Kyriakos Matsis Avenue, Ayioi Omoloyites 1082 Nicosia, Cyprus +357 22889000
Dubai and Sharia'a investment funds	Stuart Walker Partner swalker@afridi-angell.com Afridi & Angell PO Box 9371 Emirates Towers, Level 35 Sheikh Zayed Road Dubai, United Arab Emirates +9714 330 3900
France	Lola Chammas Partner lchammas@lcdmavocats.com Chammas & Marcheteau 18, rue de Vienne – 75008 Paris France +33 (0)1 53 42 42 50

Jurisdiction	Contributing lawyer(s)
Germany	Georg Schneider
	georg.schneider@noerr.com
	Noerr LLP
	Brienner Str. 28
	80333 München
	+49 89 28628184
	Florian Bentele (KAGB)
	florian.bentele@noerr.com
	Noerr LLP
	Börsenstraße 1
	60313 Frankfurt
	+49 69 971477252
	Karsten Matthieß (pensions)
	karsten.matthiess@noerr.com
	Noerr LLP
	Paul-Schwarze-Straße 2
	01097 Dresden, Germany
	+49 351 8166036
Gibraltar	James Lasry
	james.lasry@hassans.gi
	Felicity Cole
	felicity.cole@hassans.gi
	Hassans
	57/63 Line Wall Road
	PO Box 199
	Gibraltar
	+350 200 79000/
Guernsey	Robert Varley
	r.varley@babbelegal.com
	Babbé Guernsey Advocates
	PO Box 69
	18–20 Smith Street
	St Peter Port
	Guernsey GY1 4BL
	Channel Islands
	+44 (0) 1481 746178
Hong Kong	Jeremy Lam
	Partner
	jeremy.lam@deacons.com.hk
	Deacons
	5th Floor, Alexandra House
	18 Chater Road
	Central
	Hong Kong
	+852 2825 9732

Jurisdiction	Contributing lawyer(s)
India	Srinath Dasari srinath.dasari@azbpartners.com Veena Ganesh veena.ganesh@azbpartners.com AZB & Partners 67–4, 4th Cross Lavelle Road Bangalore 560 001, India +91 80 4240 0500
Ireland	Mark Browne Partner mbrowne@MHC.ie Mason Hayes & Curran South Bank House Barrow Street Dublin 4 Ireland +353 1 614 5000
Isle of Man	Peter Chemaly Attorney pchemaly@simcocks.com Simcocks Advocates Limited Ridgeway House Ridgeway Street Douglas Isle of Man IM99 1PY +44 (0)1624 690352
Japan	Shigeki Tatsuno (Mr) Partner, Attorney at Law shigeki.tatsuno@amt-law.com +81 3 6888 1124 Anri Suzuki (Ms) Associate anri.suzuki@amt-law.com +81 3 6888 4724 Anderson Mori & Tomotsune Akasaka K-Tower, 2–7 Motoakasaka 1-chome Minato-ku Tokyo 107–0051, Japan
Jersey	Jonathan Bale jonathan.bale@mjhudson.je MJ Hudson 3rd Floor 22 Hill Street St Helier Jersey JE2 4UA +44 1534 712900

Jurisdiction	Contributing lawyer(s)
Luxembourg	Vivian Walry Partner vivian.walry@cms-dblux.com CMS Luxembourg Route d'Esch 70 1470 Luxembourg, Luxembourg +352 26 27 53 1
Malta	Joseph Saliba joseph.Saliba@mamotcv.com Mamo TCV Advocates Palazzo Pietro Stiges 103, Strait Street Valletta VLT1436 Malta +356 21232271
Mauritius	Sonia Xavier Associate sonia.xavier@conyersdill.com Conyers Dill & Pearman (Mauritius) Limited Level 3, Tower I Nexteracom Towers Cybercity, Ebene Mauritius +230 404 9900 Fax: +230 404 9901
The Netherlands	Reinout Slot Advocaat Partner reinout.slot@cms-dsb.com +31 20 3016 319 Clair Wermers Advocaat clair.wermers@cms-dsb.com +31 20 3016 423 CMS Netherlands Mondriaantoren – Amstelplein 8A 1096 BC Amsterdam, The Netherlands PO Box 94700 1090 GS Amsterdam, The Netherlands
Russia	Matvey Kaploukhiy Head of Group – Corporate/M&A Matvey.Kaploukhiy@gblplaw.com Tatiana Kudachkina Junior Associate Tatiana.Kudachkina@gblplaw.com Goltsblat BLP Capital City Complex Moscow City Business Centre 8, Presnenskaya Nab., Bldg 1 Moscow 123100 Russia +7 495 287 44 44

Jurisdiction	Contributing lawyer(s)
Switzerland	Dr iur. Jürg Frick, LL.M. Attorney-at-law Juerg.Frick@homburger.ch Homburger Prime Tower Hardstrasse 201, CH-8005 Zurich Switzerland +41 43 222 10 00
United States	Richard Morris Partner rmorris@herrick.com +1 212 592 1432 Herrick, Feinstein LLP 2 Park Avenue New York, New York 10016 Edward Stevenson Partner estevenson@herrick.com +1 973 274 2025 Herrick, Feinstein LLP One Gateway Center Newark, NJ 07102, USA

FURTHER ACKNOWLEDGEMENTS:

Alternative Investment Management Association

Association of the Luxembourg Fund Industry

Australian Government Website

Australian Securities and Investments Commission

Australian Stock Exchange

Autorité des Marches Financiers

Bank of England

Central Bank of Ireland

Channel Islands Stock Exchange

CIA World Factbook

Citibank

Cyprus Stock Exchange

Deutsche Börse

European Union

Financial Conduct Authority

Financial Times

Gates Foundation

Global Economics

Government of Brazil Website
Government of Singapore Website
Government of The Netherlands Website
Her Majesty's Revenue and Customs
Internal Revenue Service
Jersey Financial Services Commission
London Stock Exchange
Luxembourg Stock Exchange
National Portal of India
New York Stock Exchange
Partners Group
Principles for Responsible Investment
Private Equity Growth Capital Council
Securities and Exchange Board of India
Securities and Exchange Commission
Shanghai Stock Exchange
Shenzen Stock Exchange
Singapore Stock Exchange
Sovereign Wealth Fund Institute
States of Alderney Website
The Charity Commission
The Daily Telegraph
The Economist
The Wall Street Journal
Tom Wolfe
UK Legislation Website
United Nations Statistics Division
US Treasury Department

Index

Printed and bound by CPI Group (UK) Ltd, Croydon, CR0 4YY

23/04/2025

14660949-0001